# Uncle John's
# BATHROOM
# READER®
# PLUNGES
# INTO
# GREAT LIVES

## The Bathroom Readers'
## Hysterical Society

San Diego, CA

# UNCLE JOHN'S BATHROOM READER PLUNGES INTO GREAT LIVES

For information, write
The Bathroom Readers' Hysterical Society
5880 Oberlin Drive, San Diego, CA 92121

e-mail: *unclejohn@advmkt.com*

Cover design by Michael Brunsfeld
San Rafael, CA *(brunsfeldo@attbi.com)*

ISBN: 1-59223-020-2

Printed in the United States of America
First printing: May 2003

10 9 8 7 6 5 4 3 2 1 03 04 05 06

## Project Team:

Allen Orso, Publisher
JoAnn Padgett, Director, Editorial & Production
Stephanie Spadaccini, Project Editor
Amanda Wilson, Project Manager
Georgine Lidell, Inventory Manager

# THANK YOU!

*The Bathroom Readers' Hysterical Society sincerely thanks the people whose advice and assistance made this book possible.*

| | |
|---|---|
| Bernadette Baillie | Dan Mansfield |
| Lauren Bensinger | Kristen Marley |
| Michael Brunsfeld | Mana Monzavi |
| Victoria Bullman | Steve Muck |
| Michele Crim | Janet Murie |
| Jackie Estrada | Janet Nelson |
| Eleanor Fisher | Jay Newman |
| Rita Haeusler | Mike Nicita |
| Becky Kaapuni | Ellen O'Brien |
| Gordon Javna | Ken & Kelly Padgett |
| Chris LaCouture | Arnold Schmidt |
| Paddy Laidley | Sydney Stanley |
| Kate Lapin | Jennifer Thornton |
| Paula Leith | Charlie Tillinghast |
| Allan MacDougall | Cindy Tillinghast |

# CONTENTS

*Extra-long articles suitable
for an extended sitting session
are marked with an asterisk.*

# INTRODUCTION

Last week I was driving up to the *L.A. Times* festival of books in Los Angeles, and as I aged in traffic (for those of you who don't know first hand, yes, the traffic really is THAT bad), I was growing ever more excited about meeting all of our great fans and BRI members that we expected to stop by our little booth. Well, not only was I not disappointed when I arrived, I was positively flushed with pride from the glowing reviews I received from our many dedicated (and satisfied) readers. I felt like Sally Field at the Oscars. "You love us…. You really love us."

So I hope that with our newest book, *Uncle John's Plunges into Great Lives*, we continue to hold up our end of the bargain—providing the best and most entertaining reading for bathroom readers everywhere.

Now to this book. Can I get a spotlight over here?

We wanted to have as a title *Great Lives and Those Not-So-Great Lives That Were Significant and Need to be Talked About More*. This wouldn't fit on the cover. So we settled on the shorter version *Plunges into Great Lives*, with "great" meaning notable or important, and not necessarily wonderful (because let's face it, many people that left a mark didn't leave it in pretty cursive). So our expectation of this book is to introduce you to many new people, some of them familiar and some of them not so, and the original, interesting, and sometimes downright bizarre stuff they did during their time.

Read about…
- Chris & Daulton's Excellent Adventure
- Did They Die With Their Boots On?
- The League of Comic Book Creators!
- A Nerd Who Changed the World
- The Secret Life of a Hairdresser
- The Last Schmaltz

Despite the typical turbulence (and with no time to move about the cabin, anyway), the runway is in site and we're putting down the landing gear. (You know you've been traveling too much when you start making airplane metaphors.) Yes, the book is almost finished. Soon things will return to normal. JoAnn can be reintroduced to her family (as soon as the rescue dogs are able to locate her buried somewhere under the avalanche of paper in her office). Amanda can get back to body-bending yoga positions and food that will go bad if stored in a desk drawer. And as always, I can reflect on the experience (they all work much harder than I do) of putting this book together—and trying to come up with a way to top ourselves for the next one.

So please enjoy. You may find some of the stories in this book inspiring, some amazing, and some even disturbing. But above all, we hope you will find all of the articles entertaining. Some of our highly perceptive readers have noticed that our voice is slightly unique from our partners up at the BRI office in Ashland (well, what can you expect when you live in a place where you can wear flip flops to work and pick up a new wetsuit at the drug store?). But both styles share the same informative, enlightening, and just plain funny tone that keep our readers coming back flush after flush.

Let us know how you feel—your thoughts, opinions, and input on what goes into our books is appreciated, and if you have specific questions about any of our *Plunges Into...* series, drop us a line at unclejohn@advmkt.com.

Now it's about time—no more excuses. Join the Bathroom Readers' Institute at www.bathroomreader.com. No spam. Just a monthly newsletter (lovingly crafted by our beloved "–Jay–"), a nifty membership card, and some great discounts on Uncle John's books and merchandise.

Take a load off and just read. And as always, go with the flow...

—Uncle Al and
the Bathroom Readers'
Hysterical Society

# HERMITS OF HARLEM

*Do you find it hard to part with those back issues of* National Geographic *or* Sports Illustrated? *Is your garage filled to overflowing with stuff you'll never use again? You may be suffering from Collyer Brothers Syndrome.*

On March 21, 1947, a telephone call came into the 122nd Street police station in Manhattan. A male voice said, "There is a dead man on the premises at 2078 Fifth Avenue." The police knew the house. It was home to the legendary and mysterious Collyer brothers. A patrolman was sent to investigate. Thus began one of the strangest tabloid stories in New York history.

## THE UPPER UPPER EAST SIDE

Homer and Langley Collyer were the sons of a wealthy gynecologist from an old New York family. In the early 1900s, the family moved into a three-story brownstone mansion in Harlem, then a fashionable neighborhood. Homer became a lawyer and Langley studied engineering. All seemed right with the Collyer family.

But there were a couple of odd things about the Collyer boys. For one thing, Langley never worked. For another, the boys never moved out of their Harlem home, even after their parents died in the 1920s. In fact, it's likely they never left New York City during their entire lives.

For a while, the Collyers seemed at least seminormal. Homer, the older brother, walked the eight miles back and forth to his law office every day. Langley studied music and tinkered with inventions, like his handy-dandy vacuum for cleaning out the inside of a piano. In the meantime, Harlem went from being an upper-middle-class neighborhood to a predominantly African American working-class enclave.

## THE COLLYERS HUNKER DOWN

As their Harlem neighborhood changed around them, the brothers gradually withdrew from the world. They stopped paying their bills and didn't object when their telephone, electricity, gas, and water were cut off. (For years, Langley fetched their water from a park four blocks away.) Afraid of intruders, they built barricades of junk in front of the windows and doors and booby-trapped the house by trip-wiring massive piles of newspapers and trash.

## HOMER STAYS HOME

Homer was almost never seen after he suffered a stroke and became blind and paralyzed. He was cared for exclusively by Langley, who only fed him a diet of 100 oranges a week, black bread, and peanut butter, thinking it would cure his brother. He explained his prescription this way: "Remember, we are the sons of a doctor."

Langley would leave the house only at night, dressed in shabby clothes and pulling a cardboard box on the end of a long rope. He gathered food for Homer and collected things.

## FAME OF SORTS

Articles about the strange recluses began to appear in the newspapers. Once, a crowd of 1,000 gathered outside the Collyer home while Con Edison workers forced their way in to remove two old gas meters.

## HERE'S HOMER!

Then came the anonymous tip that someone had died at the house. When the police arrived, a small crowd had already gathered. The front doors were forced open, only to reveal an impenetrable wall of boxes and junk from floor to ceiling. Finally, the police entered the house through a second floor window. Inside was a junk-filled maze of tunnels. Deep inside one of them was the body of 65-year-old Homer Collyer, who'd apparently died of starvation.

## BUT WHERE'S LANGLEY?

No one had seen Langley for days. He didn't even attend Homer's funeral. In the meantime, searchers began cleaning out the house. Among other things, they found the jawbone of a horse, 14 pianos, the dismantled components of an old Model T, baby carriages, pictures of a pinup girl from 1905, plaster statues, telephone directories, tin cans, chandeliers, 13 Oriental rugs, and some unfinished knitting left by Mother Collyer in 1929. But, above all, there were old newspapers. Tons and tons of them. Langley had collected every single edition of every New York City newspaper from the year 1918 on—30 years' worth.

**Legendary director Alfred Hitchcock never won an Academy Award.**

## AT LONG LAST LANGLEY

After 18 days of junk removal, Langley's body was found hidden under a massive pile of newspapers just a few feet from where Homer died. He had apparently set off one of his own booby traps while delivering dinner to Homer and was crushed to death. The coroner said that Homer died some time after Langley. So the police figured out that when Langley was killed, Homer lost the source of his food and slowly starved to death, trapped in his house, unable to see or walk. The house had no telephone, so he couldn't call anyone—and he couldn't even reach a window to call for help.

## FRONT PAGE NEWS

The story became a wild sensation; it even made the front page of *The New York Times*. Thousands of people walked or drove by the Collyer house, but they didn't stay long because of the smell. Over the next several weeks, 140 tons of junk were removed from the house, after which the house was torn down. The place where the Collyer house stood was eventually turned into a small park. In 1990, it was formally named Collyer Brothers Park.

## AND THAT'S NOT ALL

One more thing that was named for the kooky Collyers was their syndrome—also known as "compulsive hoarding," a clinically recognized obsessive-compulsive disorder. When he was asked, Langley said he was saving the newspapers so Homer could catch up on the news when he regained his sight. Experts might tell you that it was a way to keep anxiety at bay—a way for the Collyers to keep their lives at 2078 Fifth Avenue safe and intact.

And though they never knew it, they'd performed an important service for the moms of America. For years after the deaths of Homer and Langley, mothers could tell their children, "Clean your room, it's worse than the Collyer brothers' house in here."

\* \* \*

### A TIP FROM HOWARD HUGHES

"Wash four distinct and separate times, using lots of lather each time from individual bars of soap."

Joan of Arc's actual name was Jehanne Darc. The apostrophe was added later by an English historian.

# COURT CASE

*When a knockout blow almost killed one player and nearly destroyed the life of another, the NBA learned that sports violence had gone way out of bounds.*

At the Los Angeles Forum on December 9, 1977, the score was tied at halftime, 55–55. It was a ho-hum basketball game between the Houston Rockets and LA Lakers, when a routine tussle between Rocket Kevin Kunnert and Laker Kermit Washington blew up into a brawl. Washington saw a blurred figure running toward him at high speed. Afraid he'd be hit from behind, the 6'8", 250-pound player instinctively turned and threw a hard, right-handed punch. "The hardest punch in the history of mankind," is what assistant Laker's coach Jack McLoskey called it. The haymaker hit the Rockets' captain, Rudy Tomjanovich, just below his nose. The crack of Washington's punch reverberated through the Forum. Tomjanovich fell into a pool of his own blood, and the crowd grew silent, afraid he'd never get up again.

## BLOWOUT

That flash of a fist changed the two player's lives. Tomjanovich had been running at top speed to stop the fight when he was hit, and doctors compared the impact to a crash of two speeding loco-motives. The near-fatal collision shattered Tomjanovich's facial bones, dislocated his skull, gave him a cerebral concussion, and caused spinal fluid to leak from his brain. He missed the rest of the 1977–78 season while undergoing five surgeries to reconstruct his broken facial bones—a job that the surgeon compared to "gluing a shattered egg back together."

Washington was suspended for 60 days and ordered to pay a $10,000 fine, a punishment that many found far too light. But he couldn't escape angry fans. He and his family were deluged with hate mail and death threats. When Washington returned to play that season, the Lakers—who'd previously considered him one of their most valuable players—traded him off to Boston.

Both of the players, their teammates, and even the NBA did their best to move on from a brutal, life-altering moment. It was anything but easy.

---

Poet Dante Rossetti put an original manuscript in his wife's coffin; 7 years later, he retrieved it.

## WHEN NICE GUYS FINISH FIRST

The two players so changed by that game in the LA Forum had both beaten long odds to make it to the pros. Kermit Washington, 26, grew up in inner-city Washington, D.C. Rudy Tomjanovich, 29, was from Hamtramck, a poverty-tainted suburb of blue-collar Detroit, Michigan. Tomjanovich knew the humiliation of living on welfare; Washington saw school friends die in gang violence. These two underprivileged kids grew into brilliant athletes. In 1977, they were two friendly guys known as good family men and superachievers living out their dreams as popular NBA players.

## NBA DREAMS

Tomjanovich had joined the Rockets in 1970. As the starting small forward he was known for his mid-range "bankshot." By 1977, when the Rockets tangled with the Lakers, "Rudy T" was a favorite with Houston fans, a four-time All-Star, and captain of his team.

Kermit Washington joined the Lakers as a power forward in 1973; 1977 had been one of his best seasons with the team. He'd become invaluable as a rebounder and as the unofficial protector of their highest scorer, Kareem Abdul-Jabbar. When opposition players elbowed or pushed the 7'2" Abdul-Jabbar to keep him from shooting, Washington was the Laker's "enforcer," the player who tussled with anyone who harassed his teammate.

## NBA NIGHTMARES

On the night in question, the Rockets had just scored a basket in the second half. After a missed shot, Rocket Kevin Kunnert went after the rebound. Washington grabbed Kunnert's jersey (in retaliation for Kunnert's earlier jostling with Abdul-Jabbar) and Kunnert threw an elbow at Washington's shoulders. So far the scuffle wasn't much different than most of the 41 others that had taken place in the 1977 season. Then, according to Washington and Abdul-Jabbar, Kunnert aimed a second blow at Washington's head (a charge Kunnert has always denied). Abdul-Jabbar, seeing a brawl brewing, tried to break up the fight. He grabbed Kunnert—unfortunately pinning his arms at the moment Washington threw a punch that landed above Kunnert's eye and brought him to the ground. Rudy T saw his teammate in trouble and ran down the court to stop the fight. Washington saw someone coming up behind him in a blur—and threw a straight right that broke Tomjanovich's face.

The NBA had already been worried that season. The game wasn't doing well in ticket sales or TV ratings, and violence wasn't helping. Officials also feared that (since unlike hockey and football, basketball players wear no padding or protective masks) someone could be badly injured when big, angry guys threw wild punches. Rudy Tomjanovich's injuries were an NBA nightmare come true.

Media reporters labeled the two players: Tomjanovich was the victim, Washington was the thug. Rudy T struggled through months of pain and surgeries to put on his Rocket jersey the next season and play the game he loved. In the 1978–79 season he averaged 19 points a game and made the Western Conference All-Star team. But there was less joy in his success than he'd expected. Tomjanovich felt that fans (with their well-wishing and applause) pitied him as a victim, when in reality they admired his courage. And Tomjanovich had a legacy from his injuries—headaches, dental pain, and nightmares slowed him down. He sued the Lakers for failing to control their player, winning a $2 million settlement, but it was a tainted victory. After only three more seasons with Houston, Rudy T retired early—his playing dreams ended.

Kermit Washington suffered socially and psychologically. He felt guilty for what had happened to Tomjanovich, but he was sure that no one understood his position. Since his college days, Washington had been a respected, popular man and deservedly so. Now, though he felt he'd acted in self-defense when a man came running at him, he was despised as a thug. As he wrote later: "I had to have FBI agents sit next to me at the games for fear of being attacked. I was warned not to order room service (in my hotel) for fear of being poisoned."

The video replays of Washington's black fist smashing into Tomjanovich's white face aired endlessly, further complicating the situation. Washington felt that he hadn't even started the violence and that if he hadn't been a black man duking it out with two white men, he'd never have become the guy everyone loved to hate. To solve his problems, he soldiered on as a superachiever. It took time and trades, first to Boston, then to San Diego, and finally Portland. As a Trailblazer, Washington reestablished his popularity and even made it to All-Star.

**After tasting vanilla in France, Thomas Jefferson was the first person to import it to the U.S.**

## LIFE AFTER HOOPS AND HOOPLA

The two men couldn't avoid some contact, and Washington took a chance to apologize to Tomjanovich in 1987, but resentments lingered on both sides. As for the NBA, Commissioner O'Brien had already imposed stricter penalties on players involved in fighting. What had once been a maximum penalty of $500 and a five-game suspension had changed to $10,000 with suspensions that could last indefinitely. The NBA stuck with those tough penalties and added an extra referee. They were determined to curtail violence in the sport.

After he could no longer play on the court, Rudy T stayed with the Rockets as a scout, assistant coach, and finally, head coach. As head coach he led the Rockets to two NBA championships and it seemed he'd left the problems of the 1977 season far behind. But it wasn't until he finally dealt with a long-term drinking problem that Tomjanovich finally put aside his feelings about the victim label and put to rest the resentments he had harbored toward Washington.

For Kermit Washington the Forum fallout was even harder to take once he was off the court. He'd dreamed of coaching for the NBA, but no NBA coaching or assistant coaching positions opened up for him. Every time violence occurred in sports, the video of his flying fist would play on TV. Washington was told his violent reputation was still alive, making it unlikely he'd be hired. On May 14, 2000, almost 25 years later, Washington wrote a piece for *The New York Times* about what it was like to walk in his sneakers.

Sportswriter John Feinstein picked up on Washington's story and wrote a book called *The Punch: One Night, Two Lives, and the Fight That Changed Basketball Forever*, detailing the effects of the violence on the two men and on basketball. The best-selling book brought publicity to Washington's Project Contact, a charity that the generous player developed to bring doctors, nurses, and medicines to poverty-stricken Africans. It also publicized Tomjanovich's inspiring victories over physical pain and alcohol. Best of all, publication of *The Punch* brought Tomjanovich and Washington together to become friends. The friendship between the two basketball greats, along with the NBA's recognition of the danger of fighting, are two of the best things that finally emerged from one horrific haymaker.

Presidents Thomas Jefferson, John Adams, and James Monroe all died on July Fourth.

# ON BIOGRAPHIES

*Although Uncle John wrote this book on the subject, he thought he'd share the thoughts of some others.*

"There is properly no history; only biography."
—**Ralph Waldo Emerson**

"The literary tribute that a little man pays to a big one."
—**Ambrose Bierce**

"Great geniuses have the shortest biographies."
—**Ralph Waldo Emerson**

"There was never yet an uninteresting life. Such a thing is an impossibility. Inside of the dullest exterior there is a drama, a comedy, and a tragedy."
—**Mark Twain**

"Every great man nowadays has his disciples, and it is always Judas who writes the biography."
—**Oscar Wilde**

"Many heroes lived before Agamemnon; but all are unknown and unwept, extinguished in everlasting night, because they have no spirited chronicler." —**Horace**

"A well-written life is almost as rare as a well-spent one."
—**Thomas Carlyle**

"Biography lends to death a new terror." —**Oscar Wilde**

"We have escapist fiction, so why not escapist biography?"
—**John Kenneth Galbraith**

"Just how difficult it is to write biography can be reckoned by anybody who sits down and considers just how many people know the real truth about his or her love affairs."
—**Rebecca West**

"The art of Biography
Is different from Geography.
Geography is about maps,
But Biography is about chaps."
—**G. K. Chesterton**

"There never was a good biography of a good novelist. There couldn't be. He is too many people, if he's any good."
—**F. Scott Fitzgerald**

# SEX AFTER 70

*America's most famous sex therapist, Dr. Ruth Westheimer, gave everyone the power to say "orgasm"—and even to have a few. Here's the amazing story of how a refugee from the Nazi Germany became a media superstar at age 72 and made the world safe for sexually frank little old ladies.*

Even as a young sprout, Karola Ruth Siegel never seemed to stop talking. She was the cherished only child of loving parents, and they all lived together in a peaceful home in Frankfurt, Germany—until the night of November 16, 1938, when her father was arrested by Hitler's SS.

The terrified 10-year-old Karola was sent to a children's refugee camp in Switzerland. Her mother told her that when her father was released (supposedly within six months), they would come to get her. Instead, Karola stayed in Switzerland for six years—and never saw her parents or grandparents again.

### STARTING OVER

After the war, the then 16-year-old Karola immigrated to Palestine and changed her first name to Ruth. When the UN's 1947 decision to divide the land into Israel and Palestine led to bitter guerrilla fighting between the Jews and Arabs, Ruth decided to join the Haganah, the Jewish rebel army.

### RUTH LOCKS AND LOADS

In the army, she learned how to assemble and disassemble machine guns with her eyes closed, how to throw a hand grenade, and how to shoot. In fact, she was an expert marksman, which is why she was stationed at the Israel-Palestine border. Her job was to watch from a rooftop as Israeli soldiers checked each car entering Israel. If the occupants didn't know the password, they were to be shot immediately. Thankfully, she never had to shoot anyone.

But she was hit herself once, when a bomb went off outside the youth hostel where she lived. The residents had been told to go to the hostel's underground shelter, but Ruth paused on the way to grab a book to read. Three people were killed that day. Ruth was among the injured. The top of one of her feet was shattered, leaving her with the limp she still has today.

*Hannibal* is the first in a two-book deal in which Thomas Harris stipulated there will be no editing.

## BETTER THAN NOTHING

She married and moved to Paris. She was studying psychology at the Sorbonne when, in 1956, the West German government paid her 5,000 marks (about $1,500 at the time) as part of a restitution program for those who had suffered from Nazi war crimes. Ruth saw it as a way to bankroll a longed-for move to New York.

Within five years of the move, Ruth acquired a master's degree—and a new husband, Manfred Westheimer.

## SPEAKING OF SEX

When she first started working at Planned Parenthood in New York during the late 1960s, she was shocked by the casual discussions of sex all around her. But once she relaxed, she found the subject matter so enjoyable that she decided to make sex education the focus of her career. She officially earned the title of *Dr.* Ruth in June 1970, after receiving her Doctor of Education from Columbia University Teachers' College in New York.

She opened a sex therapy practice in 1975 and started lecturing on sexual issues. The lectures led to a 15-minute radio show, *Sexually Speaking*, which was a smash hit and quickly expanded to an hour. America just couldn't get enough of the little old lady who wasn't afraid to say "scrotum."

Soon she had her own TV show and got celebs like Roseanne Barr and Burt Reynolds to blab about their sex lives. She was everywhere in the 1980s: on magazine covers, in movies, on TV shows, and in commercials. Her own show went off the air in 1991, but only after forever changing the mass media's comfort level with talk about sex.

Westheimer continues to practice sex therapy in New York. And you should be so lucky as to get an appointment to see her.

\* \* \*

"[Dr. Ruth] has become the Julia Child of sex." —Gloria Steinem

"If you don't have a man, you need spaghetti." —Oprah Winfrey

Englishman Humphry Davy created the technology for the lightbulb in 1800, before Edison.

# COMPUTING & COWS

*Long before Gateway, Charles Babbage, "father of computing,"
showed an interest in cows.*

Charles Babbage (1791–1871) was, for a while, the Lucasian Professor of Mathematics at Cambridge, a position of distinction once held by Isaac Newton—and more recently by Stephen *A Brief History of Time* Hawking.

Babbage is best known for having invented a sort of Victorian-age, steam-powered calculating machine and the "Analytical Engine," a forerunner of the modern-day computer. But Babbage's interests didn't just lie there—they got up and moved around.

Babbage spent his lifetime experimenting. When he was young, he almost drowned while testing an invention for walking on water. When he grew up, he once had himself baked in an oven at 265°F for "five or six minutes without any great discomfort." He even figured the odds of a man actually rising from the dead as 1 in $10^{12}$. On another occasion he had himself lowered into Mt. Vesuvius so he could see the molten lava up close.

If, in his countryside ramblings, he came across a pig, he would stop to measure its heartbeat (which he would then list in his *Table of Constants of the Class Mammalia*).

His experiments led to all sorts of inventions. Take, for instance, the ophthalmoscope—that little light your doctor uses to look inside your eye. That was Babbage. Speedometer? Babbage. Standardized postal rates? Babbage. Skeleton key? Babbage. His tour de force came one day at the opening of the Manchester-to-Liverpool railroad line, while he stood with a railway company official waiting for the train. What about a device to sweep obstacles off the tracks in front of the engines? Huh? And so the "cow-catcher" was born. Pure genius.

In his later years Babbage came to dislike people in general. As far as we know, they felt pretty much the same about him. In 1861 at age 70, he said that he'd never spent a happy day in his life, and would gladly give up the rest of his life if he could live for just three days—500 years into the future. Babbage died at his home in London on October 18, 1871.

---

**The bagpipe was introduced to Scotland by the Celts and Romans.**

# GODS OF SILICON

*The modern computer was built one step at a time, as one inventor built on the work of another. Meet four of the giants on whose shoulders later innovators stand.*

## JACK ST. CLAIR KILBY: MICROCHIP MAN

In July 1958, Jack Kilby had been at his job just a few months at Texas Instruments. The entire plant shut down for a company-wide two-week vacation. Kilby hadn't earned a vacation yet, so virtually alone in the lab, he worked feverishly to come up with something to justify his employment.

### Let's See...

At the time, the current that ran through electronic devices was conducted by transistors, the circuits of which required workers to hand-solder wires to hundreds, sometimes thousands, of miniscule transistors, resistors, capacitors, and other microscopic gizmos, which—as you can imagine—was labor-intensive, expensive, and prone to errors.

### Micro-Management

With this in mind (and two weeks of quiet time), Kilby managed to etch the entire circuit—transistor, wires, capacitors, resistors, and all—into one single sliver of germanium crystal. These "integrated circuits" made room-sized computers obsolete. And they were unbelievably cheap to make; cheap enough to create a proliferation of electronic devices, including radios, microwaves, cell phones, VCRs, and TVs. Not only that, but Kilby and another TI scientist invented the handheld calculator—the first mass-market usage for the microchip we know and love today.

### You Win Some, You Lose Some

Kilby snagged a Nobel Prize in Physics in 2000 for his work. When CNN asked him if he had any regrets about what his work hath wrought, he answered, "Just one...electronic greeting cards that deliver annoying messages." Kilby is still a consultant for TI.

## RAY TOMLINSON: E-MAIL GURU

Ray Tomlinson was just goofing off at work one day when he created the way a lot of us communicate these days. After graduating from

MIT in 1965, he went to work at Bolt Beranek and Newman, the company that had contracted with the U.S. government to build ARPANET—the experimental military communications system that would later become the Internet.

### Where He Was @
In 1971, Tomlinson was trying to figure out a way to send messages to other engineers on the project. He knew of a message-sending program that could send messages between users of the same ARPANET machine, but he also knew of another program that could send files from one remote computer to another—so why not messages? He tinkered some more and figured out how to use them both to get what he wanted. And he chose a symbol for message address lines to denote mail sent through ARPANET to remote machines: today's ubiquitous @.

He didn't consider his new message-sending convention to be a big deal; in fact, as *Forbes* reported in 1998, a BBN coworker said that when Tomlinson showed him his work, he said "Don't tell anyone! This isn't what we're supposed to be working on."

### Traffic Jamming
But electronic mail caught on like wildfire. It wasn't the programming that was the breakthrough, it was the idea. Suddenly two users could send terse, information-filled messages to each another without the need for social niceties or for both to be available to chat at the same time. The number of e-mail messages sent grew by leaps and bounds on ARPANET. By 1973, a study found that 75 percent of all traffic on ARPANET was e-mail. Today we send millions of e-mails every day—it's changed the way we do business, talk to one another, and even the way we think.

### Just Another Day at the Office
But Ray Tomlinson didn't get rich quick—in fact, he didn't get rich at all. If he'd decided to patent his idea and charge even a fraction of a cent for each e-mail sent, he'd be a billionaire by now. Instead he continues to work at BBN, content with his place in history as a man whose work will probably outlive his name.

### JIM CLARK: LET'S GET GRAPHIC
Clark left school at 16, joined the navy, and ended up getting a doctorate in computer science. He was teaching at Stanford in

1978 when he came up with his life-changing idea. At the time, computers required thousands of lines of slow-reading code to produce 3-D graphics. Clark had a better idea—he built a chip specially modified to work with graphics rather than code. The resulting "Geometry Engine" was a revelation for engineers and architects that generated instantaneous computer designs instead of painstakingly hand-drawn blueprints.

Clark and a few colleagues founded Silicon Graphics, Inc. in 1982, a company that grew to a billion-dollar technology behemoth that put 3-D technology into the hands of desktop computer users.

### Chairman of the Bored
By 1994 he was bored at SGI and looking for something new. With Marc Andreessen, the brilliant University of Illinois student who'd developed the Mosaic Web browser, he founded Netscape Communications Corp. and started building his next billion-dollar company. When Netscape went public (early, against conventional business wisdom, before they'd even shown a profit), its shares rose from $6 to $24 on the first day of trading. Three months later the stock traded at $70. Jim Clark was a billionaire, and so were a lot of other people.

### Clear Sailing
Clark put part of his earnings into a healthcare information and technology company, WebMD, where he continues to be a director. He's also invested in building and sailing giant high-tech-enabled "smart boats," sailboats in which every component from mast to jib is automated and controlled by Silicon Graphics computers. Hey, it beats slaving away over a keyboard.

### TIM BERNERS-LEE: WEB WEAVER
The World Wide Web might not have happened if Tim Berners-Lee had kept better office files.

### Enquiring Minds
In 1980, the man who would create the ubiquitous "www" that sits in that topmost bar on your computer screen was into a six-month job as a software developer at CERN, the European Laboratory for Particle Physics in Geneva, Switzerland.

He'd left some of his notes at home in England. Wouldn't it

be great, he thought, if there was a piece of software that kept track of all the details in all his documents "that brains are supposed to be so good at remembering but that sometimes (his) wouldn't"? There wasn't such a program—so he wrote it himself and called it "Enquire." Of course, it only worked on his own personal files.

## Just a Click Away

But Berners-Lee could see that Enquire had possibilities beyond that. He envisioned a system of open documents, all written in a common language and all linked together...which turned out to be those underlined words or phrases that we click on to take us to a different page or site.

## Weaving His Web

He wrote a quick-and-dirty coding system called HTML (for hypertext markup language); came up with an addressing system that gave each file on his "web" a unique address, which he called a URL (uniform resource locator); and wrote a program that allowed documents with a URL to be accessed by computers across the Internet: HTTP (for hypertext transfer protocol). Finally, Berners-Lee took the step that would bring the whole world to what he would name the World Wide Web—the browser.

## Thanks, I'm Just Browsing

The browser was the key to the Web. Up to this point, geeky computer types could send and receive information packets across the Internet, but doing so required a lot of technical knowledge the average person just didn't possess. Berners-Lee's browser made it as simple as clicking on a bit of colored, underlined text. And click the masses did—the load on the first Web server at info.cern.ch multiplied by 10 every year from 1991 to 1994. By 1996, the number of Web and the Internet users had hit 40 million. At one point the rate of users was doubling every 53 days.

## Untangling the Web

Berners-Lee himself hasn't profited at all from his creations. He manages the nonprofit W3 Consortium (which oversees development of web technology standards) from a plain, tiny office at MIT. The protocols he created are a household name—but Berners-Lee is content to keep working behind the scenes.

**Artist Paul Gauguin worked on the Panama Canal in 1887.**

# CHEWING GUM KING

*Meet the man who put the chicle in Chiclets.*

People have been chewing gum (and gumlike substances) since ancient times. The Greeks chewed mastiche, made from the resin of the mastic tree. The ancient Mayans first chewed chicle over 1,000 years ago. Native Americans chewed the sap from spruce trees and the American settlers picked up the habit from them, adding beeswax to the sap. At the time our story begins, in 1870, people were chewing gum made from flavored and sweetened paraffin wax.

### THE GUM-TOTING BANDIT

Amateur inventor Thomas Adams was discussing a business proposition with his houseguest, the infamous General Antonio Lopez de Santa Anna. (Santa Anna, if you remember, was the man responsible for the massacre at the Alamo 34 years earlier.) Now he was living in exile on New York's Staten Island—we kid you not!—and trying to raise money so he could build an army to march on Mexico City and seize power.

Anyway, Santa Anna had a scheme to sell Mexican chicle, made from the sap of the sapodilla tree, to Americans who he thought could use it as an additive to natural rubber to reduce its cost. At the time, natural rubber was *mucho* expensive and if someone could figure out a way to reduce its cost, they'd be instant millionaires. The general had brought a large quantity of chicle with him and wondered if Adams could do something with it.

### CHICLE AND RUBBER DON'T MIX

Adams spent more than a year fiddling with the stuff, trying to make things like rain boots and toys—and failed every time. He was just about ready to throw the entire batch of chicle into the East River when he remembered how much Santa Anna enjoyed chewing it. He decided to mix up a batch of chicle gum in his kitchen that evening and gave it a try. He quickly realized that gum made from chicle was smoother, softer, and far superior in taste to the paraffin gums that were currently in vogue.

---

**Communist leader Karl Marx once reported for the *New York Daily Tribune*.**

## CHEWSY CUSTOMERS

Adams rolled the chicle gum into balls and wrapped them in colored tissue paper. He called his product "Adams New York Snapping and Stretching Gum," and he visited drugstores in his neighborhood to see if they'd take it on consignment. Within days the purchase orders started to come in; Adams had to set up an operation to make the gum in large quantities. It eventually became impossible for him to keep up with all the orders, so he invented a chewing gum manufacturing machine which he patented in 1871.

## MILESTONES IN GUM

In 1875, Adams added licorice flavoring and called the new gum "Black Jack." It was the first flavored chicle gum on the market and the first gum to be offered in sticks. Black Jack was still being manufactured well into the 1970s.

In 1888, the company introduced the very first vending machines in America. Installed in New York City subway stations, they dispensed Black Jack and the company's new Tutti-Frutti gum. In 1899, Adams created a monopoly by merging the six largest chewing gum manufacturers into the American Chicle Company. One of the company's most famous products, Chiclets, was invented by a candy salesman who wrapped chicle in a hard candy shell. Chiclets became part of the American Chicle Company in 1914.

During WWII, the demand for chewing gum outstripped the chicle supply, so scientists developed new resins and synthetic gum bases as a substitute. Today, per capita consumption of chewing gum in the U.S. totals in excess of 195 million pounds a year.

That's 175 sticks of gum per person per year. (Are you doing your bit?)

## POSTSCRIPT

Santa Anna never did profit from chicle sales or raise an army as he had hoped. He was allowed to return to Mexico shortly before his death in 1876. Thomas Adams died in 1905, and his sons ran the business until the American Chicle Company was acquired by Warner Lambert in 1960.

**The first type of umbrella was invented by the ancient Egyptians to shield the sun.**

# TRIPLE THREAT QUIZ 1
# FAD INVENTORS

*Fads: Weird objects of intense desire one day, embarrassing
reminders of how carelessly you spend your hard-earned cash the
next. But for every fad, there's some guy who said to himself over a
beer, "Hey, I bet you people would actually buy that," and then made
a million bucks with it.*

We've got five fad inventors below. See if you can match each one, not only with the fad, but with the historical fact about the fad as well. It's a mix-and-match-and-match quiz that we call the Triple Threat. Have fun! (And if you can't figure out which guy invented the Rubik's Cube, by the way, there is just no hope for you.)

Match these inventors...        With these fads...

1.  Enro Rubik                  a)  Hula-Hoop
2.  Richard Knerr and Arthur    b)  Rubik's Cube
    "Spud" Melin                c)  Tetris
3.  Gary Dahl                   d)  Frisbee
4.  Walter Frederich Morrison   e)  Pet Rocks
5.  Alexey Pajitnov

And these historical facts...

i.  This fad sold 40 million units since it was created in 1985,
    but the inventor didn't make one red cent off of it until 1997—
    because of Soviet-era governmental contracts far more puzzling
    than this puzzler (he's done quite nicely since then, however).

ii. The "inventors" of this fad actually just spun a new variation
    on an old theme, as versions of this fad gadget date back to
    ancient times. However, their plastic version of this toy sold
    more than 20 million units in the first six months after its

---

**Famous people from Arkansas: Maya Angelou, Johnny Cash, and Douglas MacArthur.**

release in 1958. A fictional version of its invention is at the center of the plot for the Coen Brothers movie *The Hudsucker Proxy*.

iii. This fad was invented in 1974 but didn't become popular until the next decade, when it became one of the symbols of the 1980s, along with Michael Jackson and Miami Vice. There are more than 43 quintillion ways to do this fad the wrong way (43 quintillion, in case you're wondering: 43,000,000,000,000,000,000).

iv. This fad symbolizes the 1970s; the creator of this fad bought the major component for a penny and sold the completed product for $3.95, which is a heck of a mark-up. This fad was so popular that it got the inventor on *The Tonight Show* with Johnny Carson not once but twice. The fad was over almost as quickly as it began—invented in April 1975, it was declared passé by Christmas—but it lasted long enough to make its inventor a millionaire.

v. Yale University maintains that an undergraduate from the 1820s gave this fad its name, but a rather more likely story is that the name comes from a baking company in Bridgeport, Connecticut, which went out of business the same year the inventor was granted a patent. The inventor of this fad is from a family of inventors; his father invented a type of car headlight.

Answers:
1-b-iii
2-a-ii
3-e-iv
4-d-v (The first Frisbee was most likely an empty pie tin from the Frisbie—with an I—Pie Company)
5-c-i

**The Woodstock concert was not held at Woodstock, but at Max Yasgur's farm in Bethel, New York.**

# JOAQUÍN!

*Joaquín didn't need no stinkin' last name. His first name alone struck fear into the hearts of California miners during the gold rush—and inspired a legend. But what was the truth? Was there a real Joaquín?*

Joaquín the bandito could strike anywhere, backed by his loyal gang of six murderous desperadoes...or was it 12? Or maybe 60. Anyway, he'd slit your throat and steal your bag of gold in the same instant, he was impervious to bullets, and he left his pursuers eating dust when he made his getaways. At least that's the story that's been handed down.

### THE MADRE OF ALL BANDITS
Day after day in early 1853, newspapers reported a crime wave in Calaveras County and the Southern Mines region in Central California. The crime spree included robberies and murders, all courtesy of a gang of Mexican banditos led by a wild, unstoppable leader called simply "Joaquín." As Mexicans from all over California joined his ranks, reports of their crimes spread to other parts of the state. Joaquín would help himself to whatever he found—gold, cash, saddles, guns, or horses. Anyone who tried to stop him was cut down. Sometimes only bodies with empty pockets remained to testify to his crimes. At other times, wild shootouts would send men running for their lives.

### BODY COUNT
All told, Joaquín and his gang probably murdered between 24 and 29 men (19 of them Chinese) during a seven-week spree. The facts are sketchy; the newspaper reports and rumors were confusing. For a little while, every crime in California was blamed on Joaquín. A dead miner, a lost horse, a missing bottle of beer...it must've been Joaquín!

### TREATY? WHAT TREATY?
Mexicans had good reasons to hate the miners who flooded California during the gold rush. California had once been part of Mexico, but in the 1840s Mexico lost "Upper California" to the

---

Delmonico's created the Baked Alaska dessert to commemorate Seward's purchase of Alaska.

U.S. The peace treaty guaranteed that Mexicans in California could become American citizens and keep all their property, but that never happened—the U.S. Constitution continued to limit citizenship to whites. And when gold was discovered and treasure-hunters overran the state, a law was passed that prohibited natives of Mexican ancestry—the original citizens of California—from prospecting for gold.

## MY ANTIHERO!

But don't think of Joaquín as a great Mexican avenger or hero—remember that most of his victims were Chinese, a group not particularly notable for their gunslinging experience, and therefore easy prey. Joaquín just wanted gold, and he'd take it where he could get it.

The miners screamed for protection. Rewards were offered and posses formed. The result? Innocent Mexicans were hung, shot, or expelled from town, their houses burned to the ground.

And all the while, Joaquín's legend grew. He was rumored to be south of Los Angeles heading back to Mexico... then on the coast near Santa Barbara...then up north again. He was everywhere! But in late July, the saga ended.

## JOAQUÍN'S LAST STAND?

In May 1853, the California Rangers recruited a Texan named Harry Love to lead a posse 20 strong. The deal was that if they captured Joaquín—dead or alive—within 90 days, they could claim a $1,000 reward, *mucho dinero* in those days. The fact that they had no idea what Joaquín looked like didn't stop them from turning over every rock in California.

In July, with their contract running out, they came upon four men sleeping in a dried-up creek bed. One of the Rangers pointed and cried, "This is Joaquín, boys!" and the shooting started. Two of the four were killed. And because the hand of one of the dead men was missing a digit, Captain Love announced that the dead men were none other than Three-fingered Jack and the dreaded Joaquín.

Three-Fingered Jack? He also became a legend, but only after he was killed by Love. Manuel "Three-Fingered Jack" Garcia,

---

"Can't act. Can't sing. Balding. Can dance a little." —MGM on Fred Astaire's first screen test.

who'd lost a finger on his right hand, was an outlaw—and an extremely nasty one—but he'd never been associated with Joaquín before that day.

## PICKLING HEADS FOR FUN AND PROFIT

Love chopped off both heads and the hand with the missing finger as evidence of the kill. Before he could preserve the body parts, one head started to rot, so Love threw it away. He pickled the other head and the hand in jars of whiskey to preserve them. Joaquín's alleged head and Jack's alleged hand toured the country and people paid good money to see them. The head ended up on permanent display in a San Francisco saloon until the earthquake of 1906, when it was lost forever.

## STILL A MYSTERY MAN

Joaquín was never heard from again. The two survivors of the shootout had been captured, but they disagreed about the dead man's identity. One kept silent; the other, with a six-shooter pointed at his head, declared that the corpse was indeed Joaquín.

## P.R. I LOVE YOU

Five years later, a newspaper reporter wrote a lurid novel about a Joaquín Murieta, thus giving the bandit the last name that's been associated with him all these years—but is in no way provable. The writer portrayed Joaquín as a Mexican Robin Hood, who had been a decent man, driven out of the mines by greedy gringos who whipped him, murdered his brother, and raped his sweetheart. If he turned to crime after all that, who could blame him? The *California Police Gazette* picked up the story, and within a few years, the legendary Joaquín was born anew—not as a bloodthirsty thief, but as a hero, fighting for justice for his people.

* * *

Other Western names for a gunfighter are buscadero, gun-man, gun toter, gunny, gun shark, gunslinger, leather slapper, pistolero, quick-draw artist, shootist, short-trigger man, and tie-down man.

Mary Jenkins Surratt was the first woman to be executed by the U.S. government.

# THE OTHER BABE

*She was a whiz at sports—and she'd be the first to tell you. Brash and supremely confident, her aim was "to be the greatest athlete that ever lived."*

Babe Didrikson Zaharias said that she got the nickname "Babe" early in her teens from boys who were amazed at her long-distance homers. But as she grew older, observers noticed more Ty Cobb in her, a darkness and a rage that made losing intolerable. It was an unnamed hostility that seemed to fuel her competitive fire.

## TEXAS TOMBOY
Mildred Didrikson was born in Port Arthur, Texas, in 1911. She was a natural athlete. In high school she played virtually every sport except football. But that didn't win her any popularity contests. Her prima donna attitude, which included boasting and constant attention seeking, alienated most of her classmates. Did she care? Doubtful. She had better things to do.

## HOOPS, AND WE DON'T MEAN EARRINGS
Basketball was her first stepping stone. At school she played for the All City and All State teams, after which an insurance company hired her as a typist (85 wpm) so she could keep her amateur standing and play on their basketball team.

## A TEAM UNTO HERSELF
In 1932, she entered the Amateur Athletic Union women's national track and field competition as an individual contestant. She caused a sensation at the opening parade when she marched as the entire team representing the Employers Casualty Insurance Company of Dallas. She won six events, broke four women's world records, and, with 30 overall points, scored eight points more than the University of Illinois, the second place winner.

## SHE WUZ ROBBED!
Her performance qualified her for the 1932 Olympics, which began just two weeks later in Los Angeles, California. Olympic

---

Surratt was hanged in 1865 for conspiracy in the assassination of President Lincoln.

rules limited her to three events. She took two gold medals—for the javelin and hurdles—and a silver in the high jump. She cleared the same height as the top finisher in the high jump, but her jump was considered a foul because she went over the bar headfirst—the judges called it "diving." (Babe's "diving" style was legalized soon after that.) Foul or not, the world couldn't help but notice her. Babe was an overnight sensation.

## BABE TURNS PRO
She lost her amateur standing after a picture of her appeared in an automobile ad. Her folks needed money, so Babe turned professional. She didn't hesitate to capitalize on her own abilities or to turn a profit from her name. She spent the next two years promoting herself: a brief stint in vaudeville playing the harmonica (while running on a treadmill); pitching in some Major League spring-training games; and touring, first with a billiards exhibition, then a men and women's basketball team called Babe Didrikson's All-Americans, and finally as the only nonbearded member of an otherwise all-male, bearded baseball road team called the House of David.

## THE GREATEST, BUT...
There was very little that she couldn't do. In addition to basketball, baseball, billiards, and track, she played tennis, golf, and handball, and she skated, cycled, swam, and bowled. When someone asked her if there was anything she didn't play, she wisecracked, "Yeah, dolls."

Anyone as talented as Babe Didrikson was bound to attract a lot of press. Famed sportswriter Grantland Rice called her "the greatest athlete of all...for all time." Other writers condemned her for not being feminine. She lived in the olden days when female athletes were thought of as unseemly, or even freakish. But not for a moment was our Babe a feminist. She didn't care about women's liberation—all she wanted was to play sports.

## THE SECRET TO GOOD GOLF
When asked how she could regularly drive a golf ball some 250 yards though she didn't weigh more than 145 pounds, she said, "You've got to loosen your girdle and let it rip."

Babe got serious about golf in 1933 and won the Texas Women's Championship in 1935. After which, the U.S. Golf

Association ruled that "for the best interest of the game," Babe was not an amateur because she had competed professionally in other sports.

At the 1938 Los Angeles Open, she was paired with George Zaharias, a "bad guy" wrestler who was making a fortune as "the Weeping Greek from Cripple Creek." They married 11 months later, and George took over as her manager and advisor.

The Golf Association reinstated her as an amateur in 1945; in 1946, she won an amazing 13 consecutive tournaments. The next year, she was the first American to win the British Amateur. For three straight years (1945–47) the Associated Press named her the Female Athlete of the Year. She turned pro in the summer of 1947, after winning 17 of 18 tournaments. In 1948 Babe won her first U.S. Women's Open, the World Championship, and the All-American Open.

With George and Hall-of-Famers Patty Berg and Fred Corcoran, she founded the Ladies Professional Golf Association in 1949. She continued her impressive performance on the LPGA tour for the next several years.

### THE 19TH HOLE

Shortly after winning the inaugural Babe Zaharias Open in Beaumont, Texas, in April 1953, Babe learned she had cancer of the colon. Surgeons removed the tumor, but discovered the cancer had spread into her lymph nodes. Her cancer was inoperable. The next year she won her third U.S. Women's Open—by 12 strokes, mind you—on the way to five titles and her sixth AP Female Athlete of the Year award.

But the pain in her lower spine, caused by the cancer, became unbearable and she stopped golfing. On September 27, 1956, she died in Galveston, at the age of 45.

She's remembered to this day as the athlete whose pursuit of greatness changed women's sports forever.

\* \* \*

"The formula for success is simple: practice and concentration, then more practice and more concentration."

—Babe Didrikson Zaharias

---

**Henry Ford was fascinated with soybeans and used them for automotive paint and parts.**

# DEM BONES

*How Lucy's skeleton shook the family tree.*

Lucy (about 3'6" tall and 60 to 65 pounds) was 21 years old when she died in what is now Hadar, Ethiopia. She checked out quietly, perhaps from accidental drowning or from an illness, but she rested in silence for more than 3 million years.

## DARWIN GETS INTO HOT WATER

Lucy's modern-day story begins in 1859 with Charles Darwin's book *Origin of Species*. Darwin theorized that nonhuman species survived by adapting to their environment and changing over time—they "evolved." Since the idea contradicted Church doctrine that God created everything perfectly in six days, Darwin cautiously wrote just one sentence hinting at evolution: "Light will be thrown on the origin of man and his history." Pretty tame, but that comment enraged Creationists, who fervently believed man was created in God's image. It also fired up researchers who were determined to prove Darwin right—man had evolved from a more primitive species. They set out to find the missing link between man and the species most like man's closest relative—the apes.

## WHILE LUCY SLEPT

By 1974, when Lucy was discovered, scientists had already figured out that humans began as primitive apelike beings and gradually became more human. They had fossils showing that *Homo sapiens* (humans) evolved 500,000 years ago. Our likely ancestor was *Homo erectus*, who evolved 1.5 million years ago. Erectus had a smaller brain and a more primitive appearance, but he stood erect (*H. erectus*, get it?), walked on two legs, and used fire to cook. He had an even smaller-brained ancestor, *Homo habilis*, who lived 2 million years ago. Habilis also walked upright and used tools; his name means "handy man." But who were the mamas and papas of *H. habilis*? Scientists knew what kind of fossil to look for. Humans were bound to be smarter than any ape or chimp, so researchers went digging for a big-brained chimp or ape-legged human ancestor. Meanwhile, rains in Hadar were steadily eroding the slope where Lucy's bones lay buried.

## LUCY IN WAITING

On November 30, 1974, paleoanthropologist Don Johanson was about to quit searching for fossils because of the 110-degree heat. Before returning to camp, he and a colleague took a cursory look at one last slope because Johanson was "feeling lucky." He was about as lucky as a paleoanthropologist can get. He picked up a piece of fossilized bone on the ground, then another, and another. The fossils formed the partial skeleton of a very primitive, female apelike creature. That night, celebrating their discovery, the researchers knocked back beers while "Lucy in the Sky with Diamonds" played in the background. During a night of partying, the Hadar expedition named their new find "Lucy."

## WHY THEY LOVED LUCY

Scientists loved Lucy. Forty percent of her skeleton was recovered, making hers the oldest, most complete remains ever found; she was more than 3 million years ancient. Her nearest competition in completeness was the skeleton of a Neanderthal man, but he was a mere baby of 75,000 years! Even more than her age or completeness, Lucy's anatomy blew their minds. Lucy was a hominid—that is, she walked upright like a human—but she wasn't human. She seemed to be evolution's missing link, half-human and half-ape (or rather half-chimp). Her arms were long like a chimp's, but her hands had fingers curved like a human's. Her skull and upper body were chimplike, but her narrow, short pelvis and her locking knee joint allowed her to walk upright like a human.

Why did Lucy leave scientists scratching their heads? She was the half-human, half-ape they'd expected, but she had the wrong halves in the wrong places! Scientists expected the missing link to have a big brain in an apelike body. Lucy had a small, chimp-sized brain with a lower body like a human's. For years people had believed it was the human brain that separated man from beast—now it seemed to be our pelvis and locking knee joints!

After years of studying her skeleton, Dr. Johanson and colleague Dr. Tim White officially categorized Lucy in 1979 as an entirely new species of hominid. She was an *Australopithecus afarensis*, which translates as "southern ape from East Africa." White and Johanson classified Lucy as an ape, but also as a hominid. They believed she was related to chimps yet also related to *H. habilis* and *H. erectus*, not to mention us noble *Homo sapiens*. Lucy's story made her an instant celebrity. She was more than a million years

The books were carried on the backs of camels trained to walk in alphabetical order.

older than handyman habilis, and could easily be his ancestor. International headlines heralded the idea that science might have found our great, great-great-great-great…grandma.

## LUCY TAKES A STAND
The world also wondered why little-brained Lucy decided to stand up on her own two feet. There's no certain answer. Walking on two legs, or "bipedalism," had evolutionary disadvantages. If Lucy had stayed on all fours, she could have run faster with fewer aches and back pains. But walking upright gave A. *afarensis* advantages that may have overshadowed problems. Females could cover long distances while having their hands free to care for their offspring; males could forage for food—and carry it home to their mates. Lucy's upright stance opened a whole new vista on evolution. Before her discovery, the focus was on competition between species over territory—survival of the fittest. Yet more than 3 million years ago Lucy and her species may have changed the course of evolution because of the advantages of cooperation. Standing upright would help Lucy and a mate form a nuclear family. Lucy could nurture the kids while her larger, stronger mate foraged for food. Lucy and kin may have pioneered family values!

## IS IT COUSIN LUCY?
Lucy inspired researchers to dig up more roots of the human family tree. In the early 1990s in Aramis, Ethiopia, not far from Hadar, fossils of *Ardipithecus ramidus* were found. Living as far back as 4.4 million years ago, A. *ramidus* walked upright, but its skull and teeth are more chimplike than Lucy's and its brain even smaller. A new evolutionary pattern had been discovered—or had it? In 2001 a skull discovered in Kenya shook the family tree again. This skull introduced a new species of hominid, *Kenyanthropus platyops* (flat faced man of Kenya). Platyops lived at the same time as Lucy but had more pronounced cheekbones, smaller teeth, and a less protruding jaw, making his skull more human. Researchers must determine whether platyops, or another species, is our direct human ancestor—making Lucy a mere distant cousin whose line is now extinct.

Even if she isn't our direct ancestor, Lucy is still evolutionary royalty. Her bones prove that humans had chimplike relatives; they tell us a lot about how we evolved—and what makes us human. For such a silent little thing, Lucy has an awful lot to say.

# CALL HER MADAME

*Trained in the innocuous art of making wax models, Madame Tussaud's waxworks took a turn for the gruesome when the French Revolution came to town.*

Madame Tussaud was born Marie Grosholtz in Strasbourg, France, in 1761. She grew up in Paris, where she learned wax modeling from Philippe Curtius, a doctor with a penchant for the art form. While working with Curtius, Tussaud met and created wax models of the distinguished personages of the day, among them Voltaire and Benjamin Franklin—the originals of which are still on display today.

## A ROYAL INVITATION

When Curtius's exhibitions caught the interest of the royal family; King Louis XVI invited Marie to come live at his opulent palace at Versailles, to help in the artistic education of his sister. Marie spent nine years there, but when the Revolution began, she headed back to Paris.

## LET THEM EAT WAX

Paris was in chaos. Because of her royal connections, Marie was thrown into prison. Her head was shaved in preparation for a meeting with Madame la Guillotine, but the revolutionaries found a better use for her—making death masks of those who weren't as lucky as she was. The likenesses, created from just recently severed heads, included Marie's former employers, Marie Antoinette and Louis XVI. Like a grisly prototype of a wax museum, the heads were put on display—and people flocked to see them.

## ON THE ROAD

Curtius died, leaving Marie his wax collection. She married François Tussaud, with whom she had two sons. By now France was in the terrible economic straits that follow any revolution. To make ends meet (or even hang out in the same neighborhood), Marie packed up her oldest boy and her collection of wax figures and went on tour. For the next 33 years, she and her waxworks visited every corner of England, Scotland, and Ireland. In pre-television days, it was the only way that the country folk could get to see the likenesses of people they'd only heard about, like Napoleon and Marie Antoinette—not to mention their own King George IV.

## SETTLING DOWN
Finally, in 1835, she and her wax portfolio settled in London and established Madame Tussaud's Wax Museum there. By now her younger son had joined her (but not the hubby she left behind). She worked almost to the end of her life at age 89, and then her sons, and then her grandsons, and so on, kept the business going.

One of Tussaud's most popular attractions was the Chamber of Horrors, which was devoted to wax heads of infamous murderers of the day. It was so renowned that convicted criminals donated clothing to dress their wax twin after their inevitable executions.

## THE WHOLE BALL OF WAX
Marie Tussaud died in 1850, but her molds and museums live on. The present London location opened in 1884, where many of her original molds survive, despite a fire in 1925 and a bomb (which destroyed more than 350 head molds and the movie theater) in 1940 during the first night of the London blitz.

Today, Tussaud's is still going strong. Gallery locations have sprouted up everywhere, from Hong Kong (where action superstars Jackie Chan and Michelle Yeoh are big attractions) to Las Vegas (home of all the Vegas greats in wax, including Liberace, Wayne Newton, and Siegfried & Roy).

\* \* \*

Where can you find Fred Astaire, C. G. Jung, Marilyn Monroe, Mae West, Lenny Bruce, and Shirley Temple together?

The cover of the Beatles' 1967 album, *Sgt. Pepper's Lonely Hearts Club Band.*

---

Aristotle believed that the most important purpose of the human brain was to cool the blood.

# THE ROUND TABLE'S CENTERPIECE PART 1

*How the Algonquin Round Table—that daily gathering of the fastest minds and the tartest tongues of Jazz Era New York—got started.*

Anyone who held the job of theater critic for *The New York Times* would be hated and feared by the poor slobs who put up shows on the Great White Way of Broadway, but Alexander Woollcott added a little something extra to the job description—the ability to cut actors and playwrights to ribbons before they knew what hit them.

This is a man who once likened a play to "a taste of lukewarm parsnip juice" and who panned a play called *Wham!* in one word: "Ouch!" Not only did Woollcott have the power to close your play in a weekend, he'd do it with a quip that was more memorable than the play itself.

## EUGENE WHO?

The only thing worse than being panned by Woollcott was being ignored by him; in 1919, that was the fate of a young playwright named Eugene O'Neill. The next year, Woollcott would praise O'Neill as "a playwright of real power and imagination," but this particular year, Woollcott wasn't giving Eugene O. the time of day, and that fact was driving O'Neill's agent, John Toohey, crazy.

## THE FIRST CELEBRITY ROAST

Toohey decided to take revenge. He organized a luncheon to be held at the Algonquin Hotel, a favorite watering hole for New York's finest writers and wits. Toohey sent invitations—on which he intentionally misspelled Woollcott's name—to some of the most cantankerous brains in the city. Among them was the dynamic duo of Dorothy Parker, theater critic for *Vanity Fair* and perhaps the only reviewer more acidic than Woollcott (she'd be fired from *Vanity Fair* in 1920 because her reviews were getting too nasty), and Parker's managing editor and dear friend, Robert Benchley. Toohey invited them and other similarly droll folks to

---

**Mark Twain referred to the accordion as the "stomach Steinway."**

let Woollcott have it while they all sat around drinking their lunches out of martini glasses and snacking on popovers to soak up the booze.

## THE MAN WHO CAME TO LUNCH

Unfortunately for Toohey, the plan backfired. Woollcott had a monstrous ego, but he could take it as well as he could dish it out. In fact, he was so delighted at the quality of his savaging at the hands of Parker, Benchley, and the rest that he suggested they all reconvene at the Algonquin the very next day for more of the same. They did, and did again the day after that, and the day after that, and so on. And so was born the famous Algonquin Round Table, a.k.a. the Vicious Circle.

## THE PLAYERS

The Algonquin attracted luminaries from all fields of literary endeavor. Aside from the charter members, other regulars included playwrights George S. Kaufman, Marc Connelly, and Robert Sherwood; novelist/playwright Edna Ferber (the author of *Giant* and *Show Boat*); newspaper columnists Franklin Pierce Adams ("FPA") and Heywood Broun; and *New Yorker* editor Harold Ross. The group also included eventual movie star Harpo Marx—yes, he could talk, and very well, too—but not his brother Groucho, who avoided the table because, as he put it, "The admission fee is a viper's tongue and a half-concealed stiletto."

Whatever. All of it made for good reading. Adams would recount the vicious, merry verbal battles in the column he wrote for the *New York Herald-Tribune*, and it wasn't long before literary tourists starting hanging out at the Algonquin just to get a glimpse of the Vicious Circle in action.

## THE MAN WHO CAME TO DINNER

Through it all Woollcott remained the heart of the Round Table, and like his fellow lunch-mates, used the friendships and notoriety born there for his own benefit. With Kaufman he wrote two moderately popular plays, *Channel Road* and *The Dark Tower*. But his most famous "collaboration" with Kaufman came when he served as the inspiration for *The Man Who Came to Dinner*, which Kaufman

---

**What country did St. Patrick come from? No one knows for sure, but it was probably Scotland.**

wrote with fellow Round Tabler Moss Hart. The play was based on a weekend trip Woollcott took to Hart's vacation home, during which he demanded, in rapid sequence: cake, a milkshake, and the heat turned off. Woollcott was so delighted that he played the title role in touring productions of the play. Woollcott would also parlay his fame onto the national stage in 1929, by becoming the host of the popular radio show *The Town Crier*.

## CHECK, PLEASE!

It was Woollcott who gave the Round Table its start in 1919 by applauding those who had come to savage him, so it shouldn't be entirely surprising that its end coincided with his own. Attendance at the Round Table started to drop in the 1930s, as many of the principals drifted away or headed to Hollywood to pursue writing careers for the movies, but the true end came in 1943, after Woollcott's death from a heart attack (which he had while on the air). The members of the Round Table met at the Algonquin for a final time to have a drink in Woollcott's honor only to discover, in so many words, that the thrill was truly gone. Harpo Marx later described it as "our strangest gathering," and perhaps it was so because the Round Table's center of gravity was no longer there.

To get aquainted with the rest of the Round Table crew, read "Slights of the Round Table Part II," page 120.

\* \* \*

## DENOUEMENT

A plaque on the Algonquin (the "Gonk") identifies it as a "literary landmark." There is a small display of Parker books and photos, and the hotel sells souvenir Round Table coffee mugs, snow globes (!), and cuff links. A painting of the Vicious Circle by Natalie Ascencios was unveiled in November 2002, for the hotel's 100th anniversary. Stop by if you can. Spend the night. Have a drink at the bar. And think.

\* \* \*

"There is only one thing in the world worse than being talked about, and that is not being talked about." —Oscar Wilde

---

Samuel Morse, inventor of the telegraph, was a successful landscape and portrait painter.

# NAME'S THE SAME

*All the twosomes described below have the same famous name.*
*Can you figure out what name each duo shares?*

1.  One of the stars of *Second City Television*, a.k.a. SCTV
    (Hint: He played opposite Rick Moranis in The Great White
    North skits), and the founder of the Wendy's fast food chain
    (*Hint:* He used to appear in his own commercials).

2.  The TV actor best known for his role as Mr. French, the
    butler/nanny on *Family Affair*, and the British-born son of
    the 16th-century explorer/cartographer who was born
    "Giovanni Cabotine."

3.  Reagan's Secretary of the Interior who infamously tried to ban
    the Beach Boys from performing in Washington because rock
    and roll encouraged drug use and attracted "the wrong ele-
    ment," and the 18th-century inventor who perfected the
    steam engine.

4.  The Native American actor and Oscar nominee for his role in
    *Dances With Wolves*, and the British-born author of *Our Man
    in Havana* and *The Third Man*.

5.  The TV actor who played patriarch Jock Ewing on *Dallas*, and
    the cartoonist who created *Garfield* the cat.

6.  A late, far-from-great senator from Wisconsin, and the manager
    of the New York Yankees from 1931 to 1946.

7.  An American boxer at the beginning of his career, and a 19th-
    century abolitionist.

8.  That same American boxer now, and a 20th-century shah
    of Persia.

8. Muhammad Ali

Answers: 1. Dave Thomas; 2. Sebastian Cabot; 3. James Watt;
4. Graham Greene; 5. Jim Davis; 6. Joe McCarthy; 7. Cassius Clay;

---

**Martha Washington was the first American woman commemorated on a U.S. postage stamp.**

# CHRIS AND DAULTON'S EXCELLENT ADVENTURE

*In 1975 two spies managed to steal top-secret info from the CIA and sell it to the KGB. Were these espionage agents slick, dangerous men in the mold of James Bond? No, they were two ex-altar boys who floundered through high school on their way to becoming college dropouts.*

C hristopher John Boyce and Andrew Daulton Lee were young Catholic altar boys serving in the same parish. They grew up in Palos Verdes, a wealthy suburb of Los Angeles, California. Chris and Daulton (as Lee was called), were best friends, but very different. Chris was the golden boy, tall and good-looking with a high IQ and an intense, idealistic philosophy. Daulton was a poor student who worried about his short stature and the fact that his ears stuck out. But he had assets—like his fast-talking style, his entrepreneurial skills, and a supply of drugs that gave him a "high" status on campus. While Chris mulled over the political ramifications of good and evil, Daulton was trying to think up the best ways to improve his "budding" marijuana business or how to make a move on a sexy cheerleader.

## TURN ON, TUNE IN, TURN TRAITOR

What they had in common was a love of adventure. Their parents could afford to indulge them in exotic hobbies, and Chris and Daulton bonded over falconry. Training birds to hunt was a pastime for Daulton, but it was a passion for Chris. He loved falconry's primitive connection to nature and the high-flying freedom of the birds.

They also shared the disaffection common to their generation. Both had dropped their ties to Catholicism. Daulton fell in with the 1970s fascination with the drug culture; he became a "snowman," first dealing cocaine and later, heroin. Chris took up the politics of protest against the government's war in Vietnam and the corruption of Watergate. But while his contemporaries were busy with their antiwar rallies or burning their draft cards, Chris Boyce used his status as a privileged son to protest in his own, unique way.

---

Queen Isabella of Spain was the first woman to appear on a U.S. postage stamp.

## WHEN GOOD OLD BOYS GO BAD

In 1974 Chris's dad, an ex-FBI agent, got tired of watching his son drift in and out of different colleges. He made some calls to pals in the FBI, and Chris was hired on at the aerospace company TRW. Dad's connections also got Chris a top-secret clearance. Within a year, the alienated, pot-smoking 21-year-old was working in a high-security section of TRW called the "black vault."

Inside the black vault, where the CIA's most sensitive secrets were recorded, Chris copied and distributed telex messages, known as TWXs or twickses. He worked on the Rhyolite and Argus projects, which used satellite spy technology to monitor military bases and missile launches in China and the Soviet Union. He learned that the CIA was working against its democratic ally Australia by not sharing promised intelligence and by engineering the removal of Australia's socialist-leaning prime minister.

Chris decided to launch a personal protest against the misdeeds of his government. To punish the U.S. for its abuse of power—and make a few bucks at the same time—he would sell U.S. spy secrets to its biggest rival, the Soviet Union.

## THE FALCON TAKES OFF

In 1975 Chris offered to give Daulton detailed secrets from the Rhyolite and Argus projects. Daulton could sell the secrets to the Russians, thereby keeping Chris's identity secret, then the two would split the profits. Daulton, always eager for easy money, traveled to Mexico, strode into the Russian Embassy; and bragged that he had secrets they'd want to pay for. He showed a KGB agent computer cards from the National Security Agency crypto system and paper from the crypto machines. The agent liked what Daulton brought him. He gave Daulton $250 and the code name Luis. The anonymous provider of the films, Chris, got the code name Falcon. The Soviets told "Luis" to get a small camera for "Falcon" and promised to pay the budding spies a nice chunk of change for photos of secret documents. The adventure had begun.

## INSIDE THE BLACK VAULT

For Chris, stealing satellite intelligence from the most powerful nation in the world turned out to be easier than rolling a joint.

---

Upon McKinley's assassination, Teddy Roosevelt became the youngest U.S. president at age 42.

Life in the black vault was one long cocktail party. The intelligence elite used the guarded isolation of the black vault to indulge in gossipy boozing. Sometimes the higher-ups drank daiquiris or mai tais that they blended in the CIA's document shredder. Other times they sent underlings like Chris out on liquor runs. The TRW guards knew that Chris used a government satchel to carry in alcohol for his bosses. They never looked inside the satchel when he left the black vault, so they never discovered that Chris used the booze satchel to carry secret documents out of TRW. The documents returned to the black vault inside a plastic bag that was buried in the dirt of a potted plant. Sometimes Chris didn't even take documents out of the building to photograph them; if he was alone in the black vault, he could take his photos right there—with the small Minox camera that Daulton bought him.

## FROM RUSSIA WITH LOVE

Daulton had more problems selling classified info than Chris had stealing it. When he swaggered into that Russian Embassy, he'd entered one of the most spied-on buildings in the world. The KGB knew they were being spied on, of course, so they set up other meeting places. Daulton was obviously an inexperienced, reckless show-off—so the Soviets tried to control him, pressing him to stay in less flashy hotels and be less conspicuous. They were paying a lot of money for TRW's satellite information, but they were having trouble convincing the erratic Daulton that their rules were serious. Once, when Daulton violated the command of staying away from the embassy, he was hustled into a car, driven for a few miles (all the while wondering if his young life was over), then tossed onto the road while the car was still moving.

## I'M WITH STUPID—AND SNEAKY

Chris Boyce enjoyed outfoxing the government, but he worried about getting caught, especially because of Daulton's instability— and his deepening addiction to heroin. Chris also suspected (correctly) that Daulton wasn't giving him half of the KGB money as promised. In an attempt to go around Daulton, Chris met with the Soviets on his own. The Russians wined and dined him and made him feel important. They urged him to return to college and take

The youngest elected U.S. president was John F. Kennedy at age 43.

classes that would make him valuable to the CIA—and even more valuable as a Russian mole. In December 1976, Chris left TRW to return to college. But as a parting present to himself, he also took along photos of the company's latest projected spy satellite system, Project Pyramider. The Soviets would pay $75,000 for them. In spite of his misgivings about his buddy, Chris figured "Luis" could deliver one last batch of CIA secrets to the KGB. Then their excellent adventure would be over.

## DAULTON'S LAST ADVENTURE

In January 1977, Daulton Lee waited for a rendezvous with the KGB but they didn't come quickly enough to suit him. He needed immediate cash to set up a big drug score, so he ignored all the warnings about going to the Russian Embassy. He wrote the message "KGB" on the cover of his Spanish-English dictionary, tried to attract the attention of the guards, and threw his message through the railing of the fence. He attracted attention, all right.

A local cop saw the nervous young American throw something onto the embassy grounds. Could it be a bomb? Daulton was arrested and interrogated by the Mexican police. Then they discovered the photos of U.S. documents that bore the heading "Top Secret." They called in the American authorities, who demanded to know how Daulton got classified documents. Daulton Lee protested that he was a patriot. Chris Boyce had given him phony CIA information to dupe the Soviets. But the Snowman couldn't fast-talk his way out of this one. Both adventurers were convicted of espionage. Daulton got a life sentence. Chris got 40 years.

## WAS IT ALL A SETUP?

The CIA claimed its high-tech spy system Rhyolite and its new project Pyramider were severely compromised, but some theorists believed Chris was set up by the CIA to disseminate misinformation. Otherwise how could he have stolen all those secrets so easily? Few Americans wanted to believe that lax security was to blame. Could TRW and the CIA really be so arrogant and incompetent?

## THE FURTHER ADVENTURES OF CHRIS

Let's leave that interesting question for a moment and follow Chris Boyce to prison. Two years into his sentence, prison officials showed the movie *Escape from Alcatraz*. Chris watched Clint Eastwood and simply copied his "papier-mâché" method of escape. In penitentiary arts and crafts classes, Chris learned the craft of papier-mâché. Using prison materials he made a dummy and put it in his bed so guards doing bed check wouldn't know he'd gone. On January 21, 1980, Chris went over the fence with a makeshift ladder. He cut the razor wire fence with rose pruning shears. He survived in the woods eating wild foods he'd learned about in the prison library. Showing a prison escape movie to prisoners? Could the prison officials have been so arrogant and incompetent?

## HUNTING THE FALCON

For 19 months Chris stayed a fugitive—hiding in the woods of Idaho, Montana, and Washington. But he needed money, so he decided to finance his latest adventure by robbing banks. Federal marshals finally got a tip and caught up with him in Washington State. He was rearrested and taken back to prison. The new convictions for bank robbery added 28 years to his sentence.

New York Times reporter Robert Lindsey wrote *The Falcon and the Snowman*, a best-seller that was made into a film starring Tim Hutton as Chris and Sean Penn as Daulton. But there was no glamour for the daring spy kids who were serving hard time.

Daulton Lee was paroled in 1998. Chris Boyce was paroled in March 2003. Both aging spy kids are back in circulation.

\* \* \*

## EARLY ESPIONAGE

- Egyptians had a well-developed secret service.
- Sun Tzu's *The Art of War* (c.500 B.C.) has large sections on deception and intelligence gathering.
- Political espionage flourished in the Middle Ages. Bishop Pierre Cauchon of Beauvais, a spy for the English, betrayed Joan of Arc, and Sir Francis Walsingham developed a political spy system for Elizabeth I.
- Joseph Fouche is credited with developing the first modern political espionage system.
- Frederick II of Prussia is regarded as the founder of modern military espionage.
- Nathan Hale and Benedict Arnold achieved fame during the American Revolution as spies, and both sides during the Civil War used spies.

# LEAGUE OF COMIC BOOK CREATORS!

*Meet the guys who put the Biff! Bang! Pow! into your comic books.*

B y day, they were mild-mannered writers and artists. But at night…well, they stayed mild-mannered writers and artists, for the most part. But! They also thought up some of the most popular comic book characters the world has ever known! And they used lots of exclamation marks while doing it! Come meet the men behind the *Men of Steel*, the *Dark Knights*, and the mutants. They aren't secret, just not very well known.

### SUPERMAN

**Joe Schuster & Jerry Siegel:** Schuster & Siegel created *Superman* in 1936, when the Cleveland duo (Siegel born there, and Schuster having moved there at age nine from Toronto) tried selling the Man of Steel as a comic strip to the newspapers. No one bought it until 1938, when DC Comics gave *Superman* a tryout in its Action Comics book. The rest is history, and Schuster & Siegel would go on to fame and fortune, right? Guess again. Sadly for the duo, DC Comics retained all rights in the Superman character (it came with the creative territory in those days), and so while the publishing company was making millions from *Superman*, Schuster & Siegel were not. They weren't doing poorly—in 1940 *The Saturday Evening Post* noted that the two of them were making $75,000 a year between them—but the two knew a raw deal when they saw it.

They sued DC Comics in 1946, and in 1948 received a relatively small settlement (a reported $120,000). But the flip side of the settlement was that the duo's byline, previously on every *Superman* story, vaporized as if hit by heat vision. Schuster left the comic book field outright, and Siegel's work slowed to a trickle. In the 1970s, while Hollywood geared up for the *Superman* movie starring Christopher Reeve, Schuster & Siegel again raised a stink about how poorly they had been treated by DC and sued the company once more. Although the courts decided they didn't have a case, DC was pressured by the comic book community into providing both men with a $35,000 a year stipend for as long as they lived, which in the case of Schuster was to 1992, and Siegel, 1996.

## BATMAN
**Bob Kane:** Like Schuster & Siegel, Kane handed over his comic book creation, *Batman*, to DC Comics, where the Caped Crusader made his first appearance in 1939. However, unlike *Superman's* creators, Kane maintained a small percentage of the take every time the cash register rang up a *Batman* sale. How did he do it? He had a lawyer in the family, who advised him to retain his copyright interests (Kane maintained he was a minor when he sold *Batman* to DC, and therefore legal representation was necessary, but he was born in 1916, and 23 is pretty old to be a minor).

Whatever Kane's exact age, keeping that stake in the *Dark Knight* did good things for his income and his leisure time. Although Kane's name was kept on all the *Batman* stories, Kane handed off most of the work to underlings in what was one of the biggest open secrets in comics. Kane himself headed to Hollywood to create animated TV shows (*Courageous Cat*) and to advise in the development of the campy 1960s Batman TV series. He had a cameo in 1997's *Batman and Robin*, as did his wife. He passed away in 1998.

## THE X-MEN, THE INCREDIBLE HULK, AND MORE...
**Jack Kirby:** Kirby, who started working in comics in 1938, was arguably the most prolific comic book character creator around. Characters he created or cocreated include the X-Men, the Incredible Hulk, and the Fantastic Four (major films based on the characters are out or on their way in all cases), as well as Captain America, Iron Man, the Silver Surfer, and Thor (the last one, admittedly, with a little help from Norse mythology). Some comic fans also give him a shared credit for Spider-Man, but officially the webslinger is Marvel Comics bigwig Stan Lee's baby. Most of Kirby's greatest creations are associated with Marvel Comics, but Kirby worked off and on for a number of comic book publishers, including Marvel rival DC; he bounced between the two majors for much of his career. He was also not above doing grunt work. In the mid-1950s, when worries about the morality of comic books

caused the industry to collapse and the superhero genre was gutted (350 comic book titles stopped publication), Kirby spent time drawing romance comics (hey, he had kids to feed). Kirby's artistic output throughout his career is staggering—more than 24,000 pages of comic book art. That's a lot of heavily muscled men in tights by any standard. Kirby passed on in 1994.

## TEENAGE MUTANT NINJA TURTLES

**Kevin Eastman:** Remember the early 1990s, when the Teenage Mutant Ninja Turtles were everywhere and you would have given a limb to go back in time and stop whoever it was from creating them? With a crowbar if necessary? Well, that year would have been 1984, and the person you'd want to, er, stop, would be Kevin Eastman, a college student who drew a "ninja turtle" to amuse his friend Peter Laird. The two of them collaborated to bring out a black-and-white comic book featuring the katana-swinging reptiles, and in relatively short order the characters had their own hit TV show and three hit movies. Eastman became rich in a way that comic book creators from the 1930s and 1940s could only dream of.

So what does a comic book geek do with fat wads of cash? He becomes a super comic book geek. In 1991, Eastman purchased *Heavy Metal* magazine, the seminal adult-comics magazine best known for its illustrated space adventures featuring chesty women with or without clothes. Not content merely to illustrate pneumatically enriched hotties, Eastman also married one—Julie Strain, 1993 *Penthouse* pet of the year and six-foot-one queen of B-movies, with whom he collaborated for a movie based on *Heavy Metal* called *Heavy Metal 2000*. Thus making him the hero of every comic book–reading male with a pulse, and probably a few without one.

## SPAWN

**Todd McFarlane:** McFarlane made his fame by creating Spawn, a super-violent comic character who deals with the devil in order to come back to earth and wreak vengeance upon those who did him wrong in life (of which there are, as one suspects, many). However, had things gone another way, we might know Todd McFarlane not for comic books but for baseball. McFarlane played baseball through high school in Canada, and at one point was recruited by the Seattle Mariners and played on a Canadian semiprofessional team associated with the major league team. He also got a scholarship to play baseball at Eastern Washington University. There he studied graphic arts—you know, just in case that whole baseball thing struck out.

Good thinking on McFarlane's part. Pro baseball passed him by, and McFarlane turned to comic books. In 1984 he started getting gigs with DC and Marvel, the latter for which he helped to revive the flagging *Spider-Man* series. In 1991, McFarlane formed his own comic book company and released *Spawn*; comic book fans went nuts and snapped up 1.7 million copies of the debut issue, making it the most successful independent comic book ever. McFarlane eventually expanded the Spawn character into movies, TV series, and action figures, keeping tight control of the property every step of the way.

Not that he forgot about baseball. In 1999, McFarlane used some of the riches spawned by *Spawn* and bought the 70th home-run ball from Mark McGwire's 1998 season for $3 million. He then toured it and other homerun balls hit by McGwire and Sammy Sosa that season in stadiums around the country to raise money to fight Lou Gehrig's disease. Which makes him kind of a superhero himself, we'd say.

* * *

## AND WE THOUGHT THEY WERE KID'S STUFF...

One of the highest prices ever paid for a comic book to date was for *Action Comics #1*, the 1938 comic book that introduced Superman and triggered the birth of many other costumed heroes. The price: $137,500 (including commission).

Other early editions are also estimated at some stellar prices: *Detective Comics #27* (1939), the first appearance of Batman and commissioner Gordon, at $30,000 to $300,000; *Captain America #1* (1941), origin of Captain American and Bucky, at $6,000 to $100,000; and *Daredevil #1* (1964) at $159 to $2,700.

Karl Benz invented the first gas-powered auto in 1885. It also had three wheels.

# THE BIG KAHUNA

*Sure, his name is impossible to pronounce, but he united and ruled over his own island paradise. What have you accomplished lately?*

Today, kahuna means many things, including "somebody who's good at what they do." Back in 1758, when some kahunas—the mystic priests of ancient Hawaii—saw Halley's Comet, they predicted that a great leader was about to be born, one who would defeat his rivals and rule all the islands.

## THE LONELY CRAB

The legend goes on to say that the king ordered his newborn grandson, Paiea (which means "hard-shelled crab"), to be put to death. The decision no doubt created some tension at the next family luau, but the old man figured, why take chances? In true epic fashion, the infant was spirited away and secretly raised to be a great warrior. He took the name Kamehameha (pronounced "ka-may-hah-may-hah"), which means "the very lonely one" or "the one set apart."

## ONLY ONE CROWN TO GO AROUND

While Kamehameha was growing up, his mean, old grandfather died and his uncle succeeded to the throne. When the uncle died, the island of Hawaii was divided between Kamehameha and his cousin Kiwalao, who was crowned the new king.

Kamehameha got a title, too. As Guardian of the War God, he had to tend to the god's shrine so that it would be all spiffed up when the king needed it to offer human sacrifices to the god. That was supposed to be the extent of his duties. So when he sacrificed a rebel chief to the war god himself, Kiwalao got royally ticked off and Kamehameha had to flee for his life. After forming an alliance with five other minor kings, he returned with a vengeance—and a pretty sizable army. Cousin Kiwalao was killed in battle, and Kamehameha wound up ruling a large chunk of Hawaii.

## THANK GODDESS!

But Kamehameha wasn't some laid-back surfer. He wanted it all.

---

The first human blood transfusion on record was performed by Jean-Baptiste Denis in 1667.

For the next ten years, he waged war with the other islands, bringing more and more of them under his rule.

Hawaii's government was a lot like feudal Europe. If a king won territory, he doled out pieces of it to lesser chieftains, who showed their gratitude by serving the king. In Kamehameha's case, it also helped that an eruption of Mount Kilauea (which is still the world's largest active volcano) destroyed a few hundred of his enemies. Everyone saw this as clear evidence that Pele, Hawaii's fire goddess, favored him over the other guys.

## THANKS, I NEEDED THAT
The day came—as the story goes—when Kamehameha landed his war canoe on the shore among a group of fishermen. The fishermen ran in terror, which infuriated the king. He attacked them until one of the fishermen did an extraordinary thing—he cracked the king over the head with a paddle.

What seemed like a pretty dumb move turned out to be a blessing that made the king stop and think. And when he thought about it, he was ashamed. So "the law of the splintered paddle," which protected the innocent against attack, became one of Kamehameha's most famous legacies.

## UNITED, YES—BUT WHAT A MESS
Things were going great in the building-the-empire department. After a while, Kamehameha controlled all the islands except Kauai and Niihau, which eventually were ceded to him peacefully after the king struck agreements with their local rulers. For the first time in its history, Hawaii was united under one leader.

However, all those years of war had wrought devastation. Fields had been ruined, people were starving, and, to make matters worse, those darn Europeans had begun to visit, bringing gifts like measles, smallpox, and pneumonia. Hawaii was not only a mess, but it had started to look like a juicy takeover target in the eyes of England, Russia, and the U.S.

## WHY WE CALL HIM GREAT
Kamehameha proved himself as forceful a ruler in peace as he'd been in war. He held his people together as they replanted and

In 1916 Jeannette Pickering Rankin became the first woman to serve in Congress.

rebuilt their economy. Even though he abolished some of the human sacrifices that were supposed to increase his mana (power), the old religion and gods were still respected as much as they'd always been.

As for the Europeans and Americans, Kamehameha dealt fairly with them—even allowing a few to settle and start cattle ranches. At the same time, he made sure his islands remained independent of these would-be colonial powers.

## ALOHA...

In 1819, when Kamehameha became very ill, his chief advisor suggested that a human sacrifice be made to save the king's life. But the Big K wouldn't allow it. When he died in his palace surrounded by his wives and children, a pig was cooked and offered to the gods instead.

The actual burial site of the first Kamehameha, now called Kamehameha the Great, is not known. According to an ancient practice, the king's flesh was removed from his bones and laid to rest in the sea. A minor chieftain took his bones to a secret cave, where they remain hidden to this day.

\* \* \*

## GOING FOR THE GOLD...AND SILVER AND BRONZE

At the 1924 Olympics in Paris, 20-year-old first-time Olympic athlete Johnny Weissmuller found himself on the starting block of the 100-meter freestyle—right between defending champion (and legendary surfer) Duke Kahanamoku and Duke's 19-year-old brother, Sam.

Weissmuller was afraid the two Hawaiians had cooked up some special strategy to swim a team race against him. (Weissmuller's reputation had preceded him to the Olympics; the previous February he'd set a world record that would last 10 years.) But to his surprise, Duke turned to him and said: "Johnny, good luck. The most important thing in this race is to get the American flag up there three times. Let's do it." And they did. Johnny came in first, Duke second, and Sam third.

Weissmuller, of course, went on to play Tarzan in the movies in the 1930s and 1940s. Duke Kahanamoku went to Hollywood, too, usually typecast as a Hawaiian king. Look for him in *Mister Roberts*, playing—what else?—"Native Chief."

# SAGA OF ABELARD AND HELOISE

*Life is funny. One day you've got the world on a string—a beautiful lover, a successful career. The next day, well, you wouldn't wish Peter Abélard's next day on your worst enemy.*

Toward the end of the Middle Ages, the Catholic Church ran pretty much everything in Europe. In a world of plagues, famine, and feudal barons, the Church was often the only safe haven. If you wanted to study, you went to a monastery—that's where the books were. If you wanted to learn, you went to the priests—that's who the teachers were.

## OUR HERO

Take Peter Abélard, for instance, a Church cleric and the most popular teacher in France. (The group of students who gathered to hear him speak eventually evolved into the University of Paris… but that was many, many lectures later, in the 12th century.) The Catholic Church's clerics weren't priests but had to follow some of the same rules—like celibacy.

Abélard, in his late 30s, ran afoul of this particular rule when he seduced his landlord's niece, 17-year-old Héloïse, who was known for her brilliant mind, as well as her good looks. Héloïse's guardian, her uncle Fulbert, had a room to let and Abélard needed a place to stay. The parsimonious Fulbert thought his niece might get some free tutoring sessions from the new tenant. She did—but the curriculum wasn't what her uncle had had intended.

Fulbert encouraged Abélard to work with his niece day and night. Months passed before Fulbert caught the couple in bed and threw Abélard out of his house. Abélard and Héloïse were soon the talk of the medieval town.

## TEENAGE RUNAWAY

When Héloïse managed to get word to Abélard that she was pregnant, he helped her sneak away and took her to live with his relatives. Héloïse gave birth to a son. She returned to Paris and proclaimed that she was proud and content to remain Abélard's lover. She didn't want to get married. Fulbert insisted on a wedding, but marriage would bring Abélard's career as a teacher and philosopher to a screeching halt, because he could no longer be part of the Church's hierarchy (that darn celibacy rule again).

## DON'T MESS WITH UNCLE FULBERT
Abélard's compromise was to marry Héloïse but to keep the marriage secret, which didn't satisfy Uncle Fulbert. What good was a secret marriage in restoring family honor? The furious Fulbert got revenge in the worst possible way. He hired a gang of thugs to waylay Abélard and castrate him.

## PICKING UP THE PIECES
Justice in those days was swift and vengeful. The thugs were caught, tried, then blinded and castrated. Uncle Fulbert got off lightly; all he lost was his property. Now that celibacy wasn't an issue for Abélard, he joined a monastery and became a full-fledged priest. Héloïse became a nun. Both withdrew from city life to live in religious communities, but Abélard continued to lecture.

## YOU'VE GOT MAIL
Abélard and Héloïse probably never saw each other again. We know about their sad story, their accomplishments, and even about their wild exploits (like the time they made love in a convent's dining room) from their letters. Some of the letters, oozing with passion and sadness, were written to each other; others went to friends. You can read them, too, if you want—they're still being published today.

## A REBEL TO THE BITTER END
In academic circles, Abélard's real claim to fame was that he used confrontation and questions to make his students think. This was unusual in the 12th century; other priests thought he dared to question the Church. One of Abélard's books actually listed contradictions between the Bible and Church authorities. His point was that by careful questioning, students could reach the truth. The Church found his teachings so blasphemous that Abélard was

forced to burn his own book. But he kept writing and teaching… and making enemies. Finally he was labeled a heretic. More books were burned and the Pope condemned Abélard to silence—sheer torture for him. The sentence was lifted before long, but Abélard was old and ill by then; he died on the way to Rome, hoping to explain himself directly to the Pope.

## A ROMANTIC, BUT KINDA CREEPY, ENDING

Héloïse lived for 20 years after Abélard's death. She became an abbess. She corresponded with many of the famous men of the day—even some of Abélard's old enemies. When she died, she was buried beside her husband. One story says that when the grave was opened to take her body, the body of Abélard opened its arms to embrace her for eternity.

\* \* \*

According to Napoleon, men were the masters of women: "Nature intended women to be our slaves. They are our property." But when he wrote to Josephine, the master's control seemed to be slipping.

> To Josephine,
>
> I love you no longer; on the contrary, I detest you. You are a wretch, truly perverse, truly stupid, a real Cinderella. You never write to me at all, you do not love your husband; you know the pleasure that your letters give him yet you cannot even manage to write him half a dozen lines, dashed off in a moment! What then do you do all day, Madame? What business is so vital that it robs you of the time to write to your faithful lover? What attachment can be stifling and pushing aside the love, the tender and constant love which you promised him? Who can this wonderful new lover be who takes up your every moment, rules your days and prevents you from devoting your attention to your husband?
>
> Napoleon

# QUEEN OF THE CATTLE RUSTLERS

*You may remember her as Butch Cassidy and the Sundance Kid's companion, as played by Katharine Ross in the movies. But historians and scientists have recently uncovered evidence that "Etta Place" was an alias—used by an even more notorious woman of the old West.*

Butch Cassidy and the Sundance Kid weren't as good-looking as Paul Newman and Robert Redford, but all the same, a gorgeous babe named Etta Place hung out with them for at least 10 years. Her identity had been a mystery to old West historians for nearly a century, until…

### MATCH.COM
In 1992, a series of computer photograph analyses linked Etta Place to another colorful figure with ties to Utah's past—Ann Bassett, the so-called Queen of the Cattle Rustlers.

First of all, the physical descriptions of Place and Bassett (provided by the esteemed Pinkerton National Detective Agency) matched almost identically. Besides mentioning their beauty and self-assurance, the Pinkerton report noted that the two women were also highly intelligent, expert horsewomen, good with guns, and as "loose" as ladies got in those days.

### COINCIDENCE? MAYBE.
The descriptions were considered coincidence all these years. But when their photographs were compared by the Computer Research Group at Los Alamos National Laboratory, the results showed that the two women were virtually identical; the chance that the two women were different people was 1 in 5,000. Pretty good odds.

The odds improved mightily when the analyst noticed something unusual with his naked eye—an elongated area at the top center of Ann's forehead that seemed to be missing hair—a tiny scar. And Place had precisely the same mark. The conclusion: Beyond all reasonable doubt the two were the same person. Etta Place was really Ann Bassett, Queen of the Cattle Rustlers.

---

In George Washington's time, U.S. life expectancy was 34.5 years for males, 36.5 for females.

## WILD CHILD

Ann Bassett was born on a ranch in Browns Park, Utah, on May 25, 1878. Her childhood was filled with every aspect of ranch life—and all the freedom she wanted.

In 1894—two years after her mother's death, in an attempt to curb her wildness—Ann's father enrolled her in St. Mary's Catholic School in Salt Lake City, Utah. The nuns tried to tame her, but after a year they had to ask her to vacate the premises. So Ann went back home. There's evidence that she spent some time as a schoolteacher, which would have given her the experience to handle overgrown boys like Butch and Sundance.

## BUTCH MEETS GIRL

Butch Cassidy visited the area sometime in 1896, and soon he and Ann were seen hanging out together. It's thought that Ann first started using the alias "Etta Place" during the winter of 1896–97, when Butch took her home to meet the family—that is, the Wild Bunch—at Robber's Roost, the gang's outlaw hideout in southeastern Utah.

## ANN RUSTLES UP SOME CATTLE...

But back in Browns Park, Ann's family ranch was in trouble. A large cattle company (no doubt run by a man in a black hat who twirled his moustache) was trying to run off the smaller ranchers. The Bassetts were warned to sell their land or else, but they stayed, as did one of Ann's old boyfriends. When he was killed, she took it upon herself to avenge him. She hunted stray cattle that wore the big cattle company's brand, and when she found them, she'd either shoot them or herd them into the Green River where they'd get stuck in the mud or be carried downstream. She even seduced the manager of the operation—who lost his job, but gained a wife. Their marriage lasted a few stormy years.

## ...AND IS CROWNED QUEEN

Ann Bassett was brought to court twice for cattle rustling; the first trial ended in a hung jury, the second got her a "not guilty" verdict. The trials made her famous. After a reporter for a Denver, Colorado, newspaper called her the "Queen of Rustlers," she became known to all as "Queen Ann."

William Henry Pratt: the real name of actor Boris Karloff.

## NOW YOU SEE HER, NOW YOU DON'T
Meanwhile, the Wild Bunch left Utah and congregated in Texas in the fall of 1900. A February 2, 1901, article in Utah's *Vernal Express* noted that "Miss Annie Bassett left on this morning's stage for Texas." Right after that, Miss Etta Place turned up in Texas.

## NEXT?
She took up with Butch and Sundance again, this time spending more time with Sundance. The trio took off for New York (with a reported $30,000 in loot), and from there, sailed to South America. Pinkerton records indicate that Place and Sundance returned to the U.S. in July 1902. Six months later Ann reappeared in Vernal, Utah, and the newspaper reported that she had been "traveling" for two years. (When unmarried women "traveled" in those days, it was often to cover up a pregnancy. But the rumor that Ann spent at least some of that time having a baby remains unproven.)

## THE LADY VANISHES
After a few more south-of-the-border rendezvous in the early 20th century with Sundance, and possibly Cassidy, no more was ever heard of Etta Place. Ann Bassett married cowboy/prospector Frank Willis in 1923 and eventually settled in the small town of Leeds, Utah, where she died in 1956.

Ann wanted her cremated remains to be scattered in her beloved Browns Park, but Frank drove there and found he "didn't have the heart to throw Ann out." He never did throw her out. Her ashes remained in the trunk of his car until he died in 1963, after which, courtesy of some family members, Ann found her way back to Browns Park, buried in an unmarked location.

\* \* \*

## BUTCH AT THE BOX OFFICE
After two plum roles (playing Elaine in *The Graduate* and Etta Place in *Butch Cassidy*) Katharine Ross seemed destined for big-time stardom, but too many bad choices in roles slowed her skyrocketing career. She still appears in films and on TV and she's been married to actor Sam Elliott (who had a bit part in *Butch*) since 1984.

# MY THOUGHTS ABOUT ME

*Some people seem to have captured their lives in a thought.*

"I had ambition not only to go farther than any man had ever been before, but as far as it was possible for a man to go."
—**Captain James Cook**

"The object of war is not to die for your country but to make the other bastard die for his."
—**General George S. Patton**

"Nothing is particularly hard if you divide it into small jobs."
—**Henry Ford**

"Any coward can sit in his home and criticize a pilot for flying into a mountain in a fog. But I would rather, by far, die on a mountainside than in bed. What kind of man would live where there is no daring? And is life so dear that we should blame men for dying in adventure? Is there a better way to die?"
—**Charles Lindbergh, Jr.**

"The life that is unexamined is not worth living."  —**Plato**

"My goal is simple. It is complete understanding of the universe, why it is as it is and why it exists at all."
—**Stephen Hawking**

"The first and most important thing of all, at least for writers today, is to strip language clean, to lay it bare down to the bone."
—**Ernest Hemingway**

"Today Europe, tomorrow the world."  —**Adolf Hitler**

"You cannot shake hands with a clenched fist."  —**Gandhi**

"Dream as if you'll live forever. Live as if you'll die today."
—**James Dean**

"Fast is fine but accuracy is everything."  —**Wyatt Earp**

"Along this track of pathless ocean it is my intention to steer."
—**Christopher Columbus**

---

Jan Paderewski was told he couldn't be a good pianist because his middle finger was too short.

# TRIPLE THREAT QUIZ 2
# SPORTS FOUNDERS

*NASCAR didn't just come out of nowhere, you know—it's not like one day people looked up and there was the Talladega racetrack and a bunch of guys in heavily-decaled cars making a bunch of left turns.*

Yes, someone thought up NASCAR, same with basketball, volleyball, and a lot of other very popular sports. Who? We provide the names. You guess the sport and the fun historical fact that goes with it. Ready? Break!

Match these sports founders...     With these sports...

1. Abner Doubleday          a)  NASCAR
2. Bill France, Sr.          b)  Volleyball
3. William G. Morgan         c)  Basketball
4. James Naismith            d)  Baseball
5. Jim Foster                e)  Arena football

And these historical facts...

i.  This sport's founder was once arrested (but never convicted) of trying to get around gas-rationing laws in 1946. He was very chummy with the FBI, and he volunteered the use of his personal planes for the bureau's use. He was also vice chairman for Democrats during Nixon's second election campaign.

ii. The founder of this sport, a longtime sports marketer, literally developed the original plans on the back of an envelope. This is also the only sport to be patented, thus assuring that no other competitors can use the same game format. The current league features teams in the U.S. and Canada as well as a development league.

---

**Original name of rock group Creedence Clearwater Revival: The Blue Velvets.**

iii. This famous sport's "founder" almost certainly didn't actually invent the sport in the mid-19th-century, as initially claimed by sports researchers. References to this particular sport appear in newspapers more then 15 years before this founder was supposed to have made up the game; moreover, this founder's obituary in *The New York Times* makes no mention of him inventing the game, concentrating instead on his Civil War service. He's buried at Arlington National Cemetery.

iv. This sport was based on a German game called "Faustball," in which the loser had to give his soul to the devil (no, not really—that's just a Goethe joke for you). This founder developed this game as a less-strenuous alternative for another game on this list—the founder of which he had been school-mates with and whom he worked with at the YMCA.

v. The founder of this sport had brains and brawn. He held degrees in philosophy, religion, and physical education—as well as being a medical doctor—and was also awarded his university's medal for being the "best all-around athlete." Although his sport became an instant hit, he never pursued fame and fortune from it, choosing relatively obscure academic positions instead.

5-e-ii
4-c-v
to basketball. At least that was the intention.)
3-b-iv (Volleyball) was supposed to be a less strenuous alternative
2-a-i
1-d-iii
Answers:

# UBER-ATHLETE

*If Jim Thorpe had been born in the 1980s instead of the 1880s, he'd be the star athlete at his school right now, he'd be training for the next Olympics, and he'd end up with a lot more money than he did. Some highlights from the life of the man who's been called the greatest athlete of the 20th century.*

• A descendant of the famous warrior Chief Black Hawk, James Francis Thorpe was part Irish, part French, and mostly Native American. He was born in a one-room cabin on an Indian reservation in Oklahoma, into the Thunder clan of the Sac and Fox tribe. His Indian name was Wa-Tho-Huk (Bright Path).

• In grammar school, Jim and his twin brother, Charlie, always came in first and second, respectively, in sports. When Charlie died of pneumonia one winter, Jim stopped going to school. In an effort to get him to go back, his father walked the 23 miles to school with him. But Jim didn't stay long—he ran the 23 miles back home the same day.

• The next year, enrolled in a boarding school in Kansas, Jim heard that his father had been hurt in a hunting accident. It took him two weeks to walk and run the 125 miles home.

• Jim's father enrolled him in a vocational program—to become a tailor, of all things—at Carlisle Indian School near Harrisburg, Pennsylvania. Not long after his arrival, Jim was walking across the sports field where some students were practicing the high jump. He asked if he could give it a try and easily made the jump, not realizing that the bar was set higher than anyone at the school had ever jumped before. When the school's athletic director heard about it, he convinced Jim to join the track and field team. The coach was none other than Glenn Scobey "Pop" Warner, the father, if you will, of Pop Warner Football.

• In 1911, Thorpe helped Carlisle win a national football championship, even beating top-ranked Harvard in front of 30,000 fans on Cambridge turf.

---

**The Ford Fairlane was named after Henry Ford's estate in Dearborn, Michigan.**

• Warner encouraged Thorpe to compete in the 1912 Olympics in Sweden. While the other athletes practiced constantly on the 11-day voyage across the Atlantic, Jim spent his days napping in a hammock. When one of the trainers complained about it, Warner said: "Leave him alone. Jim does all his training in his head."

• At the Olympics, he won gold medals in the pentathlon and decathlon events—a feat that's never been equaled to this day. As Sweden's King Gustav V was congratulating Thorpe, he said, "Sir, you are the greatest athlete in the world." To which Thorpe replied shyly, "Thanks, King."

• Jim returned to the U.S. with $50,000 worth of trophies and was greeted with a ticker-tape parade in New York City. He recalled: "I heard people yelling my name and I couldn't realize how one fellow could have so many friends."

• He got a lot of offers to join professional sports teams, but Pop Warner convinced him to return to the Carlisle football team. During the 1912 season, Jim scored a total of 198 points, including 25 touchdowns, and helped them win the championship once again.

• When a reporter discovered that Thorpe had played two seasons of semiprofessional baseball, the Olympic Committee stripped him of his medals and removed his name from the record books. But the silver medal winners refused to accept his gold medals; as one of them said: "Those belong to Jim."

• In 1913, Jim signed a contract to play professional baseball for $5,000 for the New York Giants. In one baseball game in Texas, on a field located on the border with Oklahoma and Arkansas, he hit three home runs in three different states. He hit the first one over the left field wall and into Oklahoma. He hit the second one over the right field wall and into Arkansas, and he hit the last homer within the park.

• After leading the Canton Bulldogs football team to championships in 1916, 1917, and 1919, he was elected the first president of the American Professional Football Association, which later became the NFL.

**In the War of 1812, the British burned the White House and most of Washington, D.C.**

• Thorpe played a few bit parts in several films, including the James Cagney classic *White Heat*. He also worked as a casting director, recruiting American Indians for Westerns. He sold his life story for $3,000 in the 1930s. It was made into a film in 1951, *Jim Thorpe—All American*, and starred Burt Lancaster.

• In 1950, Thorpe was selected by America's sportswriters as the most outstanding athlete of the first half of the 20th century.

• Jim Thorpe died of a heart attack on March 28, 1953. At the time of his death, he was a bouncer in a Los Angeles bar and lived in a trailer in Lomita, California. His wife was very disappointed to hear that Oklahoma wasn't interested in creating a memorial for her late husband, so she worked out a deal with two struggling communities in Pennsylvania with the unlikely names of Mauch Chunk and East Mauch Chunk, near the Carlisle Indian School. They agreed to merge and take Thorpe's name. He's buried at a memorial site there, in Jim Thorpe, Pennsylvania.

• One of the people who had competed against him in the 1912 Olympics was Avery Brundage, who placed sixth in the pentathlon and failed to finish the decathlon. Brundage later became the head of the United States Olympic Committee and the head of the International Olympic Committee. He always blocked any effort to reinstate Thorpe, and it wasn't till 1982, after Brundage had died, that Thorpe's medals were finally returned to his family and his records restored.

Score one for the uber-athlete.

\* \* \*

"Our lives were lived in the open, winter and summer. We were never in the house when we could be out of it. And we played hard. I wasn't content unless I was trying my skill in some game against my fellow playmates or testing my endurance and wits against some member of the animal kingdom." —Jim Thorpe

# HIS OWN
# WORST ENEMY

*Marcus Reno led the only unit that survived the Battle of the Little Bighorn, and he paid dearly for it for the rest of his life.*

From the moment he entered West Point at age 17, Marcus Reno rubbed his superiors the wrong way. His lax attitude earned him enough demerit points (1,031) to set a West Point record. The school was ready to toss him out, but Secretary of War Jefferson Davis intervened; he sympathized with Reno because of his own impressive West Point demerit record.

## THE WAR YEARS

A few years later when Davis was chosen to be president of the Confederacy, Reno got the chance to fight against the man who saved his young career. The Civil War was the high point of Reno's career. He fought with distinction at Williamsburg, Malvern Hill, Antietam, and Kelly's Ford. He came out of the war a major general.

## COME HOME, ALL IS FORGIVEN!

Now West Point wanted him to come back—this time as an instructor. He'd been a cavalry officer for eight years, but the academy wanted him to teach infantry tactics. Reno fired off a huffy letter of protest, and the Point withdrew its offer. Instead, the army sent Reno to New Orleans to put in some hard time on cavalry patrol. Never one to learn from past mistakes, Reno again lodged a protest, which resulted in another mark against his name.

After a year of hard work and no promotion, Reno—convinced that his talents were being overlooked—sent a letter to President Andrew Johnson. And that's how Reno ended up out West, as far away as the military establishment could send him.

## MARCUS MEETS HIS FATE

In the summer of 1869, Reno arrived in Fort Leavenworth, Kansas, and reported to Lt. Col. George Armstrong Custer to be appointed major in the Seventh Cavalry. He distanced himself from his fellow officers, feeding his reputation as a humorless disciplinarian

General Robert E. Lee was offered command of both the Union and Confederate armies.

and a loner. When his wife died in 1874, he turned more and more frequently to the bottle. By the time of the Little Bighorn campaign in 1876, Reno was a broken man.

## YOU GO FIRST—BE THERE IN A MINUTE

Custer ordered Reno to attack first, promising that he and the rest of the command would soon follow. Reno led his cavalry unit toward the Indian village along the banks of the Little Bighorn River, and a large band of warriors came out to meet them. Reno ordered his men to dismount and fight on foot.

The number of Indian warriors kept growing, and there was no sign of reinforcements. Reno ordered a retreat to the woods. As even more warriors joined the battle, Reno ordered another retreat—this time to a more defensible position on the high bluffs along the river. In the chaos of the retreat, Reno had to leave a lot of men behind. The ones who made it to the bluffs fought off wave after wave of attacks for the next 36 hours. When the dust had settled, a third of Reno's battalion was dead.

## BLAME IT ON RENO

Marcus Reno had fought as bravely as any man present, but his actions on that day seemed erratic to the big brass. They needed a scapegoat, and all eyes slowly turned to the malcontented Reno. At the official inquiry Reno was completely exonerated on the charge of cowardice. But the mere accusation seemed to unhinge him; his actions became more and more unsettling.

## I HAVE MET THE ENEMY AND HE IS I

After a few tacky incidents involving the fair sex, the army dishonorably discharged the now-broken—and always drunken— Major Reno. His last 10 years were lived in a state of near-constant inebriation. He died in 1889.

Almost a hundred years later, in 1967, Reno's case was reopened and the army changed his records to indicate that he had been honorably discharged. Which might have been nice if the major had still been alive—and sober. The board also ordered the reinternment of his remains in the sacred ground of the Little Bighorn Cemetery.

## BUT WHAT ABOUT RENO?

And if you thought the town of Reno, Nevada, was named for this sorry character, the answer is no—it was named for another Civil War hero: Major General Jesse Reno, who was killed in Maryland at the Battle of South Mountain in 1862.

---

The real name of Albanian-born Mother Teresa was Agnes Gonxha Bojaxhiu.

# ROCK STARS

*Two men with funny names who carved history in stone and put South Dakota on the map.*

## GUTZON BORGLUM

In 1927, Gutzon Borglum was one of America's foremost sculptors. He was 60 years old, had been fired from his last job, was a fugitive from justice, and was deeply in debt. But that summer work began on Borglum's masterpiece, a scupluture designed to last for millenia.

## AT HOME WITH MOM AND DAD…AND MOM

He'd been born in a log cabin in Idaho, the son of three Mormon parents—Gutzon's father was married to two sisters. Which was fine in Idaho, but when the family moved to Omaha the situation became embarrassing. Gutzon's father sent his second wife away and Gutzon never saw his mother again.

His unconventional childhood was so painful that Borglum never spoke or wrote of it. The entire subject was a Borglum family taboo.

## THE THINKING MAN'S SCULPTOR

At 23 Borglum married a woman his mother's age, Lisa Putnam, an artist he'd met in Los Angeles, California. She helped him develop important contacts in society and the art world. They moved to Paris, where Borglum met the famous sculptor Auguste Rodin.

Gutzon's younger brother, Solon, was also an artist. At first, Gutzon concentrated on painting while Solon took up sculpture. At the 1900 Paris Exhibition, Solon's sculpture was the toast of Paris. Soon after, perhaps due to sibling rivalry, Gutzon abandoned painting and began sculpting. Shortly thereafter, he also abandoned his first wife, leaving her in Europe while he shipped back to the U.S. On shipboard, he met his second wife, Mary Montgomery.

Borglum became a huge success as a sculptor. As a measure of his success, Borglum has more statues in the U.S. Capitol's Statuary Hall than any other sculptor. Commissions came in steadily from the wealthy and influential people Borglum cultivated, among them Teddy Roosevelt, which explains in part how Teddy joined Washington, Jefferson, and Lincoln on a mountainside.

## HERE COMES TROUBLE
In 1915, an elderly Confederate widow, president of the Atlanta chapter of the United Daughters of the Confederacy, contacted Gutzon about sculpting a Confederate memorial on the great granite face of Stone Mountain, Georgia. Gutzon surveyed the site and proposed a colossal spectacle—Lee and his army marching across the cliff. He had no idea how he would project the image onto the rock, how the workers would carve on the steep face, or how he would remove the thousands of tons of granite. And for their part, the Daughters had no idea how they would raise the millions of dollars in projected costs.

Enter the Ku Klux Klan, which had reorganized itself in 1915 on top of Stone Mountain. The Klan raised money for the memorial. Why Borglum joined the Klan is unclear; self-promotion may have been the primary reason. His political views were as erratic as his personality. At times, he wrote poisonously anti-Semitic diatribes, but as soon as Hitler came to power and took measures against the Jews, Borglum was one of the first to speak out against it. Borglum had no trouble befriending anyone so long as they were wealthy or influential, preferably both. (He also had no difficulty making enemies due to his arrogance and temper.)

## HAPPY BIRTHDAY, ROBERT E!
Robert E. Lee's portrait was unveiled on Stone Mountain on what would have been his 100th birthday, in 1924. Carving had already begun on Stonewall Jackson's portrait and the space was cleared for Jefferson Davis. But a faction of the Klan wanted Borglum off the Stone Mountain project, mostly because he was also planning "a great Union Memorial in South Dakota."

## THE GREAT ESCAPE
Borglum was fired. Enraged, he ordered his crew to break up the model for the memorial and drop it over the cliff. The Stone Mountain Association raised a posse and chased Borglum through the back roads of Georgia with an arrest warrant for "willful destruction of association property." After an all-night chase,

---

**Vincent van Gogh didn't start drawing until he was 27 years old.**

Borglum slipped across the border into North Carolina, out of reach of the Georgia law.

The new sculptor, Augustus Lukeman, who was hired to complete Stone Mountain blasted away most of Borglum's work (the head of Lee). By 1928 he had only completed Lee's horse Traveler, the heads of Davis and Lee, and the outlines of their bodies. Two more sculptors were hired before the memorial was completed in 1972.

## FOUR PRESIDENTS GET STONED IN SOUTH DAKOTA

Meanwhile, South Dakota needed a tourist attraction. Easterners cruised through the state on their way to Yellowstone but they weren't stopping and spending. Doane Robinson, head of the South Dakota Historical Society and its poet laureate, wanted to borrow the idea of Stone Mountain—and its original artist. What would suit South Dakota? Frontiersmen carved into one of the cliffs of the Black Hills? Gutzon Borglum had far grander notions.

## TEDDY AND THE BIG SHOTS

A national theme was needed, not only to suit Borglum's grandiose dreams, but for a far more practical reason: to attract national funding. Borglum proposed George Washington as the country's father, Abraham Lincoln as the savior of the nation, and Thomas Jefferson and Theodore Roosevelt as embodiments of national expansion for the Louisiana Purchase and the Panama Canal, respectively. The Roosevelt choice was controversial—Borglum's old pal had been dead for only a few years and history hadn't had time to weigh in. But Congress had been discussing a Teddy Roosevelt memorial and Borglum grabbed the chance to get some federal money for his project.

## PLEASING SOME OF THE PEOPLE SOME OF THE TIME

After touring the Black Hills for an appropriate site, Borglum chose Mount Rushmore for the quality of its granite and for its southeastern exposure. Work began in the summer of 1927. Money turned out to be a continual problem—exacerbated by the onset of the Great Depression. The project got federal funding but with it, it also got politics. Southerners wanted Abraham Lincoln removed; Democrats wanted Woodrow Wilson added; Eleanor Roosevelt wanted Susan B. Anthony. Borglum stood firm.

Ferdinand Porsche, known for building sleek sports cars, designed the original Volkswagen in 1936.

## MOUNTING RUSHMORE

Experienced miners did the sculpting while Gutzon and his son, Lincoln, supervised. The miners jackhammered and dynamited 400,000 tons of rock to within three inches of the final surface. Structural problems developed. Jefferson was originally to have been on Washington's right, but a bad cut ruined that head and it had to be blasted off. The second Jefferson is tilted upward, giving him a dreamy look. It wasn't intentional; it was necessary to avoid cracks in the rock. Washington's nose was deliberately left one foot longer than scale because Borglum thought it would add another 100,000 years to the life of the monument. (The National Park Service estimates the figures will last for 20,000 years.)

## UNFINISHED BUSINESS

The presidential portraits were to have been busts, but the plans to complete Mount Rushmore died with Borglum in 1941. War was looming in Europe, and the government decided not to appropriate any more money to the project. Lincoln Borglum cleaned up the site, packed up his materials, and left. Like many of the men who blasted and carved Rushmore, Lincoln's lungs were scarred by granite dust. He continued working as a sculptor, dying in 1986. The visitor's center at Mount Rushmore is named for Lincoln Borglum, not his father.

Mount Rushmore had cost just $900,000. And South Dakota got its wish. Tourism is now second only to agriculture in the state's economy.

## KORCZAK ZIOLKOWSKI

He was a promising young sculptor when he started work for Gutzon Borglum on Mount Rushmore early in 1939, as assistant to "first assistant" Borglum's son, Lincoln, but he didn't like taking orders. After just 19 days, Gutzon Borglum fired Ziolkowski.

When Lincoln gave Korczak the news, Korczak slugged him and the two men began pummeling each other. The other workers had to jump in and break it up. Lincoln Borglum ended up in the hospital. Korczak apologized and left, but the incident may have led to Korczak's ambition to out-Borglum Borglum.

---

Film star and racing enthusiast Steve McQueen invented (and patented) the bucket seat in 1969.

## ANOTHER MONUMENTAL JOB

Ziolkowski returned east and continued his studio sculpting. In 1942, he volunteered for service in WWII and was wounded. After the war, he was asked to sculpt government war memorials in Europe, but his heart drew him back to the Black Hills. In 1947, he filed a mining claim on a mountain near Custer, South Dakota. A Sioux chief, Henry Standing Bear, had long dreamed of a monument to Crazy Horse, the Sioux leader who defeated Custer at Little Bighorn. With Standing Bear's blessing in 1948, Korczak began work on his mountain. His model showed Crazy Horse mounted on horseback, his left arm pointed forward.

## KEEP IT TO YOURSELF, OLD-TIMER

Korczak's imagination wasn't constrained by what Crazy Horse actually looked like because the great chief had never permitted any photographs to be taken of him. When the model was unveiled, two Indian survivors of Little Bighorn said that it looked nothing like Crazy Horse. The project went ahead anyway. When finished, the Crazy Horse Memorial will dwarf Borglum's work on Mount Rushmore at 641 feet long by 563 feet high. At ten times the volume of Mount Rushmore, Korczak Ziolkowski had begun the largest sculptural project ever attempted.

## NO END IN SIGHT

Ziolkowski worked on Crazy Horse for the remaining 36 years of his life. When he died in 1982 at age 74, his wife and seven of his 10 children took up his work; work that may take the rest of their lives. Carving Crazy Horse's face (87 feet, 6 inches) alone took 50 years. There is no projected completion date.

\* \* \*

## FOOTNOTE TO FAME

Mount Rushmore is named for a New York City lawyer, Charles Rushmore, who was sent by his British clients to investigate their mining claims in the Black Hills in 1885. Years later, Rushmore donated generously to the monument that would immortalize "his" mountain.

---

In *Gone With the Wind,* if dates and battles are correct, Melanie's pregnancy lasted 21 months.

# SEDUCED AND BEHEADED

*Beware of drinking too much at parties! You could "be headed" for trouble!*

I t's not all that easy writing about ancient historical figures, especially when their stories conflict with reality. But we're gonna give it a try. The questions we'll be asking: Did Judith of Bethulia really exist? And why is this great Jewish heroine celebrated in the Catholic and Greek Orthodox Old Testament but not even mentioned in the Hebrew Bible? Most puzzling of all, how did a fierce woman-warrior become the inspiration for cheesy holiday pancakes?

## A BIBLE STORY

Judith was a widow who lived in a town called Bethulia in ancient Judea during the reign of Nebuchadnezzar II, the king of Assyria. She didn't have a husband, but on the plus side she was beautiful and very rich. No doubt about it, Judith had it all.

Around 593 B.C., Judith nearly lost it all. King Nebuchadnezzar II proclaimed from the coziness of his throne in Nineveh that he wanted all Jews to desert their God and worship him. To that end, he sent his armies to conquer Judea. Bethulia refused to surrender, so the Assyrian general, Holofernes, cut off its water supplies. Soon the Israelites were dying of thirst and beginning to consider the possible advantages of Assyrian slavery. But not Judith. She said her prayers, put on her best dress, packed up some delicious eats from her farm, and rode out to the Assyrian camp.

## ONE SMART COOKIE

When she was brought before the general, she pretended to be totally impressed. She flattered Holofernes and praised him for his military savvy. She gave him tips on how to conquer her people (make them break God's laws and turn away from their faith). She probably even complimented Holofernes on his cute uniform. Judith was so sweet and helpful that Holofernes invited her to his tent for a bit of…er…banqueting. Not only did the beautiful

---

For her role in *Cleopatra*, Elizabeth Taylor was the first woman to get a $1 million film contract.

Jewess seem eager to be seduced, she even brought her own food and wine to the party. What a cheap date!

## IT'S THE CHEESE

As the story goes, Judith fed the general salty cheeses that made him thirsty for the wine that she poured freely. The unsuspecting Holofernes was tickled—but soon he was pickled! When Holofernes finally passed out, the wily Judith drew his sword and lopped off his head. Then she put it in a sack and brought it to the Hebrew soldiers. They stuck her trophy on the Bethulia city walls. The Assyrian troops took one look and fled.

## SHE CAME, SHE SAW, SHE GAVE A DINNER PARTY...

Here's where we get into some scholarly studies, but bear with us, it won't hurt a bit. The big question is: If Judith was a great heroine of the Jewish people (her very name means Jewess), why did the conference of rabbis who met in the first century A.D. to canonize the Hebrew Bible refuse to include the Book of Judith?

It could have been guilt by association. Judith's book, though originally written in Hebrew, became part of the Septuagint, a collection of spiritual texts written in Greek. None of the Greek Septuagint was included in the Bible because it wasn't thought to be divinely inspired—only Hebrew or Aramaic texts were.

It could have been the fact that no one has ever found the legendary town of Bethulia that Judith saved. It could have been the fact that King Nebuchadnezzar II wasn't Assyrian, he was the king of Babylon, and the city of Nineveh was destroyed by the time of his reign. He also never had a general named Holofernes—though there was a Phoenician general named Holofernes who waged war with Israel some 300 years after old Nebbie had passed on.

Finally, it could have been the fact that, after the beheading incident, Judith supposedly lived in peace and prosperity until her death at 105. Because, in reality, Nebuchadnezzar successfully conquered the Israelites. Brave Judith would have been exiled with the rest of her countrymen who "wept by the waters of Babylon."

## THE NOT-SO-USUAL STORY

Just in case Judith's story isn't unprovable enough, there's a second version in which every Jewish bride had to sleep with the Assyrian governor before marriage. Enraged at Assyrian exploitation, Judith gave a cheesy soirée for the sleazy guv—in which he drank too much and lost his head.

## SO WHAT GIVES?

What really happened and when? The Book of Judith was written around 160 B.C. when the Jews were fighting Antiochus IV, the King of Syria who wanted them to worship him and his pagan gods. Some scholars think that the accurate story is the second one. Judith's decapitation of the governor may have been rewritten into Judith decapitating a general; that way her story could inspire hope in the ranks of the outgunned Hebrews who were defending their faith against Antiochus's superior army.

Other scholars believe Judith's victory over a despotic king is a historical fact, but that the names and dates got jumbled in translation. They point out that arrogant King Antiochus IV put the screws to the Israelites in ways that square with events in the Book of Judith. And traditionally, Judith's tale has always been told in connection with the Maccabees, the Jewish family that led the revolt against Antiochus and his mighty Syrian army.

## SO NOW YOU KNOW...

Judith is remembered during Hanukkah, a holiday that celebrates a Jewish triumph over Antiochus. In 165 B.C., Judah Maccabee recaptured the temple of Jerusalem from the king and rededicated it to the Jewish faith. Today's Hanukkah dish of potato pancakes or "latkes" have evolved from a Hanukkah tradition of cheese latkes, pancakes that commemorated Judith's cheesy headhunting party.

\* \* \*

Babylon achieved its greatest fame under Nebuchadnezzar II (630–562 B.C.). Under his rule, Babylon became a great city of 250,000 people with grand palaces, temples, and houses. He is perhaps best known for the Hanging Gardens of Babylon; the legend is they were built for his wife who missed the greenery of her mountain home. It also is said that Alexander the Great, dying of a fever, found relief in the gardens.

# FAMOUS AFTER 50

*Proof that it's never too late to start on the rocky road to success.*

## COLONEL SANDERS

Born September 9, 1890, Harland Sanders had been a farmer, a streetcar conductor, a soldier, a railroad fireman, a justice of the peace, an insurance salesman (wait while we catch our breath…), a steamboat operator, and a service station owner. He was also a good cook. Soon, folks were coming to his service station in Corbin, Kentucky—not for gas but for the food he served on his own dining room table. Business got so brisk that Sanders opened the 142-seat Sanders Café, to which he soon added a motel. The best-selling dish was the chicken, fried in a batter that included a secret blend of those now-famous 11 herbs and spices.

### Adventures in Good Cooking

In 1939, Sanders Café was listed in Duncan Hines's definitive roadside restaurant guide *Adventures in Good Eating.* That same year, Kentucky's governor made Sanders an honorary colonel for his contributions to the state's cooking. The Colonel's upward mobility slowed when gas rationing in WWII forced folks to stay home more, and it ground to a halt when a new interstate highway bypassed the road the café was on. Sanders had to sell the business in 1956; he survived on $105 a month in Social Security checks.

At least he still had his secret recipe. At 66, he started traveling the country, sleeping in his car and cooking his chicken for restaurants. If they liked it, Sanders made a handshake deal that gave him a nickel for each chicken the restaurant sold. At first business was slow; in two years, only five restaurants signed on as franchisees. Eventually, word got around and by 1964, more than 600 restaurants were selling Colonel Sanders' fried chicken. (The colonel was so protective of his recipe that he had two separate suppliers, each of whom knew just half the secret ingredients. Sanders alone would combine them before sending them to his franchisees.)

### Kentucky Fried Fortune

When the business got too big for him to handle, he sold his interest for $2 million and, at 74, became the public face of Kentucky Fried Chicken. By 86, he was an internationally recognized

---

First Lady Barbara Bush was known as "the Silver Fox."

celebrity. Colonel Harland Sanders died at 90, but his recipe is still "finger-lickin' good."

## GRANDMA MOSES

Anna Mary Moses never had time to paint when she was young. She'd been born on a farm in upstate New York in 1860; she married a farmer and worked alongside him planting, harvesting, and raising chickens—and lots of children. Anna Mary was 67 when her husband died. And it wasn't until her late 70s—when she found housework becoming too strenuous—that she took up art. At first, she did original needlework pictures, which she exhibited in the local drugstore in Hoosick Falls, New York.

### Painting the Town (and the Farm)

As fate would have it, an art collector named Louis Caldor stopped into the drugstore and saw Anna Mary's work. He encouraged her to take up painting. Soon she was painting primitive scenes of American life in the 19th century, based on her childhood memories of apple butter, soap making, sleigh rides, and country Christmases. Caldor was charmed, but when he tried to interest other art mavens in Mrs. Moses's work, they told him it was a waste of time and money promoting an artist who was pushing 80.

Anna Mary was into art for art's sake, so she kept painting and got better and better. By 1939, three of her paintings were exhibited in New York's Museum of Modern Art. Her career took off the following year with a show at Gimbel's department store in Manhattan. Now known as "Grandma" Moses, Anna Mary was baffled by the high prices (up to $20,000 each) her works were fetching.

### Mrs. Moses Goes to Washington

Soon her paintings were being shown worldwide. In 1949, she received an award from President Truman, and she gave her painting *July Fourth* to the White House—where it still hangs. She even was commissioned to do a painting of President Eisenhower's farm. In the last years of her remarkable life, Grandma Moses produced hundreds of paintings—she completed 25 of them after her 100th birthday. She died at 101, one of the most celebrated and beloved American painters of the 20th century.

## MARY KAY ASH

Mary Kay Ash once said that "a woman who will tell her age will

**The people in Grant Wood's *American Gothic* painting are ostensibly father and daughter.**

tell anything." She lived up to her own motto; sources put her birth year as anywhere from 1910 to 1918. In any event, she was straddling the half-century mark when she made a decision that turned an ordinary saleswoman into the queen of cosmetics.

### An Overachiever Is Born

Mary Kay was born to sell. As a child growing up in Texas, she out-sold all the other kids in Girl Scout cookies and tickets for school events. She was an honor student and racked up trophies for debate and public speaking. There was no money for college, however, so she got married instead. After three children and a divorce, she went to work in 1938 for Stanley Home Products selling door to door. She moved on to the World Gift Company in 1952, where her sales abilities earned her a spot on the board of directors and the title of national training director. She quit in 1963 after one of the men she'd trained was promoted over her (and at twice her salary).

One month later, she took her life savings of $5,000 and bought a formula for a skin softener she had used for years made by a hide tanner. "Beauty by Mary Kay," the company's original name, set up shop in a Dallas storefront; nine of her friends were the first employees. During the first year, the company earned $200,000 in profits; by the second year that number had jumped to $800,000, and Mary Kay had a sales force of 3,000 women.

### Think Pink

Mary Kay Cosmetics soon became famous for its motivational techniques and incentives like pink Cadillacs and diamond jewelry. The company has been honored by *Forbes* magazine as one of the "100 Best Companies to Work for in America." In 1996, Mary Kay Ash was inducted into the National Business Hall of Fame by *Fortune* magazine.

Today, the company she started with $5,000 brings in billions of dollars annually. Mary Kay Ash died in 2001, wealthy and well respected. At 50 (plus or minus), Mary Kay had turned a hard knock into a big break.

### LAURA INGALLS WILDER

Life had been hard on Laura. As a child, she and her family lived at the edge of poverty. Her sister, Mary, was left blind after a high fever at 14. A few years after her marriage to Almanzo Wilder, he came down with a severe illness, probably polio, and was left

---

**Ben Franklin used the pen name Richard Saunders to publish *Poor Richard's Almanack*.**

crippled. Their baby son died shortly after birth. Fire destroyed their home in South Dakota. So when they heard of cheap land in the Ozarks, they loaded up a covered wagon and made a $100 down payment on a farm near Mansfield, Missouri.

Despite all the hard times, Laura had lots of good memories. So at 63, she turned her adventures and misfortunes into an auto-biography. She knew she could write a little; she'd sold articles to a farm weekly, *The Missouri Ruralist*, on canning, raising chickens, growing apples, and other aspects of farm life. How hard could it be to write her memoirs?

## Laura's Life Story

Wanting to preserve her stories of frontier life, Laura took out a pencil and a blue-lined tablet and wrote *Pioneer Girl*. She showed the draft to her daughter Rose, a successful writer, and like a dutiful daughter, Rose typed it up and sent it to various publishers, all of whom agreed it was a great story—and turned it down flat. But a friend of Rose's, a children's book author, thought the story would make a good children's book. So *Pioneer Girl* again made the rounds of publishers and this time the children's department of Harper & Brothers Publishers expressed interest. So Laura rewrote her story as children's fiction, starting with her first childhood memories in the big woods of Wisconsin.

## Little House, Big Success

*Little House in the Big Woods* was published in 1932 and sales were good despite the Depression. The Ingalls family's story of courage through hardship suited the times and served as an inspiration. *Little House in the Big Woods* was a huge success and a favorite in schools as a way to study the lives of the pioneers. At 65, Laura Ingalls Wilder was suddenly famous. And then, of course, the series of *Little House* books became the popular TV series *Little House on the Prairie*, which first aired in 1974 and placed in the Nielsen Top 20 for the first seven seasons of its eight-season run.

Laura continued to write throughout her early 70s. Her royalty checks paid her more than the farm had ever brought in. She wrote eight novels in all, four of which won a Newbery Medal, an award given to outstanding children's books. At 76, she decided that she'd told all her stories. It was time to resume living life instead of writing about it.

Laura Ingalls Wilder died at 90.

---

**What do Charlie Chaplin, Albert Einstein, Bob Dylan, and Pablo Picasso have in common?**

# THE MAN BEHIND THE FROUFROU

*How an Italian-Polish kid from the Midwest became the toast of a couple of continents and the butt of one or two jokes. Say what you will about Liberace...he knew how to play the piano. You could do better?*

## A STAR IS BORN

Little Wladsiu Valentino Liberace was born in 1919, just outside Milwaukee, Wisconsin. Four years later, Walter (as the family called him) was playing the piano by ear, and by the time he was seven, he was attending music school on a scholarship.

In high school, his extracurricular activities consisted of cooking and dressing up (no surprise there). In fact, he won a school prize for originality by dressing up as Greta Garbo. Some of the other kids called him a sissy, but that didn't keep Walter down.

## IT'S MAGIC!

He was trained as a classical pianist, but he played practically everything else, too. He soloed with the Milwaukee Symphony and the Chicago Symphony while still in his teens, and he played in some local honky-tonks. After reading a self-help book called *The Magic of Believing*, Liberace started putting some positive principles into action. He dropped the name Walter altogether; from now on, he'd be known just as "Liberace" to his audiences and "Lee" to his friends. He got his teeth capped and started to dress for success—in a tasteful tuxedo at first. He moved to New York— and the nightclub scene—in 1940. A rave review in *Variety* in 1945 led to a string of dates across the country.

He was playing at the Hotel del Coronado in San Diego, California, in 1950 when a TV producer discovered him and offered him a chance to work in the then fledgling television industry. His first show was a summer replacement for the *Dinah Shore Show*, but after two years it became one of the most popular shows on TV.

## HI, MOM!

By 1954, *The Liberace Show* had gone national. Lee, still in the conservative black tuxedo, sat down at his oversized, candelabra-

**They're all left-handed.**

topped piano, and between songs—everything from "The Beer Barrel Polka" to "Clair de Lune"—schmoozed like crazy with the camera. Audiences came to expect the nod to his brother, George, the orchestra conductor, and the loving mention of their mom.

## HELLO?

In a strange societal quirk only the 1950s could produce, Liberace was adored by millions of women. They talked about his refinement, his gentleness, his devotion to his mother—but they didn't get exactly why he was so refined and gentle, or why his mom was pretty much the only woman in his life. "Gay pride" was as yet unborn, still just a twinkle in Liberace's eye. There were, of course, the usual publicity stunts, the rumors that he was engaged to this woman or that, but in the end it was his mom who cooked for him and ironed every last ruffle in every last shirt.

## THE CANDELABRA KID

Career-wise, in the early 1950s, Lee was pure gold. He played Carnegie Hall in 1953, and filled Madison Square Garden in 1954. Then it was on to Las Vegas where, at $50,000 a week, he was making more money than any other entertainer on earth. Of course, a lot of that was going for costumes. (It was a simple gold lamé jacket—and the attention he got when he wore it—that started the extravagant wardrobe he'd later refer to as "an expensive joke.")

## NOT A GOOD YEAR

But by 1957, "the Guru of Glitter" was beginning to suffer from overexposure, in more ways than one. That was the year the scandal sheet, *Confidential*, ran a story about Liberace putting the moves on a press agent (male). Lee sued for libel, denying that he was a homosexual. He won the case by proving he was nowhere near the scene of the crime.

That same year, a four-week run at the RKO Palace was canceled after two weeks because ticket sales were slow. Was Liberace's glitter getting a little tarnished?

## BYE, MOM!

Things went from bad to terrible. A couple of years later, *Top Secret Magazine* divulged the unsavory facts of Lee's break with his mother. Until then, he'd been a model son, more than a mother

---

**In 1972, Arnold Schwarzenegger appeared on TV's *The Dating Game*.**

could ask for. But now, at age 39, according to Mom, he'd taken up with "a gang of hillbillies and freeloaders." (Living the high life in Palm Springs—and loving it.)

## ALL THE WAY TO THE BANK
The press wasn't through with Liberace, the guy they called "the Sultan of Schmaltz." This time the *London Daily Mirror* had a go, describing him as "this deadly, winking, sniggering, snuggling, chromium-plated, scent-impregnated, luminous, quivering, giggling, fruit-flavored, mincing, ice-covered heap of mother love." Did they really think they could get away with it? The litigious Liberace sued and won. And that's when he coined the famous phrase "I cried all the way to the bank!"

## LIFE GOES ON
The 1960s flew by. His career rebounded. Lee was presented to the Queen of England, got his star on the Hollywood Walk of Fame, appeared on the very campy TV show *Batman*, played a casket salesman in the movie *The Loved One*, and was audited by the IRS for deducting his costumes as a business expense—a dispute he won handily. Oh, and more Vegas!

The 1970s consisted mostly of more Vegas and tours. Lee was the highest-paid performer in the world and he didn't mind letting people know. It was somewhere around this time that he told audiences, "Remember that bank I cried all the way to? Well, now I own it."

Between engagements, Lee found the time to write three books: a cookbook, an autobiography, and *The Things I Love*, all about his homes, jewelry, and costumes.

## LIB'S LAST DECADE
The 1980s didn't start out well at all. Liberace barely had time to recover from the death of his mom in 1980 when he was sued for $113 million in palimony by Scott Thorson, his former live-in bodyguard, chauffeur, secretary, and more. Even though the entertainer still denied being gay, he settled the case out of court in 1984. Thorson got $95,000, then picked up a little extra change by selling his story to the *National Enquirer*.

Liberace, "the Candelabra Kid," died of AIDS-related complications on February 4, 1987.

\* \* \*

"I'm just here to help people have a good time." —Liberace

Seventeen-year-old Warren Beatty was a rat-catcher for the National Theater in Washington, D.C.

# A NERD WHO CHANGED THE WORLD

*When he was young, no one would have taken him for a man who would ignite sweeping changes in the world. He was, in today's parlance, a dork—plump, shy, and frequently lost in his own thoughts. But, oh, what thoughts they were!*

Adam Smith's book, *The Wealth of Nations*, is considered the foundation of free enterprise—better known as "capitalism" today. Even though it was published more than 200 years ago, it's still used in economics departments in colleges around the world. And why not? Smith's radical ideas not only toppled great aristocracies and created—and destroyed—huge fortunes, they were the theoretical framework around which great nations like America were built.

## A BRAIN IS BORN
Adam Smith and his great brain were born in Scotland in 1723. His father died while Adam was still in the womb, which turned the little fella into something of a mama's boy. He was kidnapped as a child by gypsies who wanted to make him their own, but was soon rescued by his uncle. That was the last dramatic thing that ever happened to him. He never married, and he lived with his mother until her death. He was, by all accounts, a cheerful soul.

## THE PROFESSOR
At Glasgow University in the 1750s, Smith began working out the theories that would make him famous. His lectures examining the ethical foundations of humankind and their various economic systems were so dazzling that he taught students from as far away as Russia.

## THE ABSENTMINDED PROFESSOR
Even though his lectures were brilliant, he was not a great public speaker. He spoke with a stutter and was terribly disorganized, often stopping in the middle of a sentence to shuffle notes or go off on a sudden tangent that would take him so far out there that he couldn't

Oliver Cromwell banned the eating of pie in 1644.

find his way back to the point he'd been trying to make. And because he was so paranoid that his students would steal his brilliant ideas, he'd often stop in the middle of a lecture, fix note-takers with a baleful gaze, and declare that he hated "scribblers."

Outside the classroom, both his mind and his body wandered. He'd take long walks in the country, talking animatedly to himself the whole time. Once, he walked 15 miles in his bathrobe.

Another time he fell into a large hole in the ground because he wasn't looking where he was going.

## MR. SMITH GOES TO JEFFERSON

His first book, *The Theory of Moral Sentiments,* may sound like pretty snooze-worthy stuff, but it made him famous. It opened doors that led him into the company of other great thinkers of the day— from France's Voltaire to America's Thomas Jefferson. He soaked up what he learned from them (they say he was a better listener than talker), and over the next 10 years he crafted his ground-breaking masterwork.

## SO FAR, SO AMAZING

*The Wealth of Nations* came out in 1776, and it was as revolutionary as the British-American struggle going on that same year across the pond. The book was so far ahead of its time, it was as if someone announced on the news tonight that he'd discovered how to time travel.

By using examples plucked from around the world—case studies of Holland fisheries and Irish prostitutes in London— Smith convincingly made a case for free trade. It was simple: If the government would keep its filthy hands off the economy, we could all go about getting rich. Competition would keep prices low, and supply and demand would correct any economic short-falls. Everyone would look after their own self-interests, which would benefit society as a whole.

## HERE'S THE DEAL

So what's the big deal, you're saying? Listen. In the feudal wasteland of the 18th century, governments could grant monopolies to their favorite merchants and prohibit competitors from going into business. A lot of countries forbade imports as unfair competition, despite consumer demand. Artisan guilds prohibited members from moving around to find work. In a lot of businesses it was illegal to introduce labor-saving machinery and those who tried to use it could be thrown in jail. There were no corporations, no freelancers, no going into business for yourself without greasing the palms of some king or duke or another. So, to put it mildly, Smith's book was monumental. And so was he.

## BUT WHAT ABOUT GREED?

Smith knew that businessmen are prone to greed—we told you he was no dummy. He noted that people in the same trade couldn't resist concocting "a conspiracy against the public." But he also pointed out that the buyer profits as much as the seller, just by getting the consumer items he or she needs.

## POWER TO THE PEOPLE

Smith heralded a new kind of freedom. He virtually founded a secular faith called individualism—and *The Wealth of Nations* was its bible. One historian said: "Next to Napoleon, [Adam Smith was] the mightiest monarch in Europe." In fact, the leaders of the French Revolution took up his ideas, as did the growing wave of citizens looking to throw off monarchies all over Europe.

## OUR LOSS, OUR GAIN

*The Wealth of Nations* was Smith's last great hurrah. He died at home on July 17, 1790, after a painful bout with what a friend called "chronic obstruction of the bowels." His notes indicate that he was planning two more blockbuster books, one on the theory and history of law and one on the sciences.

Since ideas come from many different sources, it's difficult to trace a straight line from Smith's book to the economies of the world today. But it's safe to say that there's a lot of Smith in the free market economies of Europe, the U.S., Canada, etc. In fact, a careful reading of the U.S. Constitution reveals some highly Smith-like suspicion of government interference in its citizens' daily pursuit of happiness.

* * *

"No society can flourish [where] the far greater part of its members are poor and miserable." —Adam Smith

---

**James Bond creator Ian Fleming worked with Navy Intelligence during WWII.**

# MIGHTY ATOM

*How a 5'4" asthmatic Jew survived Nazis, the Ku Klux Klan, and a bullet between the eyes.*

He could pound nails with his hands and yank them out with his teeth. He bent steel bars across the bridge of his nose and once towed an airplane by his hair. Doctors told him he would be dead before the age of 18, but Joseph Greenstein had the last laugh—he was still popping chains with his chest at age 91. Physical conditioning, mental concentration, and spiritual awareness all combined to make this larger-than-life little strongman one of the most memorable performance artists of all time.

## DOCTORS, SHMOCTORS!
Joseph Greenstein was born three months premature in 1893 to a poverty-stricken family in Suvalk, Poland. Polish doctors were so sure he would die that they offered Mrs. Greenstein some money to use the body for medical studies. Little Joseph survived—saddled with a variety of respiratory illnesses—and when he was 14, a team of doctors again predicted his imminent death from tuberculosis.

## WANT A LIFESAVER?
According to Greenstein's biography, the very same day that he was given this death sentence, he was beaten up by a circus employee who caught him sneaking into the big top. After the beating, Joe crawled into a circus wagon that belonged to a Russian strongman who called himself "Champion Volanko." The first thing Volanko did was to find the bully who'd beaten Joe up and break his nose. Then the strongman took the anemic teenager under his wing.

For the next 18 months, Joe traveled with Volanko and the Issakoff Brothers' Circus—from Poland to the Ukraine to Bombay—gratefully studying the wizardly strongman's health regimen and his secrets of strength and endurance.

Reinvigorated, Greenstein returned to Poland, married his sweetheart, and began a career as a wrestler. When Eastern Europe was swept by a wave of anti-Semitism and a soldier randomly massacred a Jew in his town, Greenstein tracked and murdered the killer. Soon after, promising to send for his new wife and family, he left for America.

## JOEY THE KID
He made his way to Galveston, Texas, got a job as a dockworker, and spent his free time wrestling for money. As Kid Greenstein, he applied headlocks and hammerlocks along the west Texas coast for a cool $10 per match. At 19, he traveled to Yokohama, where he spent two months studying jujitsu. He returned to Texas in 1912.

## AIN'T THAT A SHOT IN THE HEAD?
With money he'd earned from wrestling, Greenstein sent for his family. In October 1914, a demented Texas local developed an obsession with Greenstein's wife, Leah. Standing 30 feet away, the crazy Texan shot Greenstein between the eyebrows, knocking him to the ground. Joe survived—doctors determined that the .38 caliber bullet hadn't entered his skull, but was flattened by it on impact. The feat made it into the Houston papers, under the headline "Kid Greenstein Stops Bullet."

## MIND OVER MUSCLE
The near-death experience sparked Joe's interest in the mental powers associated with strength and survival. He started studying psychology, hypnotism, and anatomy, and he became convinced that if the body was trained, the instinctual inner voice could be ignored—the voice that said "Don't be ridiculous, you can't…lift that heavy thing…lie on that bed of nails…stop that bullet with your forehead…." His mastery over that voice formed the cornerstone of his future.

## LEOPARD SKIN—IT GOES WITH EVERYTHING
Even though he was only 5'4" and 145 pounds, he fixated on becoming a modern-day Samson. He started wearing a leopard-skin outfit, stopped cutting his hair—and practiced pulling weights with it. One day he borrowed a friend's Packard (that's a car to you youngsters) and towed it uphill with his hair. Later he developed a hair-fastening mechanism consisting of combs and

metal plates that enabled him to pull five cars at one time, drag a 2,000-pound piano with six people on it, and stop an airplane (like the one flown by Lindbergh) from taxiing down the runway—a stunt that proved so dangerous and temporarily disfiguring that he never repeated it and warned others not to try it. (His advice was disregarded by one California stuntman whose scalp was torn off when he attempted to repeat the stunt.)

## HAIR TODAY...

It wasn't just his hair that did the heavy lifting. Eventually, Greenstein could chomp through steel chains, bend inch-thick pieces of steel across the bridge of his nose, twist horseshoes across his thighs, and drive 20 penny nails through a two-and-a-half-inch-thick board with his bare hands. And he could lie on a bed of nails while supporting a 14-man Dixieland band on his chest.

By 1927 he was booked on vaudeville tours as "the Mighty Atom," performing bizarre stunts like changing a tire without any tools and swinging four women in the air with his hair.

During his vaudeville years Greenstein developed an interest in the Kabala, a mystical Hebrew path to divinity. He became convinced that Judaism was at the root of his supernatural powers and fashioned himself onstage like a biblical hero, wearing sandals, a tunic, and a leather strap with the Star of David. He also devoted considerable study to "naturalistic" studies, or what we would now call holistic, or alternative, medicine. Which led him very neatly into his next career.

## CLEANING UP HIS ACT

Good thing, too—by the time of the Great Depression, the world had gotten tired of strongmen, and vaudeville was virtually dead. Greenstein developed a line of health products, among them Gold Piece Soap (made with lemon and coconut oil) and Mighty Atom Pep-O-Lax ("Real cleanliness begins with internal cleanliness"). Much of the radical advice he provided audiences during his street-corner sales pitches—drink lots of water, avoid junk food, cheese, red meats, fats, sugar, and preservatives—is now accepted (even though they're not usually followed) by the general public. To sell his message, Atom set up a Coney Island storefront, then

---

**John Hanson was the first U.S. president under the Articles of Confederation.**

tried his hand at a health resort, and eventually took to the streets in his Atomobile, an ancient truck serving as a stage, warehouse, and traveling museum that housed photos and memorabilia of his exploits.

## TAKING ON THE KLAN AND THE NAZIS

According to Joe Greenstein, there were no "little men," only men who limited themselves. Once, when he was kidnapped by the Ku Klux Klan—who beat him and tarred and feathered him—he tracked down his attackers and chased them with a butcher knife. He didn't catch them, but he definitely scared the heck out of them. In 1938, he tore down an anti-Semitic sign in New York City and single-handedly took on a crowd of angry Nazis. After being clubbed by them, Greenstein grabbed the knife out of one man's hand and broke another's nose.

Despite all the bigotry and violence he faced in his life, he stayed deeply in love with America and the opportunities it had provided.

## THE ATOM DIES...

Old age didn't slow him down. In 1972, at the age of 91, bearded and draped in his famous leopard-skin ensemble, Greenstein dazzled an audience at Madison Square Garden by bending horseshoes and driving spikes through metal with the palm of his hand. Five years later, the indestructible Samson succumbed to cancer.

## THE ATOM LIVES!

In 2001, Universal Pictures optioned the movie rights to a biography of the mighty little guy (one of the producers likened Greenstein's life story to "Forrest Gump meets Jackass"). If they don't let the option run out and if they can find the backing, a century after his birth, the mystical Jewish strongman will still be in show business!

* * *

### ME? JEALOUS?

When Russia's Mikhail Gorbachev was at the height of his popularity in the U.S., someone asked President Ronald Reagan if he was jealous. Reagan answered: "I don't resent his popularity or anything else. Good Lord, I costarred with Errol Flynn once."

Audrey Hepburn, whose mother was a duchess, was born Edda van Heemstra Hepburn-Ruston.

# KING OF CANADA

*For 22 years he ran Canada with a little help from his friends,
who were often with him in spirit.*

The ancient Romans wouldn't go into battle or, for that matter, schedule an orgy, if their soothsayers didn't give the go-ahead. Of course, civilization has progressed from there. We now have polling and focus groups to provide the omens. Politicians leave it to market researchers to make their decisions for them.

### MEDIUM? WELL...
During the 20th century, mediums who were prominent in pop culture weren't to be taken seriously in determining worldly weighty affairs of state. Right? Even though the likes of Rasputin, Edgar Cayce, and Jeanne Dixon managed to capture the attention of the powerful leaders of their day.

### TOP DOG
But in Canada particularly, mediums and their methods have always been highly suspect. What a surprise, then, when Canadians found out that the country's longest-standing prime minister, William Lyon Mackenzie King, had been regularly in touch with more than the beating pulse of their nation. He was also in touch with quite a few pulses that had ceased to beat, including that of his favorite dog, Pat.

### A POLITICAL FAMILY
King—or Rex, as he was known to his intimates—was born in 1874. His grandfather, William Lyon Mackenzie, had not only been the first mayor of Toronto and a member of Upper Canada's Legislative Assembly, he'd led the short-lived Rebellion of 1837, Canada's civil war in a teacup. The Rebellion helped lay the foundation for the national Liberal Party, the Canadian cousin to America's Democratic Party.

### A HARVARD MAN
King also propelled himself toward politics by his academic studies at the universities of Toronto, Chicago, and Harvard. He specialized

Robert Frost used to milk cows on his farm late at night to avoid doing so early in the morning.

in law and political economics, and he earned five degrees, including a Ph.D.

## RUBBING ELBOWS WITH THE ROCKEFELLERS

Even while he was in college, King was honing his backroom political skills and working on and off in labor negotiations. He lost an election early in his career (probably due to his lack of personality), but followed that up with a successful run with the John D. Rockefeller Foundation. Right out of the gate he settled a strike against Rockefeller mining interests in Colorado. He and John Jr. remained lifelong friends.

## MONEY ISN'T EVERYTHING

King had grown up in genteel Victorian poverty, but the family was very well connected socially, in part through the church. They were devout Presbyterians, as was King throughout his life. In fact, at one time he seriously considered making the church his career. But the political arena—and other things—beckoned.

## LADIES MAN

This devoutness interfered a little bit with his social life, which consisted of what he called "worse than wasted" times in the company of the ladies, not all of whom were exactly ladies. Although he never married, King remained a nice-looking fellow—but pudgy and slightly dull—throughout his life, counting several women among his closest confidantes.

## THE CAREER IS LAUNCHED

He won his first election in 1908 and the following year was appointed Minister of Labor. He lost the 1911 election and also the 1917 election. Despite these losses, in 1919 he was elected leader of the Liberal Party. From there it was a short hop to the prime ministership.

## HOW DEPRESSING

He lost his bid for reelection in 1930, just as the Depression was taking hold. He was devastated, but over the next five years, while waiting for his political fortunes to improve, he began to be drawn to spiritualism, which was sort of a fad at the time. But King took it seriously. In fact, some of his best friends have been quoted as suggesting he had absolutely no sense of humor.

## HI, MOM!

In 1932 King met a famous medium named Etta Wreidt who put him in direct contact with his mother, his grandfather, Sir Wilfrid Laurier (his mentor), and various other luminaries of the Beyond. In 1933 he tried the ouija board but was unimpressed—but he loved those séances. Eventually, he dispensed with a medium and took over himself. He also read tea leaves and studied numerology. All this, of course, unbeknownst to the world (if they had beknownst it, his career would have been dirt).

## AN ANSWER FOR EVERYTHING

In 1934 he visited the Beyond looking for the skinny on the next election. When the information turned out to be wrong on all counts, King decided that a "contrary entity" was making light of him. In short, an evil spirit had deliberately misled him.

In the 1935 election, after his competition had crashed on the reef of the Depression, King won his greatest majority ever. The "lying spirit" that had bedeviled his communications was gone; the Beyond was King's turf once more. As was the prime ministership. And when he wasn't prime-ministering, he was having long heart-to-heart conversations with Leonardo da Vinci and Louis Pasteur, the latter of whom told him how best to treat Pat the Dog's heart condition.

## MOM AND DAD SPEAK

During WWII, King swore off otherworldly advice. Especially after his mother had earlier told him that war would be averted, and his father confided that Hitler had been assassinated by a Pole.

"Hitler is dead, that by a Pole," was the exact message.

## DEAR DIARY...

King's daily jottings in his journal came to light after his death in 1950. If they'd been revealed during his reign as Prime Minister, it would have shattered his career. But whereas most politicians in a fix like that might go on to start a law firm or teach at a college, King had a much more interesting career to fall back on: "The Amazing Rex, Sees All, Knows All."

# IT CAME FROM BENEATH THE SWAMP

*The murderous mystery of the Lindow Man.*

Any murder mystery fan knows that a lonely bog can be a useful place to stash a victim. Over the past century, hundreds of dark, mummified bodies have been discovered in the peat bogs of northern Europe and the British Isles. The corpses show signs of violence, and some have been weighted down to keep them submerged. But as the old saying goes: "Murder will out." In the case of the Lindow Man, the "outing" of the murder took almost 2,000 years.

## MUMMY SOLVES A MURDER

In 1983, Andy Mould was working the peat shredder at the Lindow Moss Peat Company in Cheshire, England, watching for rocks or large pieces of wood that might jam the shredder, when he came across the skull of a middle-aged woman. Police were sure Andy had helped solve a local murder. Poor Mrs. Reyn-bardt, who lived near the Lindow bog, had been missing since 1960. Authorities had long suspected her husband of doing her in—now, they'd have the evidence to arrest him.

## AN OLD LADY, BUT NOT HIS

Frightened by Andy's find, the husband confessed that he'd killed his wife, cut her up, and tossed her in the bog. Though Mr. Reyn-bardt was convicted of murder, the skull was never used as evidence against him. Oxford scientists determined that it belonged to a woman who'd been in the bog since A.D. 210. The local residents were astounded to learn that their bog was an ancient burial site.

## MUMMY COMES OUT

The next year, Andy found a human foot. This time, along with police, an archaeologist was called to the scene. Experts searched the area and found a male body. The Lindow Man (or Pete Marsh,

---

Actor Daniel Day Lewis's father was the Poet Laureate of England.

as the British tabloids jokingly dubbed him) had definitely been murdered. The victim's skull was bashed in, he was strangled, his neck broken, and his throat slashed. He was dead, all right.

Pete Marsh's ultraviolent end stirred international interest. But there was no hue and cry for the cops to find his killer. Poor old Pete had no hope of justice. He'd died around A.D. 100 and he'd been bogged down (so to speak) for nearly 2,000 years.

## PICKLED PETE

How had Pete's body survived that long? In the peat bogs, cold water that's low on oxygen lays under dense vegetation. Without warmth or oxygen, the putrefaction bacteria that causes bodies to decay can't survive. Peat bogs are also acidic; they "pickle" the skin until it's dark and leatherlike. Lindow Moss bog not only preserved old Pete, it mummified him, too.

The Lindow Man was no beauty. His face and body were flattened by the weight of the peat pressing down on him for all those years. Still, he was in darn good shape for his age—which made him one of the world's greatest archaeological finds—as well as one of the world's most interesting murder victims.

## PETE'S VITAL STATISTICS

Scientists swarmed over the Lindow Man, using modern forensics to follow a crime trail almost 2,000 years cold. Examining the victim himself, they learned that he was about 5'5" tall and probably weighed about 160 pounds. He'd been between 25 and 30 years old, muscular, fit, and in good health on his last day on earth. He was naked except for a fox fur armband, but traces of fox fur in the bog made it likely that he'd once worn a fox fur cape.

Pete was most likely a man of high rank; he was fit, well fed, and sleekly groomed. His close-cropped hair, mustache, and sideburns were all preserved by the bog. His skin was decorated (traces of blue-green paint remained), but it was smooth, minus any scars that might indicate that he'd been a warrior. And Pete Marsh was no peasant; he had well-manicured fingernails, still perfectly preserved, on hands that had never done much manual labor. He'd eaten burned griddlecakes at his last meal, and there were traces of mistletoe pollen in his stomach as well.

---

**Ulysses S. Grant once received a $20 speeding ticket for riding too fast on his horse.**

## DID THE DRUIDS DO IT?

Some scholars believe that the Lindow Man was a Druid. As a Druid, he would have guarded the spiritual, legal, and intellectual traditions of the Celtic people who occupied Britain at the time. After they were conquered by the Romans, the Druids disappeared from the earth, leaving no written records of their own. But Roman writers reported that Druids painted their skin, used the mistletoe plant in their sacred rituals, and sacrificed human beings to their gods to ensure fertility, practices that make the Druids our number one suspects.

## CLUES TO MUMMY'S LAST DAYS

Beginning with his burned meal, Pete's last day went downhill from there. His last vision may well have been an axe or hammer raining blows down on his head. Once unconscious, he was strangled or garroted with enough force to break his neck vertebrae. After he was strangled, a blade sliced his throat, piercing his jugular vein and draining him of blood. Finally, Pete was dumped face-down in the bog. So much for the good old days.

Pete could have been a wealthy man mugged for his money. Or killed in a crime of passion. Some historical sleuths make the case that the Lindow Man's violent end was a punishment for a crime. But many more believe that his last meal, which included mistletoe (sacred to the Druids), along with his triple killing and burial in the bog, are proof of a human sacrifice to the Celtic gods.

## FREEZE-DRIED IMMORTALITY

The Lindow Man's body has been freeze-dried to keep it mummified. His face has been reconstructed based on radiographs of his skull, and he turns out to be a good-looking fellow. His face isn't primitive or savage—he could easily be a guy you meet on the modern streets of London. But in fact, he stays indoors these days in a dim, quiet corner of London's British Museum.

\* \* \*

Besides the British Museum, several other museums display bog bodies: the National Museum of Ireland, the Drents Museum (multiple bodies including Yde Girl and the Weerdinge Men), the Silkeborg Museum (home of the famous Tollund Man), the Moesgård Museum, and the Landesmuseum (Windeby Girl).

---

In 1929, Herbert Hoover was the first president to put a phone in the White House's Oval Office.

# SERIAL KILLER #1

*Herman Mudgett. Yes, we know you've never heard of him. That's sort of the idea when you're a serial killer, now, isn't it?*

Personally, we don't have much good to say about serial killers. First and most obviously, killing people is just plain wrong, unless it's self-defense, or a war, or your stuffed animals have told you that Jesus wouldn't mind.

But more than that is the fact that we think serial killers, as a class, simply exhibit poor form. While it's all very fun and ironic to follow the exploits of crazed murderers as if they were sports heroes (the gruesome collection of Serial Killer trading cards several years ago made this point rather forcefully), the metaphor is in fact entirely wrong. Outside of hockey, the aim of sports is not to actually brutally murder your opponent, and even if it was, your opponents would generally not be terrified student nurses.

Fact is, serial killers go for the easy targets, under false pretenses. They're not like the gangsters in the 1920s, when if you saw a guy in a pinstripe suit coming at you with a violin case, you knew you were gun butter—and that you probably had it coming. Serial killers lure you in, offering sex or money or candy or whatever, a terminal bait-and-switch, and the next thing you know, you're dead, your pancreas is being fried up, and some guy is using your skull for a candle holder.

## MEET MR. MUDGETT

Mudgett (or Henry Holmes, his alias at the time) operated in Chicago at the time of the 1892 Columbian Exposition, and he is a perfect example of this concept. Mudgett killed women in a baroque chamber of horrors he had secretly built into his mansion/hotel on 63rd Street (how does one manage to build a secret chamber of horrors? By changing contractors frequently during the construction process, so no one person—besides Mudgett—knows the set-up of the entire house), and he lured them into the place by offering them jobs. He needed a secretary, you see, someone who could take dictation, file, and then die.

President James K. Polk's wife, Sarah, banned dancing and alcoholic beverages at the White House.

## IF IT'S TUESDAY, IT MUST BE BETSY

During two years, Mudgett had something on the order of a hundred secretaries, a fact you'd think someone would notice ("You're Ethel? What happened to Helen? And, come to think of it, what happened to Bonnie, Daisy, and June?"), but apparently no one did. Maybe they thought that Mudgett was a harsh boss. Well, and he was. More to the point, however, this was 1892, and the sort of woman who had to work out of the home was also the sort of women who was less likely to be missed. Mudgett also went out of his way to "employ" new arrivals to town, who had the added benefit of no one to look out for them.

## A MAN OF MANY INTERESTS

Mudgett was not just a crazed whacko who liked killing people, mind you. He was a crazed whacko who liked killing people and taking their money. Before he offed his victims, he would gain their trust (often by making them his mistress—so these days not only would he be liable for murder, he'd also be slapped with one hell of a sexual harassment suit) and then convince them to give him their life savings. His rationale, perhaps, was that once he was done with them, they wouldn't need it anyway.

## SAY AHHH!

As it happens, Mudgett had a long history of gruesome money-making schemes. While he was in medical school, he would steal cadavers, burn them horribly with acid, and them set them in a place that had a lot of insurance in hopes of extorting a settlement of some kind—not unlike the old "cockroach in the salad bar" maneuver, except in this case the "cockroach" used to be someone's Uncle Ted.

## GORY DETAILS

This is not to say it was all just business for Mudgett. No, he was, in fact, seriously screwed up. Abusive parents, early episodes of animal mutilation, all the classic signs of total bonkerness. His torture chamber on 63rd Street was just that. Mudgett used his medical expertise to perform horrifying "experiments" on his victims, most of which, as you might imagine, ended quite badly for the patient.

After he had had his fun, Mudgett disposed of the evidence in a special cremation oven in the basement (oh, sure, it's a furnace...), or, if he chose to sell the bones to a local medical school, as he did from time to time, there was always the lime pit.

## WHAT TIME IS CHECK-OUT?

No one knows how many people Mudgett killed; estimates go up into the hundreds. Beyond the "secretaries," Mudgett also offed guests at his hotel—like a roach motel, they checked in but didn't check out. His cover was the Columbian Exposition, a huge World's Fair taking place a few blocks away; it attracted a vast number of people from faraway places. They wouldn't be missed, at least not by anyone local who might put two and two together. And he never got caught. Not for the murders in Hotel Hell, in any event.

## MR. MUDGETT'S BUDGET

Mudgett's downfall came in the form of Benjamin Pitezel, the Igor to his Dr. Frankenstein, whom a penny-pinching Mudgett (hey, murdering hundreds of people costs money!) decided to kill for insurance purposes. Wouldn't you know, the insurance company had suspicions, as did Pitezel's wife. Mudgett's response was to try to kill off every member of Pitezel's family, a tactic that he apparently seemed to think wouldn't look in the least bit suspicious. He murdered three of Pitezel's kids before the cops got him in Boston. At which point they worked backward, found Mudgett's hotel (now a smoking ruin—another insurance scam) and the evidence of his terrifying serial murders. Mudgett was tried, convicted, and, on May 7, 1896, hanged. Mudgett's last words were to the effect that he had really only killed two women. Odd statement to make as your last on this planet, considering that even only one murder was more than enough to stretch your sorry neck.

## NOTHING BUT THE BEST

There's no doubt Mudgett was a horrible man who preyed on the weak and the innocent. The worst thing about it was that he was as good at it as anyone in his line of work—possibly the best ever. That is, that we know about. The real best serial killer of all time we probably will never know about. Think about that the next time you meet a smooth-talking stranger.

# NOBODY FAMOUS

*"I'm nobody / Who are you? / Are you nobody, too?"*

Emily Dickinson, the woman who called herself "nobody," was born into a wealthy family in 1830 in Amherst, Massachusetts. She went away to school at age 16 for one year but—explaining only that it was her father's wish—she returned home and stayed there for the rest of her life. She never married. She dressed all in white and rarely left home. In later years she saw very few people. Sometimes she'd only talk to her visitors from behind a slightly opened door. If you look in a dictionary under "recluse," you can see her picture.

## SCRIBBLE, SCRIBBLE...

As a candidate for fame, Emily was one heck of a long shot. Her family entertained the cream of New England society, but Em couldn't network to save her life. By the time she died in 1886, her only real legacy was what she called her "scribblings"—her letters and poems.

After Emily died, her sister Lavinia found a box filled with hundreds of poems. (Eventually more than 1,750 were published.) Some writings were carefully handwritten into homemade books. Other immortal works were scrawled on scraps of papers or included in letters to friends. They brought her everlasting fame, but they also brought a clamor from readers and scholars who wanted to know all the personal details of the poet's intensely private life.

Her poems were nothing like the flowery, conventional poetry of the time. They were striking, original, and unexpectedly truthful. Her work held so much insight that readers wondered how a solitary female, rattling around her parents' house all day, learned so much about life...and especially about love.

## WILD NIGHTS

Some of Emily's poems shocked her 19th-century audience. Like this one:

> WILD Nights! Wild Nights!
> Were I with thee,

Wild nights should be
Our luxury!

Futile—the Winds
To a heart in port,—
Done with the compass,
Done with the chart.
Rowing in Eden!
Ah, the sea!
Might I but moor
To-night in thee!

That might not seem so sexy today, but at the time, it was hot stuff—and it stirred undying curiosity. How could a sheltered spinster—and a direct descendant of the Puritans—know so much about passion? More juicy still, who exactly did she want to spend those wild nights with?

## THE LIKELY CANDIDATES
Scholars like to say that Dickinson's reclusive behavior was the result of an unhappy love affair. They single out three married men.

Reverend Charles Wadsworth, a Calvinist preacher, was a romantic figure, a thoughtful, brooding man. He's known to have visited Emily only twice, in 1860 and in 1880. But the two wrote back and forth for decades, and in one letter to him Emily called Wadsworth her "dearest earthly friend."

How about Samuel Bowles? He was a literary dude, editor of the Springfield *Daily Republican* newspaper. Emily sent him her poems to read and he printed four of them. The two had a long correspondence in which she hinted at strong feelings for him. Sam sometimes visited Emily's brother, who lived right next door to her. Did he also secretly visit Emily?

And what about Judge Otis Phillips Lord, a brilliant and influential man and a friend of Emily's father, who regularly visited the Dickinson home? Emily openly admitted to loving him. "I confess that I love him—I rejoice that I love him." After his wife's death (when Emily was 47 years old), the judge and Emily really did fall for each other—she even considered marrying him. And some people speculated that Emily had secretly been in love with him for years before his wife died.

## IF YOU KNEW SUSIE

Then again, maybe Emily never left home because she was in love with someone who lived right next door! Emily and her brother's wife, Susan Dickinson, had been childhood friends. They lived only "a lawn apart," but Emily sent Susie scads of loving and even erotic letters. ("Oh Susie, I would nestle close to your warm heart, and never hear the wind blow, or the storm beat, again. Is there any room there for me, darling, and will you love me more if ever you come home?") Which could be more than Victorian expressions of ladylike friendship. Susan's husband, Austin Dickinson, was openly unfaithful; Susan's marriage was not happy. Did Susan find love and consolation with Emily? Did they partake in "the love that dare not speak its name" at the time?

## EMILY ON E-MAIL?

Whoever was the object of her affections, no doubt about it, Emily was one hot letter writer. And who knows how many more theories there'd be if she'd had Internet access?

For now, scholars can guess that Emily was more than a pathetic recluse suffering from a broken heart. If Em was single and solitary, maybe it was because she knew her genius was great, and she wanted to focus on her work. Could it be that poetry was the big love of Emily's life, after all?

\* \* \*

"Hope is the thing with feathers." —Emily Dickinson

"How wrong she was! The thing with feathers turns out to be my nephew. I must take him to a specialist in Zurich." —Woody Allen

\* \* \*

After reading one of T. S. Eliot's books of poetry, a critic said: "He's written better, but he's written verse."

# PRINCESS WARRIORS

*The Greeks had their Amazons—women who could equal any man in battle. Ancient Vietnam had Trung Trac and Trung Nhi, who fought in a Vietnam war that took place 2,000 years ago.*

Vietnam was part of the Chinese Empire in A.D. 39—it had been for 150 years. China had allowed the local aristocrats to keep their land as long as they paid taxes to the empire and took their orders from Chinese bureaucrats, like a certain local governor named Su Ding.

When civil war broke out in China, Su Ding saw an opportunity to squeeze extra tribute out of Vietnam without any pesky Chinese officials looking over his shoulder. But the people he was squeezing objected. So he killed one of the local landowners, Thi Sach, thinking it would frighten the rest into submission.

## WHY WE CALL HIM SU DING-A-LING
Su Ding's plan backfired badly; he'd picked on the wrong aristocrat. Thi Sach's widow was a woman named Trung Trac, one of two daughters of an old noble family. Trung Trac swore an oath, not just to avenge her husband, but to take vengeance for the 150-year-old Chinese invasion and to restore Vietnam's Hung Dynasty (from which she was descended) to the throne.

In A.D. 39, she and her younger sister, Trung Nhi, rebelled against the Chinese occupation. Legend says they killed a tiger and wrote their proclamation on parchment made from its skin, which doesn't sound so silly once you get to know them.

## ON THE RIGHT TRAC
In those days, Vietnamese women could inherit property and become leaders. In fact, both the Trung sisters were raised to be warriors. Trung Trac became the leader of the rebellion and Trung Nhi its top military commander. They raised an army of 80,000 people, both men and women, and trained 36 women—yes, women—to serve as its generals.

There were 65 Chinese-occupied fortresses in Vietnam, and the Trungs' rebel army took every one of them away from the Chinese troops. Ex-governor Su Ding was so thoroughly terrified

Hungarian Lazlo Biro, who patented the ballpoint pen, was also a sculptor and hypnotist.

that he disguised himself as a commoner and joined the crowd of Chinese who were speedily heading for home.

## TWO QUEENS IN ONE

Trung Trac and Trung Nhi became coqueens of Vietnam and stood their ground against the Chinese army for three years. When the sisters saw the end of their brief reign in sight, rather than find out what the Chinese did with defeated enemies, they drowned themselves in the Hat-Giang River, which, along with all their other exploits, gave them immediate legendary status.

Even though it took another 900 years for Vietnamese forces to defeat the Chinese army and set up an independent state, the stories and ballads about the heroic Trung sisters survived it all. The country still holds an annual festival to honor them, 15 days after Tet, the Vietnamese New Year.

\* \* \*

All the male heroes bowed their heads in submission;
Only the two sisters proudly stood up to avenge the country.
—15th-century poem

\* \* \*

## WATCH YOUR FANNY

Besides having one of the most interesting names in Olympic history, Fanny Blankers-Koen of the Netherlands was one of its most stellar athletes.

At the 1948 London Olympics, having already won the 100-meter dash, she was now up against hometown girl Maureen Gardner in the 100-meter hurdles.

At the gun, Gardner got a perfect start; it took Blankers-Koen five hurdles to catch up. When she did, she hit that last hurdle and had to stumble across the finish line. Who'd won? While the two athletes waited impatiently, the band struck up "God Save the King." Fanny figured she'd lost. But in fact the band was playing because the British royal family had just arrived.

Fanny had won after all.

Not such a nutty professor, Jerry Lewis invented and patented a video monitor system in 1956.

# FIVE 5TH BEATLES

*John, Paul, George, and Ringo got by with a little help
from these friends.*

For a while there, it seemed like everyone around the Fab Four was claiming to be the "Fifth Beatle"—disc jockeys, session musicians, journalists, and probably the guy down the street that used to beat up Paul McCartney for his lunch money. (Oh, come on. You can tell Paul was a pushover.)

But forget about them. We've got the genuine articles here— five Beatle compatriots who can make a legitimate claim to the title because of who they are or what they did. Come meet the "Nearly Fab Five."

## PETE BEST

Pete Best has the best claim to being the Fifth Beatle because he's the only one who actually was a Beatle. He was the band's drummer from August 1960 to August 1962, and played with the Beatles during the band's notorious stints in Germany, at the Star Club in Hamburg. Best was a mediocre drummer by most accounts (you can hear some of his drum work if you own the Beatles's *Anthology I* collection) but he had other valuable qualities. He was popular with the fans, especially the female ones, and his mother Mona did a good job as the group's unofficial promoter, which helped give the band some early visibility. Be that as it may, when the Beatles got a record deal, producer George Martin told manager Brian Epstein that Best wasn't a good enough drummer for recording sessions. This coincided with the feelings of the other members of the band, who wanted to ditch him anyway. Epstein got the job of sacking Best, whose seat was then, of course, filled by Ringo Starr. Some Pete Best fans weren't amused and rioted at a concert; George Harrison ended up with a black eye.

Epstein immediately placed Best with another band he managed, Lee Curtis & the All Stars, but that didn't last long, and Best spent most of the early and mid-1960s bouncing around low-rent bands whose major goal was capitalizing on Best's former relationship with the most popular band in the world. Eventually Best himself got tired of it, left the music industry, and got a job at a bakery, and then later worked as a civil servant in Liverpool. After

---

**Jerry Lewis's video assist invention is used throughout the film industry today.**

he retired in the 1990s, Best hopped back on the road with a new band, and now spends his time playing gigs and making appearances in which he again capitalizes on his former relationship with the most popular band in the world. And why not? If John was the smart one, Paul the cute one, George the quiet one, and Ringo the funny one, it's okay for Best to be known as the fired one.

## BRIAN EPSTEIN

Even though he was the Beatles' manager from 1961 to 1967, before he met the Beatles, he'd never managed a musical group before—he was the record department manager of the North End Music Store, which his family owned. Epstein was also something of a frustrated creative type; he had attended theater school for a couple of years before ditching it and working in the store. When he saw the Beatles perform in Liverpool's Cavern Club in 1961, he figured he could help make them stars. His first order of business was to give them a new look—it was Epstein who put the previously blue-jeaned and leather-jacketed Beatles into their snazzy Pierre Cardin suits and gave them all matching mop-top haircuts. He even taught them how to take that cute bow at the end of their sets. His next order of business was to get them a record contract, which he did in less than six months.

Epstein also managed Gerry & the Pacemakers and Cilla Black, among others, but he was often accused of neglecting his other clients and their careers. It was true, Epstein was completely devoted to the Beatles, not just to their career, but to them personally, as friends.

Once the band stopped touring in 1966, there was little for Epstein to do. It also didn't help that the Beatles had come to believe Epstein had botched a number of business deals for them. Epstein, who had dabbled in drugs for some time, died in 1967 from an overdose—the jury is still out as to whether the overdose was an accident or a suicide. Whichever it was, many Beatle observers (including John Lennon) pinpoint Epstein's death as the moment the band starting moving toward its breakup.

## GEORGE MARTIN

Martin was the producer of all of the Beatles' albums, including the original recording of "Let It Be." ("Let It Be" was subsequently fiddled with by Phil Spector, who added a lot of strings and such; the album is considered by many to be the Beatles' least popular album.) On the surface, Martin was an odd person to produce the Beatles. When Brian Epstein played the Beatles' demo work for Martin, he was the head of Parlophone Records, a small and underfunded division of EMI.

Martin turned out to be inspired choice for the Beatles. Rather than hammer the Beatles into a preexisting idea of what they should sound like, Martin gave the band room to experiment and the opportunity to develop their own material. After the Beatles' first single "Love Me Do" did only middlin' business, Martin was going to make their next single a song from an outside writer, but he allowed them to try another original. It was "Please Please Me," which went to number one. (The other song Martin had planned, "How Do You Do It" was given to Gerry & The Pacemakers and also went to number one, so Martin's ear for hits isn't in much doubt.) He also had the technical experience the Beatles needed; although the band is credited with innovative experimentation with tape loops and overdubs on *Revolver* and *Sgt. Pepper's Lonely Hearts Club Band*, Martin had been fiddling with both for years. (*Mock Mozart*, a 1955 comedy record with Peter Ustinov, featured extensive overdubbing.)

During 1963, a Martin-produced band was number one on the British charts seven weeks out of every ten—but the company was incredibly stingy when it came time to give Martin a raise. He left in 1965 to form his own production company, although he continued to produce the Beatles and other artists (including Cilla Black) for EMI. After the Beatles broke up, Martin continued to work with Paul McCartney and Ringo Starr, and has since worked with a weirdly eclectic group of musicians ranging from Celine Dion and Elton John to Kate Bush and Ultravox.

Martin was knighted in 1996 and retired from production work in 1998 as the most successful producer of all time.

## NEIL ASPINALL

Aspinall got to know the Beatles by way of renting a room in Pete Best's house, and he became the band's road manager, schlepping them around Liverpool. When Best was fired from the band in 1962, Aspinall planned to quit in protest, but Best talked him out of doing it. This turned out to be a good deal for Aspinall, who eventually morphed into a sort of catchall assistant for the band, up to and including contributing to albums. He played instruments on "Within You Without You" and "Being Mr. Kite" and was one

---

**Countess DuBarry, mistress of King Louis XV, invented the fish bowl.**

of the vaguely drunken sounding mates bellowing along on the chorus of "Yellow Submarine" (previous musical experience: none).

Aspinall had been studying to be an accountant when he first started driving the band to and from their local gigs, so who better to be managing director of Apple Corps, the Beatles' record company/business/big black hole of cash. This was no easy task, since the band itself managed Apple as if they were taking scads of hallucinogenic drugs (and—surprise—that's just what they were doing), but Aspinall hung in there and continued in the role even after the band broke up, since the need to administer the Beatles' affairs didn't end once the four of them stopped working together. At this point, it's arguable that he spends more time thinking about the Beatles than any other person in the world.

## MAL EVANS

A prime example of a big lug more or less stumbling into an interesting life. Mal Evans was a telecommunications engineer in Liverpool who started hanging out at the Cavern Club in the early 1960s and was eventually asked to be a bouncer. It was in this "throw the drunks out" capacity that he got to know the Beatles and Brian Epstein. In 1963, Epstein asked Evans to become the Beatles' roadie, assisting Neil Aspinall with the setup of the band's equipment. After the band stopped touring in 1966, Evans, like Aspinall, became something of a catchall assistant; you can see him lurking around in the famous "rooftop concert" in the *Let It Be* documentary (which Aspinall produced), and he was also called upon to throw in random musical bits, including one of the many piano stabs at the end of "A Day in the Life."

Evans also fancied himself something of a music producer, although his track record in this regard is not so stellar. He brought the band Badfinger to the attention of the Beatles (who signed them to Apple) and helped produce one of their albums. Subsequent producing attempts were pretty bad. His production work on Who drummer Keith Moon's solo album was bad enough to be thrown out in its entirety. After the Beatles broke up, Evans moved to Los Angeles and it's there he died in January 1976. How? While the Beatles once wrote that "Happiness Is a Warm Gun," sadness is an unloaded rifle drunkenly pointed at a member of the Los Angeles Police Department.

# ALL SHAKERED UP

*Ann Lee didn't have any trouble convincing her followers that she was God. But it's tough to spread a religion when one of your key beliefs involves lifelong celibacy. Not only is it no fun, but you're not going to produce a lot of new followers.*

If you stumbled into an 18th-century Shaker church meeting, you'd see something that looked more like a psychedelic trip: shaking, howling, drooling, singing, and speaking in tongues. All of these activities were pretty normal for the folks who called themselves the Shakers. And if that weren't unusual enough, the Shakers were led by a woman whose followers thought she was God herself.

## NO SEX PLEASE, WE'RE BRITISH
Ann Lee was born in Manchester, England, in 1736, at the beginning of the Industrial Revolution. As a child, she worked in textile mills instead of going to school. In fact, she was completely illiterate—but that didn't stand in her way. Ann was secure in her beliefs, and they were pretty strange considering she came from a family of humble, regular folk. Ann believed sex was sinful, even for procreation. She wished aloud that she could stay single and chaste all her life.

## ANN GETS OFF TO A SHAKY START
And so she dumped the Church of England in 1758 for a group of former Quakers. The new sect, known as the Shaking Quakers (because of their propensity to shake uncontrollably during worship), had broken away from the Quakers' Society of Friends because of their beliefs that they could communicate with the dead and that the end of the world was near at hand.

Ann took to the Shaking Quakers (later shortened to "Shakers") immediately. Who needed sex when a meeting could send a girl into religious ecstasy? At the time, the eccentric sect was attracting a lot of attention in 18th-century England—and not the good kind. Shakers' houses were set upon by mobs, their windows broken and their poor little butts kicked.

The Canadian province of Alberta was named for Queen Victoria's daughter.

## SORRY, HONEY, I HAVE A HEADACHE
Under pressure from her family, Ann married a blacksmith named
Abraham Stanley in 1762. Despite her misgivings about sex, Ann
and Abe conceived four children, all of whom died in infancy.
Her grief bound her even more tightly to her strange new faith
and her notion that sex led to no good. She spent most of her
time meditating and praying.

## ANN SEES THE LIGHT
After some years, the Shakers' meetings got so lively (and Ann so
outspoken on the evils of "fleshly lusts") that she was jailed in
1770 for "profanement of the Sabbath."

Her prison term gave her even more time to meditate, and
this is where she had a doozy of a religious vision. She wasn't just
Ann Lee, human zealot, and God wasn't just a manlike being, but
a mother-father figure. The father half had already appeared on
earth as Christ. And she, Ann Lee, was God's female component.
And you could call her Mother Ann.

## COMING TO AMERICA
But no one treated her any better just because she was God. She
was imprisoned repeatedly, once for 14 days with no food, in a
prison cell so small she couldn't lie down. And she wasn't safe
outside jail either. More than once, she managed to escape murderous mobs—a deliverance she attributed to God's intervention.

Is it any surprise that Mother Ann had a vision in 1774,
telling her to escape to the New World of America, the place
where the Quakers had found refuge? Ann and eight other
Shakers (including her aforementioned husband, Abraham)
settled near Albany, New York, and hunkered down, waiting for
her prophecies of the Second Coming of Christ and the end of the
world to come true.

## ONCE UPON A TIME IN AMERICA
But the Americans weren't all that glad to see the Shakers,
especially because they were—ahem—English and pacifists in a
country soon to be at war with—ahem—England. The Shakers
were just too far out, what with the wild dancing on Sundays,
their refusal to marry and procreate, and that strange, zealous

As he requested in his will, actor Bela Lugosi was buried in his *Dracula* cape.

woman who called herself God. At one point, American revolutionaries tried to get Ann captured by the British army. When that failed, she was thrown into jail for five months.

## TAKING THE SHOW ON THE ROAD
When she was released, the Shakers ventured out on a two-year missionary journey. They visited big East Coast cities, hoping to spread the word of…Ann. Once again they were set upon by angry mobs—beaten, stoned, dragged by their hair, driven out of every town. But like some kind of Energizer Bunny of the Lord, they kept preaching, inspiring hundreds of followers to show up at their revival meetings and then follow them back to New York. After all, a fierce belief in celibacy pretty much eliminated the chances of the pitter-patter of newborn Shaker feet, which left converting adults as the only way to spread their religion.

## LIFE AFTER DEATH
Mother Ann died from natural causes a year later, without witnessing the Second Coming of Christ or the end of the world. Her followers founded isolated celibate communes in Kentucky, New York, and Ohio. They lived simply—in much the same manner as today's Amish or Mennonites. To bring in some dough, the Shakers grew and sold seeds, dried fruit, and vegetables. They also made simple, sturdy, rustic furniture that's now highly prized by antique hunters.

Their religion mostly died out with the Civil War. At its peak, there were about 6,000 Shakers living in 19 communities between 1830 and 1840. Currently there are fewer than 20 Shakers, now known as the United Society of Believers in Christ's Second Appearing. They live in the only remaining Shaker communities, located in Canterbury, New Hampshire, and Sabbath Day Lake, Maine. Today, more people have sat in a Shaker chair than have ever heard of the strange, compelling Ann Lee, the woman who thought she was God.

* * *

## ANN LEE'S WIT AND WISDOM
"Clean your room well; for good spirits will not live where there is dirt. There is no dirt in heaven."

"The devil tempts others, but an idle person tempts the devil."

—Ann Lee

In 1841, Prince Albert brought the first royal family Christmas tree to Windsor Castle.

# SECRET LIFE
# OF A HAIRDRESSER

*The world's most famous hairdresser, and possibly the richest, was one of the fiercest street fighters in postwar London.*

Vidal Sassoon was a nice Jewish boy, and one of those rosy-cheeked children of the Blitz (the near-constant German bombing of London), whose parents evacuated him during WWII. When he got back home in 1946 at age 17, he had dreams of being a "footballer." But his mum said no. Get a real job—a profession. So he apprenticed himself to a top hairdresser.

## SORRY, KID, THE WAR ISN'T OVER

But to Sassoon's surprise, even after that long, dirty war, there still seemed to be groups of fascists on every London street corner, preaching hate against the Jews. Their leader, a Nazi sympathizer named Oswald Mosley, had spent most of the war in prison for his profascist rabble-rousing. Now Mosley and the hundreds of other British fascists who were interned with him in 1940 were back on the streets as if nothing had changed.

What had changed under the Nazis, though, was the face of Europe. Pictures of Auschwitz and Buchenwald and Dachau were coming to light. While the fascists were loudly questioning the very existence of concentration camps, some Londoners were realizing that their war wasn't over. They had to fight back.

## NEVER AGAIN!

So 43 Jewish ex-servicemen who called themselves "the 43 Group" started up a crudely armed paramilitary force that eventually grew to more than 1,000 Jews and gentiles, men and women—including Vidal Sassoon. Their one and only aim was to prevent the fascists from gaining a political stronghold. That meant breaking up their meetings and chasing them from street corners where they were preaching their poison. They armed themselves with the same weapons the fascists used: brass knuckles, broken bottles, knives, razors, smoke bombs, and blackjacks. As a result, there were large, bloody conflicts in meeting halls and on the streets of London.

In the process, the 43 Group earned themselves the animosity of the police, the press, and even the Jewish establishment. On the bright side, they also scared the heck out of their fascist foes.

---

In 1836 Alabama was the first state in the U.S. to declare Christmas a legal holiday.

## HE HAD CHUTZPAH
Sassoon would tell you that he was just a foot soldier in his home-grown army, but his buddies remember him as a guy who'd stand firm in a fight, just the sort you wanted standing next to you when the fists and the potatoes studded with razor blades started flying.

## POLICE BRUTALITY? HARUMPH!
You'd think the police would have helped out a bit, but in general they sided more with the pro-Nazis. Aside from their more reprehensible beliefs, fascists stood for law, order, and discipline, just like the police are supposed to. One night Sassoon and his group—the police right on their heels—chased some fascists into a pub. The cops arrested the 43ers and beat some of them up. After a night in a cell, they told the judge about the police brutality. His answer was: "Those sorts of things do not happen in Britain, now go home and be good boys."

## HAIRY SITUATION
Sassoon often showed up at work battered and bruised from a night's fighting. One morning, after a particularly violent encounter, he went to work with a badly scratched face. One of his clients said, "Good God, Vidal, you look terrible. What happened to you?" "Nothing much," he said. "I just fell over a hairpin."

## TIME WELL SPENT
After five years of fighting, the 43ers disbanded. They had, with their unrelenting passion, achieved their goal. There are still fascist parties in England today, but none of them pose the threat of those postwar days.

## HAIRDRESSER TO THE STARS
Sassoon went on to be *the* hairdresser of the 1960s, as famous as any icon of the day. He laid down his scissors in the 1970s and created a range of hair products that amassed him a gazillion-dollar fortune—part of which now funds the Vidal Sassoon Center for the Study of Antisemitism and Xenophobia at the Hebrew University in Jerusalem.

\* \* \*

"Violence for its own sake is nonsense, but in defense of one's children and one's elders is a necessity." —Vidal Sassoon

President Franklin Pierce decorated the first official White House Christmas tree in 1856.

# TRIPLE THREAT QUIZ 3
# VIDEO GAME MAKERS

*You know, before they had video games, kids would actually have to go outside and play. How barbaric! Fortunately we live in a much more civilized time, and the five fellows below are ones you can, um, thank for that.*

Each of these guys invented some of the most popular games, consoles, and video game characters of all time. Your job is to match the man to the game and the correct historical trivia fact. No joystick required!

Match these game makers...        With these video game classics...

1. John Carmack              a) Pac-Man
2. Nolan Bushnell            b) Doom
3. Shigeru Miyamoto          c) Pong
4. William Higinbotham       d) Atari
5. Toru Iwatani              e) Mario Brothers

And these historical facts...

i. He created the first version of this game on an oscilloscope at the Brookhaven National Laboratory in 1958. It is generally regarded as the first "video game," although some video game geeks complain that it's not really a video game, since you can't hook an oscilloscope to a TV monitor. These people need to be introduced to that fascinating nonvideo concept known as a "life."

ii. The creator of this famous part of video game history would later go on to create the Chuck E. Cheese chain of restaurants, in which children would eat pizza, play video games, and be "entertained" by a frankly terrifying animatronic rat. He

Ancient Egyptians slept on headrests made of stone.

resigned from the restaurant chain when it went bankrupt in 1984, although both he and the restaurant have since recovered.

iii. The main character of this video game hit was inspired by a bit of Japanese folklore and was so popular that it caused a shortage of Japanese yen; at the height of its popularity, 12,000 consoles were assembled in one day, and it is the cause of possibly the worst Top 10 song ever, by Buckner and Garcia. An urban myth has the inventor of this game leaving the game manufacturer in a huff about royalties, but it's not true (he's still with the company).

iv. This game maker is regarded as the "Spielberg of Video Games" because of his ability to keep coming up with hugely popular game titles. To say video games are his life is an understatement; he even married a woman he met at the video game company he works at. For all his creativity (or perhaps because of it), he was a slacker at college, legendarily attending fewer than half his classes.

v. This game became enormously popular for its nonstop action but also because players were encouraged to create "mods"—modifications of the game's source code that allowed people to make new versions of the game (the marines famously created a mod). This inventor's side gig is called Armadillo Aerospace, which is an attempt to create rockets for space tourism.

Answers:
1-b-v
2-d-ii
3-e-iv
4-c-i
5-a-iii (The song was "Pac Man Fever." Listening to it is like running the tips of your fingers across a power sander.)

The average player height in the NBA is 6' 7.4".

# HERO TO THE MAX

*The Nazis tested his love of country and justice to the limit, but he never broke. He was the legend of the French Resistance—but who exactly was the mysterious Max?*

He was known by the code name Max. During the Nazi occupation he forged a fragmented Resistance movement into a disciplined secret army that made the Germans pay a heavy price for their occupation of France. Naturally, Hitler made Max's capture a high priority. The leader of the Resistance knew the secrets of every pocket of anti-German activity. If the Gestapo could only break Max, the Nazis could crush the French Resistance. There was just one problem...who was Max?

## THE UNLIKELY HERO

As a young man few would have picked Jean Moulin as the hero-most-likely-to-save-his-country. His father's political influence got him a civil service job with the Prefect (government administrator) of Savoie, even though Moulin would much rather have been an artist or cartoonist. He had socialist leanings that sometimes got him in trouble and a marriage that failed in less than two years. What Moulin really seemed to excel at was a sophisticated good time. He loved skiing and playing tennis, and he was known to be a swell dancer.

By 1939 he'd settled down—more or less. He became a suc-cessful (many said brilliant) prefect himself working at an influential post in Chartres, outside Paris. Jean still loved the artistic life, and he kept up his taste for wine, women, and song, but kept it separate from his civil service ambitions.

Meanwhile, Hitler's Germany invaded Poland. Soon after, France and Britain declared war on Germany. Germany took Norway, Den-mark, and the Low Countries in short order. France would be next.

## AN OFFER HE COULDN'T REFUSE

On June 17, as the Nazis made a brutal incursion into Chartres, they massacred a group of unarmed Senegalese French soldiers. To cover up, they ordered Moulin to sign an official statement that the Afro-French troops had raped and killed some women in the area. When Moulin refused, he was arrested and tortured. That night, afraid that under more torture he would do as the Nazis asked, Moulin cut his own throat with a piece of broken glass. A guard found him and rushed him to the hospital. The Germans had wanted the prefect under their control; they didn't want to be accused of causing his suicide.

## THE "PREFECT" ESCAPE
The Nazis made sure Moulin "retired" from his job as prefect. Moulin could have turned to a career in art and lived quietly through the war, but he'd only just begun to fight.

Using his civil service skills, Moulin created the alias Joseph-Jean Mercier. He gave Mercier a birth date similar to his own. With his new identification papers, Moulin (as Mercier) visited the exit permits office. There he asked the junior clerk a question to get him out of the room. Left alone, the former prefect simply stamped his false passport with an exit permit. He escaped France and made his way to England so he could "serve my unhappy country."

## YOUR MISSION SHOULD YOU CHOOSE TO ACCEPT IT
In London, Moulin met with French General Charles de Gaulle. From his exile in Britain, de Gaulle was organizing a Free French movement whose soldiers fought the Germans from outside France. De Gaulle had also called on those remaining in France to resist the German occupation. Though the general was Catholic and conservative and Jean Moulin was still a socialist—and a bohemian—their mutual devotion to France made them allies.

Moulin volunteered to return to France as de Gaulle's emissary and unite the Resistance—no easy task. Resistance groups were as divided as French politics. The communists, socialists, moderates, and right-wingers had all set up their own anti-German cells, and each of them wanted to take power once France was finally free.

After a quick course in coding and decoding and a few brief lessons in parachuting, our hero was dropped by the Royal Air Force into France.

## CLARK KENT AND SUPERMAX
For the next 18 months, Moulin led a double life. Back at home he was the retired prefect-turned-art-dealer whose main preoccupation

seemed to be skiing. But in Lyon, Moulin was the political leader of the French Resistance. And he became best known by London's code name for him, "Max."

Surviving as a secret agent and an undercover political leader took all of Max's skill. He'd memorized the details of his false life and was always prepared to repeat them to the Germans when questioned. He made sure he stayed in locations that had several entrances so if the Gestapo knocked on one door, he could sneak out another. He constantly moved his headquarters from one secret address to another.

While the Germans hunted him, Max managed to funnel money, arms, and agents into the Resistance. By controlling the money and the arms, Max forced the squabbling leaders of the different political factions (and these guys never learned to love on another) to unite under General de Gaulle's authority in the National Resistance Council.

## CHERCHEZ LES FEMMES

With London's help, the Secret Army sabotaged German-controlled railroads, canals, telephone, and telegraph systems. In February 1943, Moulin returned to London. There, General de Gaulle awarded him the Croix de la Libération and appointed him delegate general for Free France. But though the general recognized Moulin's great achievements, not even de Gaulle knew everything. While the hunted Max was uniting the Resistance, he was also carrying on affairs with three women at the same time! Ooh, la la, and vive la France!

But by May 1943, Max began to tire—and it wasn't just from too many mistresses. The precarious unity that he'd forged was already fraying. As the authority caught in the middle, he had to deal with anger from all camps. Worse, he saw one after another of his closest compatriots arrested.

And the Germans had put Klaus Barbie, "the Butcher of Lyon," in charge of the local Gestapo unit. Barbie, vicious even by Nazi standards, tortured members of the Resistance until they turned on their compatriots. Max was afraid that Barbie was closing in on him. He hoped to leave France and fight the war from overseas—but he never got the chance.

In 1976, Sarah Caldwell became the first woman to conduct at the Metropolitan Opera.

## BETRAYAL

On June 21, Max attended a meeting with Resistance leaders in a doctor's home in Caluire. The Germans, led by Barbie himself, broke up the meeting demanding to know which one of the men was Max. Moulin had been betrayed. When he got no answer, Barbie wasn't worried. He took the group to his headquarters and tortured them until someone finally identified Moulin as Max.

Then it was Moulin's turn. Barbie and the Gestapo tortured Moulin until he was near death. Finally he was beaten so badly that he lapsed into a coma. He died a few days later, on a train bound for a concentration camp. He must have kept silent because the Gestapo was never able to use anything he knew against the Resistance movement.

## MAX'S LAST VICTORY

Who betrayed Max? Each of the political factions in occupied France blamed the others. However Barbie found out about Max, he got far less from him than he'd hoped. By holding out under torture, Max gave de Gaulle a huge victory. He saved the Resistance, a force worth (as General Eisenhower would later say) "fifteen divisions." And as for Max himself, he passed from a hero into a legend.

## WHAT HAPPENED TO BARBIE?

For his crimes, especially for Moulin's death, Hitler awarded Barbie the "First Class Iron Cross with Swords." After the war, Barbie was tried and convicted in absentia and given the death penalty. But the American intelligence community employed him and helped Barbie, his wife, and his children escape to Latin America, where he enjoyed a prosperous career. He established residence in Bolivia, where he obtained citizenship in 1957, and lived for a while under an alias. He worked for dictatorships in Bolivia and Peru as an interrogator and torturer. Because he was responsible for the torture and deaths of over 26,000 people, Barbie was a wanted man in France. Nazi hunters identified him in Bolivia at least as early as 1971 but it took until 1983 with a change in the political government in Bolivia before he was deported to France.

Tried in Lyon in 1987 and sentenced to life imprisonment for his crimes against humanity, he died in prison in 1991.

---

**Sir Isaac Newton was ordained as a priest in the Church of England.**

# A PATRIOT'S SECRET LIFE

*When the personal becomes political...*

M arch 23, 1775. British troops were camped near Boston and British ships were ready for action all along the Eastern seaboard. Relations between the American colonists and the British Crown were at the breaking point.

## RABBLE-ROUSER
In St. John's Church, in Richmond, Virginia, some delegates to the second Virginia convention were counseling prudence and hoping for a peaceful settlement of their disputes. But not Patrick Henry. Henry was calling for militias to be raised and armed—a virtual declaration of war against the superpower of the 18th-century world. The greatest orator of the American Revolution rose from his seat and delivered the speech that would ring through history:

> The war is actually begun!... Is life so dear, or peace
> so sweet, as to be purchased at the price of chains and
> slavery?... I know not what course others may take;
> but as for me, give me liberty or give me death!

The daring statement could have cost him his head. But liberty and death had become very personal to Patrick Henry.

## HOW HE GOT THERE
Patrick Henry married Sarah Shelton in 1754. He was 18 and she was just 16. He tried his hand at both farming and shopkeeping, but failed at both, eventually turning to bartending in his father-in-law's tavern, studying law in his spare time. In 1760, he was admitted to the bar and within a few years had a very successful practice. In 1765, he was elected to the Virginia House of Burgesses at the age of 29. Meanwhile, at home, his little family was growing.

## THE MADWOMAN OF SCOTCHTOWN
In 1771, Henry purchased Scotchtown Plantation. Soon after giving birth to her sixth child that same year, Sarah fell into a

---

The patent name for the first computer mouse was "X/Y Position Indicator for a Display System."

depression. From there, her mental condition deteriorated; her behavior became violent. Her husband had to make a decision. The first mental hospital in North America had just opened in Williamsburg in 1773. The asylum had 24 cells, each with barred windows that looked onto a dim central passageway, a mattress, chamber pot, and an iron ring in the wall to which the patient's leg and wrist restraints were attached.

## COMMITTED

But Henry couldn't bring himself to lock Sarah up there. Instead, he confined her to the basement of Scotchtown. In a whitewashed room with a dirt floor, she was strapped down and cared for continuously by a slave woman. She existed this way for three years, until she died in early 1775 at the age of 37. Her servants buried her, but because of superstitions regarding the mentally ill, they never disclosed her grave site. It was just a few weeks after Sarah's death, with an intensity sharpened by grief, that Henry delivered his call for "liberty or death." Less than a month after his defiant call to arms, the "shot heard round the world" was fired in Lexington, Massachusetts. The American Revolution had begun.

## PATRIOT'S POSTSCRIPT

Two years later Patrick Henry married Dorothea Dandridge, who was more than 20 years his junior, and had 10 more children. Henry served as the first governor of Virginia, and continued his radical ways in the cause of individual liberty, even opposing the adoption of the U.S. Constitution as too much government.

To the end of his life, he never mentioned his first wife again. He died on June 6, 1799, after his doctor urged him to drink liquid mercury, hoping it would cure a bowel malignancy.

## POSTSCRIPT

Patrick Henry died at the age of 63 on June 6, 1799. He is buried in the family cemetery at Red Hill. On his gravestone are carved the words, "His fame is his best epitaph."

Beside Patrick Henry is buried his second wife, Dorothea Dandridge Henry. Other family members are interred in the cemetery in marked and unmarked graves.

**The first "mouse" was patented in 1970 by Douglas Engelbart.**

# THAT WOMAN IS A SCANDAL!

*There are all sorts of ways to become a scandalous woman.*
*Just ask these ladies.*

## NINON DE LENCLOS

Ninon de Lenclos had affairs with some of 17th-century France's most important men, including (and this is not an exhaustive list): Gaspard de Coligny, Marquis d'Andelot; Louis de Bourbon, Duke d'Énghien (the Great Condé); Pierre de Villars; and both the Marquis de Sévigné and his son, Charles de Sévigné (talk about a family affair). She knew everyone who was everyone, and we mean that in the biblical sense.

But de Lenclos was not just some shameless political groupie. She was a major player in France's intellectual and political circles. Independently wealthy and an author herself, de Lenclos hosted some of Paris's most intellectually stimulating salons for decades, drawing luminaries such as Molière (whom she encouraged as a young man, and you can take that any way you like) and Racine. Her intellectual influence even reached out beyond the grave—in her will, she left money to her accountant's son so he'd be able to buy the books he desired. The boy's name: François Marie Arouet, who would become rather better known by his pen name, Voltaire.

Not everyone approved of de Lenclos's libertine attitudes and lifestyle. Anne of Austria, who happened to be queen of France at the time, was so incensed by de Lenclos's behavior that she had the woman confined to a nunnery in 1656. Ninon was released shortly thereafter, however, in no small part due to the intercession of another Queen, Christina of Sweden.

De Lenclos would have the last laugh on Anne. First she published a ripping justification of her life in 1659's *The Coquette Avenged*, and then she befriended Madame de Maintenon, who would eventually marry Louis XIV—Anne's son. To this day in France, de Lenclos is a symbol of female intellectual and sexual freedom, proving that sometimes a little scandal is a good thing.

## LADY SARAH CHURCHILL: QUEEN ANNE OF ENGLAND

She was relatively uneducated for a royal, not particularly bright, in chronically poor health (she was what was at the time euphemistically called "stout"), suffered the heartbreak of a series of miscarriages and children who died young, and was married to a pleasantly bland drunkard who was nevertheless so ineffectual they didn't even bother to make him king when Anne became queen in 1702. In short, exactly the sort of person who could use a good friend. What she got instead was Lady Sarah Churchill.

Which isn't to say Lady Churchill wasn't Anne's friend. They were friends since childhood, and, if you want to believe the rumors, rather more than friends as well (Lady Churchill's official title at court was—no joke—Lady of the Bedchamber. Apparently this officially wasn't supposed to imply anything). Sexually connected or not, the two women were deeply devoted to each other, down to calling each other endearing pen names in letters—Anne was "Mrs. Morely," while Lady Churchill was "Mrs. Freeman." Anne lavished Lady Churchill with gifts and favors, including a rather nice estate named Blenheim.

But friends aren't also supposed to push an outside political agenda on you to manipulate affairs of state—that's just rude. Alas for Anne, Lady Churchill most certainly did have a political agenda. A prominent and passionate Whig partisan, Lady Churchill pushed for Anne to include Whig ministers in her government, something the queen was not inclined to do. Nevertheless, Lady Churchill pushed and pushed and finally annoyed Anne enough that she—what's the euphemism?—"fell from favor" around 1707. In her place rose one Lady Abigail Masham, a cousin of the queen (and, as it happens, a tool of the Tories, the competing political party at the time). Lady Churchill was entirely dismissed in 1710, after which she lived in Germany for a time, not returning to England until her queen and former confidante died in 1714.

## RACHEL JACKSON

The wife of Andrew Jackson, who became president of the U.S. in 1829. What's so scandalous about marrying Andrew Jackson? Well, nothing...unless you're technically still married to someone else, which Rachel was, to one Lewis Robards.

Mind you, it wasn't Rachel's fault. Robards had sued for divorce in 1791, on the grounds (erroneous at the time) that his wife had taken up with Jackson. Rachel and Jackson, thinking that the divorce was final, married that same year. In fact, Robards delayed finalizing the divorce until 1793. The Jacksons got married again in early 1794, just to be sure.

The irregularity of Jackson's marriage would come to haunt him later, as it became an object of gossip and mild political scandal when he entered public life. Jackson, of course, never took kindly to innuendoes about his wife, and came to blows on the matter a number of times (and on other matters, too—honestly, it was pretty easy to get into a fight with Andrew Jackson). He even killed a man, Charles Dickinson, in a formal duel brought about in part by Dickinson's disparaging comments about his wife's honor. Dickinson was regarded the better shot and actually plugged Jackson square in the chest, but Jackson was craftier. He held his fire until after Dickinson pulled the trigger, and then, by the rules of the duel, Dickinson was obliged to hold still in one spot until Jackson returned fire.

Jackson coolly lined up his shot—and misfired. It was decided that the misfire didn't count, so Jackson lined up the shot again. This time, he blew a hole in Dickinson's gut. The 1806 duel would also become a point of scandal for Jackson, and he would carry Dickinson's bullet in his chest until he died. But from Jackson's point of view, his Rachel's honor was avenged, so there you have it.

## CHRISTINE KEELER

The center of the most famous sex scandal of 20th-century Britain, Keeler was a pretty teenage runaway working as a showgirl in a London nightclub when she made the acquaintance of Stephen Ward. Ward was a doctor who liked nothing better than to hobnob with Britain's politically powerful—hobnobbing which often involved a distinct lack of clothes except for the occasional mask or whip.

It was through Ward that the young Miss Keeler made the acquaintance of John Profumo in 1961. Profumo was a successful older man who just happened to be the Conservative Secretary of State for War, and the two of them engaged in an illicit (and in Profumo's case, adulterous) affair. In 1962, details of the affair emerged; Profumo's consorting with a young woman (labeled in the press as a "call girl," no less) would have been bad enough without another intriguing wrinkle, which was that while Keeler was spending time with Profumo, she was also consorting with Eugene Ivanov, a bigwig at the Soviet Embassy. It being the Cold War era, this presented an entirely new set of troubles for Profumo. He resigned in 1963. Dr. Ward, who was on trial for living off the "immoral earnings" of Keeler and others, committed suicide.

Keeler did nine months in prison on an unrelated offense and then more or less dropped out of sight, although the details of the "Profumo Affair" were the basis of numerous media tie-ins, including the 1989 film *Scandal*. Keeler resurfaced in 2001 to promote her book about the affair, *Truth at Last: My Story*, in which she contends that Dr. Ward was a Soviet spy who used her to get information on Profumo about nuclear warheads, and that Ward once tried to kill her while she was water-skiing in order to keep her quiet.

## JUDITH CAMPBELL EXNER

This scandalous woman, known for her two-year affair with President John F. Kennedy, has the unusual distinction of having become scandalous on a time delay. Her involvement with Kennedy did not become common knowledge until 1974, more than a decade after JFK was assassinated in Dallas in 1963.

Exner met JFK in 1960 through the good graces of none other than Frank Sinatra, whom she had dated after her divorce from her first husband, actor Bill Campbell, in 1958 (she took on the "Exner" after marrying pro golfer Dan Exner in the 1970s). Exner would write in her 1977 tell-all autobiography that she and Kennedy began their affair the night of the 1960 New Hampshire primary; the next morning Exner woke up to roses from Kennedy and the news that he'd won the primary. It was also during this time that she got to know mob boss Sam Giancana; her connection between the two men served as fuel for rumors that Kennedy bought the Chicago vote in 1960, with Exner acting as intermediary. (Exner maintains she was not sleeping with Giancana…at that time, anyway. They did hook up later, after Kennedy had been assassinated.)

Exner's involvement with JFK became known in 1974, when she testified before the Church Committee on CIA assassination attempts, thus ensuring her presence in endless conspiracy theories about Kennedy's murder (although Oliver Stone thinks she's in the clear). Exner died in 1999 of cancer.

Hugh Hefner and Bing Crosby had ancestors on the *Mayflower*.

# YA GOTTA HAVE HEART

*Americans often confuse her with Filipina shoe-fetishist Imelda Marcos. Wrong! While Imelda was collecting those shoes, Corazon Aquino was battling Imelda's husband, Ferdinand, for presidency of the Philippines.*

Born in 1933 into a family that had made its fortune in sugar and rice, Corazon (which means "heart") Aquino grew up in the midst of wealth and power. Her father was a congressman and her grandfather was a senator, but she never thought she'd be called upon to be a politician herself. She was educated at fancy private schools in Philadelphia and New York, held degrees in French and math, and thought about studying law. However, when she married politician Benigno "Ninoy" Aquino, Jr., in 1954, she settled for being a wife and mother.

## THE PARTY ISN'T OVER TILL I SAY SO

She basked for a while in the glory that was Ninoy. He was a political wunderkind. He'd already been the youngest mayor of his town (at 22) and the youngest governor of his province (at 29). He was shaping up as a powerful threat to President Ferdinand Marcos, who was nearing the end of his second term, which was constitutionally mandated as the maximum anyone could serve.

That should have cleared the field for Ninoy to step in. But in one swift move in 1972, Marcos declared martial law, installed himself as permanent president, and jailed most of his political enemies, including Ninoy. Eight years later, Ninoy was released. Marcos allowed him to visit the U.S. for heart surgery but warned him that if he returned to the Philippines he would face a death sentence.

## AVERAGE AMERICAN HOUSEWIFE

Ninoy and Cory settled in a Boston suburb, but they kept a sharp eye on the First Couple of the Philippines. As Ninoy recuperated he grew more restless every day, and for good reason. In a country where seven out of ten Filipinos were certifiably poor, Ferdinand and Imelda were looting the National Treasury to the tune of $5 billion. Not even a death sentence could keep Ninoy from going back.

---

Lenin's embalmed corpse has been on public display since 1924.

## SWIFT INJUSTICE
In 1983, leaving Cory at home in Boston, he boarded a plane
bound for the Philippines. When his plane landed, soldiers hustled
him away at gunpoint and shot him right there on the tarmac.
Marcos had killed off the only man who could threaten his position.

## CORY FOR PRESIDENT!
It took Ninoy's supporters a few years to talk Cory into running
for president in Ninoy's place. When she finally agreed, Marcos
said he wasn't worried—he even called for an immediate election.
Yet he couldn't have been as confident as he seemed because on
the February 1986 election day, his thugs went around ripping up
ballots, paying for votes, and intimidating voters at gunpoint.

## TANKS VS. NUNS
It set the country aflame. Thousands of people flooded the streets
in protest. The election was condemned by Filipino Catholic bishops
and by the U.S. Senate. Two of Marcos's high officials rebelled,
declaring Aquino the true winner. The tanks that Marcos had sent
to disperse the crowds ground to a halt in front of a group of
rosary-clutching nuns kneeling in their path. His loyalists were
defecting in droves. All the world was watching.

Just one day after Marcos had himself falsely inaugurated, he
had to flee to Hawaii, exiled forever. Reports vary on the number
of pairs of shoes that his wife had to leave behind, but according
to the former First Lady herself, the precise number was 1,060.

## CORY AS PRESIDENT
Hailed as the savior of her country, Cory had a lot to live up to—
too much, in fact. She faced heavy odds. Guerrilla war continued
to threaten the Philippines, as did massive poverty. Cory served
two terms (and survived seven coup attempts). She left office in
1992, succeeded by General Fidel Ramos, a military man who had
thrown his support behind her presidency in 1986—and who had
saved the Aquino government from the aforesaid attempted coups.

Cory hadn't been a perfect president, but she'd tried to govern
her people fairly. She lives in the Philippines today, a powerful
and admired symbol of righteous rule.

---

**A team of specialists is necessary to "maintain" Lenin's body.**

# SLIGHTS OF THE ROUND TABLE PART II

*Think you can keep up with the greatest wits of the 20th century?
Then meet your lunch partners.*

Sitting down with the wits at the Algonquin Round Table was not for the faint of heart. They called themselves "the Vicious Circle," and if you decided to sit in on one of their lunches you'd be likely to find its members laughing at you as much (if not more) than they were laughing with you. Their potential for painfully sharp criticism, especially for each other's work, was immense. Edna Ferber, a Round Table regular, called the group "the Poison Squad," and noted: "They were actually merciless if they disapproved. I have never encountered a more hard-bitten crew."

But then she also noted: "If they liked what you had done, they did say so publicly and whole-heartedly." Indeed, the wits of the Round Table not only lunched together but worked together, too, collaborating on plays, hiring one another for magazines, quoting each other in newspapers and magazines, and generally boosting each other to the outside world just as much as they tore into each other in the privacy of their own social club. Yes, it's sort of passive-aggressive, but no one ever said witty people were stable.

## DOROTHY PARKER
Arguably the Round Table's most famous wit, which is saying something. But to go back to that "witty does not equal stable" crack a few sentences ago, Parker was also an object lesson for the fact that being witty also isn't the same as being happy. Parker really wasn't; she attempted suicide on multiple occasions (including one time when, apparently without anything more conventionally toxic to ingest, she downed some shoe polish). She battled depression and addiction the whole of her adult life. Even her famed wit caused her headaches. In 1920 she was fired from *Vanity Fair* magazine, where served as the drama critic, because her reviews were too mean. She was, in short, a poster child for the whole concept of "crying on the inside."

But on the other hand, you don't have to be Dorothy Parker, you just have to read her. And her wit had its payoffs, too. Like

---

Bluesman Bo Diddley's real name is Ellas Otha Ellas Bates.

that *Vanity Fair* firing—it opened the door for her to become a fixture at a hip new magazine called *The New Yorker* back in the day when it was still young and struggling. (A key anecdote from this era had *New Yorker* editor Harold Ross asking Parker why she hadn't filed a story. She replied that "someone else was using the pencil.")

At *The New Yorker*, Parker penned a book review column under the nom de plume of "The Constant Reader." This is where she got in some of her best lines. Such as, "This is not a book to be tossed aside lightly, but to be hurled with great force." Of the works of *Winnie the Pooh* creator A. A. Milne, Parker commented: "Tonstant Weader fwowed up." Parker's penchant for the poison-tipped barb was balanced by the keen sense of feminine desperation that surfaced again and again in her other writing, most famously in the 1929 O. Henry Award–winning short story *Big Blonde*, about the slow decline of a party girl, and in her three volumes of poetry, some of which was itself in the form of one-liners ("Men seldom makes passes / At girls who wear glasses").

In the 1930s, Parker headed to Hollywood to set her wit to screenplays, and grabbed an Oscar nomination for 1937's *A Star Is Born*, starring Janet Gaynor, which she cowrote with her then-husband Alan Campbell (a 1954 version with Judy Garland used the same script, polished by fellow Round Tabler Moss Hart). Parker returned to New York in the 1960s, after Campbell's death, and died herself in 1967. Interestingly, she willed her estate to Martin Luther King, Jr., whom she greatly admired—a far-from-ironic final gesture from a woman who knew her irony.

## ROBERT BENCHLEY

A founding member of the Round Table and a great friend of Parker's. The two of them worked together at *Vanity Fair* (he was the managing editor when she was the drama critic), and again at *The New Yorker*, where he was the drama critic and she the book critic. Their friendship would outlast the Round Table, and would always remain platonic, but the two loved to kid about their relationship. One time Parker jokingly suggested they run off together, and Benchley asked what they would do with her husband. Parker replied, "Ship him off to military school."

But Benchley wasn't just Parker's straight man. He was an accomplished humorist in his own right, specializing in short, absurd humor pieces, the most famous of which, *The Treasurer's Report*, starts out as a staid recitation of financial figures and quickly derails into hysterical chaos. His 1935 short film, *How to Sleep*, nabbed him an Academy Award; Alfred Hitchcock was so impressed with Benchley that he cast him as a star of his 1940 film *Foreign Correspondent* (for which Benchley also cowrote the script). Thereafter, Benchley made a reasonably good living playing himself (or, more accurately, vaguely fictional versions of himself) swilling cocktails and tossing bon mots in various movies.

Benchley's short stories and humorous writings were well regarded, but Benchley stopped publishing them in 1938, when he was 49, because he maintained that humorists really weren't very funny after the age of 50 (Dave Barry, take note). Benchley would die in 1945 at age 56, and not at all humorously, from a cerebral hemorrhage. Benchley's heirs would go on to be literary figures in their own right; his son Nathaniel wrote books for children and novels for adults; his grandson Peter wrote *Jaws*.

### EDNA FERBER
The Round Table's other female regular, but don't think Ferber was standing in Parker's shadow—Ferber had quite the career long before she toddled over to the Algonquin to snack and snipe. In 1924, she nabbed the Pulitzer Prize in literature in 1924 for *So Big*, a weeper about a determined woman raising her child in difficult circumstances. The book was made into a movie more than once by Hollywood.

In fact, these days Ferber is better known not as an author but as source material for classic plays and movies. *Show Boat*, her 1926 novel, was made into a Tony Award–winning musical, which itself was the basis for three different movie adaptations, and her 1952 novel *Giant* is the source of James Dean's final film, for which Dean posthumously received one of the film's 10 Academy Award nominations. Ferber would keep knocking out novels into her seventies (*Ice Palace* was her last, in 1958—made into a movie starring Richard Burton). She died in 1968, of cancer.

### GEORGE S. KAUFMAN
For proof that the citizens of the Round Table got well into each other's business, one doesn't have to look any further than Kaufman. A famed playwright who rarely wrote plays by himself, Kaufman collaborated with Circle mates Edna Ferber and Alexander Woollcott, and cowrote two plays that became Marx Brothers movies, featuring Table-mate Harpo Marx. But his most successful plays

---

Karl Marx and Friedrich Engels wrote *The Communist Manifesto* while in England.

were written with Moss Hart, who wasn't a Round Table regular—until he started writing with Kaufman. Their greatest plays are still immensely popular and include *You Can't Take It with You* and *The Man Who Came to Dinner*, which was a lovingly sarcastic tribute to Woollcott. It's entirely reasonable to say that if Kaufman didn't spend much of his time sniping at his pals at the Algonquin, a substantial chunk of 20th-century theater simply wouldn't have been written—or cowritten, at the very least.

## FRANKLIN PIERCE ADAMS

If it hadn't been for Adams (or "F.P.A.," as he was known), the Algonquin Round Table would have been nothing more than a collection of talented but largely obscure wits tanking it up at a conveniently located hotel bar. But as it happens, Adams just happened to be the preeminent newspaper columnist of the 1920s, churning out a daily column for the *New York Herald-Tribune* called "The Conning Tower." The column was a collection of light verse, quips, comments, and observations, primarily from F.P.A., but also by selected contributors—say, the folks at the Algonquin Round table. It was a good deal for everyone. F.P.A. got column inches, the Round Table regulars got famous, and everyone got a little tipsy and stuffed themselves on lunchtime snacks. Which is not to say that F.P.A. didn't get in his own digs—one time when a fan approached Alexander Woollcott to sign a first edition of one of his books, Woollcott said, "Ah, what is so rare as a Woollcott first edition?" F.P.A. replied: "A Woollcott second edition."

As famous as F.P.A. was as a columnist, he became a household word in America starting in 1938, when he was asked to be a panelist on the popular radio show *Information, Please*. Proving that literary fame is nice, but to become really famous—even back then—you needed to be multimedia.

\* \* \*

To learn more about the man who might be called the "centerpiece" of the Round Table, read "The Round Table's Centerpiece Part I," page 31.

---

**Actress Laura Dern's grandfather, George Dern, was Secretary of War under FDR.**

# TOONSMITHS

*How did all those* Looney Tunes *cartoons get to be so darn funny? Blame these five guys.*

Anyone who's ever stared glassily into the boob tube on a Saturday morning while cramming an entire boxful of sugar-encrusted breakfast cereal into their face will not be surprised to learn that four of the top five animated shorts (per the 1994 book *The 50 Greatest Cartoons*) were from the famed Warner Bros. animation studio—home of Bugs Bunny, Daffy Duck, Roadrunner, Wile E. Coyote, as well as other cheerfully violent anarchistic characters. The fab four cartoons, in case you're curious: *What's Opera Doc?*, *Duck Amuck*, *One Froggy Evening*, and *Duck Dodgers in the 24 1/2th Century*. What might surprise you is that these toons have something else in common—the creative team of director Chuck Jones, writer Michael Maltese, voice actor Mel Blanc, layout artist Maurice Noble, and composer Carl Stalling (who did the music for two of the four). When it came to pure, whacked-out cartoon madness, doled out in explosive six-to-seven minute increments, Jones, Maltese, Blanc, Noble, and Stalling were the best there ever were. So who were these nutbags, anyway?

## CHUCK JONES

Arguably the greatest animation director in history, Jones's entry to the animation world was humble enough. His first animation job, in the 1930s, was as a cel washer—he scraped paint off the clear sheets animators drew characters on so the sheets could be reused. As an animator, Jones kicked around various studios for most of that decade, and he managed to get fired from the Ub Iwerks studios (Iwerks animated *Mickey Mouse* for Disney) not once, but twice before signing on with the Leon Schlesinger studio in 1936. This studio was eventually bought by Warner Bros. It was here Jones directed his first short, *The Night Watchman*, in 1938.

His early work actually isn't much good. It leans heavily on a Disneyesque cuteness that gets old fast. By the mid-1940s, Jones started letting his shorts play fast and loose, developing the quick, violent, and funny pace we've all come to love. Between 1948 and 1958, he was directing some of Warner Bros.' best work (including the four cartoons previously mentioned) and creating characters like Roadrunner, Wile E. Coyote, Marvin the Martian, and Pepe LePew. Pepe LePew, in fact, brought Jones his first Oscar in 1949 (for the short *For Scent-imental Reasons*), a sweet vindication for Jones, since his producer, Edward Seltzer, hated the smelly skunk.

When Warner Bros. closed its animation studio in 1963, Jones jumped ship to MGM and tried his hand at *Tom and Jerry* shorts, substantially changing the look and feel of the characters while doing so. (The critical opinion about this era of *Tom and Jerry* shorts is mixed.) During this period Jones also directed the famous *The Grinch Who Stole Christmas!* cartoon special, and received another Oscar for the animated short *The Dot and the Line*. In the 1970s—the dark ages of animation by any estimation—Jones went independent and created a number of television cartoon specials. In the 1990s he was lured back to Warner Bros. to create a batch of animated shorts designed to capitalize on the enduring popularity of his previous work. He received an honorary Academy Award in 1996 and died in 2002, at age 90.

## MICHAEL MALTESE

Chuck Jones may have directed all those great cartoons, but it was Maltese who wrote all the gags, creating the unique combination of broad physical comedy (think Daffy Duck getting his beak blasted off in the great Hunter's Trilogy—*Rabbit Fire, Rabbit Seasoning,* and *Duck! Rabbit! Duck!*—which also featured Bugs Bunny and Elmer Fudd) and biting, knowing wit (think any of Bugs's numerous asides). Homages to scenes Maltese wrote pop up even in contemporary animation—one scene in 2001's *Monsters, Inc,* in which the monster Sully responds woozily to trash being compacted, is a direct and acknowledged steal from a similar scene in the Maltese-written 1952 short, *Feed the Kitty*. Given the amount of laughter his works create, it's not out of line to suggest Maltese was one of the funniest writers in 20th-century film—and underappreciated both in his time and in ours. Oddly enough, Maltese didn't want to be a writer. He started off in the 1930s as an "inbetweener"—an animator whose job it is to create the frames of animation in between the lead animator's main drawings. In 1939, he was more or less dragooned into being a story writer at Warner Bros. Some of his early work was controversial—a final gag he wrote for the 1941 cartoon *The Heckling Hare* was "blue" enough to get the director fired. (The director, Tex Avery, landed on his feet just fine and made some fabulously wild cartoons for MGM.) After working with director Fritz Freling, Maltese hooked up with Jones and they started their run of famously anarchic cartoons, cocreating the Roadrunner, Wile E. Coyote, and Pepe LePew.

The Jones-Maltese collaboration continued when Jones moved to MGM—Maltese wrote several of the *Tom and Jerry* cartoons Jones directed, imbuing them with a Roadrunner-like zing. During the 1960s, Maltese also ventured into television animation by becoming the head writer at the Hanna-Barbera studios, which was busy cranking out "limited animation"—the awful "look, we're hardly moving" style that defined Yogi Bear, Snagglepuss, and the Flintstones. Hanna and Barbera assumed that if the writing was good enough, no one would notice the lame animation, which was correct thanks to Maltese and his crew. Maltese retired in 1973 and spent his waning years fiddling around with comic books for Gold Key Comics, although he and Jones reunited briefly for a couple of cartoon shorts in the late 1970s. Maltese died in early 1981.

## MAURICE NOBLE

It's not an insult to say that Maurice Noble's work on Warner Bros.' animated shorts got shoved to the background. That's because Maurice Noble's work was the background—as the layout artist, Noble was responsible for the look and feel of the space the animated characters ran around in. If you ever admired the clean, impressionistic design of *What's Opera Doc?*, or the crazily precarious cliffs and spires the Roadrunner zoomed around on, you've been grooving on Noble's contribution.

Noble's own story is one of the most interesting among this crew. An art-school dropout, he was earning $90 a week designing department store displays when he took a job at the Walt Disney Studios—not because he was that interested in animation, but because it would be a $10 a week raise, a real consideration during the Depression. While at Disney, Noble worked on backgrounds for a number of shorts, but most famously for *Snow White and the Seven Dwarfs*. Noble's tenure at Disney came to an end after he and other artists went on strike. After the strike was settled,

Noble was assigned a new office—literally a broom closet (he had to stand on a chair to see out his window). He also wasn't assigned any work, and was therefore laid off because he wasn't doing anything.

Then Pearl Harbor happened, and Noble joined the army, where they put him to work setting up short propaganda films (produced by director Frank Capra) for the troops. Eventually, Noble joined Capra's outfit and worked directly under Major Theodor Geisel—better known by his pen name, Dr. Seuss. The two formed a friendship that would work out nicely for both. After the war, Noble freelanced, then got the call to join Chuck Jones's Hollywood animation unit. Their collaboration began in 1952.

Jones and Noble characterized their relationship as strictly professional, but even so, it was very close. Noble joined Jones at MGM and codirected a number of shorts with him, including the Oscar-winning *The Dot and the Line*. He also worked on the Grinch special with Jones and Geisel, and a number of other Dr. Seuss specials produced by Geisel. Later, Noble did some writing for the *Tiny Toons Adventures* TV series and produced a series of student-created shorts known as Noble Tales. He died in 2001.

## CARL STALLING

Not the best-known orchestral composer of the 20th century, but based on the popularity of *Looney Tunes*, arguably the most heard. Stalling, a former movie theater organist, got his start in film composing at the beginning of the sound era and worked with Disney on some of his earliest sound cartoons. Along the way he invented something called the "click track," a tempo indicator that film composers use to this day to score films. Stalling worked with Disney through the 1920s, helping Walt create the Silly Symphony line of cartoon shorts, but he left in 1930 to join Ub Iwerks animation studio. When that folded in 1936, he jumped over to Warner Bros. as the animation department's musical director.

From 1936 through 1958, Stalling scored almost every cartoon from the studio (assisted by Milt Franklyn, who succeeded him when he retired). Stalling used a combination of his own work and selections from the vast Warner Bros. musical library. When Stalling did the latter, he would often pick music whose titles corresponded with the action. When Sylvester the Cat slapped Tweety Bird between two slices of bread, Stalling would use music from the song "A Cup of Coffee, a Sandwich, and You." He

---

**In one demonstration, over 200 monks were thrown in the air by an electrical jolt.**

retired in 1958 and died in 1974. A CD of his cartoon music, the *Carl Stalling Project*, was released with great fanfare in 1990.

## MEL BLANC

The voice of nearly every single notable character in the Warner Bros. cartoon canon—and some outside of it, too. A little-known fact is that Blanc provided Woody Woodpecker's famous (and annoying) laugh, and after he signed an exclusive contract with Warner Bros. in the 1940s, Blanc sued Woody's creator, Walter Lanz, for continuing to use his voice. Just about the only major cartoon voice Blanc didn't do for Warner Bros. was Elmer Fudd (by Arthur Q. Bryans), and he did that after Bryans passed away.

Blanc's interest in voice work started early. After high school in the mid-1920s, he got a gig in his hometown of Portland, Oregon, doing a radio show called *The Hoot Owls*. After this, he went to Hollywood to make his mark in movies but didn't do very well. It wasn't until 1937 that he made his first voice-over appearance: Porky Pig (then Warner Bros.' big star) in *Porky's Romance*.

At the time Blanc started doing voices, most animation voice acting was done by whoever was around at the time; animators often ended up doing their characters' voices (most notably Walt Disney, who supplied Mickey Mouse's voice). Blanc changed that by becoming Warner's "go to" guy for voices, providing most of the vocals for hundreds of Warner Bros. shorts and specials from 1937 until his death. While Blanc was providing the voices for Bugs, Daffy, and others, he was also enjoying a successful run as a featured player on Jack Benny's radio show, playing Carmichael the Polar Bear, Professor LeBlanc, and the voice of Jack Benny's car. After the Warner Bros. heyday was over, Blanc continued to stay busy in voice acting, as the voice of Barney Rubble on *The Flintstones*, and later as Heathcliff the cat and Twiki, the sidekick android on the live-action series *Buck Rogers in the 25th Century*.

Unlike most of Blanc's compatriots, his role in the cartoon process was well-known; in 1961, after a car accident that nearly killed him, Blanc surfaced from a coma to find thousands of get well cards waiting for him, many sent simply to "Bugs Bunny."

When Blanc passed away in 1989, Warner Bros. took the unusual step of placing a two-page ad in *Variety*, showing all the characters he had voiced, their heads bowed in mourning.

**"Happy Birthday"** was the first song to be performed in outer space.

# WHO SAID THAT?

*Uncle John's quiz on notable quotes from famous folks!*

1. "First they ignore you, then they laugh at you, then they fight you, then you win."
   *Hint:* Political and spiritual leader of India

2. "The future belongs to those who believe in the beauty of their dreams."
   *Hint:* First lady and famous American humanitarian.

3. "Good people do not need laws to tell them to act responsibly, while bad people will find a way around the laws."
   *Hint:* Greek philosopher's whose thoughts greatly influenced Western civilization.

4. "Once you eliminate the impossible, whatever remains, no matter how improbable, must be the truth."
   *Hint:* English literature's brainiest detective.

5. "A doctor can bury his mistakes but an architect can only advise his clients to plant vines."
   *Hint:* Most influential architect of his time.

6. "Anatomy is destiny."
   *Hint:* Austrian originator of psychoanalysis.

7. "There is nothing worse than a brilliant image of a fuzzy concept."
   *Hint:* Legendary pioneer of photography and the environmental movement.

8. "I'll sail to Ka-Troo. And bring back an It-Kutch a Preep and a Proo. A Nerkle a Nerd and a Seersucker, too."
   *Hint:* This Pulitzer Prize–winning author is believed to have invented the word "nerd."

**It was sung by the *Apollo IX* astronauts on March 8, 1969.**

9. "Most people would sooner die than think; in fact, they do so."
   *Hint:* British philosopher, mathematician, and social reformer.

10. "He who slings mud generally loses ground."
    *Hint:* Governor of Illinois and American ambassador to the United Nations.

11. "That's one small step for man, one giant leap for mankind."
    *Hint:* The first person to set foot on the moon.

12. "I am one of those who think, like Nobel, that humanity will draw more good than evil from new discoveries."
    *Hint:* A Nobel Prize–winning physicist killed by overexposure to radiation.

13. "Dorothy was so happy to wake up in Kansas. Not I! I'd have looked for another cyclone and stood in its path!"
    *Hint:* This Kansas native was happier in Hollywood as one of TV's best-loved comediennes.

14. "A lie gets halfway around the world before the truth has a chance to get its pants on."
    *Hint:* Prime Minister of Britain, led his country to victory in WWII.

15. "Once you're dead you're made for life."
    *Hint:* He's been praised as rock and roll's greatest dead guitarist.

16. "If you can count your money, you don't have a billion dollars."
    *Hint:* American business executive who became one of the richest men in the world.

17. "All diplomacy is a continuation of war by other means."
    *Hint:* A founder of the Chinese Communist Party and premier of Communist China.

18. "Posterity: you will never know how much it has cost my generation to preserve your freedom. I hope you will make good use of it."
    *Hint:* The sixth U.S. president.

---

**Tonight Show** veteran Ed McMahon is a retired Marine fighter pilot.

19. "Assassins!"

    *Hint:* Famous conductor insulting his orchestra for murdering their music.

20. "When I played ball, I didn't play for fun...It's no pink tea, and mollycoddles had better stay out."

    *Hint:* The great baseball player known as the Georgia Peach.

21. "You can't say that civilization don't advance, however, for in every war they kill you in a new way."

    *Hint:* The cowboy humorist who was part Cherokee Indian.

22. "Biography lends to death a new terror."

    *Hint:* Famous British playwright and renowned wit (who surely wasn't complaining about Uncle John's Biographies).

Answers:
1. Mahatma Gandhi (1869–1948); 2. Eleanor Roosevelt (1884–1962); 3. Plato (427–347 B.C.); 4. Sherlock Holmes (created by Sir Arthur Conan Doyle) 1859–1930; 5. Frank Lloyd Wright (1868–1959); 6. Sigmund Freud (1856–1939); 7. Ansel Adams (1902–1984); 8. Theodor Seuss Geisel a.k.a. Dr. Seuss (1904–1991); 9. Bertrand Russell (1872–1970); 10. Adlai Stevenson (1900–1965); 11. Neil Armstrong (1930–); 12. Marie Curie (1867–1934); 13. Vivian Vance (played Ethel Mertz on *I Love Lucy*) 1909–1979; 14. Sir Winston Churchill (1874–1965); 15. Jimi Hendrix (1942–1970); 16. J. Paul Getty (1892–1976); 17. Zhou Enlai (1898–1976); 18. John Quincy Adams (1767–1848); 19. Arturo Toscanini (1867–1957); 20. Ty Cobb (1886–1961); 21. Will Rogers (1879–1935); 22. Oscar Wilde (1854–1900)

---

**Bill Haley's "Crazy Man, Crazy" was the first R&R record single to make the Billboard Top 20.**

# ON HER TOES

*That's how a girl from an Oklahoma Indian reservation made it to
center stage as America's first prima ballerina.*

Elizabeth Marie Tall Chief was born on the Osage reservation
in Fairfax, Oklahoma, in 1925. But forget about the possible
disadvantages of such an upbringing. The tribe lived on top
of one of the richest oil fields in North America. Betty Tall Chief
(as our heroine was called) spent her first years in a 10-room house
on a hill overlooking the reservation.

Dad was a full-blooded Osage, Mom was Scots-Irish with a
streak of stage mother. She saw to it that Betty and her sister,
Marjorie, started studying ballet almost as soon as they could walk.

### A FAR CRY FROM OK

By 1930, the reservation's oil supply was becoming depleted, and
anyway her mom wanted the girls to be musical film stars, so in
1934, the family moved to Los Angeles. The girls studied first with
Ernest Belcher (the father of—for fans of Hollywood musicals—
dancer Marge Champion), then with Madame Bronislava Nijinsky,
the sister of the world-famous dancer Vaslav Nijinsky. The training
at Nijinsky's was rigorous—serious ballerina stuff—and Betty and
Marjorie ate it up.

In school, the kids made fun of Betty's last name, so she
changed it to one word: Tallchief. At age 15, as a student of Nijinsky's,
Miss Betty Tallchief danced her first lead—at the Hollywood Bowl.

### THE BIG APPLE BECKONS

After high school, Betty was accepted at the Ballet Russe de
Monte Carlo, a Russian troupe that moved its headquarters to
New York when WWII broke out. All she had to do was work
hard and try not to step on any Russian toes (literally *and* figura-
tively). Some of the Russian dancers jealously guarded the best
roles and weren't above retaliations like putting ground glass in
the toe shoes of young Americans.

### THE "RODEO" COMES TO TOWN

When Agnes de Mille started rehearsing the company for the
debut of her ballet, *Rodeo*, she gave Betty two gifts: the first, a
teensy solo in *Rodeo*; the second, the suggestion that Betty change
her name to Maria.

Jimmy Stewart was awarded the Distinguished Flying Cross and the Croix de Guerre in WWII.

## ON THE WAY UP
After her first lead performance, a *New York Times* dance critic called Maria "a real discovery." He spoke of her "easy brilliance" and that "when she has grown up…she can hardly escape being Somebody."

Meanwhile, somebody else with a capital *S* was watching. And at the first opportunity, he snatched her away from Ballet Russe for his own ballet company—later renamed the New York City Ballet.

## B-MUSED
George Balanchine had already had two ballerina wives; in 1946, Maria became the third. Under his tutelage, she quickly worked her way up to prima ballerina. Eventually, as Balanchine kept adding new ballets for her to perform, she was dancing eight performances a week. At the point of physical exhaustion, she stopped working long enough to look around. When she did, she was surprised to find out that she was famous.

## MAKING HEADLINES
The American public adored her—even if they'd never seen her dance. She was the essence of grace, talent, and beauty—and how could she be more American? Foreign audiences clamored to see her, as much for her exoticness as for her talent. The headline in a Paris newspaper read *"Peau Rouge danse a l'Opera"*—literally, "Redskin Dances at the Opera." But Maria still found fame, even of the dubious "redskin" variety, gratifying.

## SPLITSVILLE, BUT CIVILIZED
A second visit to Paris in 1952 gave Maria a chance to visit Marjorie, who'd joined a European ballet company and had married a Russian dancer/choreographer. Marjorie wasn't anywhere near as famous, but Maria was still envious—Marjorie was about to give birth to twins.

Even though Maria thought of her own marriage as a perfect—if not very passionate—arrangement, it came to an end that same year. It was an amicable annulment (on the grounds that Balanchine didn't want any children)—amicable because Maria was smitten with a dashing Russian aviator and Balanchine was ready to take on a new, even younger wife-protégé, Tanaquil LeClerq.

---

The Carpenters' "We've Only Just Begun" was originally a radio spot for a California bank.

## TWO MORE HUBBIES AND A FAIRY

Maria stayed on at the ballet, married her fly-boy, and divorced him a little less than two years later because he didn't have the slightest understanding of how hard a ballerina has to work. Dalliances followed—with a Texas millionaire and an Olympic sailor named Buzz, who turned out to be the scion of a wealthy Chicago family. Maria and Buzz married in 1956; Buzz stayed in Chicago to work in the family business, while Maria continued to dance in New York and wherever else the ballet took her.

During this time Balanchine choreographed the Christmas favorite *The Nutcracker*, tailoring the role of the Sugar Plum Fairy for Tallchief.

## SEMIRETIREMENT

As younger ballerinas took over her roles, Maria started teaching some of Balanchine's classes. In the mid-1960s, Jackie Kennedy asked her to teach a private class for girls that included Caroline Kennedy, a few of her cousins, and Maria's own daughter, Elise.

A ballerina's shelf life is a lot longer than most athletes. Tallchief danced until she was 41. But she'd seen the writing on the wall—it said "Suzanne Farrell," an 18-year-old who was Balanchine's new favorite dancer.

Even though she credits Balanchine with most of her success, let us not forget that it was Tallchief's talent and charisma as a dancer that brought his New York City Ballet to the world's notice.

## CATCHING UP ON THE FAMILY

After more than 10 years of marriage, Maria finally moved to Chicago to settle down with her husband and daughter. The small-scale classes she taught there eventually evolved into the Chicago City Ballet.

Pretty sensational life for a little girl from the reservation, wouldn't you say?

* * *

## NOBODY SAYS NO TO MR. B!

Only one protégé ever turned Balanchine down—that would be Suzanne Farrell (nee Roberta Sue Ficker) when Mr. B. was 64 and she was 23. Farrell married fellow dancer Paul Mejia, whom Balanchine paid not to show up for work, which ticked Farrell off no end. She made the mistake of giving Balanchine an ultimatum, and Balanchine banished them both from the New York City Ballet forever.

**Elton John is Sean Lennon's godfather.**

# A GRIMM TALE

*Mirror, mirror, on the wall,*
*Who collected more fairy tales than them all?*

It's a Cinderella story. Once upon a time (1785, actually) in a kingdom far, far away (Hanau, Hesse, now Germany) a boy was born whose life's work has thrilled and enchanted children to this day. His name was Jacob. The following year, Jacob's brother, Wilhelm, was born. The two became so inseparable that they are known today simply as the Brothers Grimm.

## IN FOR THE COUNT

The boys led a happy, comfortable childhood until 1796 when their father, who'd been town magistrate, died. Mother Grimm and her six children were suddenly poor. With the help of a kindly aunt, the brothers were admitted to a school at the palace of a count. The other students were members of the nobility or pages working in the palace. Students and teachers alike treated Jacob and Wilhelm as if they were country bumpkins.

But the brothers worked hard on their studies and impressed their teachers. In those days, only the nobility were permitted to attend universities, but the university at Marburg admitted the brothers when the count granted them special permission. Though both brothers studied law, their hearts were in books and literature.

## THE FROG KING

In 1806, Jacob Grimm was clerking in the Hessian war office when Napoleon's French army marched in and took over the government. Jacob managed to keep his job because he could speak French. (He wanted to quit because he hated the French, but he needed the money.)

Later, with Napoleon's brother Jerome installed as King of Westphalia, Jacob was put in charge of the royal library. The library had 12,000 books and only three people in the entire kingdom were permitted to read them—King Jerome, his queen, and Jacob the librarian...and the king and queen didn't read much. Jacob's only specific instruction was to write "Library of the King" on the

---

**In 1891, Samuel O'Reilly used Edison's electric pen as a model for the first electric tattoo machine.**

door. After that, he could just hang around the library and get paid for it.

## JUST PLAIN FOLK

In a sort of passive opposition to French occupation, Jacob and Wilhelm began collecting and writing about German folktales in scholarly journals. They hated being forced to speak French and seeing paintings and books looted from Hesse and taken to France. They grumbled about the spying of the French secret police and the high taxes imposed by the French, which ate up their meager incomes. They wanted the fairy tales they collected to help maintain the German heritage they felt was being lost.

The Grimms wanted their tales to be authentic tales of the German Volk using their simple phrases. One hundred years earlier, a Frenchman named Charles Perrault had collected eight French tales, but Jacob and Wilhelm were unimpressed. They wrote, "There is nothing more difficult than using the French language to tell children's stories…without pretentiousness."

## SPINNING YARNS INTO GOLD

In December 1812, while Napoleon's army was getting trounced in Russia, the Grimms' first collection, *Children's and Household Tales*, was published. It included 87 stories (though the final edition would include more than 200). The brothers had collected the tales from the common people—peasants, soldiers, fishermen, and servants. These were fanciful fables of gnomes, elves, and witches passed down in cottages and spinning rooms, but never before written down. The Grimms took down the tales exactly as they were told to them.

The book was a great success; but it also had its critics. In Austria it was banned as being too "superstitious." Some stories were criticized as being too violent or otherwise inappropriate for children. While Jacob maintained the stories were not for children, Wilhelm agreed with the critics and he edited later editions of the tales to make them more G-rated. Stories of children being killed and eaten were removed, as were references to out-of-wedlock sex. (Rapunzel's premarital pregnancy, for example. Oh, you didn't know?)

## WHAT BIG WORDS YOU HAVE!

The Grimms worked on other scholarly pursuits related to language. Jacob Grimm wrote the lengthy *German Grammar*, explaining how languages had changed over the centuries and how Indo-European languages were related. He even devised a rule on language similarities known as "Grimm's law."

Together the brothers started producing a German dictionary that not only gave current word definitions and usage, but also etymology. They worked in tandem: Jacob worked on the letters A through C; Wilhelm did D. That was as far as they got in 20 years of work. The massive dictionary was finally finished 100 years after their deaths.

## HAPPILY EVER AFTER

Throughout their lives, the brothers were happiest when together. They often worked together on the same projects. They taught at the same university. They lived together. Even when Wilhelm married in 1823, Jacob lived with Wilhelm, his wife (who had been the source for many of their tales), and their children. When Wilhelm, who had a heart condition, traveled to spas for treatments, Jacob wrote him long letters telling him how much he was missed. Wilhelm died in December 1859. Jacob followed in September 1863.

Today it's almost impossible to imagine children's books (much less Disney movies) without the stories the Brothers Grimm collected. *Cinderella, Snow White and the Seven Dwarfs, The Sleeping Beauty, Hansel and Gretel, Little Red Riding Hood, The Frog Prince, Rapunzel, The Bremen Town Musicians, Rumpelstiltskin*, and many more might all have been lost and forgotten but for Jacob and Wilhelm Grimm.

\* \* \*

"In olden times when wishing still helped one, there lived a King whose daughters were all beautiful, but the youngest was so beautiful that the sun itself, which has seen so much, was astonished whenever it shone in her face." —The Brothers Grimm

# IT'S NEWS TO NELLIE

*Was Nellie Bly a woman ahead of her time or was she just trapped in a society when women were less than second-class citizens?*

In 1885, the *Pittsburgh Dispatch* ran a column called "What Girls Are Good For." It argued that women should not vote or work, but make their "home a little paradise" and play "the part of an angel." One of the readers was a 20-year-old girl who knew first-hand the dangers of being dependent on a man. Born 13th out of 15 children in a small Pennsylvania town, she'd quit school and moved to Pittsburgh at 16 to get away from an abusive stepfather. Because there weren't a lot of job options for young women then, she'd been working at a series of low-paying jobs. The column's unrealistic view so outraged her that she wrote an angry anonymous letter to the editor signed "Lonely Orphan Girl."

The editor was so impressed by her letter that he advertised in the Sunday classifieds looking for her. When she showed up at the paper, he offered her a job. She wrote two stories for the paper as the Lonely Orphan Girl: "The Girl Puzzle" about the difficulties of poor working girls, and "Mad Marriage," calling for the reform of Pennsylvania's divorce laws. She was hired. In those days it was unseemly for women writers to use their real names, so Elizabeth Cochrane took the name Nellie Bly from a Stephen Foster song.

## NELLIE AND THE NEWS

Nellie wanted to expose unsafe working conditions in the sweatshops and write about the poor. However, a lot of the businesses Nellie wrote about also advertised in the paper, and they complained about her reports and threatened to withdraw their advertising. Her editor wanted her to concentrate on flower shows and other fluff pieces, but instead, Nellie went to Mexico to write about the plight of the poor and government corruption there. When the Mexican government realized what she was up to, she was ordered out of the country. Her articles later became a book, *Six Months in Mexico*.

One day, Nellie left a note for her editors that said "I am off for New York. Look out for me. BLY." She moved to New York

---

**Twilight Zone's well-known theme was from Marius Constant's compositions.**

City thinking that she could easily get a job with Joseph Pulitzer's *New York World*, but she couldn't even get an interview. After four months, she still hadn't found a job and she'd run out of money. In desperation she talked her way past the guards at the *World* and into the office of the managing editor. She so impressed him that he gave her a $25 retainer until she could be hired.

## NELLIE AT THE NUT HOUSE

Her first assignment was to get herself committed to a women's insane asylum. Her journal of that experience exposed the horrific conditions at the asylum and the cruelty and abuse of patients by the staff. She also noted that many of the people being held there weren't even crazy—like women whose husbands had them committed just to get rid of them, and women whose only mental problem was that they didn't speak English.

She wrote, "I always made a point of telling the doctors I was sane, and asking to be released, but the more I endeavored to assure them of my sanity, the more they doubted it…" She called the place "a human rat-trap…it is easy to get in, but once there it is impossible to get out." Not quite. Nellie was fortunate enough to have a boss who came to get her after 10 days.

Her book *Ten Days in a Madhouse* made her famous and prompted much-needed reforms. And because she was very pretty, worked in a male-dominated industry, and took huge risks, she was popular with readers. The newspaper gave her her own byline, something previously unheard of for a newspaperwoman—and in a time when few men were accorded the honor.

After her trip to the asylum, she went undercover as a chorus girl, a maid, and an unwed mother. To get the story on poor treatment of women prisoners, she even got herself arrested for theft.

## AROUND THE WORLD WITH NELLIE

Meanwhile, her editors dreamed up another publicity stunt to boost circulation—but they wanted one of their male reporters to do it because a woman would need an escort. The idea was to see if someone could travel around the world in less than the 80 days it took Phileas Fogg, the character in Jules Verne's *Around the World in Eighty Days*. Nellie insisted that she could beat whoever they sent and that she'd do it for another newspaper if necessary. She got the assignment. Unescorted, she traveled by steamship, rail, horse, and rickshaw with only a small satchel and a checked coat that would become her trademark. Her articles created a sensation—readers couldn't wait to get their hands on the next installment. *The New York World* capitalized on the excitement by running a contest to see who could guess the exact amount of time it would take her. Nellie arrived back in New York 72 days later, beating Phileas Fogg's fictional time by more than a week. She soon realized how much the newspaper had profited from her reporting. Disappointed that her editors didn't give her a raise, thank her, or otherwise acknowledge her contributions, she resigned.

## NELLIE GOES INTO BUSINESS
In 1895, Bly married 70-year-old millionaire Robert L. Seaman, probably more as an investment than for love. He was 40 years her senior and died soon after their marriage. Nellie took over his manufacturing business and instituted reforms to help the workers; she added unheard-of benefits such as paid health care, a gymnasium, and a library. The business prospered, but the accounting staff was busy embezzling most of the profits, so the company was forced into bankruptcy in 1910.

## SOME VACATION THAT TURNED OUT TO BE
Nellie went to Europe for a long vacation—long enough to be there at the start of WWI. She became—what else?—the first female war correspondent, and her reporting from the front provided a vivid look at the war's cost in human terms. She spent four years reporting in Europe, and upon her return home she went to work for the *New York Evening Journal*, writing an advice column.

The one-time "Lonely Orphan Girl" also did a lot of charitable work for the city's poor, focusing on helping unwed mothers and abandoned children. She died of pneumonia in 1922, at the age of 55. Newspapers around the world carried her obituary and *The New York World* wrote:

"Nellie Bly was THE BEST REPORTER IN AMERICA."

**Elvis Presley made only one TV commercial—for Southern Maid Doughnuts in 1954.**

# A DOTTY IDEA

*Elbert Botts's brainchild wasn't just a bump in the road.*

Y ou may have run over Elbert Dysart Botts's invention today. Never heard of him? Well, he's the innovative guy who developed Botts Dots, the raised reflective markers seen on roads and freeways throughout America.

## MEET DR. BOTTS
Botts earned his doctorate in chemistry from the University of Wisconsin and taught for 16 years at San Jose State University. When WWII broke out, he went to work for the government as a chemist. Then he landed a job as a chemist in research and development at CalTrans (the Californian Department of Transportation), where he was assigned the task of creating reflective paint for freeways that could be seen in heavy rain.

## YIKES, SPIKES!
That's when Botts dreamed up the idea of raised markers, which he called Reflective Pavement Markers, or RPMs (known by the nickname "Botts Dots"). Unfortunately, the ceramic markers cracked apart after being rolled over, exposing the spikes that held them to the road surface, which—as you might have guessed—was bad news for tires. But one of Botts's former students came up with a solution. He developed a durable, fast-drying epoxy that replaced the spikes.

## FOLLOWING THE DOTTED LINE
Elbert Botts retired from CalTrans in 1960 and died two years later at age 69. Even though he never got to see his invention installed on warm-weather roads all over the country (he died three years before the first Botts Dots were installed in Northern California in 1963), we hope he knows that from now on, every time we hear that "thump-thump-thump" under our car wheels, we'll be thanking him for keeping us awake and out of everybody else's lane.

Nearly 50 percent of the newspapers in the world are published in the U.S. and Canada.

# EVERY DOG
# HAS HIS DAY

*How two moments in one night—one beautiful, one terrible—changed a homeless immigrant into the man Teddy Roosevelt called "the most useful citizen of New York."*

Jacob Riis sat by the river and thought seriously about killing himself. After all, he thought, no one would notice and no one would care. Then, as if he'd been sent right out of central casting, a little dog who'd been following Riis around that day crept into his lap and licked his face. Said Riis: "The love of the little beast thawed the icicles in my heart." The dog's affection lifted his spirits enough so that he was able to go on.

### GIVE ME YOUR TIRED, YOUR POOR...

He'd come to America in 1870 from Denmark at the age of 21. He arrived penniless and stayed that way, just one of thousands of Americans. The country was in the middle of a depression; thousands were out of work and homeless. He managed to find a few odd jobs from time to time, but that was all. He lived on the street, except during winter when he availed himself of what was called a police lodging house. The lodging houses were dirty and crowded, and people had to sleep on the bare floor, on newspapers or a plank of wood. But at least they had a roof over their heads. Months of hunger and homelessness had brought Riis to the river.

### SAD, SAD STORY

Later that night, Riis tried to sneak the little dog into the lodging house under his coat, but the desk sergeant saw it and made him put it outside. As he slept, Riis was robbed of a small gold locket that he'd saved and treasured as a memento from home. When he realized it was gone, he complained to the desk sergeant. The sergeant got angry, accused Riis of being a liar, and ordered one of his officers to throw him out into the street.

It gets worse. The little dog, of course, was waiting outside. When he saw Riis being pushed out the door, he bit the cop on

---

**A Virginia man fashioned an eight-mile long chain of chewing gum wrappers over 38 years.**

the leg. The cop let go of Riis, grabbed the dog who had just saved Riis's life—and smashed his head against the steps. In that moment, all of Riis's despair was transformed into anger. He vowed that somehow he would find a way to avenge the death of that little dog.

## THE UNIVERSE PROVIDES

And find it he did. He heard about a writing job at a news agency, was hired, and by 1877, his reputation was so formidable that the *New York Tribune* and the Associated Press hired him as a police reporter. His beat was police headquarters on Mulberry Street, one of the worst slums in the city. Knowing that pictures could tell his story better than any words, he took up photography. He used a flashlight to light his shots until the invention of flash powder, which enabled him to photograph the interiors of tenements and the streets and back alleys of the slums at night.

He came out of those tenements and alleys with heartrending photos like *Blind Beggar* or *Home of Italian Ragpicker*—photos that would change forever the way American society viewed the immigrants who were arriving in boatloads every day.

## MURDER, HE WROTE

In 1888, Riis was hired as a photojournalist by the *New York Evening Sun*. His work there—and his first book, *How the Other Half Lives, Studies Among the Tenements of New York*—was a groundbreaking exposé of society's indifference to the plight of the immigrant poor, the oppressed, the exploited, and the downtrodden. He blamed much of the misery and crime in the slums on the greed of landlords and building speculators. He called it "premeditated murder as large-scale economic speculation." His reporting inspired shock and horror among New York's rich and middle classes.

It also captured the interest of the New York Police Commissioner, Theodore Roosevelt, who would later become governor and then the 26th president of the U.S. Riis took Roosevelt with him on some of his forays into the dark corners of the city. When Roosevelt was elected governor of New York, he closed the lodging houses and made sure that Riis's concerns became official business.

**Actress Kathleen Turner's father was a POW of the Japanese during WWII.**

## FOR THE LITTLE GUY

Riis traveled all over America conducting "magic lantern" shows, where he projected his photos onto a large screen. A reporter wrote: "His viewers moaned, shuddered, fainted and even talked to the photographs he projected, reacting to the slides not as images, but as a reality that transported the New York slum world directly into the lecture hall."

He usually concluded his lectures with the declaration, "My dog did not die unavenged!"

## PHOTO FINISH

Riis wrote several other books, including *Children of the Poor* (1892), *Out of Mulberry Street* (1898), *The Battle with the Slum* (1902), *Children of the Tenement* (1903), and his autobiography, *The Making of an American* (1901).

Jacob Riis has been credited with precipitating many of the reforms that improved the living conditions of the poor during what is now known as the Progressive Era. Health and sanitation laws were passed and enforced. Landlords were forced to make repairs and improvements. Laws were passed requiring modern improvements to new residential construction. The Mulberry Bend slums were eventually razed, largely due to his efforts. He also started the Tenement House Commission and the Jacob A. Riis Settlement House. By the time he died in Barrie, Massachusetts, on May 26, 1914, he was known as the "Emancipator of the Slums."

Riis's work has proven to be an invaluable resource to historians and social scientists ever since, but many of his photographs would be lost today if it weren't for a photographer and historian named Alexander Alland. In 1946 he searched for and found Riis's original glass plate negatives in the attic of the Riis family home before it was torn down. They are now part of the collection of the Museum of the City of New York.

\* \* \*

"I'd look at one of my stonecutters hammering away at the rock, perhaps a hundred times without as much as a crack showing in it. Yet, at the hundred and first blow it would split in two, and I knew it was not that blow that did it, but all that had gone before."

—Jacob August Riis

Poet Robert Frost's full name was Robert Lee Frost.

# PRINCE OF HUMBUGS

*Who said there's a sucker born every minute? It turns out that it wasn't Phineas Taylor (a.k.a. P. T.) Barnum after all.*

It was one of Barnum's envious competitors who coined the famous, "There's a sucker born every minute." In fact, P. T. greatly respected his customers and would have been more likely to say there's a "customer" born every minute.

He did say, "Every crowd has a silver lining," and he'd be the first to admit that he'd spent his life bringing crowds together so that he could separate them from their silver.

## THE SIX-FOOT MAN-EATING CHICKEN!

They called him "the Shakespeare of Advertising," because he believed in the power of publicity. He used it to profit from the public's taste for what he called "humbug," which Barnum himself defined as "putting on glittering appearances...to...arrest public attention and attract the public eye and ear." He proudly called himself "the Prince of Humbugs," because he could deceive people in such a way that they were greatly entertained, even though most of the attractions he promoted didn't even come close to the tremendous buildup he gave them.

Like the Six-Foot Man-Eating Chicken he advertised—which turned out to be a six-foot man...eating chicken.

## A LESSON IN MARKETING

The master showman was born in Bethel, Connecticut, in 1810. His father died when he was 15, leaving him to make his own way in the world. Through hard work and pluck, he saved enough to start a weekly abolitionist newspaper in 1829. He called it the *Herald of Freedom*. In 1831, he was thrown into jail for denouncing a Protestant minister in the paper. To his delight, he went to jail an unknown newspaper owner, and 60 days later, came out a hero and a martyr. This taught him another valuable lesson—that there's no such thing as bad publicity.

### Joice Heth

Barnum moved to New York in 1834 and began his career in show business when he discovered Joice Heth, a woman who claimed to be 161 years old and a former slave who'd been a nurse to George Washington. Heth entertained audiences with stories and songs about the young George and drew very large crowds because, as one of Barnum's handbills proclaimed, she "was the first person who put clothes on the unconscious infant, who, years later, led our heroic fathers on to glory, to victory, and freedom."

Eventually the public's interest in Joice Heth waned, so Barnum—ever resourceful—started spreading rumors that Heth was in fact not a person at all, but a robot. One of Barnum's anonymous letters to the newspaper said, "Joice Heth is not a human being. What purports to be a remarkably old woman, is simply a curiously constructed automaton, made up of whalebone, India-rubber, and springs ingeniously put together, and made to move at the slightest touch according to the will of the operator."

Of course, this attracted even *more* people, including earlier visitors who wanted to determine for themselves whether they'd been duped the first time—while Barnum continued to rake in the cash. Eventually Heth died and Barnum cashed in on her again when he had a public autopsy performed to determine her actual age. It turned out that Heth couldn't have been much more than 80 years old. Barnum declared that he was "shocked" to find out he'd been duped.

## THE AMERICAN MUSEUM

In 1841, Barnum opened the American Museum, located on Broadway in the heart of New York City. It became one of the most famous places of amusement in the entire world, where "500,000 natural and artificial curiosities from every corner of the globe" were on exhibit. The collection included minerals, fossils, animals, natural wonders, minor deceptions, and elaborate hoaxes. Also on display were a wide range of physical "freaks," including people he claimed were the world's tallest, shortest, heaviest, thinnest, hairiest—you get the drift.

### Tom Thumb

Charles S. Stratton was a dwarf who was only five years old when Barnum began exhibiting him as General Tom Thumb. A little man of many talents, he appeared in costume—as Napoleon, Hercules, Samson, and a variety of other characters—while he sang, danced, and told jokes.

In 1844, Barnum took Tom on the first of two European tours

---

Helena Bonham-Carter's great-grandfather was U.K. Prime Minister Herbert Asquith.

where he was presented to Queen Victoria of England, Queen Isabella of Spain, and King Leopold of Belgium. At the invitation of King Louis-Philippe I of France, Tom rode in a royal procession in a miniature carriage drawn by four matching Shetland ponies.

In 1863, Tom married another dwarf, the lovely Miss Lavinia Warren, in a grand ceremony. A few days later, they were guests of honor at a White House reception hosted by President Lincoln. After the marriage Barnum often exhibited them with a normal-sized baby for dramatic effect, though they never actually had a child of their own.

## Anna Swan and Commodore Nutt
Barnum liked to exhibit giants and dwarfs together in order to accentuate their differences. Anna Swan was eight feet tall and said to be "the tallest woman in the world." She was often paired with George Washington Morrison "Commodore" Nutt, who at 29 inches tall was even smaller than Tom Thumb and billed as "the shortest man in the world."

Barnum built carriages for both Anna and Commodore Nutt so they could travel around New York City attracting large crowds that would follow them to the American Museum. Anna's huge carriage was pulled by two Clydesdales, while Commodore Nutt's was shaped like a walnut and pulled by two Shetland ponies.

## Zip, the Pinhead
"The Missing Link" and "Zip, the Pinhead" was William Henry Johnson, a black dwarf who was a microcephalic, which means he had a very small head. Though he was born in the U.S., Barnum claimed he was a member of a previously undiscovered African tribe. Johnson wore a fur-covered ape suit and cavorted about as people threw him coins, which to their great amusement, he threw right back at them.

After Barnum's death, Johnson managed his own very lucrative career and continued to exhibit himself well into the 1920s. He lived to be 84, finally passing away in his large and comfortable home in Connecticut in 1929. He was reported to have said on his deathbed, "I sure fooled 'em a long time."

## Jo-Jo, the Dog-Faced Boy
Fedor Jeftichew was born in St. Petersburg, Russia, and suffered from a genetic disorder that caused him to have thick, long hair covering his entire body. Barnum promoted him as "Jo-Jo, the Dog-Faced Boy" who "looks like a man, barks like a dog, and

---

**Actor George Clooney is the late singer Rosemary Clooney's nephew.**

crawls on his belly like a snake." Advertising posters proclaimed him "the most prodigious paragon of all prodigies secured by P. T. Barnum in 50 years. The human–Skye terrier. The crowning mystery of nature's contradictions."

### The Bearded Lady
Thanks to Barnum's talent for promotion, Josephine "Madame" Clofullia became the most famous bearded lady of the nineteenth century. Josephine greatly admired Napoleon III and styled her beard after his. Supposedly, Napoleon was so flattered when he learned of it that he sent Madame Clofullia a large diamond, which she wore in her beard whenever she was on exhibit.

### The Tattooed Man
Constentenus, "the Tattooed Man," was covered with 388 "Oriental" designs. In one of the more fanciful stories Barnum made up about his attractions, he claimed that Constentenus was captured by the Khan of Kashagar and forcibly tattooed as an alternative to death.

### The Ossified Man
Barnum exhibited Jonathan Bass for years. Bass suffered from a disease that caused bone to develop in his muscles, tendons, and ligaments, and which eventually immobilized him to the extent that he had to be fed a liquid diet. He reportedly died when he was dropped by an attendant who was carrying him.

### The Siamese Twins
Chang and Eng Bunker were one (actually two) of the few human oddities that were famous in their own right before Barnum got ahold of them. They were smart, literate, and loaded with business savvy. The twins agreed to a six-week run at the American Museum after forcing Barnum to design the contract on their terms, not his. The brothers saw Barnum for what he was and called him on his own "humbug." They went back into retirement after their limited engagement with the museum.

### Jenny Lind
In a rare foray into the entertainment mainstream, Barnum hired Swedish opera singer Jenny Lind to come to the U.S. in 1850 to give 150 concerts for what was then a princely sum of $1,000 per concert. When she asked Barnum why he hired her before he had

even heard her sing, Barnum replied "I have more faith in your reputation than in my musical judgment." Barnum did such a fine job of promoting the tour that when Jenny Lind's ship arrived in New York, there were 30,000 people there to greet her—even though no one in the U.S. had yet heard her sing.

## WHAT, AND QUIT SHOW BIZ?

Barnum retired from show business in 1855, but it wasn't long before financial difficulties forced him to go back to work. In 1871, he created the "Greatest Show on Earth," a traveling circus, menagerie, and collection of sideshows. In 1881, Barnum merged with James A. Bailey, his most successful competitor, and together they started what still exists today as Ringling Bros. and Barnum & Bailey: The Greatest Show on Earth.

### Jumbo

In 1882, Barnum bought a huge elephant from the London Zoo for $10,000. Elephants had been exhibited in the U.S. before, but Barnum billed his elephant, Jumbo, as the largest in the world. (In fact, Barnum and his elephant popularized the use of the word "jumbo" for anything oversized. Jumbo's name was from *jamba*, a West African word for "elephant.") Jumbo was a huge sensation when he arrived in New York, and later when he toured the country in his own custom-made railroad car. Three years after his arrival, Jumbo was hit by a oncoming train while standing on a railroad track. Barnum gave Jumbo's skeleton to the Museum of Natural History in New York, but held onto the hide. He had a wooden frame built and covered it with the elephant's skin—billing it as the "world's largest taxidermy job." Barnum took his stuffed animal on tour for four years, after which he gave Jumbo to Tufts University.

A tragic fire in 1975 all but destroyed the taxidermied elephant. His ashes now reside in a peanut butter jar in the athletic director's office at Tufts.

## THE OLD MASTER

A couple of weeks before his death, Barnum told reporters that the press never had anything nice to say about someone until after they were dead, so the next day *The New York Sun* ran his obituary on the front page under the banner "Great And Only Barnum— He Wanted To Read His Obituary—Here It Is."

A few weeks later Barnum was dead of heart disease at 81.

# THE JOKE'S ON US

*W. C. Fields had more pet peeves than Dr. Doolittle had pets. In his performances he harangued so many icons of American life—family, children, and dogs, to list a few—his audiences thought he had to be kidding.*

The year 1880 had few events to commend it to history. James A. Garfield was elected president that year, but less than 12 months later, he was assassinated. The standardizing of railroad track width was finally approved. That must have been important to somebody.

The future was heralded by two momentous events. One was the patenting of the first cash register, without which retail commerce would have had to wait for the invention of the credit card. The second was the birth of William Claude Dukenfield, a.k.a. W. C. Fields, the entertainer who made hatred humorous. Ironically, Fields was born in Philadelphia, Pennsylvania, the city of brotherly love.

## ORIGINAL CYNICISM
The insincerity of man was embedded in Fields at an early age. His father, when drunk, would sing religious songs and beat him, sometimes simultaneously. His mother would be sweetness and light to her neighbors' faces, then would mimic them outrageously as soon as their backs were turned. These perspectives would drive W. C. Fields's comedy throughout his life.

## APPLES AND ORANGES
He started juggling when he was 12 years old—at first, fruits and vegetables from atop his dad's produce cart—and was hired as a juggler at an amusement park when he was 14. (He is, in fact, a member of the Juggling Hall of Fame.) To set himself apart from the competition, he incorporated comedy into his act. It worked. By age 20, he was a headliner in the Ziegfeld Follies (despite the fact that Ziegfeld thought comedians distracted attention from the chorus girls). Fields must have noticed the Follies girls, though. He had a son with one, born in 1917.

## TALKING HIS WAY TO THE TOP
His first movie, *Pool Sharks* (1915), was based on one of his successful

---

Mark Twain first learned to ride a bicycle when he was nearly 50 years old.

stage skits, but his booming career didn't start until the talkies, when he finally got to use his inimitable raspy voice, sharing the screen with George Burns and Gracie Allen, and Mae West. He wrote the screenplays, too, for a lot of his movies, including *The Bank Dick* and *Never Give A Sucker An Even Break*, which he wrote under the pen names Mahatma Kane Jeeves (say it out loud) and Otis Criblecoblis, respectively.

### "AW, GEE, DONCHA LOVE ME, POP?"
W. C. put the dysfunctional family on the world's stage. Shrewish wives and spoiled, lazy children were constantly caricatured in his stage and movie plots. And he played the long-suffering, henpecked husband and beleaguered father who delivered his wisecracks in the melodically nasal, sarcasm-soaked whine of a voice that became his trademark.

### TAKING THE SHOW ON THE ROAD
Occasionally, Fields would put his "family"—complaining wife, screaming sticky kids, obnoxious pet—in a car, on one of those all-American Sunday outings, so he could vent his spleen at a couple more things he hated: oblivious pedestrians and other drivers. Safe to say, he put the "rage" in "road rage" before asphalt was laid across America.

He built his stage presence around this irreverent shtick, which was surely an expression of the demons he'd been carrying around with him since childhood.

### MARITAL BLISTERS
W. C.'s own brief marriage was followed up with a caustic 30-year-long correspondence with his ex-wife, Hattie. He enclosed every alimony check in a nasty note. But by all reports, Hattie gave as good as she got. In the period just before his death, W. C. and Hattie did mellow somewhat. They may have had a change of heart or simply grown weary of sniping at each other. Whichever, the correspondence during the last year or two of his life was reasonably civil.

### TRUST NO ONE
As one of his characters once said, "If a thing is worth having, it's worth cheating for." In Fields's comedy his businessmen peddled

The bicycle was 50 feet high, with pedals a mere 48 inches off the ground.

snake oil elixirs, shares in dry oil wells, and underwater residential lots. They were all scammers without a conscience. In that regard his humor resonated with his audience's view, such scammers being the order of the day during the "get rich quick" 1920s and the "get poor quicker" early 1930s.

Years of dealing with producers, managers, agents, and other shifty backstage hustlers ingrained in Fields a distrust of employers to whom, he always said, he gave fair value but from whom he always got short counts.

## ...BUT NO ONE

W. C. drove a hard bargain himself. Because he'd made a success of himself, by himself, he believed everyone else should, too. Charity, in his view, didn't begin at home; charity shouldn't begin at all. When one of his two sons approached him to finance his college education, Fields told the young man to get a job and pay for it himself.

Ironically, he distrusted the people he hired as much as those who'd employed him. His friends learned to gauge his mood when they dropped in to visit by whether his staff was on hand. If they weren't, that meant he was in a foul mood and had fired them all.

## NOBODY'S ALL BAD

At a dinner honoring W. C. Fields in 1939, humorist Leo Rosten said of him, "Any man who hates small dogs and children can't be all bad." In fact, W. C. had a paradoxical side. He often wrote parts into his stage shows and movies for down-at-the-heel cronies from his burlesque and vaudeville days. The comedian definitely wasn't a total ogre.

If the real W. C. Fields stood up, he'd also have been found to be somewhat fond of children, notably his own grandson, and occasionally tolerant of dogs—even though, from a professional perspective, he'd be first to rail that both were scene stealers. As for the rest of the world, public and personal life tended to merge, often in an alcoholic blur.

## ANOTHER DUBIOUS CLAIM TO FAME

W. C. Fields may have been the most famous drunkard who ever lived. The Romans had wine; Fields had gin. The bottle killed him in the end, but throughout much of his life it was his best friend, almost his only friend. And to his credit, he was never seen falling-down drunk. On the other hand, by the 1920s, he was never seen cold sober either.

## DON'T TELL ME WHAT'S FUNNY

Given the content and style of his humor (including the occasional double entendre) and his real-life animus toward anything not in accord with his opinions, W. C.'s ongoing war with the censors was inevitable. The Catholic Legion of Decency was on his case, but his most ferocious censor was the movie industry's self-appointed censor, the enforcer of the industry's own code of propriety.

W. C. took the view that he alone knew what made people laugh and it had nothing to do with the political correctness of the day except, perhaps, to the extent it lampooned that correctness.

He battled the censors and didn't always win. Take *The Bank Dick*, for instance. Field played Egbert Sousé, a bank guard (the "dick" in question) who is seen entering the Black Pussy Café and Snack Bar throughout the film—until the censors insisted that Fields change the name to the Black Pussy Cat Café.

## THE PERFECT JOKE

W. C. Fields died on Christmas Day, 1946 in Pasadena, California. Maybe this was his last attempt at delivering the "perfect joke," the one that got the guaranteed last laugh. Because one of the things he hated most was commercialized holidays.

* * *

## THE QUOTABLE W. C.

"I am free of all prejudice. I hate everyone equally."

"Madam, there's no such thing as a tough child—if you parboil them first for seven hours, they always come out tender."

"You kids are disgusting! Standing around all day, reeking of popcorn and lollipops."

"During one of my treks through Afghanistan, we lost our corkscrew. Compelled to live on food and water for several days."

# TRIPLE THREAT QUIZ 4
# HOT DJS

*What sort of world is it where someone can become famous for playing music? Why, our kind of world, of course!*

The five guys listed below hit the big time by spinning discs during four decades of music history. Match them with the radio stations that made them famous and the historical facts that make them interesting. It's your own Top 5 picks!

Match these DJs...

1. Alan Freed
2. Wolfman Jack
3. Dr. Demento
4. Rick Dees
5. Rodney Bingenheimer

With the stations they're most associated with...

a) KROQ
b) KMET
c) WJW/WINS
d) KISS
e) XERB

And these historical facts...

i. This DJ is also a Grammy-nominated musical artist with one truly regrettable #1 disco hit to his name, for which he received a People's Choice Award. He also had a late-night talk show on ABC that flopped badly, but the disappointment he must have felt about that was countered by the fact that his syndicated Top 40 show airs in more than 20 countries.

ii. This DJ worked as a roadie for mediocre 1960s bands Canned Heat and Spirit before chucking a life on the road for a life behind a mic. He also has a side gig as a musical archivist and researcher, working with labels like Columbia and MCA. You can also hear him narrating the 1988 spoof-horror "classic" flick *Lobster Man from Mars*.

---

Emperor Caligula issued invitations in his horse's name and considered making it a consul.

iii.  This DJ had a TV show in the 1950s that was abruptly canceled when Frankie Lymon, a black pop star, was shown dancing with a white girl, thereby enraging the ABC network's southern stations. He once also held a dance party at a 10,000-seat arena in Cleveland—which was canceled because 20,000 uninvited dancers tried to crash the party. Hey, it was Cleveland in the 1950s. Go figure.

iv.  This DJ was a stand-in for Davy Jones on the Monkees TV show and in the 1970s had a Los Angeles nightclub where luminaries like David Bowie and Iggy Pop liked to hang out. He was also the first person to play records by The Clash, The Cure, and Nirvana, which is good, but also Duran Duran, which is very, very bad. Recently he was a featured performer on the popular Nickelodeon show *Spongebob Squarepants*, playing—who'da guessed?—a DJ.

v.  Played himself in *American Graffiti*, George Lucas's famed nostalgia wallow. During a stay in Virginia in the early 1960s, this DJ opened up an integrated dance club, which provoked the local chapter of the Ku Klux Klan to plant a burning cross on his lawn. He found fame at a Mexican station that broadcast at a brain-frying 250,000 watts, a signal strong enough to carry from Baja California to Canada. Once he played a DJ in space on an episode of *Battlestar Galactica*.

Answers:
1-c-iii
2-e-v
3-b-ii
4-d-i (The hit: "Disco Duck"; the talk show: *Into the Night With Rick Dees*; the Top 40 show is the aptly named *Rick Dees's Weekly Top 40*.)
5-a-iv

Anton Chekhov, John Keats, Frederic Chopin, and Franz Kafka all died from tuberculosis.

# THE MUSE

*The original high-maintenance love goddess, she gave as good as she got—if artistic results are any gauge. What was it about Alma that made men wild? Pay attention, girls.*

Alma Schindler moved in the highest artistic and intellectual circles in turn-of-the-century Vienna. Gustav Klimt, a pal of Alma's father and the painter of *The Kiss* (which you've seen, even if you don't think you have) gave her her fist kiss.

### VA-VA-VOOM!
She was 22 when Gustav Mahler first saw her. He was 19 years older, but he had to have her. Alma was flattered by his attention, but torn—the tempestuous cutie was already having a passionate affair with her music tutor, Alexander Zemlinsky. But when Mahler (who would eventually become conductor of the New York Metropolitan Opera) proposed a few weeks after their first meeting, Alma accepted. The two wed in 1902, making Zemlinsky the first in a long, long string of Alma's broken-hearted lovers.

### ALMA SCHINDLER MAHLER
Mahler supported his bride in fine style and the couple produced two daughters. During their years together, Mahler wrote five vastly influential symphonies, but Alma was miserable. Mahler made her give up her burgeoning composing career, and he wouldn't let her go out on the town. Alma missed Vienna's lively social whirl.

### GROUP GROPIUS, OR HOW I SPENT MY VACATION
After eight miserable years of marriage, Alma decided she needed a vacation. She took her daughter Anna to a spa resort where, somewhere between the mineral baths and the hotel rooms, Alma hooked up with young German architect Walter Gropius (future founder of the Bauhaus school of design). Mahler hadn't exactly been ringing Alma's chimes in the bedroom. Passionate Gropius did—the two embarked on a steamy affair during Alma's vacation, after which she took the train back to Vienna and her husband. But Gropius wasn't ready to give her up so he wrote her a blistering

Zeppo Marx was instrumental in establishing the Afghan hound as a breed in the U.S.

love letter, which he mistakenly addressed to her husband. Oops! After reading Gropius's letter, Mahler had no peace. Still in love with his wife and aware of her infidelity, he was stricken impotent, which didn't help matters. What does a turn-of-the-century Viennese do in a case like that? He seeks help from none other than Sigmund Freud, who in one mammoth four-hour analysis session penetrated the roots of Mahler's problems and got his mojo working again. The Mahlers experienced a brief second honeymoon, but it was too late—a genetic heart defect began to take its toll on Gustav. He died in 1911. You could say he died of a broken heart.

## BETWEEN HUSBANDS

Alma cast her roving eye on Gropius, but he'd lost interest when he'd found out that Alma had slept with her husband right up until his death, during a period when Gropius thought of her as his property. That was okay. This was Vienna, 1912, and there were plenty of other incredibly talented fish in the sea. Like painter Oskar Kokoschka. The press called him a wild, violent beast, and he was a social persona non grata. The two began a three-year affair, during which it was said they stopped making love only long enough for Kokoschka to use Alma as a model.

## CRUSHING KOKOSCHKA

Kokoschka was obsessed with Alma, who remained a bit distant. She drove him so crazy that Kokoschka's mother threatened to shoot Alma dead if she came near her troubled son. Alma gave Kokoschka enough affection and sex to keep him on a string, during which time he painted some of the masterpieces that now hang in museums all over the world. Eventually, Alma tired of him. After announcing she was pregnant, she aborted their child, and a few months later demanded that Kokoschka volunteer for WWI. He did and in 1915 was seriously injured by a bayonet.

## ALMA SCHINDLER MAHLER GROPIUS

Having sent Kokoschka off, Alma took up with Gropius again. This time it took, for a while. They were married in 1915. During their marriage Gropius came to be known as one of the leading lights in European architecture.

---

**The state of Georgia was named for England's King George II.**

## KOKOSCHKA GOES CUCKOOSCHKA

When Kokoschka learned of their marriage, he had a life-size Alma doll made—a doll that resembled his ex-girlfriend in every intimate detail. Kokoschka walked the streets with his doll-friend and took it to parties and to the opera, and used it as an artist's model. After some months, he gave a big party with champagne and music, exhibited the doll in a stunning costume, and when dawn came he took it out to the garden, beheaded it, and broke a red wine bottle over its head.

## AND WHOSE BABY ARE YOU?

The real Alma had two children by Gropius, but in 1919 (the year he founded the Bauhaus school), he learned that his third child had been fathered by someone else. Alma had met a young poet named Franz Werfel (who would eventually write the novel *The Song of Bernadette*) two years earlier. They were mad for each other. They'd make love, then Alma would send him back to his writing desk the instant they'd finished, demanding that he improve his art to be worthy of her love. Gropius, defeated, agreed to a divorce.

## ALMA SCHINDLER MAHLER GROPIUS WERFEL

In 1929, Alma and Werfel were married—she was 50 and he was 39. He started turning out a successful string of plays, poetry books, and novels. The two fled Austria for France just a few steps ahead of the Nazis (Werfel was Jewish). In Lourdes, Werfel made a vow that if he and Alma made a safe escape, he would write a book about St. Bernadette (which he did when the two immigrated to Hollywood in 1940).

Werfel died in 1945. Alma moved to New York and settled into a lavish apartment surrounded by her trophies—love letters, Mahler's scores, Kokoschka's paintings, and Werfel's manuscripts. She enjoyed the Manhattan social whirl until her death in 1964. Though Alma herself only ever composed a few songs, she left a mark because, as she wrote in her autobiography, she held "for an instant the stirrups of her glorious knights." Oooh.

---

**The state of Louisiana was named for Louis XIV of France.**

# PATIENT, HEAL THYSELF

*Faith as a medical intervention has been around for a long time.*
*Effecting a cure by denying the existence of an ailment and relying on*
*Bible-based spiritual healing takes it a step further. Mary Baker Eddy*
*had no hesitation in taking that step.*

Nothing particularly set Mary Baker Eddy apart from other people starting life's journey in 1821 in Bow, New Hampshire. She was the sixth child in a well-to-do farm family that was about as normal as families get.

But by the end of her journey in 1910, she'd established the Church of Christ, Scientist; founded one of the world's most respected newspapers, *The Christian Science Monitor*; and become a self-made millionaire during a period when women didn't even have the vote. Over the course of it all, she outlived two husbands, divorced a third, and raised a son. Not bad for a lady who spent most of her first 40 years in her sickbed.

## WHEN ALL ELSE FAILS
The experience of her various ailments and her strong Christian faith combined to shape her writings, from which sprang Christian Science. Eddy was born to and raised in a strict Congregational Church environment. Not totally content to wait for God's healing power to kick in—nor for that matter the miraculous curative powers of the various nostrums and poultices that physicians of the day had to offer—Eddy looked to other less orthodox remedies.

## THE OTHER MAN IN HER LIFE
Enter Phineas Parkhurst Quimby. Like it or not—in her later years, she didn't—Mary Baker Eddy was more influenced by clock-maker-cum-hypnotist Quimby than any other man in her life, including her father and three husbands.

## HEY, THIS WORKS!
Quimby was remarkable for taking a view (and producing the results) that a patient's best physician is the patient. He could have easily coined the term "It's all in your head." Eddy was living proof of it, at least until Quimby died.

Hoping to improve worldwide communication, Ludwig Zamenhof created Esperanto in 1887.

For nearly 20 years, using hypnosis and placebos, Quimby experimented and refined his technique of mind over body as a means of healing various ills. He hung up a shingle in 1859 and began treating patients officially. In 1863, Mary Baker Eddy became one of those patients and in quick time she pronounced herself healed.

## QUIBBLING WITH QUIMBY

Over the next four years until his death in 1866, Quimby continued to treat Eddy periodically. But more important, she assisted him with his writings and began doing some of her own writing, usually edited by him. In later years this would lead to confusion, criticism, and even a lawsuit for alleged plagiarism initiated by a staunch Quimby advocate.

## FAITH HEALING

After Quimby's death, Eddy continued to expound on his ideas but she attributed them more to herself. Some said she did this because he wasn't around to argue. But the truth may lie elsewhere.

First, Quimby was not a particularly staunch endorser of traditional religion. In fact, he found it unsavory and self-serving. At best, he was a small "c" christian. Eddy, on the other hand, tried to meld his healing methods with her Christian faith.

Second, shortly after Quimby's death, Eddy took a fall, which, according to her, should have left her a helpless cripple. Instead, by applying Quimby's methods in a Christian context, she recovered. Ultimately, in order to get God in the equation, she had to get Quimby out. In later years, she went so far as to repudiate him as a mere hypnotist who learned his healing methods from her rather than vice versa.

## WHAT CONTROVERSY?

In 1875, Mary Baker Eddy published the book *Science and Health*, in which she set forth the tenets of Christian Science. The book has since sold more than 9 million copies. The more successful she became in spreading her doctrine, the more the controversy over the Quimby matter dogged her. Interestingly, Quimby's son, George, scoffed at the entire issue. He wrote: "Had there been no

Australian outlaw Ned Kelly wore a homemade suit of armor.

Dr. Quimby, there would have been no Mrs. Eddy." When asked why he didn't participate in the plagiarism suit, he reportedly said, "Dr. Quimby had taught that truth could take care of itself when the time came."

The Church didn't enter the fray, because it accepted that Quimby had held Eddy's work and vision in very high regard. Moreover, during the years of her close association with him, Eddy was writing prolifically, writings that almost always were edited and/or evaluated by Quimby. In short, whatever she was doing was done with his approval. Quimby may have provided the seed, but the sowing, nurturing, and harvesting were the results of Eddy's labors.

## ANY NEWS IS GOOD NEWS

It's entirely conceivable—as sometimes happens today—that the high-profile bad press helped advance the success of Christian Science. Mary Baker Eddy and her cause got a lot more than 15 minutes of fame from the publicity.

## ON A ROLL

In 1879, Eddy founded the Church of Christ, Scientist, the first world-wide church ever established by a woman. Today there are about 2,000 branch churches in 80 countries. In 1881, she opened the Massachusetts Metaphysical College, where she lectured until 1889.

In 1908, her 88th year, Eddy established *The Christian Science Monitor*, the standard for journalistic integrity worldwide. The paper is renowned for its uniquely independent reporting of news.

## SHE DID IT HER WAY

She overcame chronic illness, she bested her critics one and all (even those who were miffed that when she died a millionaire in 1910, she didn't leave a dime to charity), and she established a religion that continues to grow worldwide. In 1992, the Women's National Book Network cited *Science and Health* as one of the 75 books by women "whose words have changed the world." More than 10 million copies of this perennial best-seller have been sold and the book has been in print for more than 125 years.

Maybe it shouldn't always matter who has done what, as long as whatever is done provides benefit to the affairs of humanity.

---

Queen of England for 10 days? Lady Jane Grey, from the 10th to the 19th of July 1553.

# UNABASHED BANDIT

*For Ronnie Biggs, fame came as naturally as his tendency to nick
goods from the back of a lorry.*

No bolder rogue than Biggsie has ever thumbed his nose more vigorously or publicly at the crème de la crème of British police forces.

Yet, by his standards (or anyone else's) Ronnie was a crook, and only average at that. Like most crooks, when he wasn't stealing, he was doing time for stealing—pencils, cars, pharmaceuticals— just about anything that wasn't nailed down. Among his peers, he was considered a reliable bloke. He had some of the essential criminal skills, could be depended on to do his set tasks, and was never known to inform on confederates or, as they would say in the London underworld, grass a mate.

### IT'S A LIVING

Ronnie Biggs was born in 1929, the youngest of five children, in a poor, crime-ridden section of south London, a section where thievery was as much a part of the elementary school curriculum as the alphabet. His first conviction came when he was 15, which was understandable since he was still learning the ropes as a thief. By 1963 he was a career criminal of sorts, nothing spectacular, but he was making a living. What little legit work he had was as a house painter, a useful occupation he'd likely picked up in prison.

### HAPPY BIRTHDAY, RONNIE

Then a fellow lag (ex-con) named Bruce Reynolds, with whom Ronnie had served time, made an offer Ronnie couldn't refuse, a role in Britain's Great Train Robbery of 1963. As befit his status, Ronnie's role would be minor. He was to make sure two trainmen minded their manners in peaceable fashion while the remainder of the robbers relieved the train of nearly three million pounds ($3.8 million at that time). Ronnie thought it would be a profitable way to spend his 34th birthday.

## IT'S A CRIME

Sixteen men were involved in the robbery of the Glasgow-to-London mail train, the objective being to steal a load of used bills destined to be destroyed. Using a ruse to stop the train in a remote rural area, the thieves worked so fast that some of the train crew were unaware that a robbery was taking place. Not all took part in the actual robbery; some were responsible for obtaining vehicles, others for arranging hideouts, and at least one to follow train schedules.

Alas, as luck would have it, most of the 16 robbers, including Ronnie, were rounded up within a few months. Ronnie was just beginning to get famous, but for now he had to share his fame with 15 other villains, including two who managed to elude capture for several years.

## A LONG SENTENCE

The biggest robbery in British history drew the longest sentences for its perpetrators, though not a single gun had been brandished during the entire exercise. Little of the money had been recovered. Among other shares still tucked away was Ronnie's, some £147,000. In their wisdom, the courts decided Ronnie wouldn't get to spend it until he was an old man, if then. The judge whacked down his gavel and Ronnie was escorted away to serve 30 years in Wandsworth Prison, a jailhouse so old Oscar Wilde had served part of his two-year sentence there after being convicted for committing indecent acts.

## RONNIE ON THE RUN

Fifteen months later, Ronnie was poised on top of the Wandsworth wall ready to make his leap into legend. He wouldn't see the inside of a slammer again for 35 years.

Suddenly Ronnie was on the front pages of newspapers throughout the world. The incensed—and acutely embarrassed—British police tore up the countryside looking for Ronnie. All a waste of time. Ronnie was in Paris being fitted out with plastic surgery and papers for flight to Australia, expenses that ate up a lot of his share from the robbery.

After a few years living in Melbourne, he embarked on a

The first man to translate the entire Bible into English was Miles Coverdale.

period of country hopping—Australia, Bolivia, Argentina, and Venezuela. During this period Biggs was obliged to stay conspicuously honest, making his living as a building contractor. The high cost of flight had exhausted his loot and an arrest in a foreign country would almost certainly result in extradition back to England.

## RONNIE IN THE SUN
In 1974, the British police found him in Rio, basking on the beach in Copacabana. Finally, justice and British propriety would be served. The extradition proceedings were publicized worldwide. Ten years had passed; 10 years of Ronnie tiptoeing the straight and narrow. Despite the relative stodginess of that, he'd still kept some cunning and a measure of luck.

## BIGGSIE'S HAVING A BABY
As it turned out, Ronnie's Brazilian girlfriend was pregnant, which sent the Brits packing, because under Brazilian law Ronnie could no longer be deported. The shame of it all! To have found him, loudly trumpeted their success, and then to have lost him again. Ronnie had become a folk hero, famed now as a bon vivant in Rio and, in the rest of the world, famed as the consummate scofflaw.

## CELEBRITY STATUS
Unfortunately, Ronnie's loot was long gone. Brazil didn't mind his hanging around—it certainly beat the poor image that came with rumors of harboring Nazi war criminals. But by law, Biggs wasn't allowed to work. So he made do, transforming his celebrity into a paying proposition by becoming a tourist attraction. Ronnie himself said, "If you can't live off the money you stole, then at least live off your reputation as a thief."

Ronnie Biggs T-shirts and coffee mugs became stock items in Rio's souvenir shops. Up until 1999, for $60 per person, visitors could indulge in "The Ronnie Biggs Experience," a pleasant meal, a poolside party, entertainment, and urbane convivial conversation—all hosted by Ronnie himself at his small villa.

## STOLEN PROPERTY
Of course, the unrelenting British police continued their pursuit. In 1981 Ronnie was kidnapped, presumably by bounty hunters,

Flora MacDonald smuggled Bonnie Prince Charlie to safety by dressing him as her maid.

and loaded into a sack on a yacht bound for Britain. At a Barbados port of call, local officials freed him. Forty days later, he was back in Rio. Good news for Ronnie—yet another boost to his one-man tourist industry. Bad news for the Brits, who finally backed off. Ronnie was lost to them but not forgotten.

## GIVE A BLOKE A BREAK

But by the end of the century, in grave health, Biggs decided to spend his last years in Britain. "Let bygones be bygones," he reasoned.

The British court took a different view. Ronnie went promptly from Heathrow Airport to the hoosegow. The ambitious young turks around the British courthouses and police stations were probably exulting in their blind faith that justice was now duly served, but the average blokes of the world were enraged at this patent inhumanity. To this day, appeals and petitions beset the British judiciary and politicians demanding Ronnie be freed. And who knows? He may yet get to lift a glass or two with his old chums in a local alehouse.

\* \* \*

"There's a difference between criminals and crooks. Crooks steal. Criminals blow some guy's brains out. I'm a crook." —Ronald Biggs

"A robber is much more high-toned than what a pirate is—as a general thing. In most countries they're awful high up in the nobility— dukes and such." —Mark Twain, *The Adventures of Tom Sawyer*

"Thieves respect property. They merely wish the property to become their property that they may more perfectly respect it."
—G. K. Chesterton

"A human being has a natural desire to have more of a good thing than he needs." —Mark Twain, *Following the Equator*

# THE LAST SCHMALTZ

*In the 1950s, when rock and roll began to monopolize the charts, Lawrence Welk waltzed into America's living rooms and remained the premier proponent of politeness and polka for 27 years.*

Lawrence Welk was born on March 11, 1903, to Ludwig and Christina Welk, German-speaking immigrants from Russia who had settled in Strasburg, North Dakota. In the fourth grade he dropped out of school to help out on his family's farm (although, with eight children, you'd think his parents could have spared one or two). In his free time, he learned to play the accordion, and within a few years was performing at barn dances and weddings.

Apparently music suited him better than farming. Lawrence had made a deal with his father—in exchange for a $400 accordion, he would stay home and work on the farm until he was 21. Of course, since home was a rural German-speaking community, that meant Welk never learned English until he moved away—giving him his lifelong signature accent.

## GETTING A FIZZY SIGNAL

Welk left home the day he turned 21. Within three years, he had his own band, the Novelty Orchestra (later renamed the Hotsy Totsy Boys and, still later, the Honolulu Fruit Gum Orchestra). They played gigs in ballrooms, hotels, and on radio stations across the Midwest. In 1938, according to a legend perpetuated by Welk, a radio listener gushed that the band's music was "effervescent, like champagne." (Or it might have been a fan letter that used the phrase "light and bubbly"—stories contradict.) However it actually happened, Welk had finally found the perfect metaphor. From then on, his group was known as the Champagne Music of Lawrence Welk.

Continued success took the band across the country and eventually to Southern California, where a 1951 late-night appearance on local television caused a flood of calls to the station, who knew a good thing when they saw it. Welk's local show ran for four years, until ABC started airing it nationally in 1955.

---

**Currer, Ellis, and Acton Bell? Pseudonyms for Charlotte, Emily, and Anne Bronte.**

## BUBBLING OVER WITH ENTHUSIASM

Audiences loved Welk's wholesome variety show of barbershop quartets, ballroom dancers in cowboy outfits, and endless cascades of bubbles. At the same time that the pelvis-gyrating Elvis Presley was shocking audiences with his (gasp!) sex appeal, Welk was banning cigarette and beer advertising on the show. Welk refused to hire comedians for fear of raunchy antics, and he once fired a favorite female performer for showing "too much knee." The idyllic show, with Welk's trademark phrases "ah-one an' ah-two" and "wunnerful, wunnerful," may not exactly have been pulse-pounding entertainment, but his fans were devoted and the show maintained high ratings for decades.

## DON'T WORRY, STAY SAPPY

Not even the cancellation of the show in 1971 burst Welk's bubbly attitude. Ratings still soared, but sponsors weren't interested in selling to his sedate audience. So Welk campaigned on his own for the show, leading to deals on more than 250 independent television stations in the U.S. and Canada. New shows were produced for syndication until 1982. Just goes to show that *Star Trek* wasn't the only TV show saved by a cult of devoted fans.

By the time of his death in 1992, Welk had amassed a business empire—a music library, resorts in California and Missouri, a home video line, and several record labels. At one point, Welk was the second richest performer in show business, outearned only by Bob Hope. Not bad for a squeaky-clean bandleader who started his career unable to read music, and an emcee whose heavy accent led to memorable malapropisms, such as the time he instructed his band, "Pee on your toes!"

Remember him the next time you're enjoying a glass of bubbly.

\* \* \*

Nobody knew how to make money from radio until New York station WEAF broadcast the first "commercial" in 1922. The five radio programs cost $50 plus the long distance access fee. That same year, a Massachusetts car dealer was ordered to "cease and desist" doing direct radio advertising, because it was interpreted to be against the law.

First African American to win a Wimbledon title: Althea Gibson, women's champ, 1957 and 1958.

# IT'S THE PRINCIP-LE

*He was the spark that ignited WWI. Depending on your view of history, he was either a hero or a terrorist.*

June 28, 1914, was a beautiful sunny day in Sarajevo. But Gavrilo Princip didn't notice. He sat alone and disconsolate at a sidewalk café. He and his friends had just tried—and failed—to kill Archduke Franz Ferdinand, the heir to the imperial Austro-Hungarian throne.

## VISITING ROYALTY

Ferdinand and his wife, Sophie, had arrived by train earlier in the day. The archduke knew that a visit to the Bosnian capital was dangerous—there was a lot of unrest among the populace—but he also knew that it was his duty to go there and "show the flag." Appearances were an important part of keeping his crumbling empire together.

The Sarajevo police—120 of them—were stationed along the motorcade route. Princip and the other members of the assassination team had spaced themselves out and blended into the crowd.

As the open car carrying the archduke and his wife approached, one of Princip's coconspirators, Nedjelko Cabrinovic, threw a bomb. But it bounced off the car and landed in the street, exploding under the car that followed and injuring two passengers and several onlookers. While Cabrinovic was being arrested, the archduke's car sped off, eliminating any chance of a second assassination attempt.

## THE CAUSE

As Princip sipped his coffee, he must have reflected on how and why he'd arrived at this moment. He believed that by ridding itself of the archduke, Serbia could assert its independence from the Austro-Hungarian Empire and unite with neighboring Bosnia. Ferdinand had already indicated that he intended to give Serbia a greater voice in running its own affairs—but that isn't what the radicals wanted—a compromise would spoil their plans for complete independence. The archduke had to be eliminated.

## THE YOUNG BOSNIAN

Gavrilo Princip was born in 1894 in Bosnia, the son of a postman and the fourth of nine children. He attended school in Sarajevo and Tuzla. When Austria-Hungary seized his homeland in 1908, he joined Mlada Bosna ("Young Bosnia"), a radical student group dedicated to freeing Bosnia from the grip of the Austro-Hungarian Empire. Gavrilo attempted to join the Serbian army, but was turned down for being too small and weak. He was recruited by a Serbian revolutionary organization called the Black Hand in 1912.

## THE ARCHDUKE'S ARCHENEMY

The leader of the Black Hand was Colonel Dragutin Dimitrijevic, also known as Apis ("the Bee"), the chief of the Intelligence Department of the Serbian Army. It was Apis who had hatched the plan to kill the archduke and who had recruited Princip and two other men from a coffeehouse in Sarajevo. Though it was clearly a suicide mission, it was an easy sell for the Bee because his new recruits were burning up with revolutionary zeal—and with tuberculosis (TB). At that time, TB was as good as a death sentence. The young men had nothing to lose.

The trio from the coffeehouse was brought to Serbia for partisan training and were each given a revolver, two bombs, and a small vial of cyanide. They were instructed to commit suicide after the assassination so that the plot couldn't be traced to Serbia.

## A FATEFUL DECISION

While Princip was still sitting and pondering what had gone wrong, the archduke's car arrived at city hall. When the mayor of Sarajevo began his speech as if nothing had happened, Ferdinand interrupted angrily. "What is the good of your speeches? I come to Sarajevo on a visit, and I get bombs thrown at me. It is outrageous!" Needless to say, that was the end of the day's speeches.

The archduke inquired about the injured and was told they were at the hospital. Ferdinand wanted to visit them, but a member of his staff warned that the trip might be dangerous. General Oskar Potiorek, the governor of Bosnia, scoffed, "Do you think Sarajevo is full of assassins?" All the same, Potiorek suggested that it might be prudent for Sophie to remain at city hall, but she refused, saying, "As long as the archduke shows himself in public today, I will not leave him."

Sophie should have listened to Potiorek, but this trip was one of the few times that she'd been allowed to appear with her husband in an official ceremony. Back in Austria, she was an outcast in royal circles because Ferdinand had married below his station and Sophie wasn't allowed to appear beside him in any official functions. Ironically, her participation in the ceremonies in Sarajevo was supposed to be a wedding anniversary treat.

## A VERY WRONG TURN

It was decided that they would all go to the hospital. In what can best be described as either an ill-advised display of bravado or monumental stupidity, the motorcade took the same route they'd traveled before. Along the way, the archduke's driver took a wrong turn—a fatal mistake that would put Europe on the road to war.

Princip looked up in astonishment—the royal car was passing right in front of the café where he was sitting. When the driver realized that he was going the wrong way, he stopped and began to back up slowly. Princip leaped up, stepped forward to within five feet of the car, took out his revolver, and fired two shots.

Ferdinand was hit in the neck and Sophie was hit in the abdomen. The archduke pleaded, "Sophie dear! Sophie dear! Don't die! Stay alive for our children!" But Sophie was already dead, and, within moments, Ferdinand would be dead as well.

After firing the fatal shots, Princip attempted to turn the gun on himself, but it was knocked out of his hand by an onlooker. He then swallowed the cyanide he'd been issued, but it was so old, it only made him vomit. The police arrested him and according to one account: "They beat him over the head with the flat of their swords. They knocked him down, they kicked him, scraped the skin from his neck with the edges of their swords, tortured him, all but killed him." No doubt at that point Princip was wishing they would kill him and get it over with.

## THIS MEANS WAR!

Austria-Hungary demanded that Princip and the other assassins be turned over, but Serbia refused, citing its sovereignty and right to try them under Serbian law. Eventually Serbia gave in, but by then it was too late. As a direct result of the assassination,

---

Baron Von Steuben, a Prussian, drilled Washington's troops at Valley Forge.

Austria-Hungary declared war on Serbia on July 28, 1914. Because of various treaties and defense agreements between European countries, one nation after another took sides. The end result was the Great War.

## HERO OR TERRORIST?

Meanwhile, Princip was quickly convicted of murder. But because of his age, he could only be sentenced to 20 years in prison. He died of TB in 1918 at the age of 24, in the prison hospital.

For years after, he was celebrated as a national hero of Yugoslavia. There was even a museum dedicated to Princip in Sarajevo at the corner where the event took place, along with a wall plaque and his footprints embedded in the pavement.

In the 1990s, ethnic differences resulted in war between Bosnia and Serbia. Bosnia now considers Princip a terrorist and an unwitting dupe of Serbia. The museum, plaque, and footprints are gone now, but Princip's actions that day will always be considered one of the defining moments of the 20th century.

## AFTERMATH

The ultimate costs of WWI in lives and property were staggering. In four years of war, over half of the 42 million men who were mobilized became casualities. More than eight million soldiers and six million civilians died.

And it didn't end there. The victors weren't kind to the vanquished. The allies sought revenge by forcing Germany to pay huge sums as war reparations. The German economy collapsed under the weight of those reparations, causing great disaffection and disillusionment among Germany's youth. That set the stage for someone like Adolf Hitler to come to power and drag the entire world into another world war just 20 years later.

\* \* \*

Archduke Franz Ferdinand's speech (Sarajevo City Hall, June 28, 1914): "It gives me special pleasure to accept the assurances of your unshakable loyalty and affection for His Majesty, our Most Gracious Emperor and King. I thank you cordially for the resounding ovations with which the population received me and my wife, the more so since in them an expression of pleasure over the failure of the assassination attempt."

# HEAD CHEESE

*All about James Lewis Kraft, the go-getter who made a better Cheddar.*

Cheese had been around for approximately 5,000 years when James Kraft, the second of eleven children, was born in 1874 to a Mennonite farm family in Fort Erie, Ontario, just a few miles from Buffalo, New York. Little did cheese realize the changes that were in store for it.

### SLICE OF LIFE
At 18, Kraft went to work clerking in a Fort Erie grocery store, then became a working minority partner in a Buffalo cheese factory. In 1903, while he was on a cheese-selling trip in Chicago, the company folded. Kraft was left stranded with $65. James knew cheese and he knew merchandising. He bought a wagon and a horse named Paddy and began buying cheese in bulk, repackaging it, and selling it to small Chicago retailers. Then he got the bright idea of sticking his name on the cheese before reselling it.

### A KRAFTY BUSINESSMAN
James Kraft was among the first manufacturers to focus on creating the ultimate sales tool: brand recognition. By 1911, the Kraft name was seen plastered on billboards and elevated trains all over Chicago. As the company grew, he advertised in local magazines— then went national, leaping ahead of his competition in the use of colored display advertising. By 1914, Kraft cheeses were being sold across the U.S., but James had still bigger fish to fry.

### SHARP CHEDDAR VS. DULL CHEDDAR
Cheddar was the most popular cheese in America at the time (and still is), but in those days it had problems. It tended to mold or to dry out too quickly, and the quality was often inconsistent.

After years of experimentation to obtain consistent cheeses with longer shelf lives, Kraft settled on a method that involved melting the cheese, stirring it, and letting it cool in sterile sealed containers. Well, maybe it wasn't quite that simple, but that was the gist of his 1916 patent for the "Process of Sterilizing Cheese and an Improved Product Produced by Such Process." Since then,

---

Robert A. Taft was lucky; use of initials for presidents wasn't popular until FDR's time.

the method for processing cheese has remained fundamentally the same. Kraft's processed cheese became more popular than Hula Hoops and the Beatles combined. During WWI, Kraft sold 6 million pounds of tinned cheese to the U.S. Army.

## IF YOU LIKE MUSIC, YOU'LL LOVE CHEESE

When it came to promotion, Kraft didn't miss a beat. In 1933, his company became the first to sponsor a two-hour radio show, *Kraft Music Hall*, hosted for 10 of its 16 years by Bing Crosby. James also had a hand in creating *Kraft Television Theatre*, the first commercial network program. The dramatic anthology series debuted in 1947 and ran until 1958 (five years after Kraft's death), when it was replaced by the TV version of *Kraft Music Hall*, hosted by Perry Como, who inherited all of Bing Crosby's cheesiest gigs.

## GETTING JADED

Cheese wasn't Kraft's only interest, though. He was also a rock collector, often asking his chauffeur to stop his car while he jumped out and filled cardboard boxes with gravel. But Kraft wasn't just any rock collector, and that gravel wasn't just any gravel. It was American jade, on which Kraft is still considered to be one of the foremost authorities. His book, *Adventure In Jade*, published in a limited edition in 1947, remains the most comprehensive guide available on the subject, and is considered more accessible to weekend rockhounds than scholarly geology tomes, partly because Kraft blended expertise with reminiscences of his collecting forays.

Prized among the awards Kraft gave to exceptional employees were handmade jade rings he fashioned himself in his Chicago workshop. You can still see his donation to the North Shore Baptist Church, where he served as Sunday School superintendent for 45 years. He gave the church an enormous 6-1/2-by-3-1/2-foot leaded jade window. Centered in the window Kraft placed a white cross he made from the rarest American jade.

## IN THE J. L. HOUSE NOW

Even 50 years after Kraft's death, his employees are fiercely loyal. When a *Chicago Tribune* columnist depicted Kraft's rock collecting as eccentric, letters poured in from across the country to defend "Mr. J. L." Executives today just don't inspire that kind of devotion. James Kraft truly was a big cheese whiz.

---

Composer and pianist Jan Paderewski was Prime Minister of Poland in 1919.

# PRESIDENT CUSTER

*Why did George Armstrong Custer rush recklessly into battle against
the Sioux at the Battle of the Little Bighorn? Could it be that he thought
a well-timed victory would sweep him into the White House?*

On the morning of June 25, 1876, the men of Custer's
Seventh Cavalry were exhausted. They'd raced for three
days to be the first to reach the Sioux camp along the
Little Bighorn River. Their orders were to wait until June 26,
when all three groups of an expeditionary force would meet and
take action together. But Custer didn't want to wait. He thought
he had a chance to be the Democratic Party's nominee for president that year, and the convention was just two days away. He was
ready to gamble the lives of his soldiers against 3,000 Sioux and
Cheyenne warriors on a long shot.

### THE GOOD, THE BAD, AND THE UGLINESS
He'd made a name for himself ten years earlier. Even though he'd
graduated at the bottom of his West Point class, his Civil War
record earned him a wartime promotion to general at the age of
23. In fact, Custer was the youngest man ever to wear a general's
star—and still is. But after the war, this temporary rank was
removed and he reverted to his permanent grade of lieutenant
colonel. He'd also been court-martialed on a variety of charges
(among them, going AWOL).

Still, he was a popular figure in the press, and he had
influential friends. Even better than that, he had some very
unpleasant information that would mortally wound the already
scandal-plagued administration of the Republican president,
Ulysses S. Grant.

### SKIMMING WITH SHARKS
It seems that Grant's secretary of war, William Belknap, and Grant's
own brother, Orvil, were involved in skimming money on goods
sold to the Indians and to the troops stationed on the frontier.
Custer gave the story to the *New York Herald* and before long,
Democrats in Congress were calling for Belknap's impeachment—
so loudly that Belknap decided to resign.

### EAT MY DUST, MR. PRESIDENT
Custer had had to testify before a congressional committee and
was still in Washington, but his career plans were elsewhere. A

King James I's mother and son were both beheaded.

campaign against the Sioux was planned for that summer and Custer wanted to return to his command in the west.

President Grant struck back by refusing to permit Custer to return to his post. (Grant may also have been holding another grudge against Custer, who'd had Grant's son, Fred, arrested for drunkenness while he was attached to the Seventh Cavalry.) This might have stymied someone with smaller *cojones*, but Custer just picked up and left Washington anyway. Grant retaliated by having him arrested. The press cried foul and Grant relented. Custer returned to the Seventh Cavalry—and his fate.

## GREAT WHITE FATHER-TO-BE

No one knows what back-room deals and promises the Democrats made to Custer regarding the nomination for president. What *is* known is that shortly before the Battle of the Little Bighorn, Custer told his trusted Indian scouts that if he gained even a small victory over the Sioux, he would become the Great White Father in Washington.

It's not so farfetched. The Democrats wanted a general of their own to run against the Republicans. And a lot of Democrats weren't happy with their frontrunner, New York governor Samuel B. Tilden. Custer had made himself a hero by testifying against graft and corruption; his star was on the rise. All he needed now was a victory over the Sioux to clinch the deal.

## DYING TO BE PRESIDENT

The Democratic convention was scheduled to begin on June 27 in St. Louis, Missouri. But the Little Bighorn was days away from the nearest telegraph office, so Custer would have to attack by the 25th if Washington was to receive news of his victory in time. He also wanted to attack the Sioux alone, so no other general would share the credit. He took the gamble, and would either become a martyr or the president. The story goes that the Sioux medicine man, Sitting Bull, reported that when the end came and Custer knew he had lost, Custer died laughing. But it's doubtful that the more than 200 soldiers who died with him thought it was all that funny.

## WHEW! THAT WAS A CLOSE ONE!

Samuel Tilden got the nomination. The election of 1876 was so close that it was thrown into the House of Representatives to be decided. Tilden lost by one electoral vote. Afterward—and for the rest of his life—he maintained that he'd been robbed.

The man who beat him? President Rutherford B. Hayes.

---

**Rembrandt painted more than 50 portraits of himself.**

# THE YELLOW ROSE OF TEXAS

*Was there a real woman known as the "Yellow Rose" whose eyes "were bright as diamonds" and "sparkled like the dew"?*

The first known copy of the song "The Yellow Rose of Texas" was written around 1836; the composer signed it with just three initials. Based on the verses, history's best guess is that he was a black soldier from Tennessee. But who was the Yellow Rose? The original lyrics make it clear that she was a woman of color. At that time, "yellow" was used to describe a person of mixed black and white ancestry, a mulatto. The word "rose" could describe any beautiful woman. The answer to the mystery of the "Yellow Rose" may lie in the title of a second version of the song, "Emily, The Maid of Morgan's Point."

## DEEP IN THE MESS OF TEXAS

In early 1836, Texas was in a heap of trouble. The Mexican army under General Antonio Lopez de Santa Anna was sweeping across the state crushing the rebellious Texans bent on independence for their state. On March 6, 1836, the fortress at the Alamo fell, along with all its defenders. Three weeks later, at Goliad, the Mexican army rounded up the Texans who'd surrendered under a white flag and executed them by firing squad.

The new Texas government was on the run. By April 21, the remnants of the Texas army under Sam Houston faced the much larger Mexican army under Santa Anna on the plains of San Jacinto for what became the final showdown.

Mexico was about to lose Texas forever—but Santa Anna had more important things to pursue. A beautiful woman was waiting for him in his tent—time for a siesta.

## ALL THE COMFORTS

General Santa Anna, the so-called "Napoleon of the West," was a man of lust and luxury. He had a wife in Mexico, but he loved women and was never lonely for long. He even entered into a marriage ceremony with a San Antonio girl during the siege of the Alamo so that he could enjoy her womanly comforts with the blessings of her family—before moving on to the next *señorita*. He

---

Wilson Bentley was the first person to photograph a single snow crystal in 1885.

traveled with a three-room silk tent, carpets, champagne, chocolates, a piano, and his own supply of opium. The Napoleon of the West was addicted to more than women.

## THE GAL WHO GAVE HER ALL FOR TEXAS

The woman in Santa Anna's tent at San Jacinto was Emily D. West, a free mulatto woman, not from Texas, but from Connecticut. Here's what we know about her: In October 1835, she was working at a hotel in New Washington, Texas (probably as a chambermaid). On April 16, 1836, a Mexican cavalry unit raided New Washington, looted and plundered the town and the hotel, and took captives, including Emily. She and the others were dragged off to the plains of San Jacinto. Whether Emily was attracted to General Santa Anna and willingly became his battlefield mistress or whether she was one of the unwilling spoils of war will never be known.

What is known is that on that fateful afternoon of April 21, 1836, with the armies of Texas and Mexico facing each other, General Santa Anna ordered a siesta and retreated to his tent to spend some quality time with Miss Emily.

Legend has it that on the morning before the battle, Sam Houston climbed a tree to spy into the enemy camp and saw Emily preparing a champagne breakfast for Santa Anna. He remarked: "I hope that girl makes him neglect his business and keeps him in bed all day."

## THE BRIEF BATTLE OF SAN JACINTO

The Texans attacked at 3:30 in the afternoon; by 3:50 it was over. More than 1,300 Mexicans were either killed or captured. The Texans lost nine men. Santa Anna escaped in the confusion but was captured the following day hiding in a swamp wearing a private's uniform he'd taken off a dead soldier.

## DEEP IN THE HEART OF NEW YORK

The beautiful Emily survived the battle. Her story and the song circulated through minstrel shows, barrooms, and around the campfires of the frontier. But Emily had had enough of Texas. She left in March 1837 on a ship bound for New York. From there she vanished from history—but never from song.

(To read about Santa Anna's eventual fate—and the leg he left behind the day he escaped from the Texas army—check out page 23 in Uncle John's Bathroom Reader Plunges into History.)

---

Canadian Andrew Law was the only British Prime Minister born outside the U.K.

# BANKER FOR THE LITTLE GUY

*A. P. Giannini was the first to challenge the unwritten rule that banks should only lend money to people who don't need it.*

Amadeo Pietro Giannini learned the value of a dollar the hard way. He was only seven years old when he saw his father killed in a fight with another man over exactly that amount—one lousy dollar. The elder Giannini had been a farmer; both he and A. P.'s mother were Italian immigrants. After his father's death, his mother married Lorenzo Scatena, who was in the produce business. A. P. quit school at 14 to help his stepfather, who was so impressed by his stepson that he made him a partner in the business.

## EARLY RETIREMENT
A. P. helped build the business—and his reputation—by being fair and honest. He did so well that he was able to retire at 31 by selling his half of the business to his employees. But his retirement didn't last long; a group of San Francisco businessmen asked him to serve on the board of a small savings and loan that catered to the Italian-American community, and Giannini accepted.

Back in those days, banks only loaned money to large businesses and other assorted rich folks. When A. P. couldn't convince the other members of the board to extend credit to hard-working poor people, he decided to start his own bank. He lined up some investors and started what he called "The Bank of Italy" in a converted saloon. He even kept one of the bartenders on as an assistant teller.

The Bank of Italy was the first to offer home mortgages, auto loans, and installment credit. A. P. built his business by reaching out to the immigrant poor, even going door-to-door to explain his services to folks who didn't know anything at all about banks.

## THAT'S THINKING AHEAD
In the aftermath of the 1906 San Francisco earthquake, the fire that swept the city was getting a little too close to his bank, so he

---

Eugene O'Neill was expelled from Princeton for breaking a window in the president's office.

borrowed a wagon, collected all his gold, currency, and records, and brought it all to his home. A few days later, while the other banks in town were still closed, A. P. set up shop amid the rubble with a plank stretched across a couple of beer barrels serving as his desk. The loans he extended—in many cases based on little more than a handshake—helped rebuild the city.

## THE ROAD—AND THE POND—TO SUCCESS
Giannini always worked harder and longer than his competitors. Once, when he was riding his horse out of town to visit a farmer to close a deal, he saw a competitor behind him who he knew was on his way to the same farmer's house. Giannini took a shortcut, raced ahead, dismounted his horse, swam across a small pond, and ran the rest of the way to the farmhouse to get his contract signed before the other man arrived.

## BRANCHING OUT
Because so many of his customers had to travel long distances to do business with him, he decided to open a branch of his bank in San Jose in 1909. Then he started buying up other banks and opening new ones all over California and from there, in other major American cities.

In 1928, he purchased the Bank of America, an old and very respected institution in New York City, and consolidated all of his banks under that name. He continued to open branches all over the U.S., making Bank of America the first nationwide bank; by 1945, it was the largest in the country.

## TWICE AS NICE
Giannini was a liberal in a conservative business, but he wasn't just being a nice guy. All of his innovations like loans to ordinary people and installment payments, were sound business decisions that revolutionized the banking business and generated substantial profits for his shareholders. He also helped large and small businesses that were down on their luck or out of favor. His financial backing of the California wine and movie industries was instrumental in their growth. He created a motion-picture loan division and helped Charlie Chaplin, Douglas Fairbanks, D. W. Griffith, and

Bette Nesmith, mother of Monkee Mike Nesmith, invented Liquid Paper in the 1950s.

Mary Pickford start United Artists. Giannini loaned Disney $2 million when he went over budget on *Snow White*. A. P. also is remembered for many visionary projects, including the financing of the building of the Golden Gate Bridge.

He was more than generous with his employees—literally. The profit sharing and stock ownership plans he instituted for them would guarantee their loyalty and his own success. But it wasn't money he was after; it was the good that it could do.

## A MAN OF MODEST MEANS
The man who tried to retire at 31 was still at the helm when he died in 1949, at the age of 79. His estate was valued at a modest $500,000, because although he could have amassed a huge fortune in his lifetime, he was never interested in accumulating wealth and often didn't take a salary. He used most of the money he made to start foundations that funded scholarships, and supported medical and agricultural research.

*Time* magazine named Giannini one of the most important 100 persons of the 20th century.

\* \* \*

"It's no use to decide what's going to happen unless you have the courage of your convictions. Many a brilliant idea has been lost because the man who dreamed it lacked the spunk or the spine to put it across" —A. P. Giannini

\* \* \*

## SILLY RUMORS

In his autobiography, TV producer Aaron Spelling (*Charlie's Angels, Starsky and Hutch, Beverly Hills 90210*) set the record straight about the mansion in Los Angeles, California, he shares with wife, Candy. Yes, it does have 12 bedrooms. And a bowling alley, a screening room, a sports bar, a video game/pool room, a swimming pool, and a wine cellar. But contrary to gossip, the house does not have a skating rink. How do these rumors get started?

Chez Spelling also has two rooms set aside for wrapping presents (because "Candy loves to give presents").

# HAVE I GOT
# A DEAL FOR YOU!

*When Charles Ponzi heard that "a fool and his money are soon parted,"*
*he wasted no time trying to find as many fools as possible.*

You've probably heard of Ponzi schemes, and maybe even participated in one. They can be as harmless as a chain letter that circulates among friends or as intricate and complicated as the classic financial pyramid fraud. Here's the true story of Charles Ponzi, the man who invented the multimillion-dollar investment scheme and who took it to its most grandiose heights.

## MINOR ENTERPRISES
Nothing in Ponzi's past predicted that his name would become a household word. He emigrated from Italy to the U.S., then Canada, in 1903. He first brush with crime was forgery, an escapade that netted him nearly two years in prison. Next he tried his hand at smuggling aliens into the U.S. "Hold it, buddy," said the customs man, and Ponzi was off to serve another prison sentence, this time in a federal prison in Atlanta.

## LAYING THE FOUNDATIONS FOR THE BIG ONE
Sentence served, the unrepentant Ponzi made his way to Boston, where he borrowed $200 from a furniture dealer and set himself up with an office. Five months passed, during which Ponzi duped more than 10,000 Americans of $9.5 million, of which he managed to spend about $1.5 million. This didn't put him up there with Enron, but remember, these were 1920 dollars, so his scam wasn't small change either.

Ponzi's scheme was simplicity itself. Offering 50 percent interest, he borrowed money, giving his lenders short-term promissory notes as security. With their money, he told his prospects, he would purchase and redeem international postal reply coupons (sort of official self-addressed stamped envelopes that were valued at the floating rates of an individual country's currency). He promised to earn them profits up to 400 percent from the currency fluctuations of the 60 countries that recognised the coupons.

---

Jack Johnson also invented the common household wrench.

## TAKING IT TO THE TOP

At the height of his enterprise there were probably not enough of these coupons in circulation worldwide to cover the enormous sums he was supposedly investing. No problem for Ponzi—he wasn't buying the coupons anyway. Instead, he was using the money from later lenders to pay the early lenders. That's the essence of the Ponzi Scheme.

With greed as the seed, lenders sprang up like crabgrass on a suburban lawn. Soon Ponzi needed 30 employees to handle all the business he was doing. Beginning in April 1920, he hit the big time. By August 1920, the big time hit back.

## IF IT LOOKS TOO GOOD TO BE TRUE...

As early as May, the Post Office Department started sniffing around Ponzi's operation. Ponzi opened a deposit account in the Hanover Trust Company, and as if that wasn't enough, then purchased a 38-percent share of the company itself. But even before Ponzi came along, the Massachusetts banking regulators were looking hard at Hanover's business practices. Once Ponzi started flashing his "Have I got a deal for you!" smile, they looked a lot harder.

By July 1920, federal and state authorities wanted to audit his operation. He staved them off, but he couldn't stave off that furniture dealer who had lent him the $200 and now claimed he'd been promised half the profits. Taking the dispute to court, the dealer managed to have $500,000 of Ponzi's cash frozen—at a time when liquidity was essential.

## IT PROBABLY IS

The investors panicked. On the streets of Boston near riots ensued as lenders made run after run on Ponzi's cash reserves. Until there was nothing left.

## CRAZY ABOUT MONEY

Ponzi was hauled up on federal mail fraud and state larceny charges. His lawyers were hard-pressed to come up with a defense. One suggestion—foreshadowing the legal acrobatics of today—was that he plead "financial dementia." Their defense would be that he suffered an obsession that compelled him to devise pie-in-the-

---

**Thomas Selfridge, a Wright Bros. test-flight passenger, was the first airplane fatality.**

sky ways to become astronomically rich. But common sense prevailed, and a plea bargain on the federal charges sent Ponzi off, once more, to the pokey.

## MAKING UP FOR LOST TIME
No sooner did he finish serving that sentence than the state of Massachusetts convicted him for larceny. Ponzi promptly filed an appeal, and decamped to Florida to sell some swampland. Unfortunately, he was now out of step with the times. The land rush had peaked before his arrival and state authorities were prosecuting speculators. More charges ensued.

## PONZI WINDS DOWN
Even the intrepid Ponzi had had enough. He attempted to flee to Italy but was (illegally) snatched from the ship and, after more legal machinations, was extradited back to Massachusetts to serve out his larceny conviction. In 1934, he was deported to Italy. But by then the name "Ponzi" was secure in history.

Ponzi left Italy shortly before WWII, and turned up in Rio de Janeiro, where he taught English for a living. There he died in 1949, penniless except for $75 that he'd put aside from his Brazilian government pension.

## "I AM NOT A CROOK!"
Until he died, Ponzi proclaimed himself an innocent man beset by powerful enemies—mostly people who had lost their shirts, he said, by not trusting him enough.

\* \* \*

"Politics would be a helluva good business if it weren't for the goddamned people. I would have made a good pope."
—Richard M. Nixon

A fever that Florence Nightingale caught in the Crimean War left her a semi-invalid for life.

# WHO'S YOUR DADA?

*The kind of guy who'd put a mustache on the Mona Lisa and call it art, that's who.*

Trying to describe Dada, the movement that took the art world by storm in the 1910s and 1920s, is like trying to whistle the Declaration of Independence. If you want to know what you'd think about it, here's a simple test. Go into a men's restroom and take a look at the urinal. Now imagine it upside down. Is it art?

If your answer is "of course not, you idiot," then you're not much going to like Dada. But if your answer is "maybe it is, and maybe it isn't, but hey, that upside-down urinal is pretty damn funny," then congratulations, you're a member of the Dada demographic. Enjoy the upside-downness of the urinal. But remember to use the right-side-up urinals for, well, you know.

## IT COULD HAVE BEEN "MAMA"
The name "Dada" is fundamentally meaningless. It was selected at random in 1916 from a German-French dictionary and means "hobbyhorse" in French. The practitioners didn't focus on one style of doing things, like Cubism or Impressionism, or on a specific sort of medium. There were Dada writers, painters, sculptors, poets, and maybe even a Dada chef or two (but you probably wouldn't want to nibble on any of their appetizers).

The movement's aim was to annoy and agitate. Dadaist creative types felt that the art world had gotten smug and staid and boring, and Dada was meant to be a land mine in the path of the middle-class patrons strolling through the art galleries. To this end, Dada works and artists themselves didn't have to be "good" (by any prevailing standard much of it was childish crap), they just had to make people think about what they were thinking about art.

## THE STEP-PARENTS OF PUNK
It worked. Not only did Dada directly usher in some of the most significant art movements of the 20th century, including Surrealism and pop art, but its attitude served as the template for any number

---

**Bobby Fischer was the youngest international chess grand master from 1958 to 1991.**

of other art revolutions. The Dadaists would have certainly recognized the Sex Pistols as their strung out, unhygienic stepchildren. On the flip side, Dada is also ultimately responsible for people getting away with rolling themselves in peanut butter while reciting from stereo installation manuals and calling it art. But you have to take the bad with the good, especially with an art form that has such a shaky relationship with "good" and "bad" to begin with. Who are the people responsible for launching—or, if you're feeling less than charitable, foisting—Dada onto an unsuspecting public? Here are some of the most notable perpetrators.

### Tristan Tzara

The blame or praise for Dada ultimately goes to Tzara, since it was his big idea in the first place. Romanian born, but living and working in France and writing in French, Tzara was just 20 years old when he and his pals "created" Dada. While lots of 20-year-olds write utterly nonsensical poetry, Tzara was one of the very first to do it on purpose. One of his great parlor tricks, in fact, was to cut up a newspaper article into its component words, put the pieces into a bag, shake up the bag, and make a poem from the words he pulled at random out of the bag.

Tzara eventually abandoned anarchy to become a communist in the 1930s and a member of the French resistance during WWII. Before he died in 1963, he ended up fairly respectable. There's some irony for you.

### Marcel Duchamp

Tzara was Dada's founder, but Duchamp was its superstar. He's the guy who painted the moustache on the *Mona Lisa* to enrage the shopkeepers and lawyers, and he actually did submit a urinal on a pedestal to an art exhibit (he called it *Fountain*), only to have it rejected—not because it was a urinal, but because he signed the work "R. Mutt."

But that was Duchamp all over—a monstrously talented, lazy genius who really couldn't be bothered to do much with his talent. This is the guy who, after becoming the toast of the New York art world in the 1910s in the wake of his most famous painting, *Nude Descending a Staircase, No. 2*, gave French lessons to support himself rather than bother with the hassle of painting full-time.

So it's not entirely surprising that Duchamp might have been attracted to Dada, which was by its very nature not exactly taxing on the imaginative parts of one's brain. His contribution to the movement was something that would become one of its signature forms—the "ready-made" art, in which everyday objects were held up as art, often with some cryptic or mocking epigram written on them. A 1915 ready-made was a snow shovel with the words "in advance of a broken arm" scribbled on it.

Duchamp's ascension to true artistic fame would wait until the 1960s, when a new generation of pop art artists would call him a seminal influence, and rightly so—Andy Warhol's 100 *Campbell's Soup Cans* is nothing if not a ready-made with an extra layer of irony (and paint) slathered on. Not bad for a guy who essentially slacked his way into art history.

### Alfred Stieglitz

Every club needs a clubhouse, and for Dada, the clubhouse was "291," the New York art gallery owned by Stieglitz. Stieglitz originally created 291 (named for its street address) as a gallery for his own artistic movement—the Photo-Secessionist Group, a coterie of photographers who pushed for photography to be seen as a serious art form. But after he opened 291, Stieglitz focused on other forms of modern art, which he exhibited in his gallery. Artists he showed there included Dadaist Francis Picabia, Picasso, Cézanne, Max Weber, and Georgia O'Keeffe, who would eventually become his wife and the subject of a series of his famous photo prints. There's no doubt that 291was a prime focus of Stieglitz's life—he so identified himself with the gallery that he took to signing letters "291," which would be like the president of the U.S. signing letters as "1600."

While Stieglitz's enthusiasm for his gallery, Dada, and modern art was ardent, unfortunately for him it wasn't particularly popular—many of the gallery's exhibitions were derided or, even worse, ignored. In 1917, 291 closed, a victim of critical underappreciation and WWI. Stieglitz turned his attention back to photography and actually went quite a ways to having it recognized as an art form. In the 1920s and 1930s, he'd get back into the art exhibition scene, displaying more modern art (and photography) in subsequent galleries to more appreciative audiences—and thus continuing the

Dadaist artistic tradition of (eventually) snatching success out of the jaws of critical derision.

### Francis Picabia

Dada was a multiheaded monster—groups of Dadaists were making trouble in cities all over the world—and Francis Picabia was the movement's traveling ambassador. The French-born painter, who'd already clocked artistic time in Cubism, first made it big in New York Dada circles where he hung out with Duchamp and Stieglitz.

Then, loaded with Dada stories to dazzle the natives, Picabia traveled back to Europe in 1917 and made the acquaintance of Dadaists in Paris, Zurich, and Barcelona. Eventually, and like everyone else, Picabia ditched Dadaism for other artistic forms, and switched to the surrealist and abstract styles of painting.

### George Grosz

Dada was designed to be a blow against conventional society, but it was the Berlin Dadaists who took the form and made it overtly political—those crazy Germans, huh? Grosz, in particular, had a way of using Dada techniques to satirize those in power. He spent most of WWI in a garret, churning out bitterly satirical pictures of wounded war vets, prostitutes, and other walking wounded—he'd been drafted into the army himself but quickly punted into an asylum before being discharged, so he wasn't just a spectator, as it were, in the madness of war. After the war, his caricatures became even more bitterly broad and venomous—Dada's editorial cartoons, as it were.

It would get Grosz into trouble, especially after the Nazis, who declared him "Cultural Bolshevist Number One," came to power. Grosz left Germany for New York in 1933 and became an American citizen in 1938, all the while churning out paintings and drawings filled with the horrors of war and capitalism. Ironically, Grosz would die in Germany in 1959 (after a fall down a flight of stairs) on his first trip back from exile. It's not a stretch to say it was a fairly Dada way to go.

\* \* \*

## DADAISM BY TRISTAN TZARA

"Like everything in life, Dada is useless."
"Dada is without pretension, as life should be."

# ANAGRAM THIS

*Anagramming is the art of rearranging letters to come up with some semblance of a phrase that relates to the original set of letters, like ELVIS...LIVES. Here are some goodies from Uncle John's private collection. And don't blame us—we didn't write 'em.*

GEORGE BUSH becomes...HE BUGS GORE.

GEORGE WASHINGTON becomes...GREAT SHOWING. GONE.

WILLIAM HOWARD TAFT becomes...A WORD WITH ALL— I'M FAT.

GROVER CLEVELAND becomes...GOVERN, CLEVER LAD.

THOMAS ALVA EDISON, THE INVENTOR becomes...HE LIT HOMES, AND OVER VAST NATION.

U. S. GRANT, R. E. LEE becomes...TRUE GENERALS.

MADAM CURIE becomes...RADIUM CAME.

SALMAN RUSHDIE becomes...READ, SHUN ISLAM.

ALEC GUINNESS becomes...GENUINE CLASS.

JIM MORRISON becomes...MR. MOJO RISIN'.

RONALD WILSON REAGAN becomes...RAN ON ALL-WRONG IDEAS.

GEORGE HERBERT WALKER BUSH becomes...HUGE BERSERK REBEL WARTHOG.

WILLIAM JEFFERSON CLINTON becomes...JAIL MRS. CLINTON, FELON WIFE.

---

Van Gogh's self-portrait shows a bandaged right ear—he painted a mirror image.

# GOING BANANAS

*What it's really like to be a small screen sidekick to TV's big shots?*
*Uncle John gives you the inside poop.*

Back in the 1950s, when TV was becoming a national pastime, the TV heroes had sidekicks who reappeared as regularly as those commercial breaks for cigarettes and booze.

What was it like to be in a hero's shadow every week? Uncle John peels off the TV glamour of second bananas and gives you a good look.

### VIVIAN VANCE

"When I die," Vivian Vance once groused, "People will send flowers to Ethel Mertz." True, her role as the nosy Ethel Mertz in *I Love Lucy,* made her one of the most famous actresses on the planet. But, the (actually) glamorous gal hadn't counted on being typecast as a frumpy landlady.

She was born Vivian Roberta Jones in 1909, far from Hollywood in Cherryvale, Kansas. Her religious parents discouraged her acting ambitions because they considered it sinful. So at 16, Vivian left home to take up a life of sinning on the stage. Her first time out, she had to give up and return home, but she never lost the dream. Seven years later she tried again. She changed her name to Vivian Vance (Vance was the first name of her acting coach) and moved to Manhattan where she carved out a career on Broadway, working with Ethel Merman, Jimmy Durante, and Bob Hope, and she even landed a major role in Hooray for What, starring Ed Wynn.

But while her career soared, Vivian's personal life crashed. She began to suffer frightening psychosomatic illnesses and severe bouts of depression. In 1945, in Chicago, while performing a lead role in *The Voice of the Turtle*, Vivian had a nervous breakdown and had to quit the show.

### Would You Be Ethel Louise Roberta Mae Potter Mertz?

In 1951, she was back performing *The Voice of the Turtle*, in La Jolla, California. Desi Arnaz was in the audience, and asked

---

Queen Victoria was one of the first women to use chloroform during childbirth.

Vivian to sign on to his new sitcom, *I Love Lucy*. The show would focus on the comic misadventures of Desi and his real-life wife, famous comedienne, Lucille Ball.

But Lucy had envisioned Ethel as "a dumpy fat woman in a chenille bathrobe and furry slippers with curlers in her hair." She wasn't eager for female competition; Vivian was too slim, too young, and too pretty to be her second banana. Privately Vivian agreed with Lucy that she had little in common with blowsy Ethel, but she wanted the job. She told Lucy that if a dumpy fat woman was required, "You got her. That's what I look like in the morning when I get out of bed." After a few episodes, Lucy grudgingly admitted that Vivian would do.

### When Bananas Want to Split

Along with the Lucy problem, Viv faced a Fred problem. William Frawley, (the balding actor who played Ethel's hubby Fred Mertz) was as grouchy in real life as he was on the small screen. He couldn't stand Vivian's constant rehearsing and analysis of her character. Frawley once said of her: "She's one of the finest gals to come out of Kansas, but I often wish she'd go back there." For her part, 39-year-old Vivian annoyed Frawley by complaining that the 64-year-old actor shouldn't be cast as her husband, since he was old enough to be her father.

The part of Ethel was a huge break, but it meant that Vivian would always be second banana to Lucy.

### Don't Call Me Ethel

Vivian acted up a storm for the nine years (1951–1962) of *I Love Lucy*, constantly rehearsing to improve her comic timing. In 1953, she won an Emmy for best supporting actress, and life on the set improved. Her problems with Frawley were never resolved, but Lucy grew to respect and rely on her.

She never learned to love her frumpiness, but she made peace with the role that brought her so much success. By the time *I Love Lucy* went off the air in 1962, Lucy had come to rely on Vivian's work and friendship so much that she asked her to sign on to a new series, *The Lucy Show*. This time Vance had enough clout to insist that her character be named Vivian—not Ethel!

**The comic strip character Popeye was created by Elzie Crisler Segar in 1929.**

## JAY SILVERHEELS

The role of Tonto was a breakthrough not only for struggling actor, Jay Silverheels, but for an entire generation. Silverheels made Hollywood history when he rode the range as Tonto, a Potowatomi Indian—all because he really was an Indian and not a white man with brown greasepaint on his face and a braided wig on his head.

America's most famous native American TV star was actually a Canadian, born Harold Jerome Smith on the Ontario Six Nations Reservation, a Mohawk of the great Iroquois Confederacy, in 1919, the son of a decorated war veteran. Harry was a champion wrestler and Golden Gloves boxer—but it was lacrosse that got him started. He could run so fast across the lacrosse field that he picked up the name "Silverheels." He took the J from his middle name and became Jay Silverheels (but he didn't make it legal until 1971). In 1938, the Canadian lacrosse team went to Hollywood for a tournament, where Jay was discovered by comedian Joe E. Brown.

### The Buckskin Ceiling

After joining the Screen Actors Guild, and getting a few roles as an extra, Silverheels knew he'd hit what Native American artists call the "buckskin ceiling." The featured Indian roles were going to white actors—Jay had to content himself with bit parts listed in the credits as "Indian."

In 1949, while filming the movie The Cowboy and the Indians, Jay met another "B" actor, Clayton Moore. Later that year, both men signed a contract to star in a new television series based on a hit radio show called *The Lone Ranger*. Clayton would be the hero and Jay would play his faithful Indian sidekick, Tonto. Once again Jay played "Indian." But this time it made him famous.

### Me See Much Hokum, Kemo Sabe

Tonto wore buckskin and addressed the Lone Ranger as "Kemo Sabe" (which means "trusty friend" or "trusty scout"). Silverheels hated the broken, ungrammatical lines he had to say. But for all its hokum, *The Lone Ranger* was a ground-breaking Hollywood effort—it was the first TV show to star a real Native American who was portraying a self-sufficient person with as much courage as the hero.

---

Teddy Roosevelt was saved from an assassin's bullet by a thick speech in his jacket.

Tonto's high visibility generated a lot of movie offers, but Silverheels only accepted projects that gave a sympathetic portrayal of Indians. In the late 1960s, he formed the Indian Actors Workshop in Los Angeles.

In 1979, the year before he died, Jay Silverheels became the first American Indian actor to have a star on Hollywood's Walk of Fame. But he'd likely have been prouder of his induction into the Hall of Honor of the First Americans in the Arts in 1998.

## EDDIE ANDERSON

Even his wife and relatives called Eddie Anderson by his TV name, "Rochester," the long-suffering African American manservant on TV's *The Jack Benny Show*. Benny played a vain, argumentative miser; Eddie played Benny's barely paid butler, chauffeur, and general housekeeper. Eddie had a raspy voice that sounded like a saw flailing through granite, and his hoarse arguments with his skinflint "boss" delighted audiences. Actually, Benny knew that his know-it-all butler was comic gold—and he paid Anderson handsomely for it.

Eddie Anderson was born in 1905 in Oakland, California, to a show biz family. His father was in a minstrel revue and his mother had been a tightrope walker in the circus. He sold newspapers as a kid, shouting so loudly to hawk his wares that he developed permanent laryngitis. Eddie's hoarse growl didn't stop him from entering show business, and he worked steadily in vaudeville from the time he was 14, mainly in a song-and-dance team with his older brother Cornelius.

### A Banana Gets a Break

His first big break came in 1936 when Eddie played Noah in the movie *Green Pastures*, a retelling of Bible stories with black actors in Biblical roles. But even though Eddie and the film both got good reviews, roles for black actors were scarce. So in 1937, when a radio show needed an African American to play a two-minute part, Eddie gladly auditioned.

At first glance, Benny, the show's star, wasn't particularly impressed with Eddie's acting, but he liked that sandpaper rasp of a voice. He hired Anderson to play a Pullman porter who'd never heard of Albuquerque even though his train stopped there on every run. Eddie's two-minute performance (in which he lectured Benny on the fact that there was no "Albee kurkee") was such a spectacular success that Anderson's one-shot appearance turned into 20 years of second banana fame.

### "Yeah, Boss"

Benny had his writers create a role for Eddie—a butler with the suitably British name of Rochester Van Jones. In 1949, *The Jack Benny Show* came to television.

The very early Rochester role was riddled with racial stereotypes—like a fondness for gin and too much time spent at crap games. But Eddie was never servile. (If Benny asked Rochester to do something he didn't want to do, like answer the door, the butler would just say, "Boss, you're closer to the door than I am.")

Within two years of signing on with Jack Benny, Eddie was making over $150,000 a year. The role of the poorly paid butler eventually made him the highest-paid, black performer of his day. While the TV Rochester was working for peanuts, the real-life Rochester was a savvy businessman. The one-time newspaper boy lived with his wife Maymie and their children in a huge mansion. He even had his own butler!

### The Odd Couple

Anderson and Benny had their difficulties over the years. Jack Benny was a perfectionist who occasionally checked into the hospital as a result of "nervous exhaustion." Eddie was more easy-going, and though his comic timing was perfect, his ability to show up on time was not. Which didn't help Mr. Benny's nervous condition. All the same, Benny admitted that Anderson was "one of my greatest assets."

Anderson died where he'd been born—in Oakland—in 1977.

\* \* \*

### SECOND TO NONE

After playing Igor to Vincent Price's mad scientist in 1953's *House of Wax*, Charles Bronson (then Charles Buchinsky) still couldn't get a big role. In 1968 he took off for Europe and almost overnight became the biggest box-office draw in Paris, Rome, and Madrid.

# NOT GENERAL-LY KNOWN

*Tales from the life of General George S. Patton, Jr.—including a few juicy tidbits that weren't covered in the biopic.*

• To his men he was known as "Old Blood and Guts." His family and friends called him "Georgie."

• Patton was one of the wealthiest men in the U.S. Army. He was born in 1885 on his mother's family estate, Lake Vineyard in California, 12 miles northeast of Los Angeles. The 14,000-acre estate is now known as Pasadena, San Marino, San Gabriel, and Alhambra, California.

• An only son pampered by his father, mother, and a maiden aunt, Georgie didn't attend school until he was 11.

• He couldn't read or write when he started school. Today he'd be diagnosed as dyslexic. Spelling remained a problem for him throughout his life. He compensated for his difficulties in reading by memorizing. He could recite long passages from Kipling, Shakespeare, and the Bible from memory.

• Georgie took five years to graduate from West Point. He had to repeat his first year when he failed math. When he finally graduated in 1909, he placed 46th in a class of 109.

• In 1910, he married Beatrice Ayer, a wealthy Boston socialite. Helped by her fortune, which was even greater than the Patton family's, they lived well even on the most primitive army bases. They always "dressed" for dinner and kept servants. Patton also indulged in thoroughbred horses, polo ponies, and sailing yachts.

• In 1912, Patton represented the army and the U.S. at the Olympics held in Stockholm (the fifth of the modern Olympic Games). At the time, there were two pentathlons. The more familiar one, the one that's survived to today, was won by Jim Thorpe that year (see our story on Thorpe on page 56). Patton was

---

Josef Stalin originally studied to become a priest.

entered in a new event called the "Modern Pentathlon," which had been created to showcase the skills required of army officers: horseback riding, target shooting, fencing, swimming, and running (but not away from the enemy, we presume). Patton might have won the gold medal, because he did very well in four of the events, but in the shooting contest he missed the target twice. As a result, he placed fifth, behind four Swedes.

• Despite being in the cavalry, Patton didn't use horses during the army's expedition against Pancho Villa in 1916. In one raid, Patton and his 15-man contingent rode into battle in three rickety Dodge cars. The skirmish was the first instance of motorized warfare in the history of the U.S. Army.

• In WWI, Patton commanded a tank brigade. He was shot while leading his men into battle near Verdun. The bullet entered his left thigh and exited near his rectum, taking a teacup- sized hunk of flesh out of his backside. For the rest of his life, Patton was proud of his war wound. He was even known to drop his trousers at parties to show it off. He was once thrown off a public beach for indecent exposure because he'd cut his bathing trunks high and wide in the back to display the scar.

• Because of his wound, Patton saw just two days of actual combat in WWI. Which was more experience than Eisenhower, who, despite being Supreme Allied Commander of the European Theater in WWII, had never been in combat before.

• As the Third Army crossed the Rhine in March 1945, Patton celebrated by urinating into the river from a pontoon bridge. And, as he encouraged photographing the historic yellowing of the waters, a lot of soldiers came away with souvenir pictures of the event. Winston Churchill must have relished the symbolism. A few days later he did the same thing.

• Patton wanted to be killed by the last bullet of the last battle of the last war. Instead, he died from a broken neck suffered in what otherwise was a minor auto accident in December 1945. He's buried in a military cemetery in Luxembourg at the head of his troops.

# PAGING DR. BLACKWELL!

*Elizabeth Blackwell, the first fully accredited female doctor, gave women the last laugh.*

The Blackwell family was an idealistic, humanitarian bunch—their home was a stop on the Underground Railroad, where runaway slaves could hide on their way to freedom in Canada. The same moral conviction inspired Elizabeth Blackwell to bring women into medicine. And if she had to become a doctor to do that…hey, she'd darn well become a doctor!

## THE QUEEN OF REJECTION

Her friends told her that the doctor idea was nuts. She not only had gender problems, she had money problems, too. Her father died when she was 17, leaving the family broke. Even in the 1800s, a good medical education didn't come cheap. So Elizabeth decided to be a teacher—but only in schools that would let her study the medical books in their libraries. This brought her to the notice of a doctor who ran one of those schools. He was so impressed with her determination that he wrote to 20 medical schools across the country asking them to accept Miss Blackwell as a student. Soon Elizabeth had 19 responses from prominent American medical schools—19 letters of rejection!

## A DULL DAY IN GENEVA

The 20th letter went to the tiny Geneva Medical College (now Hobart College) in upstate New York. The doctor's letter livened up a dull anatomy class when the dean of the school interrupted a lecture to tell the students that a woman had dared to apply to their school. The administration put it to a student vote—and only a unanimous "aye" would admit Elizabeth. What the dean didn't say was that the administration didn't want to offend the distinguished doctor who'd recommended her. Since the students would surely vote "nay," the school would have an excuse to reject Elizabeth's application. After all, these were prudish Victorian

---

Benito Mussolini's straight-arm salute was derived from the Roman Empire's Roman Salute.

times, when the thought of a woman dissecting a naked male cadaver was beyond shocking. The guys figured it would be a hoot to admit a woman to the school. They all voted for acceptance— including one dissenter who was "pummeled" until he also voted "aye."

## PROGNOSIS NEGATIVE

When she arrived, though, most of the faculty—and all the faculty wives—shunned her. Some students thought it wasn't so funny to have a woman in class after all. Her presence during anatomy dissection embarrassed everyone including Elizabeth. She described anatomy lab as "a terrible ordeal."

The local hospitals wouldn't let her observe on their wards, so she went to the Blockley Almshouse infirmary in Philadelphia, where she cared for destitute women who suffered everything from venereal disease to typhus.

## TAKE THAT, YOU NAYSAYERS!

Of course, everyone expected her to give up. But not Liz. She'd joined the school late, so she stayed up nights studying until she left her classmates in the dust, grade-wise. She swallowed every snub and insult. She even starved herself to save money to continue her studies.

Eventually, they all came to admire her. And she used her experience in the almshouse to write a medical thesis on typhus— a student thesis so excellent that it was honored with publication in a professional medical journal.

In a black silk dress with lace collar and cuffs, on January 23, 1849, Elizabeth Blackwell accepted her diploma while the audience applauded wildly for her. She'd graduated first in her class.

## PUNCH LINE

The outside world wasn't ready for a woman doctor, so Blackwell had to slog through decades of still more prejudice, but she made the doctor's life work for her. She eventually opened a women's medical school in New York City. By the time she died in 1910, more than 7,000 women were licensed physicians in the U.S. All because one stubborn woman made it through medical school.

---

Chaucer, Rabelais, Mark Twain, and Ben Franklin all have written about flatulence.

# ONE-IN-A-MILLION BRAZILIANS

*Aside from its fabulous music, teeny bikinis, and its irrepressible love of life, Brazil has a few more claims to fame...*

You say you don't know much about Brazil? How's this: It's bigger than the continental U.S., occupies almost half of South America, and has a larger population than all the other South American countries combined. With those odds, it's not surprising that it's home to so many talented writers, sportsmen... and...children's television hostesses

Step right up and say *alo* to a few of Brazil's most important citizens.

### JORGE AMADO
Arguably Brazil's greatest writer of the 20th century. You may have heard of Amado because of the movie version of *Dona Flor and Her Two Husbands* starring Sonja Varga as a remarried widow whose first husband comes back from the grave. No, it's not a zombie flick. In fact, Amado's books vividly reconstruct life in his Northeast Brazilian state of Bahai, with a special emphasis on the earthy, racially mixed lower classes.

Amado was something of a radical—he served in the national government as a communist—and as a result he spent time in jail and in exile, and often had his books banned in both Brazil and Portugal. But you can't keep a good writer down. Amado, who published his first novel at 19, ended up writing 25 novels, which have been translated into 48 languages. He died in 2001.

### PELÉ
Known to his mother as Edson Arantes de Nascimento, Pelé is to soccer what Babe Ruth is to baseball or Elvis is to white sequined jumpsuits—he's the king, baby, and don't you forget it. Pelé isn't a very big man—he was 5'6" and just 160 pounds in his prime, but man, could he move. He'd blow by defenders almost like he knew where they were going before they did. He reached the 1,000 goal

---

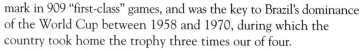

mark in 909 "first-class" games, and was the key to Brazil's dominance of the World Cup between 1958 and 1970, during which the country took home the trophy three times our of four.

Pelé retired in 1974—"retirement" apparently meaning "to go to the U.S. to play soccer for the New York Cosmos for three years for $7 million." In 1981 he made a really bad movie with Sylvester Stallone (Victory, which combined soccer with a WWII POW camp escape flick), but let's not talk about that—like, ever.

In 1999, the International Olympic Committee declared Pelé the Athlete of the Century.

## OSCAR NIEMEYER

Some architects design houses. Some design skyscrapers. But Oscar Niemeyer oversaw the design of an entire city. Brasilia, the capital of Brazil, was carved out of a high Brazilian plain in the 1950s like Washington, D.C., was carved out of a swamp in the late 1700s.

Neimeyer had some experience with building entire cities. In 1941, he planned Pampulha, a garden-laden suburb of Belo Horizonte. When Juscelino Kubitschek de Oliveira (the Belo Horizonte mayor who'd commissioned Pampulha) became the president of Brazil in 1956, he asked Neimeyer to design Brasilia as well. Neimeyer demurred from planning the whole city, but he served as chief architect, overseeing the project, and he designed the government buildings in the city as well as the soaring, circular Cathedral of Brasília, arguably his best-known and best-loved work.

## AYRTON SENNA

You can think of him as the Brazilian Dale Earnhardt—a total intimidator on the Formula One race circuit, with over 40 Grand Prix titles and three world champion titles. He won because, frankly, he scared the heck out of his competitors—he was the master of aggressive, intimidating, and ruthless driving in pursuit of the prize. He loved speed, capturing pole positions (the number-one starting position, earned by being the fastest in qualifying races) a record number of 65 times. Off the track Senna was known to be both enigmatic and deeply religious, which only added to his allure. Add to all of this a famously bitter rivalry with French driver Alain Proust, and you've got drama larger than life.

Senna died spectacularly as well in 1994, when his car smashed head first into a concrete wall at the San Mario Grand Prix at 186 miles an hour—only a day after another driver, Austrian Roland Ratzenberger, died in a similar crash (at the time of the crash, Senna was carrying an Austrian flag which he intended to unfurl to honor Ratzenberger if he won). Reporters and other drivers had noted that Senna seemed distracted in the days leading up to the crash. Whatever the reason, Senna's death sent all of Brazil into mourning.

## XUXA

Here in North America, our children's show hosts are purple dinosaurs and nice Presbyterian ministers who wear sweaters and ask us to be their neighbors. In Brazil, their children's show host is a totally hot former *Playboy* model in shiny white leather who has dated famous sports stars (including the aforementioned Pelé and Senna). Which leads to the obvious question: What's wrong with us? It doesn't look as if we're going to change that dichotomy either, since Xuxa (shoo-sha) attempted to bring her show to the U.S. in 1993, but it failed after just one season.

Meanwhile, down south, blonde and blue-eyed Xuxa has been a kid's staple for more than 20 years (the show debuted in 1982), and Xuxa herself, despite the controversial past and occasionally skimpy clothing, has been a genuine advocate for the kids. Her campaign for polio vaccination in Brazil helped bring the vaccination rate to 90 percent. Xuxa's celebrity comes with a price, including a kidnapping attempt in 1991, in which two of the attempted kidnappers were killed. Ironically, to find peace and relative anonymity, Xuxa has two residences in the U.S. (besides her houses in Rio, Buenos Aires, and Barcelona).

* * *

## THE GIRL FROM BRAZIL

Astrud Gilberto recorded "The Girl from Ipanema" for the album *Getz/Gilberto* (the Gilberto in the title being her husband, Joao) for $120, what the American musicians' syndicate paid for a single night of work. She'd accompanied Joao to New York only to act as his interpreter, she'd never sung professionally before. Joao earned $23,000 for the album. But no one will argue that it was Astrud's song that made the album the huge hit it was.

First player to hit a home run in the major leagues: Ross Barnes, in 1876.

# CIRCUS STARS

*Step right up and meet some of the more accomplished people who tamed the lions, swallowed the swords, and launched themselves from cannons.*

## GUNTHER GEBEL-WILLIAMS

He didn't run away to join the circus, he went with his mom when she joined Germany's Circus Williams as a wardrobe assistant during WWII. Twelve-year-old Gunther already had a special rapport with animals, but after Harry Williams, the owner of the circus, taught him the finer points of animal training, he went on to become fabulously popular in Europe. Williams died in 1952 when Gunther was 18, at which point the young animal trainer took over the management of the circus and added a hyphen and "Williams" to his own last name. In 1968, Ringling Bros. bought the Williams Circus outright for the sole purpose of getting Gebel-Williams for their very own.

### Perfect Attendance Award
Gebel-Williams was committed enough to his craft that in 30 years of performing, he never missed a show—that's more than 12,000 performances in front of an estimated 200 million people. And trivia fans take note: In 1995, he got a special award from Madison Square Garden for being the person who'd performed there the most in history.

### Don't Leave Home Without It
Gebel-Williams's fame reached its peak in 1977, when he became the first circus performer in history to get his very own prime-time television special. An American Express commercial later that year—featuring Gebel-Williams in a three-piece suit with Kenny, his favorite leopard, flung across his back—made him a household word. His animal-handling philosophy was a little more enlightened than the usual approach, with an emphasis on working with the animal's natural instincts.

Of course, you can't please everyone: A small group of animal-rights protestors picketed his funeral after he died of cancer in 2001.

The "S" in Ulysses S. Grant stood for nothing; his real name was Hiram Ulysses Grant.

## EDITH CLIFFORD AND EDNA IRENE PRICE

Sword swallowing—it's not just a guy thing. Two of the most famous sword swallowers were women.

### Not Just Mrs. Elastic Man

Edith Clifford, who performed from 1899 through the 1920s, got an early start, making her professional debut at age 15. She joined the Barnum & Bailey Circus in 1901 with her husband, Thomas Holmes (who was an "elastic man"), and proceeded to swallow some really inadvisable things during the course of her career, including razor blades, bayonets, saw blades, and scissors. She could also swallow a very impressive number of swords—16 is her verified record, although reports have her swallowing 24 at one time. For her pains, she's known in sword-swallowing circles (now there's a group for you) as "the Champion Sword Swallower of the World."

### The Royal Line of Queen Edna

Edna Irene Price has to settle for being known merely as the "Queen of Sword Swallowers," but don't feel too bad for her—she got into Ripley's Believe It or Not for being the very first woman to swallow a white neon tube. (We wonder just how many women were clamoring for that rare distinction, but let's not diminish her talent.) Edna knew firsthand of the potential dangers of sword swallowing—she got the job because her aunt, a sword swallower herself, died after an unfortunate sword-swallowing mishap. Price herself avoided major injury during her circus career (from the 1920s through the 1950s), and died, after retiring from the field, in 1987.

## ANDREW DUCROW

The first modern circuses—created in 18th-century England— were big on horse acts; the 42-foot diameter of the traditional circus ring, in fact, is designed specifically to give horses just enough room to gallop. And it was Andrew Ducrow who thought up the biggest horse act of all, an act he called "The Courier of St. Petersburg," in which a rider stands astride two horses while other horses (by tradition, bearing the flags of the countries through which the courier must ride to get to Russia) race between his legs. If you don't think it takes guts to let a galloping horse charge between your legs at full speed, try it some time.

## All the World's a Stage—Really!

But Ducrow was more than just a guy who was good at thinking up new ways to get horses to run around in circles. He was the son of a strong man, trained in all sorts of performing arts, including acrobatics and rope tricks. He also had a mind for business and managed Astley's Amphitheater, the first modern circus, between 1823 and 1841, during which time he was also its premier performer. Shows of the time not only included horse tricks but often full-fledged theatrical performances in which horseback riding played a large role—lots of circuses of the time featured a stage as well as a circus ring, so you could actually go to the circus and see a little Shakespeare, too.

## Andrew's Career Ends in Burn-Out, Twice

Ducrow's career came to an end in 1841 when Astley's Amphitheater burned to the ground (the third time it had done so, actually, having previously burned in 1794 and 1803). Ducrow suffered a nervous breakdown after the fire and died just a few months later.

# THE ZACCHINIS

The Zacchini family weren't the first human cannonballs (an Englishman named George Farini thought up the idea in the 1870s), but they were the first to make it a going concern. Farini's "cannon" was spring-loaded and not particularly reliable, which is not what you want to hear about a contraption designed to throw you from one side of a circus tent to the other.

## They Had Lots of Zacchinis for Launch

Ildebrando Zacchini, an acrobat, had a better idea. In 1922 he designed an air-powered cannon that was more reliable, and then set about launching his children out of it (he had seven sons, five of whom became cannon fodder). Zacchini's cannon impressed impresario John Ringling, who brought Ildebrando, his cannon, and his brood of launchable kids to America in 1929.

## One Last Fling

The Zacchinis found themselves needing to top themselves to keep the excitement level high. They did so by pulling stunts like creating the double human cannon, increasing the launch speeds to up to 90 miles per hour, and even blasting each other over objects, such as Ferris wheels (and in some instances, two Ferris wheels). Of course, sooner or later someone's going to get hurt, as

The first woman in space was Valentina V. Tereshkova.

Mario Zacchini was at the 1940 World's Fair. The net he was shot into collapsed and Mario broke several bones. As Mario himself put it, "Flying isn't the hard part; landing in the net is." Be that as it may, the Zacchini family kept at it, going through three generations before the final Zacchini cannonball, Edmondo, launched himself into the air one last time in 1991.

## THE FLYING WALLENDAS

The famous "Flying Wallendas" got that nickname because of an accident. A slip of the wire during a performance in Akron, Ohio, caused four of the Wallendas to fall to the wire, but they did so with such flair that the newspaper reported that it seemed like they were flying rather than falling.

### Talk About Pyramid Schemes

It added another layer to the Wallenda's already oversized acrobatic reputations. The family traces its history back to the 18th century, when family members formed a band of traveling entertainers in Bohemia. The modern Wallenda family started with Karl Wallenda, who apprenticed himself to another acrobat in the early 1920s and then struck out on his own in 1922. Wallenda's calling card was a three-level, four-person "pyramid" that consisted of Karl perched on a chair placed on a bar held by two men riding bikes, while Karl's wife stood on his shoulders—all on a wire suspended 50 feet in the air. The Wallendas topped that with ever more complex "pyramids," including an eight-person pyramid in 2001 that earned them a place in the *Guinness Book of World Records*.

### The End of a Wallenda

In a 1962 show in Detroit, the Wallendas were performing a pyramid when one of their number lost balance and the pyramid collapsed, killing two performers and permanently paralyzing another (Karl's son Mario). That didn't stop the Wallendas from performing the very next night. Karl kept performing until 1978, when he fell to his death at age 73. The family maintains that Karl's age was not a factor in his death—rather, they point to misconnected guy ropes.

* * *

"Life is like being on the wire, everything else is just waiting."
—Karl Wallenda

Peter the Great, tzar of Russia, practiced dentistry on his subjects.

# MASTER JUBA

*The man who invented tap dancing. Hey, somebody had to do it.*

After visiting the U.S. in 1842, Charles Dickens tried to describe a dancer he'd seen in Manhattan: "Single shuffle, double shuffle, cut and cross-cut; snapping his fingers, rolling his eyes, turning in his knees, presenting the backs of his legs in front, spinning about on his toes and heels…dancing with two left legs, two right legs, two wooden legs, two wire legs, two spring legs—all sorts of legs and no legs."

The dazzling dancer was William Henry Lane, known professionally as Master Juba. He was born a free black man in Rhode Island in 1825.

## WHITES IN BLACKFACE

Minstrel shows began in the 1830s. They introduced a lot of familiar American songs, like "Polly Wolly Doodle," "Dixie," and most of Stephen Foster's classics, against a backdrop of dances, jokes, and skits based on the ugliest stereotypes of African American slaves.

The performers were working-class white men (most of them Irish) who blackened their faces with burned cork and spoke in what was called "plantation" dialect. The shows were the most popular form of entertainment in America from 1840 to 1890. They were still performed into the 1950s, but they died out with the advance of the Civil Rights Movement.

## BLACKS IN BLACKFACE

Until the 1840s, only whites were allowed to perform in minstrel shows. Ridiculous as it sounds, when William Henry Lane started performing minstrel acts, he was required to wear blackface just like everyone else. Eventually he became popular enough to throw away the burned cork and show his own skin instead.

## JUBA IS BORN

Most slaves came from cultures in Africa that used drumming as a means of communication and personal expression. But American

---

*Muppet* Animal was modeled after Who drummer Keith Moon.

slaves weren't allowed to play drums, so they used their bodies as instruments instead. Over time, the hand clapping, foot stomping, body thumping, and thigh slapping evolved into a dance called "patting juba."

## TAP IS BORN
William Henry Lane combined patting juba with the jig and reel dances that he'd learned from his Irish neighbors. He combined them with some other ethnic dance steps—the shuffle, the slide, buck dancing, pigeon wing, and clog—into what became known as tap dancing. As his reputation grew, the promoters started to advertise him as "Master Juba, the 'dancinest' fellow ever was." Everyone else seemed to agree; he was proclaimed the greatest dancer of all time by American and European writers alike.

## TAKING IT ON THE ROAD
At the time, an Irishman named Jack Diamond was considered the best white dancer in the U.S. He and Juba teamed up, staging dance competitions across the country. Eventually, in 1845, Juba became the first black performer to get top billing over a white performer in a minstrel show.

## TWINKLE TOES
Juba went on to perform—as they say—"before the crowned heads of Europe." *The Illustrated London News* asked, "How could he tie his legs into such knots and fling them about so recklessly, or make his feet twinkle until you lose sight of them altogether?"

## THE DANCE IS ENDED
Juba liked what he saw in Europe and eventually settled in London, where he performed with an English dance company and opened his own dance studio. He met an untimely death in 1852 at the tender age of 27—but no one seems to know how he died.
Maybe he just danced his heart out.

\* \* \*

"So you can't dance? Not at all? Not even one step? How can you say that you've taken any trouble to live when you won't even dance?" —Hermann Hesse

---

Eleanor of Aquitaine brought 300 women along on the second Crusade with hubby Louis VII.

# MINER'S ANGEL

*"Pray for the dead, and fight like hell for the living." So said the toughest little old lady who ever walked the streets of America.*

She'd been born Mary Harris in 1830, in County Cork, Ireland, and immigrated to the U.S. with her family in 1835. After grade school, she learned dressmaking and trained to be a teacher; she taught school in Michigan and Tennessee. And she married George Jones in 1860 in Memphis.

## ALL IS LOST

Mary Jones might have lived out her life in obscurity, as the wife of an ironworker and the mother of four, but in 1867 a yellow fever epidemic swept through Memphis, taking with it the lives of the people Mary loved best. In her own words:

> One by one, my four little children sickened and died. I washed their little bodies and got them ready for burial. My husband caught the fever and died. I sat alone through nights of grief. No one came to me. No one could. Other homes were as stricken as was mine. All day long, all night long, I heard the grating of the wheels of the death cart.

After her husband and children were buried, Mary got a permit to nurse the remaining victims in the city. She stayed in Memphis until the plague ended.

## THE HAVES AND HAVE-NOTS

The widow Jones moved to Chicago and opened a dress shop that proved to be very popular with the wealthy ladies of Lake Shore Drive. But that didn't make Mary completely content:

> We worked for the aristocrats of Chicago, and I had ample opportunity to observe the luxury and extravagance of their lives. Often while sewing, I would look out of the plate glass windows and see the poor, shivering wretches, jobless and hungry, walking along the frozen lakefront. The contrast of their condition with

that of the tropical comfort of the people for whom I
sewed was painful to me. My employers seemed neither
to notice nor to care.

And she might have lived out her life as an obscure dressmaker,
if not for another tragedy: the Great Chicago Fire of 1871. Once
again, Mary had lost everything.

## HI, MOM!
America was undergoing the painful transformation from an agrarian
to an industrial economy. Most workers in the new America were
powerless and entirely at the mercy of their employers. They lived
and worked under horrible conditions and were often paid little
more than starvation wages. Mary had seen life from both sides
and was determined to make things better for the working class.

Her husband had been a staunch union man. She knew that
the only way workers could improve their lot was to band together
and demand change. She began to get involved in union activities
and traveled around the country helping workers organize. She'd
lost her own family, but she adopted the workers as her family.
That's when they started to call her Mother Jones.

## GO, GRANNY, GO!
Now, in the 1870s, Mother Jones was a fearless five feet tall, with
bright blue eyes, silver white hair, pink cheeks, and wire-rimmed
glasses. She wore matronly black dresses and even exaggerated her
age to seem more motherly. She was compassionate, ambitious,
and she'd stand up to anyone—governors, police, corporate executives, strikebreakers, and armed thugs. She was denounced in the
U.S. Senate as the grandmother of all agitators, but she was a folk
hero to many working-class Americans. She was present at some
of the most effective strikes of the time. In 1877, she was one of
the leaders of a railway strike in Pittsburgh that ended in violence
when the state militia fired on a crowd of men, women, and children.
The strike was broken, but its violent end inspired future struggles.

From 1890 on, Jones fought for better wages and working
conditions for mine workers. She became an official union organizer
for the United Mine Workers in 1901 and watched the membership
grow from 10,000 members to 300,000.

Brandley, Voorhis, and Day owned an underwear company now known by their initials: BVD.

During a miner's strike in Utah, *The Deseret News* in Salt Lake City called her "a ranting vixen seeking to lead a mob of destructionists into the execution of some diabolical plot."

## NEWS AT 11
The so-called vixen knew the value of street theater to attract publicity. In 1902, she led a march of miner's wives called the "mop and broom brigade" that routed strikebreakers with brooms and mops in the Pennsylvania coal fields. Imagine watching that story on the 5:30 news.

## THE CHILDREN'S CRUSADE
In 1903, to bring attention to the plight of child workers in the fabric mills, she organized and led what was called "the March of the Mill Children" from Kensington, Pennsylvania, to President Teddy Roosevelt's home on Long Island. Most of the children were physically stunted from harsh working conditions, many of their little hands missing fingers as a result of one careless moment at a weaving machine. They carried banners that said: "WE WANT TO PLAY" and the press eagerly followed the march's progress. When they arrived at Roosevelt's home, he refused to meet with them, but the publicity had done its job. Soon after, one by one, the states started passing new child labor laws.

## ARSENIC AND OLD LACE
During the 1912–13 Paint Creek-Cabin Creek coal strike in West Virginia, armed men employed by the mine-owners machine-gunned the strikers and their families. When a company guard was murdered in retaliation, Mother Jones was arrested and charged with conspiring to commit murder. She was 82 years old. A federal prosecutor labeled her the "most dangerous woman in America," and she was sentenced to 20 years in prison by a military judge. She contracted pneumonia while in prison and was set free by West Virginia's governor in May 1913. By then, she was 83. But she wasn't going to let a little jail time slow her down.

## TIME TO MOVE TO HAPPY ACRES REST HOME?
The next year, striking workers in Ludlow, Colorado, had been evicted from their company housing and had built a tent city on

---

Conchita Cintron, first female professional bullfighter, mastered 1,200 bulls starting at age 12.

public land. The Colorado militia, coal company guards, and scores of hired thugs attacked and destroyed the tent city—killing 20 people in the process. The sad event became known as the Ludlow Massacre.

Mother Jones, at 84, had been one of the leaders of the strike.

## RAISING HELL
Someone once introduced Mother Jones at a union meeting, calling her a great humanitarian. She leaped to the podium and bristled, "Get it straight. I'm not a humanitarian. I'm a hell-raiser." Whenever she spoke to the workers, she always promised to "agitate, educate and aggravate" on their behalf.

## OLD-FASHIONED AFTER ALL
For all her radicalism in other areas, Mother Jones was opposed to giving women the right to vote, because she thought it would undermine the family. She felt that a woman's traditional role as housewife and mother were much more important. "Solve the industrial problem and the men will earn enough so that women can remain home...I have never had a vote and I have raised hell all over this country!"

Her last public appearance was at her 100th birthday party in Silver Spring, Maryland, on May 1, 1930. She died soon after and was buried in the Union Miners Cemetery at Mount Olive, Illinois, under a headstone with the inscription, "She gave her life to the world of labor, her blessed soul to heaven."

\* \* \*

"Work, work, work is preached from the pulpit, the newspapers and magazines: the laboring people are anxious to divide the honor, but they won't. You never hear from the pulpit, the magazine or the newspaper headline rest, rest, rest." —Mother Jones

John Enders cultivated polio in a test tube and he—not Jonas Salk—got a Nobel prize for his work.

# IN NAME ONLY

*Their stories may be long-forgotten, but their names are on the tips of our tongues.*

## BOYCOTT

The first boycott boycotted Boycott. It happened this way: Captain Charles Cunningham Boycott, a retired British Army officer, was hired to manage the Earl of Erne's estates in County Mayo, Ireland. In 1880, after a year of bad harvests, the Irish Land League proposed rent reductions for tenant farmers. Boycott—not a very nice man—ignored the proposal and even tried to evict one farmer. The locals wouldn't stand for it. On the advice of Irish nationalist Charles Stewart Parnell, Boycott's workers left him, tradespeople refused him service at all the local stores, and people jeered him in the streets, hung him in effigy, and threatened his life. Finally, Captain Boycott fled to England. But he couldn't flee the notoriety of his name, which in quite a few languages besides English has come to mean a refusal to deal with a person or business as a form of protest.

## CARDIGAN

James Thomas Brudenell, Seventh Earl of Cardigan, was good-looking, fearless, and a superb horseman. Unfortunately, he was also an idiot who bought his way up the chain of command with his fabulous fortune. By 1854 he'd purchased his way up to major general in the British Army, commanding a cavalry brigade in the Crimean War. It was Cardigan who, during the Battle of Balaclava, led the famous charge of the Light Brigade into the Valley of Death. Although 250 of his 673 men were killed or wounded, Cardigan—first in and first out—survived the charge without a scratch. During the earl's fleeting moment of fame, the knitted vest he wore that freezing winter was named for him. It later sprouted long sleeves and three buttons up the front to become the cardigan sweater we know and love today.

## DERRICK

The device we know of as a movable crane or an oil-drilling structure was originally a gallows—but there's not much gallows humor to

---

Chuck Berry's famous duck walk came from his attempts to hide his wrinkled suit.

the story. The original Derrick raped a woman during the sack of Cadiz in 1596. He was tried, found guilty, and sentenced to be hanged. But his commanding officer, Robert Devereaux, Earl of Essex, pardoned him on condition that he take on the job of executioner at Tyburn Gallows in London. By one of those cosmic quirks of fate, Essex was sentenced to death for treason a few years later, and Derrick was appointed as his executioner. At the time, nobles were exempt from hanging, so Essex's sentence called for beheading, a technique that Derrick wasn't skilled at. Derrick struck three blows with the ax before Essex's head came off. During his career, Derrick hung more than 3,000 people and his name became associated with the gallows itself, and then to any apparatus that resembled the gallows.

## GERRYMANDERING

"Gerrymandering"—or rearranging electoral districts in tortured ways to benefit a political party—is an old American tradition that dates to 1810. Massachusetts Governor Elbridge Gerry reorganized some electoral districts to favor his party, the Jeffersonians, in the upcoming elections. One day, Gilbert Stuart—the painter who is famous for most of the portraits of George Washington that you've seen—walked into the offices of the *Boston Sentinel* newspaper. Seeing the reptilian shape of a new district, Stuart proceeded to add a head, feet, and claws to it, proclaiming that the new district looked like a salamander. "That's no salamander," said the editor, "that's a gerrymander." Gerry's questionable redistricting cost him the governorship in 1812 but gained him a vice-presidential nomination; he shared the winning ticket with James Madison. Gerry died in office in 1814, but gerrymandering lives on.

## LEOTARD

Who's that daring young man on the flying trapeze, and what the devil is he wearing? The young man was French acrobat Jules Leotard. Monsieur Leotard not only designed that form-fitting elastic garment worn by dancers and acrobats—he also invented the flying trapeze and perfected the aerial somersault. He was a circus star in Paris and London in the mid-19th century and was the inspiration for the song "The Daring Young Man on the Flying Trapeze."

## LYNCHING

"Lynching," or hanging a suspected criminal without the delay and inconvenience of a trial, comes from the name of a specialist in just that sort of mob "justice." In 1780, Captain William Lynch led a band of vigilantes in Pennsylvania County, Virginia, to search out and deal with a gang of thugs who were disturbing the peace. With no legal authority to do so, he heard a little evidence and promptly sentenced several members of the gang to hang. Lynch's name lives on in infamy because in an 1836 magazine article, none other than Edgar Allan Poe wrote that the expression "lynch law" originated with that very same Captain Lynch.

## MAVERICK

In the mid-19th century, Samuel A. Maverick, land baron, legislator, lawyer, and mayor of San Antonio, Texas, had cattle on his ranch that multiplied so fast that he didn't have time to get his "MK" brand on them. The neighbors got so used to seeing the unbranded stock roaming around that they started calling any unbranded calf "one of Maverick's." Eventually, Maverick and his sons rounded up his cattle and drove them to his ranch, but the name "maverick" stuck. By the Civil War, "maverick" was in widespread use in Texas and the rest of the West. Now "maverick" is used to brand anyone who holds himself apart from the herd, a nonconformist.

\* \* \*

### SOME MODERN SLANG

**Monkey Wrencher:** Someone who defends the environment by sabotaging (throwing a monkey wrench into) the efforts of developers, drillers, loggers, miners, and such. The term was coined by the late Edward Abbey in his comic novel *The Monkey Wrench Gang*. Ecotage is another term for sabotage on behalf of the environment.

**Easter Egg:** Used to be American slang for a child born nine months after a summer romance. Now it is more frequently used as computer terminology to describe undocumented programs—typically games or elaborate screen shows—that programmers hide in applications. Well-known examples include a pinball game hidden in Microsoft Word and a flight simulator concealed in Excel.

---

Eli Whitney created interchangeable parts to fill a large army order for muskets in 1797.

# ROYAL BAD ENDS: ROMAN EDITION

*Because no one gets assassinated like a Roman emperor.*

Starting with Augustus Caesar in 27 B.C., and continuing through to the fifth century A.D. (and including both the Eastern and Western Roman Empires after they split, Sonny-and-Cher-like, in the late fourth century A.D.), there were 115 Roman emperors, give or take a couple. Of those, about 30 died relatively natural deaths. The rest died pretty damn horribly—poisoned, stabbed, strangled, drowned, run down by angry mobs, and so on.

We sifted through these numerous atrocities and picked a few of the best. Here are some of the more notable bad ends of Roman Emperors. Don't let it happen to you!

**Claudius (death: A.D. 54):** Claudius may have been part of the plot to assassinate his predecessor, the infamous Caligula, who was stabbed to death by his own bodyguards in A.D. 41. Regardless, he was certainly a better emperor than Caligula, or at the very least not nearly as publicly depraved, and he expanded the Roman Empire into Britain among other notable achievements. Claudius's downfall came at the hands of his second wife, Agrippina. Claudius's first wife, Valeria Messalina, was executed after she participated in a "mock" wedding ceremony with a consul-designate while Claudius was away in Ostia, so Claudius was in the market. Agrippina seemed a good match—among other things, she was a sister of the now-deceased Caligula, so she had a good bloodline—by Roman standards, at least.

Unfortunately for Claudius, Agrippina came with her own political agenda and a son, Nero, from a previous marriage, whom she maneuvered into becoming the heir to the empire. Once that was accomplished, it was time to get Claudius out of the way, which Agrippina accomplished through the use of a poisoned mushroom. Nero later showed his gratitude to his mother by having her assassinated in A.D. 59 (he said it was because she was plotting against him, but it was because she kept interfering in his life); he himself committed suicide in A.D. after the senate had sentenced him to be flogged to death.

**Commodus (death: A.D. 192):** You may recognize him as the emperor who is stabbed to death in the Coliseum by Russell Crowe in Gladiator, but it didn't happen like that at all. No, he was strangled to death in his bath by an athlete named Narcissus. Incidentally, Commodus didn't smother his father Marcus Aurelius, either—Marcus Aurelius died from disease, possibly the plague, in A.D. 180. But the movie did get one thing right. Commodus was a pretty lousy emperor and more than a little nuts (among other things, he had every month in the Roman calendar bear one of his personal names, of which he apparently had many).

**Didius Julianis (death: A.D. 193):** Didius Julianus became emperor the old-fashioned way. He bought the title. Seems the previous emperor, Pertinax, died in the typical Roman way of being assassinated (he was trying to quell a rebellion by his Praetorian Guard, but things got out of hand) and left no named successor. Which left the title up for grabs. So Didus Julianus and his rival, Flavius Sulpicianus, started offering progressively richer favors to the Praetorian Guard, outbidding each other until finally the amounts were too rich for Flavius's blood. Like a cheap side of beef, Rome was sold, and Didius was emperor—in name at least.

Not everybody was happy, though—several others candidates also decided they wanted to be emperor. One of them, Septimius Severus, got both the Roman senate and the Praetorian Guard behind him and was declared emperor on June 1, 193; Didius got himself assassinated that very same day. He was emperor for 66 days, which made his one of the shorter (but not the shortest) reigns on record. Septimius Severus, on the other hand, ruled for 18 years and died peacefully in A.D. 211.

**Geta (death: A.D. 211):** One of the sons of Septimius Severus, he and his older brother Caracalla were co-emperors, for a time, at least. Unhappily for Geta, Caracalla wanted Rome for himself and had his younger sibling murdered. Legend has it that the brothers, who had always been estranged, scheduled a meeting with their mother in hopes of burying the hatchet; that's where Caracalla had his soldiers bury the hatchet, all right—right in Geta's chest. Geta is supposed to have died, bleeding, in his mother's arms. Caracalla got his, incidentally—a soldier hired by a rival stabbed him to death when he got off his horse to relieve himself on the side of the road in Syria, in A.D. 217. All the more reason to wait until you get to a designated rest area.

**Gordian I (death: A.D. 238), Gordian II (death: A.D. 238):** See, there was this emperor named Maximinus Thrax, whom apparently nobody anywhere liked, so various people in various parts of the Roman Empire took it in their heads to name their own emperors and let them pretty much slug it out. Two of them were Gordian I (who was proconsul of Africa, and very old—almost 80 at the time) and his son, Gordian II. Gordian I had been rather surprisingly named emperor at the instigation of landowners in Africa, and his confirmation was quickly approved by the senate, as was the quick addition of his son Gordian II as co-emperor. Alas, their rule was equally quick. Gordian II died in battle defending Carthage from troops loyal to Maximinus Thrax, and Gordian I, who was also in Carthage at the time, subsequently hanged himself with his own belt.

As it happens, Maximinus Thrax was killed shortly thereafter by his own troops (we told you nobody liked him), then two other emperors, Pupienus and Balbinus, were—just like that—proclaimed and assassinated. So that makes it five individual emperors bumped off in A.D. 238, what you might call a bumper year for imperial death. Gordian III, the teenage grandson of Gordian I and nephew of Gordian II, would be A.D. 238's sixth emperor, and would manage to last until A.D. 244, when he was likely killed off at the instigation of Philippus, who would then become emperor, and who was himself killed in battle in A.D. 249.

**Numerian (death: A.D. 284):** Legend has it that Carus, who battled the Persians, was killed by a bolt of lightning. While no good for him, it certainly is a refreshing change of imperial death for the rest of us.

His son Numerian also had an infamous demise. Apparently he was dead for quite a while before anyone noticed. He traveled in a closed coach for days (because of an eye inflammation) before

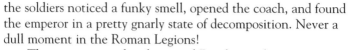

the soldiers noticed a funky smell, opened the coach, and found the emperor in a pretty gnarly state of decomposition. Never a dull moment in the Roman Legions!

The senate immediately named Diocletian the new emperor and, as his first order of business, in front of the entire senate, Diocletian accused Numerian's father-in-law, Aper, of the murder (everybody knew he did it) and personally ran him through with a sword. Never a dull moment in the Roman senate!

**Crispus (death: A.D. 326):** The eldest son of Constantine the Great and the first ruler of the Eastern Roman Empire, Crispus never got to be emperor, because his father had him put to death in A.D. 326. The most interesting explanation of this is that Constantine heard from his second wife, Fausta, that Crispus was planning a rebellion. Sadly for Constantine (and for Crispus), Fausta was lying, motivated by a desire to clear the way to the throne for her own sons by Constantine. (How typical!) And while it worked (her sons did succeed Constantine), Constantine was supposed to have been so incensed when he discovered the truth, that he had Fausta killed as well, locking her in her bath and raising the temperature until she was boiled alive like a lobster. Whether this particular lurid story is true, Fausta did in fact die in A.D. 326, shortly after Crispus.

**Petronis Maximus (death: A.D. 455):** One of the last emperors of the Western Roman Empire, Petronis Maximus was emperor when Rome was famously sacked by the Vandals. Like everyone else, he was in a rush to get out of town before the Vandals showed up. But on the way out of town, he was waylaid by a mob of imperial slaves, who attacked him, tore him apart, and threw his dismembered corpse into the Tiber river. He'd been emperor for a grand total of 77 days.

So let that be a lesson. It doesn't matter if you do get to be emperor of Rome with all the perks included; the fact is that's just one bad gig.

# LEDERHOSEN AND RUFFLES

*You've seen them—those cute (who said "cheesy"?) fat-faced, pink-cheeked figurines of innocent children? Here's the woman who created them, and why the Nazis didn't like her— or her subversive little statues.*

Sister Maria Innocentia Hummel didn't need eBay or a fancy gallery to become one of the most successful commercial artists of all time. Fifty years after her untimely death, her artwork is still generating millions from sales of prints, cards, books, calendars, gift sets, and the fanatically collected figurines that bear her name—Hummel. Despite her gift for grossing in the gazillions, Sister Hummel lived in poverty and signed her paychecks over to God.

## CUTE LITTLE REFUGEES
Americans are sentimental. After WWII, as occupiers of Germany, the G.I.s traded cigarettes and canned goods for exquisitely molded porcelain figurines marked "M. I. Hummel." The tiny statues featured children at play, with titles like *Baby and the Bee* or *The Golden Rule*. Hummel figurines struck a hopeful chord in a postwar generation longing for a simpler, more innocent time. And they were a reminder that Germany produced more than genocide and devastation.

## HUMMEL MANIA
Originally priced at $2 each, the figurines migrated back to the U.S., where an obsessive collector's market escalated the value of some pieces to a current high of $20,000. The official collector's club has more than 200,000 members in the U.S. alone. Betty Ford had a large collection and former President Reagan even has a few. Today, you can take home a new one for between $60 and $1,500.

## THE MOTHER OF THEM ALL
But outside the confines of Hummel-land, few people know that the artist behind this 20th-century collecting frenzy was a young German nun, Berta Hummel, who lived through the German depression and WWII. Her vision of the world and her enthusiasm for humanity, particularly for children, was unstoppably positive.

Mike Tyson won $20 million in 91 seconds when he defeated Michael Spinks in 1988.

## THE ARTIST AS A YOUNG GIRL

When she was 18, Berta's middle-class parents sent her to the Academy of Applied Arts in Munich, but she couldn't ignore that little voice—and no, it wasn't a Hummel—that kept telling her that her future lay elsewhere. She left Munich in 1930 and joined a convent. Her decision to live in "poverty, chastity and obedience" behind convent walls wasn't unusual—at the time, there were more than 6,000 convents with 75,000 members in Germany.

At the nunnery, she wove fabrics and sewed clothing for priests, taught art at the convent school, and illustrated religious cards. The cards were so popular outside the convent that a local publisher started selling them. The public clamored for more works from Sister Hummel and two books followed, *The Hummel Book* and a few years later *Here Comes the Bee* (bees were her symbol—get it?—B for Berta).

In 1933, the owner of the Goebel porcelain factory saw Sister Hummel's cards and made a deal to convert her illustrations into three-dimensional porcelain statues. Introduced in 1935, the figurines were an immediate hit. The frenzy had begun...almost.

## GET THOSE ANGELS OUTTA HERE!

Hitler's regime had come to power in the 1930s and wasn't comfortable with the Church—or with Sister Hummel's spiritually infused work. Sometimes the children were depicted in the real world, sometimes in a fairy tale or fantasy setting that might include (gasp!) angels.

Nazi-backed newspapers charged Sister Hummel with heresy; one even accused her of disparaging the nation's youth with "hydrocephalic [big-headed] and club-footed goblins." In punishment, the powers-that-be reduced the convent's paper ration, thus depriving Sister Hummel of art supplies.

In 1937, the sale of Hummel figurines, along with all Hummel artwork, was banned in Germany. Sister Hummel's work was condemned (along with that of modern German artists Kokoschka and Max Ernst) as "degenerate art." Her publisher's warehouse was searched and her books were burned. (You'd think that all those little figurines would have been smashed to smithereens, but the export of Hummel figurines continued because the Nazi's needed foreign money.) The school where Sister Hummel taught art was closed, she was prohibited from teaching at state schools, and the convent's taxes were increased dramatically.

## WITH THOSE WINGS, YOU DON'T LOOK JEWISH

All the same, in 1944 Sister Hummel claimed to be "perfectly happy" with her life. She continued drawing with whatever materials she could scrounge and secretly created images of angels adorned with six-pointed Jewish stars as well as a drawing that superimposed a menorah over a cross—which, if found by the Nazis, could have landed her in a death camp. In September 1945, at the age of 37, the woman who called herself the "little brush in the hands of God" died from tuberculosis.

## OH, WHAT CUTE LITTLE...SOLDIERS?

The companies that licensed Hummel's work continued to sell it after her death, issuing new works based on her drawings and modifying some of her pieces in ways she might not have appreciated—for example, the tiny children marching as soldiers in *Volunteers* is now available with an American flag. (We'll take two!)

## THE CURRENT STATE OF HUMMELDOM

If those Hummel fanatics can't get enough jollies just looking at their little statues, they can—through the official M. I. Hummel Club—take Hummel-sponsored tours, subscribe to a quarterly magazine, and get discounts on the new figurines that come out all the time!

Meanwhile, Goebel, the authorized manufacturer, still has its hand in the works, squeezing those little Hummels dry—by chasing down infringers, defending itself against antitrust claims, and in the strangest case, pitting itself against Berta's mother's estate. In an attempt to control the copyright, in 1984 the company argued that Berta was an employee of the convent and therefore all works created by her were owned by the convent. (Luckily, the judge didn't buy it.)

## ADMIT IT!

And so, Sister Hummel's legacy hums along. Although it's been dismissed as kitsch and blatantly exploited, even the most cynical among us can't deny that we need a little Hummel now and then. Don't we?

# PRESIDENTIAL CAMPAIGN SLOGANS

*We've come a long way, baby…or have we?*

| SLOGAN: | CANDIDATE: |
| --- | --- |
| "Tippecanoe and Tyler Too" | William Harrison, 1840 |
| "We Polked You in '44, We Shall Pierce You in '52" | Franklin Pierce, 1852 |
| "Don't swap horses in the middle of the stream" | Abraham Lincoln, 1864 |
| "Full-dinner Pail" | William McKinley, 1900 |
| "Get On the Raft With Taft" | William Howard Taft, 1908 |
| "Return to Normalcy" | Warren Harding, 1920 |
| "A Chicken in Every Pot and a Car in Every Garage" | Herbert Hoover, 1928 |
| "Roosevelt for Ex-president" | Wendell L. Willkie, 1940 |
| "Peace, Prosperity, Progress" | Dwight Eisenhower, 1956 |
| "In Your Heart You Know He's Right" | Barry Goldwater, 1964 |
| "A Leader, for a Change" | Jimmy Carter, 1976 |
| "Ross for Boss" | Ross Perot, 1992 |

First record to sell a million copies: *Whispering* by bandleader Paul Whiteman and orchestra.

# A SONY OF HIS OWNY

*After WWII, Japanese companies flooded the American market with
cheap, poorly made products. The words "Made in Japan" translated to
"schlock." But Akio Morita changed that.*

The Morita family had been brewing sake and soy sauce for
14 generations when Akio was born in 1921. As the oldest
son, he was expected to take over the business, but Akio
was more interested in tinkering with electronics.

His first business, Tokyo Telecommunications Engineering
Corporation, was housed in a bombed-out department store in the
ruins of postwar Tokyo. He had a partner who focused on engineering and product design, while he handled marketing, personnel,
and financing—the business end.

Their first product was an automatic rice cooker, which might
have been a hit if the postwar Japanese economy hadn't been
devastated by the war. No one could afford to buy it. That's when
Morita realized he had to look elsewhere for his markets—to the West.

### MAKING A TAPE
First on the agenda was a tape recorder. But Morita and his partner
couldn't find a source for magnetic tape, so they made their own
by grinding up magnets and sticking the powder to strips of paper
so that they could test their prototypes. They perfected Japan's first
magnetic tape recorder in 1950, and after some aggressive marketing
by Morita, it was a modest success.

### OPTICAL ILLUSION
In trying to design a pocket-size radio for the American market,
Morita found that the smallest radio he could make was still a little
too large. So he had his salesmen wear shirts with bigger pockets,
so the radio could slip in and out during demonstrations. The radios
they sold became the first commercially successful transistor radios.

### MAYBE THE BEST IDEA HE EVER HAD
Morita decided to scrap the mouth-filling "Tokyo Telecommunications Engineering Corporation" for a name that would be easy to

---

The inventor of radio, Marconi, opened the first radio broadcasting station in Writtle, England.

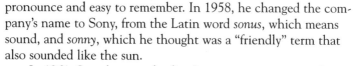
pronounce and easy to remember. In 1958, he changed the company's name to Sony, from the Latin word *sonus*, which means sound, and *sonny*, which he thought was a "friendly" term that also sounded like the sun.

In 1961, Sony became the first Japanese corporation to have its stock listed on the New York Stock Exchange. Later it became the first Japanese company to build a manufacturing facility in the U.S.

## SO, N.Y.

Morita moved his family to New York City in 1963 because he wanted to learn all he could about Americans and their culture, so that Sony could design products tailored to the American market. A lot of people in the industry thought a tape player without a record function would never catch on, but Morita knew he could make the device much smaller and more portable without it. He added some headphones and in 1979 the Walkman was born.

## MR. NICE GUY

Akio Morita's excellent communication skills and great charm allowed him to easily bridge the cultural gap between Japan and the West—he seemed to captivate everyone he came into contact with. True, he was a workaholic, but he also liked sports and remained very active throughout his life, even taking up water-skiing, scuba diving, and wind surfing in his 60s.

## SONY PICTURES, ETC.

Sony developed the first successful battery-powered portable TV, the Trinitron picture tube (which set a new standard of quality for color TV), and the first color home video recorder (the now-defunct Betamax). Not to mention these media standards: the three-inch floppy drive, 8 mm videotape, and, in a joint effort with Phillips, the audio CD. Pretty good track record for a kid who might have ended up pushing soy sauce.

In fact, Morita died of pneumonia in 1999 at age 78. At the time of his death, he was the most famous Japanese citizen in the world and Sony was the number one consumer brand in the U.S.

Lionel Rothschild, House of Commons, was the first Jewish member of Parliament in 1858.

# TRIPLE THREAT QUIZ 5
# JAZZ GREATS

*Every single one of these guys is so much cooler than any of us will ever be.*

Put all of these guys together on the same stage, and you'd have a heck of a jazz quintet—but who would be playing what? Your job: Connect the jazz great with his instrument, and then improvise the connection to the right historical tidbit. All together now...

Match this jazz great...                With his instrument...

1. Lionel Hampton        a) Drums
2. Miles Davis           b) Piano
3. Art Blakey            c) Saxophone
4. Charlie Parker        d) Vibraphone
5. Thelonious Monk       e) Trumpet

And these historical facts...

i. This jazz great started as a drummer and switched over to his most famous instrument by fiddling with it during a recording session, and then playing it on a song that became a hit. His sound was so unique that Benny Goodman had him join the Benny Goodman Quartet—making the Quartet the first inte grated jazz band in the U.S. Alumni of his own orchestra include Quincy Jones, Charles Mingus, and Dinah Washington.

ii. Here's another jazz great who started on another instrument than the one he was famous for. He was originally a pianist, but quickly changed roles after a jazz club owner in Pittsburgh suggested to him—by way of pointing a pistol at him—that he should try another instrument. He did. Later, in 1960, he and his group became the first American jazz players to perform in Japan—for the Japanese—an event that was momentous enough that it was televised across the island nation.

iii. This great was great from an early age. At age 13 he had entered—and won—the weekly amateur contest at Harlem's Apollo Theater so many times that he was banned from entering it again. At age 19 he was playing with fellow jazz greats Charlie Parker and Dizzy Gillespie. He's one of only four jazz musicians to be featured on the cover of *Time* magazine. He's also featured on a U.S. stamp.

iv. In addition to being one of the all-time jazz innovators, this great was also a skilled painter whose work has been displayed in New York, Japan, and Germany. He's also known for playing in a wide range of styles, from bebop to cool jazz to jazz-rock, but is most famous for his "modal" improvising. He once ruefully noted that a commercial he did for a Honda scooter "got me more recognition than anything else I have ever done."

v. He's credited with being the mind behind the jazz genre of bebop (along with Dizzy Gilespie), but his immense talent for jazz was tempered by his frailties. In 1946 he was institutionalized for a mental breakdown caused in part by his addictions to heroin and booze, and during the 1950s his hard living helped get him banned from playing in New York night clubs. His tumultuous life was turned into a movie in the late 1980s by one of his biggest fans—Clint Eastwood.

Answers:
1-d-i
2-e-iv
3-a-ii
4-c-v
5-b-iii

**Mary Lyon founded the first women's college in America, Mount Holyoke Seminary, in 1837.**

# RELUCTANT HERO

*Alvin York had the most important qualities of a war hero. He wasn't scared of nothing, he was well schooled in the art of hunting, and he could shoot the fleas off a dog's back from a mile away.*

Alvin Cullum York was born on December 13, 1887, in a two-room log cabin in Pall Mall, Tennessee. His father was a farmer and a blacksmith, and Alvin was one of 11 children. Like most mountain people of that time, Alvin learned to hunt at a very early age. He grew into a tall, redheaded youth who was an expert shot; he often won the weekly shooting matches that were held in his town on Saturdays. He was a wild young man who did a lot of drinking and fighting, but in 1914, after one of his best friends was killed in a bar fight, he realized the error of his ways and joined a fundamentalist church with a strong moral code that forbade violence of any kind.

### NICE TRY, ALVIN
So when the U.S. declared war on Germany in 1917, York wrote on his draft notice "Don't want to fight." But the army denied him conscientious-objector status, and during his training his commanders managed to convince him that going to war to save lives was a moral thing to do. Relieved that his moral dilemma had been resolved, he became an outstanding soldier. York was such an excellent marksman that he was promoted to corporal and assigned to train other men.

### ON THE BATTLEFRONT
On October 8, 1918, in France's Argonne Forest during the last major battle of WWI, Corporal York and 16 other soldiers led by acting Sergeant Bernard Early crept around the left flank of the German lines. Their mission: to capture machine gun positions and a rail line that was supplying the German front.

### SNEAK ATTACK
York and the others crawled undetected through the heavy brush and got themselves situated well behind the front lines. They quietly approached a group of about 20 Germans, who were eating breakfast in a small valley surrounded by hills.

The wreckage from Glenn Miller's plane has never been found.

The Americans took the enemy completely by surprise; the Germans immediately surrendered. The position they'd captured was a headquarters for a machine-gun company and when the Germans on the surrounding hills realized what was going on, they turned their machine guns around and started firing. Everyone dove for the ground, but six Americans were killed and two were wounded—among them Sergeant Early, who turned over his command to York.

## IN HIS OWN WORDS

The battle still raged. York was crouching on the ground, trying to use the prisoners as cover. As he later recounted in his diary,

> The Germans were what saved me. I kept up close to them, and so the fellers on the hill had to fire a little high for fear of hitting their own men.
>
> As soon as the machine guns opened fire on me, I began to exchange shots with them. In order to sight me or to swing their machine guns on me, the Germans had to show their heads above the trench, and every time I saw a head I just touched it off. All the time I kept yelling at them to come down. I didn't want to kill any more than I had to. But it was they or I. And I was giving them the best I had.

## A TURKEY SHOOT

As he picked off the Germans one by one, he thought of the turkey shoots back home in Tennessee. A turkey would be tied up behind a log so that the only way to hit him was to aim for his head whenever he was foolish enough to raise it up above the protection of the log. The German soldier's heads made much better targets.

## A GOOSE HUNT

> Suddenly a German officer and five men jumped out of the trench and charged me with fixed bayonets. I changed to the old automatic and just touched them off, too. I touched off the sixth man first, then the fifth, then the fourth, then the third, and so on. I wanted them to keep coming. I didn't want the rear

King Tut's third and inner coffin was made of about 243 lb. (110 kg) of gold.

ones to see me touching off the front ones. I was afraid
they would drop down and pump a volley into me.

Once again, York's training as a hunter had kicked in. He
explains in his autobiography that as a boy he'd learned when
hunting geese in flight to shoot the birds in the rear first and work
your way to the front, so that the others don't spook and scatter.

## THE WHITE FLAG

A German major who'd already been taken prisoner had seen
enough. He called to his men and ordered them to surrender. The
eight remaining Americans now had over 80 prisoners. Problem
was, they were still behind German lines. York put the German
major at the head of the line of prisoners and held a gun on him,
as he and the other American soldiers escorted the prisoners
toward the front.

Whenever they'd come across German soldiers, York would
have the major order them to surrender. When one refused, York
had to shoot him. By the time they'd reached the American lines,
they'd taken 132 German prisoners, including three officers.
Surveyors of the battle scene a few days later reported that York
had killed 28 Germans. Word of his exploits quickly spread
throughout the entire Allied armies—and to newspapers around
the world.

## SERVING UP THE "FRUIT SALAD"

The commander of the American Expeditionary Forces, General
John J. "Black Jack" Pershing called York "the greatest civilian
soldier of the war," presented him with the Congressional Medal
of Honor, and promoted him to sergeant. Marshal Foch, the
Supreme Allied Commander said, "What York did was the greatest
thing accomplished by any soldier of all the armies of Europe,"
and awarded him France's medal for bravery—the Croix de Guerre.

When York returned to the U.S., New York City threw him a
ticker-tape parade. He was inundated with offers to endorse this
and endorse that, but he refused them all, saying, "Uncle Sam's
uniform ain't for sale."

## THE RETURNING HERO

When he finally returned to his hometown in Tennessee, his
neighbors presented him with a home and a farm. He quickly married

and settled back into the quiet and simple life he'd dreamed of while he was gone. He also reverted back to his pacifist nature, and during the 1930s when war clouds were gathering once again, he spoke out against U.S. involvement. He even went so far as to renounce America's involvement in WWI—*his* war.

Eventually he realized that America couldn't stand by while Germany enslaved Europe. He started traveling the country on bond tours and recruitment drives. He even tried to enlist, but was turned down because of his age.

## YORK GOES HOLLYWOOD

Filmmaker Jesse Lasky approached York about making a movie of his life. At first, the retired sergeant refused, but he finally consented when he realized that he could use the money to build a school in his hometown. The film, *Sergeant York*, was a smash hit in 1941 and won Gary Cooper an Academy Award for Best Actor that year.

## UNHAPPY ENDINGS

York used all the income from the movie to build and support his school. And even though he was a totally on-the-up-and-up guy, the IRS accused him of tax evasion in 1951. It turned out that York owed money because he'd gotten some bad advice from his tax lawyers. The penalties, interest, and fees he owed were more than his total net worth. When word got around that York was in serious financial trouble, some friends in Congress established a relief fund for him that paid off his debts.

In 1954, he suffered a stroke that left him paralyzed from the waist down. Alvin York died at the Veterans Hospital in Nashville, Tennessee, on September 2, 1964, and was buried with full military honors in his hometown.

## A REAL MAN

Alvin York was a humble man who wore the mantle of "war hero" with a quiet dignity, and who used his fame to help the people of Tennessee. The school he founded, now called the Alvin C. York Institute, is still in operation today. Though he was honored throughout his life for his bravery on that fateful day in 1918, he said just before he died that he preferred to be remembered for what he did after the war, "for helping improve education in Tennessee, bringing in better roads, and just helping my fellow man."

Most people know about *Profiles in Courage*, but JFK also wrote *Why England Slept*.

# CRAZY ABOUT MUSIC

*He died in an insane asylum, but left the world a legacy
of musical greatness.*

When Robert Schumann's father died in 1826, his mother
insisted that he go to Leipzig to study law. He went to
Leipzig, all right, but he spent most of his time composing
music, reading and writing poetry, and knocking back the brews
with his buddies—or whatever 19th-century German artists did at
the time for fun.

### GO AWAY, LITTLE GIRL
In Leipzig, Schumann met the famous music teacher Friedrich
Wieck and his nine-year old daughter Clara, who was an amazing
piano prodigy. Robert and Clara were to become one of the most
famous couples in music history—but later, once little Clara got
puberty out of the way.

### ALTERNATE LIFESTYLE
Schumann moved in with the Wiecks (as was a custom among the
artists of the day), during which he practiced the piano daily and
composed some really terrific music. He'd hoped to support himself
as a concert artist, but—uh, oh—he started having trouble with
his hands, and in fact, the middle finger of his right hand became
paralyzed, not a good thing for an aspiring concert pianist. (No
one knows for sure, but the likely cause was the use of a mercury
treatment for a syphilitic sore—syphilis being another custom of
the day.)

Luckily, he had other talents to fall back on. His pianistic
career at an end, he decided to devote himself to composing and
writing about music. It turned out that he was a perceptive and
brilliant music critic. He was one of the first to appreciate Fredric
Chopin, declaring of the great Polish composer: "Hats off gentlemen,
this is genius."

### NOT WITH MY DAUGHTER!
By the time Clara was 17 (and an accomplished concert artist),

she and Robert decided they were in love. Whoa, said Clara's father. He forbade the marriage and even threatened to shoot Robert if he came near Clara again. It wasn't that he didn't like Schumann; he just thought a one-handed pianist had no future. In an episode straight out of a Harlequin romance, Robert and Clara swore undying love for each other, and settled for being secret pen pals for the next four years. The works Schumann created during these years established his reputation as a composer. He said they were love letters to Clara.

Eventually, the couple took Clara's father to court, suing for the right to marry without his consent. They won, and married. Clara continued to give concerts, Robert composed, and by all accounts, the two were a devoted couple.

## NO HAPPY ENDINGS
But they didn't live happily ever after. Because being a genius isn't easy. Robert was given to alternating fits of depression and creative mania. When he was up, he worked at incredible speed. He composed 130 songs on the sustained high of his first year of marriage. Music historians call this "the year of song." He wrote an entire symphony in four days. But he also suffered periodic breakdowns during which he wasn't able to compose at all.

## BETWEEN HEAVEN AND HELL
By 1852, he began to suffer from auditory hallucinations; he said he heard the voices of angels. As his condition got worse, the angels turned into devils. One night during a rainstorm he told Clara he couldn't longer control his own mind any longer and was afraid he might hurt her or their children. He ran out of the house and threw himself off a bridge into the Rhine River.

Pulled out of the water by some boatmen, he was taken to an insane asylum. In an action that today would be considered shockingly cruel, Schumann's doctors told Clara she shouldn't see him because it would be too upsetting for him. Clara went along with it. She supported herself and her children by giving concerts, and was greatly helped by the young composer Johannes Brahms who had befriended the family and lived in their home.

**The only horse to defeat Man O' War was named Upset.**

## FINAL DAYS

Schumann's condition steadily worsened and he began to refuse all food. When he grew dangerously weak, Clara was finally—after two years—allowed to visit him. In a heartbreaking scene, she helped him take some wine and spilt some on her fingers. Schumann licked the wine from Clara's hand. He died the next day.

Clara, who is considered one of the greatest concert pianists of all time, and a talented composer in her own right, lived on to 1896. Today, her husband's work is more popular and respected than ever; he and Chopin, who also died young, are considered the two great composers of the Romantic era.

## THE FINAL DIAGNOSIS?

But what, exactly, was wrong with Schumann? Some people think it was manic-depression. Others think it was the result of syphilis, whose symptoms in the later stages are similar to the disorder. Maybe it was both. We'll never know for sure.

\* \* \*

## ALL IN GOOD PUN

The Boston Pops Orchestra was in the middle of Beethoven's ninth symphony, but conductor John Williams was worried. He'd earlier found his bass section passing a bottle around, getting boozed up right before a performance! So far they were doing fine, but this particular symphony required extra effort from the basses at the end. The situation made Williams so nervous that just as he was about to cue the basses, he knocked over his music stand. The sheet music scattered. And his worst fear was realized: It was the bottom of the 9th, no score, and the basses were loaded.

Did you know they're planning to make an action movie called *The Three Bs*, based on the lives of Bach, Beethoven, and Brahms? That's right. Bruce Willis signed up to play Beethoven and Mel Gibson agreed to play Brahms. When the casting director approached Arnold Schwarzenegger and asked him if he'd like to be in the movie, too, he thought about it a minute, then nodded and said: "I'll be Bach."

---

James Madison was the only president to face enemy fire while in office during the War of 1812.

# GOSSIP MAVENS

*Darling! Scoot yourself over here and we'll tell you all about the cattiest gossips ever to hit the streets of Hollywood: Louella Parsons and Hedda Hopper.*

You know, gossip just isn't what it used to be. Sure, there's more of it—your supermarket check-out aisle would be positively bare if it weren't for all the magazines and tabloids telling who did what with whom and how often—but the gossip columnists slinging the tales of seamy celebs today just don't have the, oh, what's the word, *oomph* of the gossip columnists of the Golden Age of Hollywood. In those days, not only could a gossip columnist tell millions of slavering housewives what your next movie was, if she decided to slag that movie—and your performance in it—well, then, sweetheart, you simply wouldn't work in this town again. Back to Iowa with you, darling. Iowa, ironically, being where the most powerful of all gossip mavens was from.

## LOUELLA PARSONS

Louella Parsons was a lonely, neglected wife in little Burlington, Iowa, when one night in 1906 she decided to take in a movie at the local picture show—*The Great Train Robbery*, to be precise. Well, dearie, she was *enthralled*. Fast-forward to 1914, and Louella had left that dreary Iowa town far behind for the lights and glamour of Chicago, where she worked at the *Chicago Record-Herald* as the world's first movie columnist. The lights! The camera! The action!

### Working Girl

Then, tragedy—the *Record-Herald* was bought by William Randolph Hearst, who declared the paper didn't need a movie columnist. Out on the streets, our plucky Louella picked herself right up and headed to New York to bang out another movie column, this time for the *Morning Telegraph*. Hearst may have run her out of Chicago, but in New York, he was impressed with her style and made her a deal she couldn't refuse—a job with his New York paper, the *American*. She took the job in 1922, and in 1925 moved to Hollywood itself, the very epicenter of glitz and glamour. Our heroine Louella would work for Hearst, in fact, for the rest of her long career.

---

The first helicopter flight was in 1921 by French aviator Etienne Oehmichen.

## Witness

How did she manage a lifetime contract? Well, sweetie, normally we wouldn't pass on *gossip*, but in this case we'll make an exception. Seems that in 1924, Louella and several other notables were on Hearst's boat when movie director Thomas Ince suddenly and tragically took ill and was rushed off the boat, thence to expire. Oh, the official story is that it was acute indigestion—you know, something he *ate*—but those who were there might tell you that if it was *indigestion*, it's because he ate a *bullet*, and he ate it through his *forehead*. And that the chef of that *particular* dish was none other than Hearst himself, because he suspected Ince had a thing for Marion Davies, Hearst's own little Rosebud. It would have been such the scandal, except that Hearst hushed all the witnesses with lavish gifts—in Louella's case a lifetime contract. It's just rumor, mind you. And you know what they say about *rumors*.

In any event, Louella paid back the favor for Hearst—when that nasty man Orson Welles made *Citizen Kane*, Louella alerted Hearst to the fact that it was based largely on him ("Rosebud!"). She walloped Welles with scathing comments in her columns, and even allegedly organized a campaign to have Welles booed at the Oscars. Sure, he got an Oscar for Best Screenplay, but on the other hand, his career never *did* completely recover, did it? In her 1961 autobiography *Tell It to Louella*, she said, "I have carried only one grudge for any length of time and that was against Orson Welles."

## The Terminator

Louella could be even nastier behind the scenes, when she felt the need. On her website, B-movie actress Mamie Van Doren alleges that in the 1950s Louella Parsons launched a vicious whisper campaign against her, in part because Van Doren's manager was Parsons's own boyfriend and Louella was seeing green. Apparently Louella told some of the trashier tabloids that Mamie and her mother were, well, women of low repute. Oh, you know—hookers, darling. Scandalous—and not a bit of it true. Now you know why you wanted to stay on her good side.

## HEDDA HOPPER

But if you couldn't stay on Louella's good side—say for instance, your name was Orson—there was one other option: Hedda Hopper. Not that that was her real name. Her real name was, and this is very rich, Elda Furry. Yes! *Furry!* I know! And she came to the gossip game with a certain amount of experience on the other side of the publicity machine—she was an actress, primarily during the silent era, mostly playing the heroine's best friend, in more than 100 films. She got rid of "Furry" by marrying actor DeWolf Hopper (their son, William, had a long-running role in the early *Perry Mason* series on TV). But back in 1938 she left acting behind for a much more interesting job—gossip columnist for the *Los Angeles Times*. Her column was called "Under Hedda's Hat," because Hedda loved her hats the way Imelda Marcos loved her shoes.

### Public Enemy

Of course, she and Louella became mortal enemies—how could they *not*?—and stars who were beloved of one were less than the dust beneath the pumps of the other. And vice-versa—while Louella was busy torching Orson Welles when *Citizen Kane* was in the theaters, Hedda had him as the featured guest for a week-long sit-down on her radio program. Their rivalry eventually even spawned a movie in itself: *Malice in Wonderland*. Well, a TV movie, anyway. But it starred Liz Taylor! So *that's* good.

### Reds

Like Louella, Hedda wasn't above being petty when it suited her. Hedda had a chatty relationship with FBI director J. Edgar Hoover, to whom she wrote long letters about all the communists in Hollywood. In one 1947 letter, for example, she swiped at Charlie Chaplin and other "commies": "I'd like to run every one of those rats out of the country starting with Charlie Chaplin. In no other country in the world would he have been allowed to do what he's done." And of course, Chaplin was eventually run out of the country! Coincidence? Possibly, but then again, possibly *not*.

## HEDDA AND LOUELLA HANG UP THEIR HATS

So what happens to old gossip columnists? Why, darling, the same thing that happens to old actors and actresses—they die, or they just fade away. Hedda died in 1966, probably hatless. Louella stopped writing her gossip column in 1965 and lived out her last years in a Santa Monica nursing home. Rumor has it that she spent her final days watching old movies on the TV and talking to the images of the people whose careers she'd casually made or broken. How's that for irony? And how's that *gossip*? It's such good gossip it hardly matters if it's *true*.

---

The first U.S. patent issued was in 1790 for a process to make potash.

# KING OF KETCHUP

*Richard Nixon smothered cottage cheese with it; Japanese eat it on rice; and one ice-cream manufacturer tried to make it a flavor. Here's a story you'll relish, about the man whose name became synonymous with the condiment so popular that it's found in nearly every fridge in America.*

Hundreds of years ago, the Chinese used the brine from pickled fish as a dipping sauce. They called it "ke-tsiap." From there it made its way to Malaysia, where the name was modified to "kechap." In the 1680s, Dutch and British explorers brought the concoction back to Europe, where the upper classes spiced it up with goodies like pickled mushrooms, anchovies, kidney beans, and walnuts. Eventually, the Brits bottled it and called it "catsup." By the late 1700s, the recipe found its way to New England, where tomatoes were added to the mix. Mid-19th-century entrepreneurs exploited the American taste for sweet food and started selling catsup made with tomatoes, vinegar, sugar, cinnamon, cayenne, and salt. But it wasn't until the 1870s that H. J. Heinz came up with the recipe that our taste buds would recognize today.

### A BORN SALESMAN
Henry John Heinz was born in Pittsburgh, Pennsylvania, on October 11, 1844. His father, another Henry, had come to the U.S. from Bavaria only four years earlier. At the age of 12, H. J. began selling his mother's homemade horseradish sauce door to door.

### EXHIBIT A...THE TOMATO
At the time, the typical American diet was a pretty dreary affair, consisting mostly of bread, potatoes, root veggies like carrots, turnips, rutabagas, parsnips, and beets, and meat—usually dried, smoked, or salted. Pickles were still something that, by and large, were available only in wintertime. Tomatoes were considered an exotic Mexican fruit.

### HORSERADISH AS FAR AS THE EYE CAN SEE
By 1869, Heinz had a burgeoning condiment business and a partner, Clarence Noble. They bottled their horseradish sauce (and pickles,

---

Fanny Wright became the first female public speaker on public affairs in America.

sauerkraut, vinegar, and so on) under the name Heinz and Noble, and they delivered their goodies by horse-drawn wagons to grocers in and around Pittsburgh. They had 100 acres of garden along the Allegheny River—including 30 acres of horseradish—along with 24 horses, a dozen wagons, and a vinegar factory in St. Louis. In 1875, Heinz bought 600 acres in Illinois in pursuit of new sources of cucumbers. (A similar search drives the plot of the next *Star Trek* movie, we've heard.)

## KETCHING UP

A banking panic that same year forced the business into bankruptcy, but H. J., with his brother and cousin, bounced back. In the depression brought on by the banking collapse, 1876 proved to be a hard first year, but one in which a new product was introduced—Heinz sweet tomato ketchup. Next came red and green pepper sauces, then cider vinegar, apple butter, chili sauce, mincemeat (a finely chopped mixture of raisins, apples, and spices, with or without meat), mustard, tomato soup, olives, pickled onions, pickled cauliflower, baked beans, and the first sweet pickles (and sweet pickle relish) to ever hit the market.

## HOME SWEET FACTORY

Not only that. In an era when long hours, poor working conditions, and low pay were the norm for urban workers in America, Heinz put into practice what was then a radical notion—that workers should be treated well on the job. Conditions at his factories were often better than the workers had at home.

## TRAVELING SALESMAN

Then, long before globalization became a buzzword, Heinz sailed with his family to England, including in his luggage a bag packed with "seven varieties of our finest and newest goods." Ten years later the first overseas office opened near the Tower of London. Heinz's products eventually became so successful in the U.K. that most British shoppers thought Heinz was a British company.

## THE PRINCE OF PICKLES

By 1896, Heinz was a household name and H. J. himself had become a millionaire. How did he do it? Three years earlier, at the

A coffee pot with a sieve to strain away the grounds was not invented until 1806.

Chicago World's Fair, everyone who attended the Heinz exhibit—more than 1 million vacationers from around the world—left the fair with a free pickle pin. Although a green plaster-of-Paris pin may sound a little, well, cheesy, it proved to be one of the most effective promotional items in the history of retailing.

## HIS LUCKY NUMBER?
The ideas kept coming. Heinz's next idea proved to be another marketing coup, one of the greatest in the history of retailing, in fact. Here's how the story goes: The company was still in need of an easily recognizable slogan. So, while riding on a New York City elevated subway car one day, Heinz spotted a sign above a local store that said "21 Styles of Shoes." He decided that his own products weren't styles, but varieties. And although he had more than 57 foods in production at the time, the numbers five and seven held a special significance for him and his wife Sallie, so he adopted the slogan "57 Varieties."

## MAYBE NOT
While the story about the train is true, the part about the numbers five and seven holding some sort of special significance for Henry Heinz and his wife could best be described as a pile of horse…in this case, let's say horseradish. The story may have been an attempt on the part of the folks running the Heinz Corporation to keep the Henry Heinz mystique alive. Maybe there's a more likely explanation.

It's hard to say exactly what may have been going through the mind of the pickle peddler from Pittsburgh when he came up with it. According to some accounts, he simply liked the way the number 57 looked in print. In all likelihood, when Heinz had his epiphany on the train in 1896, he simply miscounted his products. (He actually had at least 62 at the time.) When he returned to his office, he probably already had the slogan "57 Varieties" embedded in his brain and nothing—not even an accurate product count—was going to change his vision.

In any case, it's clear that the "57" in Heinz 57 really stands for incredibly savvy marketing. He took what was for all intents and purposes an arbitrary number and attached it to his brand name. It cost him absolutely nothing. Over the last century, millions if not billions of people have probably asked themselves or others, "I wonder what the 57 stands for in Heinz 57?" You can't buy that kind of publicity.

## THERE'S A PICKLE LOVER BORN EVERY MINUTE

Now that Heinz was an instantly recognizable national brand, H. J. was ready to take things to the next level. Literally. With all the subtlety of a P. T. Barnum (or Donald Trump, to update the image a bit), Heinz erected a 40-foot-high flashing electric pickle— New York City's first electric sign (1900)—in the heart of Midtown Manhattan. And a 90-foot pickle at the end of a 900-foot pier in Atlantic City.

In the same year that the Big Apple pickle went up, there were 100 manufacturers of ketchup, but even now Heinz ketchup is the standard by which other ketchups are rated. The man who made it happen died of pneumonia in 1919 at the age of 75, but his name (and his ketchup) live on.

\* \* \*

## LET THEM EAT CHEESECAKE

When you hear the name Sara Lee, do you think of some femme in an apron slaving away over a hot oven, turning out cakes by the hundreds and thousands? Forget it.

The real Sarah Lee never went near the kitchens that made her famous. In 1935, Charles Lubin and his brother-in-law bought a chain of small neighborhood bakeries. In 1949 they parted ways, Charles retaining the company. His first solo product was a cream cheesecake named for his eight-year-old daughter, Sara Lee Lubin. The business was wildly successful, as we know. And little Sarah Lee (Lubin) Schupf grew up to become one of America's best-known and most generous women philanthropists.

**The first typewriter was produced by gunmakers E. Remington & Sons in 1874.**

# POP PHYSICIST

*One of the world's most brilliant scientific minds is trapped inside a mute hunk of paralyzed flesh. Here's the true story of Stephen Hawking, who may be the world's only celebrity physicist.*

The first time Stephen Hawking fell in love it was with mathematics. This was at St. Albans School, just north of London. His father wanted him to go on to his own alma mater, University College, Oxford, to study medicine. Since UC didn't offer math degrees, Stephen agreed—but not to the medicine; he'd study physics instead. He did so unenthusiastically, loafing through his three years there. Without even trying, he was awarded a first-class honors degree in natural science in 1962.

## HAWKING GETS COSMIC

Hawking moved on to Cambridge to get his doctorate. This time he was determined to study something he was interested in. He took on the difficult fields of relativity and cosmology—odd choices for a guy without a strong math background, but a good choice for a guy who was finally getting his way.

## HAWKING GETS DIAGNOSED

But there was something else, something ominous, happening at the same time. During his last year at Oxford, he'd noticed he'd gotten, well, clumsy. He'd fallen a few times. When he told his mother about it on Christmas break in 1962, she convinced him to see a doctor. Two weeks of hospital tests later, Stephen had an explanation—he had a degenerative nerve disease: amyotrophic lateral sclerosis, a.k.a. Lou Gehrig's disease. The doctors weren't at all hopeful—they predicted he wouldn't live long enough to finish his doctorate degree.

## ALONG COMES JANE

One month before his diagnosis, Stephen had fallen in love again, this time with Jane Wilde, a fellow student. He was straight with her about his illness. He told her that even if he lived more than the expected two years he'd soon be paralyzed. Jane pledged to

---

Derek Walcott was the first African American writer to win the Nobel Prize for literature.

stand by him. Fighting off despair at his physical condition, he worked like a man inspired, trying to finish up his doctorate so he could have enough money to marry Jane. As he worked harder and harder, his body got weaker and weaker.

## LIFE IN THE HANDICAPPED ZONE

Jane and Stephen were married in July 1965, and Hawking was awarded a fellowship at Caius College, Cambridge. As his scientific reputation ramped up, so did his disability—at first he had to use a wheelchair for long distances, then he couldn't walk at all. His uncoordinated limbs were leaden and refused to cooperate. Fortunately, he was offered a series of positions that didn't require lecturing, just research. He moved from a research fellowship to a professorship of Gravitational Physics at Cambridge in 1977.

But all the while his disability was getting worse. Jane was devoting her life to his care and to caring for their three children. Up until about 1975, Stephen could still get in and out of bed unassisted, and feed himself. When he couldn't do that anymore, he hired private nurses to come in for an hour or two a day, and he relied on friends to help move his stubborn body through life's daily tasks.

## MIND OVER MATTER

But his academic career never slowed down. In 1979 Hawking was appointed Lucasian Professor of Mathematics at Cambridge, the same post once held by Isaac Newton. He was doing incredibly heady stuff—brilliant, influential research on black holes, combining Einstein's Theory of Relativity with Quantum Theory, and arguing that space and time began with the Big Bang and would end in a black hole.

## THE REST IS SILENCE

By 1980, Stephen could no longer walk or write, but he could still speak. His slurred speech had to be translated for lectures, and he dictated papers to a secretary. But when he suddenly caught pneumonia in 1985, he had to undergo an emergency tracheotomy, after which his ability to speak was gone.

*Time* **named the personal computer "Man" of the Year in 1982.**

## FUNNY, YOU DON'T SOUND BRITISH

At first, the ideas fighting to get out of Hawking's head had to be communicated painstakingly; he'd raise his eyebrows when someone pointed to the right letter on a spelling card. For a brilliant man whose work involved writing scientific papers, this was a disaster. But his academic career was saved when a Silicon Valley programmer sent Hawking a computer program called Equalizer, which could be fitted to his wheelchair and would allow Stephen to pick from a list of words on a computer screen by head or eye movements. When he'd built an entire sentence he could send it to a voice synthesizer, which said the sentence out loud in an eerie, mechanized tone. Hawking only had one complaint about this miraculous device—it gave him an American accent.

Now Hawking could carry on a conversation, give a speech, and write books and papers. His *A Brief History of Time*, an almost mystical yet scientific examination of space and time, was published in 1988. The book spent more than four years on the *London Sunday Times* best-seller list, longer than any other book in history, and sold more than 10 million copies.

## THE TIME AFTER TIME

Hawking fell in love again, this time with one of his full-time nurses. He left Jane, his wife of 25 years, in 1990. He continues to write (*The Universe in a Nutshell* was published in 2001), lecture, do research, and make public appearances all over the world.

In 2002 he celebrated his 60th birthday. Pretty good for a man who wasn't supposed to live past 23, eh?

\* \* \*

### EINSTEIN'S BRAIN

After pathologist Thomas S. Harvey, M.D., performed the autopsy on Albert Einstein in 1955, he made off with Einstein's brain. For many years, he kept it with him in a formaldehyde-filled mason jar in his office in Wichita, Kansas. It wasn't untill 1985 that a pair of researchers persuaded Harvey to give them some tissue samples. Today, most of the brain has been sectioned for study—only the cerebellum and a piece of his cerebral cortex are still floating in a jar in Wichita.

Future publishing greats Simon & Schuster published the first crossword puzzle collection in 1924.

# COMICS ENEMY #1

*Pow! Wham! In the 1950s, comic books were jam-packed with violent villains, crypt creeps, femme fatales, and other baddies. But by far the scariest thing to ever happen to comic books was a psychiatrist named Frederic Wertham.*

Though some groused that the first newspaper comic strip, *The Yellow Kid*, distracted attention from hard news when it debuted in *The New York World* in 1895, few complained seriously about the gentle, funny strip and its brethren: *Popeye*, *Little Nemo in Slumberland*, and *Mutt and Jeff*.

But when comic books grew up and got serious in the 1930s, people started to pay attention. *Flash Gordon* and *Dick Tracy* were full of thrilling adventure—with a dash of violence thrown in. By the arrival of *Superman* in 1939, media critics were complaining that the "funny books" weren't all that funny anymore; they were growing seamy.

An oft-quoted editorial by Sterling North, literary editor of the *Chicago Daily News*, said this on May 8, 1940:

> Badly drawn, badly written, and badly printed—a strain on the young eyes and young nervous systems—the effects of these pulp-paper nightmares is that of a violent stimulant. Their crude blacks and reds spoil a child's natural sense of colour; their hypodermic injection of sex and murder make the child impatient with better, though quieter, stories. Unless we want a coming generation even more ferocious than the present one, parents and teachers throughout America must band together to break the "comic" magazine.

Yet despite such invective, comics' popularity exploded. WWII servicemen and school kids devoured *Superman*, *Batman*, and *Captain America*. By 1947, 60 million comic books were being sold per month and it seemed nothing could halt their upward trajectory.

## ENTER DR. WERTHAM

One man was ready to try—Dr. Frederic Wertham, a 53-year-old

**Cruciverbalist: a crossword puzzle devotee.**

German immigrant psychiatrist. It wasn't that Dr. Wertham was an uptight bluestocking. In fact, he was broadminded for the times.

Wertham earned his M.D. in 1921. One of his early jobs proved influential—working with a psychiatrist who held the novel theory (at the time) that doctors should investigate a patient's environment before diagnosing treatment. Wertham brought that idea with him to the U.S., where he began investigating the connections between mental health and criminal behavior.

In 1941 Wertham wrote Dark Legend, a successful study of a 17-year-old who murdered his mother. In 1949 he continued his study of criminal backgrounds with the case study round-up *Show of Violence*. At the same time, he began testifying in front of various lawmaking bodies. His article, "Psychological Effects of School Segregation," was submitted as evidence in the landmark case of Brown vs. the Board of Education and helped strike a blow against segregation.

Wertham continued working with troubled, often criminal, youths, many of whom he noticed were avid comics readers. Once he started examining the comics, the lurid sex and violence he found in them worried him. In 1948, he spoke at a psychiatric convention, charging that excessive comic book consumption had figured largely in the delinquency of the troubled youths he studied.

## FUNNY BOOK FALLOUT

Wertham's idea struck a chord in an America worried about a rising tide of juvenile delinquency. Articles criticizing comics appeared in *Time* and *The Saturday Review of Literature*. Some communities staged mass comic book burnings and protested in front of comic book stores. Others enacted laws designed to censor and control comic book dealers and publishers. In 1949 the book *Love and Death* called comics publishers "degenerates" and said that the two biggest companies were "staffed entirely by homosexuals and operating out of our most phalliform skyscraper." That same year, the Canadian government passed laws against the production of "crime comics."

In 1950 the U.S. feds entered the fray, when a Senate special committee investigated the link between crime comics and organized crime. Blaming comic books for subsequent crimes became a common gambit for young criminals who claimed that the violent comics they read about "made them do it."

---

**Popular pin-up girls were used as the model for Tinker Bell in the movie *Peter Pan*.**

## TALES OF THE CORRUPT
But the worst was yet to come for the comic companies. Still worried about the effect of comics on troubled youths—especially a new breed of gruesome horror comics published by impresarios like *Tales From the Crypt*'s M. C. Gaines—Wertham continued writing articles attacking comics throughout the 1940s. Finally he published his landmark book Seduction of the Innocent in 1954.

Today the book is a real howler, with passages that term the *Batman and Robin* stories "a wish dream of two homosexuals living together" and *Wonder Woman* as a "lesbian counterpart of Batman" who gave little girls "wrong ideas" about a woman's place in society. He even criticized Superman as giving kids the wrong ideas about physics because he could fly.

## DRAWN AND QUARTERED
But not many people were laughing in 1954. Wertham's accusation was taken seriously. The U.S. Senate convened a Subcommittee on Juvenile Delinquency that spring, and Dr. Wertham was both consultant and its chief witness.

The subcommittee was an unqualified disaster for the comics publishers. One particularly damaging exchange will serve as an example:

> **Senator Kefauver** (holding up a gory M. C. Crime SuspenStories comic cover): "This seems to be a man with a bloody ax holding a woman's head up, which has been severed from her body. Do you think that is in good taste?"
>
> **M. C. Gaines:** "Yes, sir, I do—for the cover of a horror comic. A cover in bad taste, for example, might be defined as holding the head a little higher so that the blood could be seen dripping from it..."
>
> **Kefauver:** "You've got blood coming out of her mouth."
>
> **Gaines:** "A little."

## CENSORED COMICS
In the end, the Senate decided not to pass official censor laws. But comic book producers were forced to draw up a self-regulating

code. Only sanitized comics received the Comics Code Authority (CCA) stamp of approval, marking it safe for sale to America's kids. The code restricted sex and violence, strictly forbade criticism of religion, and even restricted the use of slang terms.

Disgusted by the CCA's kowtowing, Gaines dumped his horror comic lines and concentrated on his new satire magazine, Mad. Sales of the censored comics dropped off throughout the 1950s (though some attributed this more to a new form of media that was absorbing children's attention, namely television). Marvel Comics (then called Atlas) was almost forced to fold, and DC Comics faded to a shadow of its former self. Dozens of other comics companies went out of business.

Eventually the comic book industry would recover as superhero comics like DC's *The Justice League of America*, and Marvel's *Spider-Man* and *The Fantastic Four* recharged the genre in the 1960s. But it would never again be the entertainment monolith it was in the 1940s.

## WERTHAM'S DEMISE

As for Wertham, he continued to write throughout the 1960s and 1970s, publishing books on the rise of American violence. In 1973, startlingly, he published *The World of Fanzines*, a book that praised sci-fi and comics fanzines as a praiseworthy new form of art. After its publication, New York Comic Art Convention founder and promoter Phil Seuling invited Wertham to a panel to address his "fans." Instead, Wertham was besieged at the panel by angry comics fans who accused him of wrecking comics in the 1950s. Wertham stalked out and never again wrote about comics. Wertham died in 1981.

\* \* \*

## RADIO DAYS

*The Lone Ranger* and the *Green Hornet* were the radio creations of George W. Trendle, who owned radio station WXYZ in Detroit. But Trendle's brainchildren had one more thing in common: according to the script, Britt Reid (the Hornet) was the grand-nephew of John Reid (the Ranger).

# WHEN WAYNE MET WYATT

*Every story in this book is a true one as far as we know. But here's one that may be just a Hollywood legend, the invention of a Hollywood press agent.*

Picture Hollywood's ideal of the Western lawman. He's a quiet, serious man who doesn't waste words and rarely cracks a smile, much less a joke. A cool customer, he doesn't drink much and keeps his emotions to himself. He's a man of his word, loyal to family and friends. We've just described Wyatt Earp (or that part of the legend he wanted remembered). And it's no coincidence.

## COWBOY AND THE COWBOYS

In the 1910s and 1920s, Wyatt Earp was living quietly in Los Angeles, California. It was a time when old cowhands who'd once raised cattle and hell in the old West drifted into tamer occupations like wranglers (handling horses and cattle) or stuntmen for the movies. Hollywood sets were open then—anyone could drop in— and Earp liked to visit old acquaintances there. He became friendly with silent Western star William S. Hart and tried to teach him the "fast draw."

Earp also impressed an assistant prop boy named John Ford, who would later become famous as a director. Ford would bring Earp coffee and listen to the old cowboy's tales of the famous gunfight at the O.K. Corral. Ford's conversations with Earp influenced his classic Western, *My Darling Clementine*, based on the gunfight, in which Henry Fonda played Wyatt Earp.

## THE COWBOY AND THE DUKE

In the late 1920s, Earp was approaching 80, but he retained enough of the image of the Western hero to impress another young prop man named Marion Morrison, who liked to sit and talk with Earp and hear the old man's stories. When Morrison got his first starring role, he changed his name to John Wayne. Wayne later said that Earp was the "ballsy" kind of guy Wayne tried to portray in films. Something to remember the next time you see a John Wayne Western.

**Peter the Great of Russia taxed Russians that wore beards.**

# KING OF THE ZULUS

*The man who turned the Zulu clan into a mighty nation was at heart a bullied mama's boy with a bad temper and a great need for revenge.*

The man who would be king of the Zulus entered the world in 1789, the son of Senzangakona, a Zulu chieftain, and Nandi, an orphaned Langeni princess. But Shaka was never treated like a prince. Technically, his parents belonged to the same clan in southern Africa and their marriage violated Zulu custom, which made Shaka illegitimate. And so, according to another charming custom, the tribal elders proclaimed that the mother, while pregnant, was carrying "i'Shaka," an intestinal parasite. The name stuck—and her baby was called "Shaka."

## UNWANTED: DEAD OR ALIVE
Shaka's parental units weren't getting along, so Nandi took her baby home to live with her own clan. But the Langeni weren't thrilled to see her; Shaka ended up spending a fatherless boyhood among a people that despised his mother. After mistreating Nandi and Shaka for years, the clan banished them. Eventually, mother and son found a measure of acceptance with the Mtetwa tribe— that is to say, they were tolerated. So Shaka grew into a bitter young man, storing up his hatred for the people who had mistreated him and his mother.

## WAR! WHAT IS IT GOOD FOR?
Young Shaka finally found a nice outlet for all that pent-up animosity when he was called to serve as a Mtetwa warrior at age 23. In his first battle, he and his fellow warriors defeated the Butelezi clan and won their territories—which included (heh, heh) the Zulu's land. His brilliance as a warrior didn't go unnoticed by the Mtetwa chieftain, Dingiswayo. So when Shaka's father died, Dingiswayo made Shaka the new chief of the Zulu.

## HOW DO YOU SAY "UNCLE" IN SWAHILI?
Shaka pointed his new army toward the local clans—starting with the Langeni. As each tribe was conquered, anyone left alive was integrated into the Zulu clan.

---

Actors buried in Arlington Cemetery: Fay Bainter, Audie Murphy, and Lee Marvin.

During Shaka's reign, the Zulu (population:1,500) went from one of the smallest clans in southern Africa to an awesome nation of 250,000. (It's a good thing, too, because Shaka was killing people left and right and he needed new warm bodies to replace the cold, dead ones.) Shaka ruled with an iron fist—meting out instant death to anyone who opposed or contradicted him. Any soldier caught disobeying even the slightest of the king's dictates was immediately executed. Each man entering the army had to take a vow of chastity and be prepared for tortuous physical and mental training. Shaka's army was so tight and his tactics so far ahead of their time that most battles against the Zulu weren't battles at all—they were more like little skirmishes followed by some non-Zulu waving the white flag.

## THE MADNESS OF KING SHAKA

When Shaka's beloved mother died in 1827, the king went (certifiably) insane with grief. In memory of his mother, 7,000 people were randomly executed. By royal decree, no crops could be planted for a year, and no milk—the staple of the Zulu diet—could be used. Any woman found to be pregnant was executed with her husband.

## HE WHO LIVES BY THE SWORD

It took two men to kill him. On September 23, 1828, Shaka's half-brothers stabbed the king to death with spears. They buried his body in an unmarked grave, thus ending a reign that in a mere 10 years had turned the tiny Zulu clan into the great and powerful Zulu Nation.

\* \* \*

"This is the death I have in mind for you. The slayers will sharpen the projecting upright poles in this cattle-kraal—one for each of you. They will then lead you there, and four of them will pick you up singly and impale you on each of the sharpened poles. There you will stay till you die, and your bodies, or what will be left of them by the birds, will stay there as a testimony to all, what punishment awaits those who slander me and my mother."
—Shaka Zulu, condemning those who had tormented him in his youth

---

Boxing champ Joe Louis is buried at Arlington Cemetery.

# SCHOOL'S OUT FOREVER

*A lot of self-made millionaires and billionaires didn't feel the need for a full-on education—they had millions and billions of bucks to make and they just couldn't wait.*

**RICHARD BRANSON:** That's Sir Richard Branson to you, buddy. The founder of Virgin Records and Virgin Atlantic Airways was miserable at school because of his dyslexia. He played at being an entrepreneur from age 12 (with mixed success) and he left school at 17, at which point his headmaster predicted he'd "either go to prison or become a millionaire." He hasn't been sent to jail yet. In fact, he was knighted by Queen Elizabeth in 2000.

**ANDREW CARNEGIE:** Born in Scotland, the son of a weaver, he came with his family to the U.S. in 1848. Around the same time, age 13, he went to work as a bobbin boy in a cotton mill. He started his own business at age 29, eventually building it into the Carnegie Steel Company. At one time the richest man in the world, Carnegie was what they call "a captain of industry." A strange combination of ruthless businessman and free-spending philanthropist, he gave away more than $350 million to good causes in his lifetime.

**JIMMY DEAN:** The singer-songwriter ("Big Bad John") left school at 16 and joined the Merchant Marines. He knew that fame could be fleeting, so after his prime-time TV variety show ran its course, he founded the Jimmy Dean Meat Company and kept his TV appearances to folksy sausage commercials. He sold the company to Sara Lee in 1991, but is still chairman of the board.

**WALT DISNEY:** The famous film/TV producer and theme park pioneer had always been more interested in art than in the Three R's. He left school at 16 to enlist in the army when the U.S.

---

Pavarotti likes to have a bent nail in his pocket for good luck when on stage.

entered WWI, but they wouldn't take him because he was too young. So he did his wartime bit driving a Red Cross truck. His hometown high school awarded him an honorary diploma when he was 58.

**GEORGE EASTMAN:** Eastman's father died when he was about eight years old. At 14, he took it upon himself to support his mother and two sisters. He worked his way up from office boy to clerk to founder of the company that became Eastman Kodak.

**HENRY FORD:** The founder of the "Ford Motor Company" left his family farm and one-room schoolhouse at 16 to become a machinist's apprentice in Detroit. He introduced the Model T in 1908; five years later his assembly-line mass production enabled him to sell the cars for $500 each.

**HENRY J. KAISER:** The founder of Kaiser Aluminum and Chemical Corporation and Kaiser Steel left school at 13. His later friendship with Franklin and Eleanor Roosevelt helped him understand the value of labor unions, so he ended up being an industrialist and a friend of the working man. He founded Kaiser Permanente (the first HMO) for his employees in 1942.

**KIRK KERKORIAN:** The "Father of the Las Vegas megaresort," dropped out of school in the eighth grade to become a professional boxer. He built three hotels that were the largest in the world in their time, including the MGM Grand. Today, Kerkorian is the 41st richest man in the country

**JOHN D. ROCKEFELLER:** The world's first billionaire dropped out of high school two months before graduation; he took a 10-week business course from one of those chain business schools and went on to co-found The Standard Oil Company.

**DAVE THOMAS:** The founder-spokesperson of the "Wendy's" fast-food chain started working in a restaurant at 12, after which he left home, took a room at the YMCA, and dropped out of school at 15. He worked as a bus boy and a cook, and eventually opened his own place: Wendy's Old Fashioned Hamburgers. Later in life, he studied long enough to get his equivalency diploma.

# MORE OF MY THOUGHTS ABOUT ME

*Here are more enlightening autobiographical observations.*

"I think, therefore I am."
—**Rene Descartes**

"I simply ache from smiling."
—**Queen Elizabeth**

"Deals are my art form."
—**Donald Trump**

"There is no genius without a touch of madness."
—**Vaslav Nijinsky**

"Results! Why, man, I have gotten a lot of results. I know several thousand things that won't work."
—**Thomas Edison**

"If everything's under control, you're going too slow."
—**Mario Andretti**

"Fly like a butterfly, sting like a bee."
—**Muhammad Ali**

"If you can count your money, you don't have a billion dollars."
—**J. Paul Getty**

"If I were not Napoleon I would be Alexander."
—**Napoleon Bonaparte**

"I may be compelled to face danger but never fear it, and while our soldiers can stand and fight, I can stand and feed and nurse them."
—**Clara Barton**

"Be bold. If you're going to make an error, make a doozy, and don't be afraid to hit the ball."
—**Billie Jean King**

"I skate where the puck is going to be, not where it has been."
—**Wayne Gretzky**

"Autobiography is now nearly as common as adultery and hardly less reprehensible."
—**Lord Altrincham**

"Everything that irritates us about others can lead us to an understanding of ourselves."
—**Carl Jung**

---

Liu Ch'ung, a Chinese man, had two sets of pupils in each of his eyes.

# NOT THE OATMEAL GUY

*Say "Quaker" to most Americans and they'll summon a picture of
the big, smiley guy on the oatmeal box. This isn't about him.*

Nowadays, in our easy American tolerance for religious
differences, it's hard to understand the kind of persecution
the founder of the Quakers had to undergo—and the kind
of steely courage it took to be a human religious punching bag.

## ALONG COMES GEORGE

George Fox was born in 1624 in County Leicestershire, England,
at a time when there were rumbles of religious dissent all over
Europe—France had its Huguenots, Germany its Lutherans,
Ireland its Protestants. England itself was a simmering cauldron of
discontent— the common folk were fed up with the corrupt
C.O.E. (the Church of England, to you).

## WHAT, AND QUIT SHOE BUSINESS?

George spent some time as a cobbler's apprentice, but left home at
18 in search of religious counsel. He wanted to see if the C.O.E.
priests could help him with what was particularly plaguing him—
the nature of man's relationship with God.

## A DO-IT-YOURSELFER

When their answers didn't satisfy him, Fox spent day and night
praying alone with his Bible. Eventually, he saw the light—God's
grace comes to those who ask for it, without translation from
priests and popes and kings. The C.O.E., Fox believed, was formal
and corrupt and spiritually dead. He thought he was just the guy to
swing the C.O.E. back to real, pure spiritual worship.

## GEORGE GETS EGGS-ACTLY WHAT HE ASKS FOR

At age 23, Fox started preaching. He'd go to church, listen to the
sermon, then stand up and deliver a stinging counter-sermon of his

---

Through the early 20th century, boys wore dresses often up to age 5.

own. At every stop, he was beaten, kicked, and/or egged (a favorite form of criticism in farm country). He was imprisoned eight times between 1649 and 1673.

## CUTTING OUT THE MIDDLEMAN
In his late 20s, he had a revelation. The Lord wanted him to gather true believers into a new faith without priests, a faith that depended on the mystical communication between God and his believers. He called the new faith the Society of Friends.

From then on, his fame and following spread. His sermons were said to be so affecting that those who heard them quaked with emotion—thus the name at first derisively applied to his new faith, the Quakers. Now the crowds weren't throwing eggs at him anymore—they were listening instead.

## THE QUAKER EXPLOSION
George must have been doing something right. Within a few years, tens of thousands embraced the faith, despite the fact that they were mercilessly persecuted: whipped, beaten, imprisoned, even killed. Fox was persecuted wherever he went—England, Holland, Germany, even the West Indies and North America. He was beaten again and again even in relatively tolerant America.

## THE FRIENDS' AMERICAN FRIEND
When he returned to England in 1673, Fox was imprisoned one last time. But a Quaker pal—America's own William Penn, the founder of Pennsylvania—used his influence to get Fox released.

## THE END OF A FRIEND
The Society of Friends brethren (and sistren) continued to do missionary work and preach with increasingly less persecution until King William III established the Toleration Act of 1689, which gave all C.O.E. dissenters freedom of worship (except, of course, for those darn Roman Catholics).

Sadly, Fox only lived through two years of this tolerance—he died undramatically and quietly in London in 1691.

The Chinese invented the first waterproof umbrella using wax and lacquer.

# HOOTCHY-KOOTCHY

*Almost any kind of sexy dance was labeled a hootchy-kootchy dance in the early 20th century. It was first performed at the 1893 World's Columbia Exposition in Chicago by a dancer who called herself "Little Egypt."*

More than 21 million people visited the expo to see wonders like Edison's light bulb and Tesla's coil (not a birth control device, but an electrical transformer that shoots out lightning bolts when the charge builds). Not to mention a scary new ride known as the Ferris wheel. But the attraction that stole the show was nothing more than a sexy bump-and-grind dancer.

## BELLY UP TO THE STAGE

Back in Egypt, the shapely Fahreda Mahzar and her Syrian dancing girls were second-rate belly dancers who performed at parties and weddings. When Mahzar (calling herself "Little Egypt") opened an act at the expo called "the Streets of Cairo," she caused an immediate scandal. Little Egypt called the dance the "Coochee-Coochee," and newspapers reported that the belly dance far outshone any newfangled electrical wonders.

## WHERE DID YOU SAY YOU WERE FROM?

The dance was unheard of in Victorian America, where women wore skirts down to the ankle and corsets even to bed. Little Egypt performed in a semitransparent skirt—you could actually see her legs! The exposition's PR man, future New York congressman Sol Bloom, was inspired enough to pen the best-selling tune, the "Hootchy-Kootchy Dance." You probably know how it goes: "There's a place in France, where the naked ladies dance..."

## THE DANCE OF THE NO VEILS

Within a few years there were 22 "hootchy-kootchy" dancers at Coney Island alone, and imitators across the country. In 1896 Fahreda Mahzar resurfaced after being arrested at a raid on a stag party. She'd been dancing naked as a jaybird, her specialty, for the delighted guests—for $10 a head. Those stag parties must have paid well—Mahzar died in 1908 and left an estate of a quarter of a million dollars. Not bad for a woman who today might be dancing atop a bar.

**Shirley Temple received 135,000 presents on her eighth birthday.**

# WHO STARTED THE GREAT CHICAGO FIRE?

*Mrs. O'Leary's cow has finally been exonerated. And a guy called Peg Leg Sullivan has been pegged as the culprit.*

The Great Chicago Fire of 1871 burned for two days, during which 90,000 people lost their homes, 300 people died, and property valued at $192 million was destroyed. A great city rose out of the ashes of that disaster, but the question has always remained. Who started the fire?

### THE COW STORY

According to legend, the fire was started at about 9 P.M. while Mrs. Catherine O'Leary was milking her cows (the O'Learys had a small dairy business). The story that one of the cows kicked over a lantern appeared in an article, based on rumor, that ran in the *Chicago Evening Journal* the day after the fire. The paper didn't bother to question why a cow was being milked at nine o'clock at night, when most farmers and dairy folks are in bed.

The story was picked up by other papers and quickly became a legend with a life of its own. The Chicago Board of Police and Fire Commissioners investigated the scene a month later. The commissioners were certain that the fire began in the O'Leary barn, but they couldn't determine who started it after it was proven that Patrick and Catherine O'Leary were in bed at the time the fire started.

### PEG LEG'S STORY

The alarm was raised by Daniel "Peg Leg" Sullivan, a local colorful character. According to his statement, he was standing outside a neighbor's house when he saw the O'Learys's barn on fire. He rushed over and released the animals in the barn, but the fire spread before he could do anything to stop it. Sullivan then woke the O'Learys. By the time the first fire trucks arrived, the barn was destroyed and the fire had spread to some nearby structures.

---

Queen Elizabeth I of England suffered from anthophobia (fear of roses).

## NOT SO FAST, PEG LEG!

The cow story stuck for more than 100 years, until an amateur historian recently turned up several inconsistencies in Sullivan's story. For one thing, land records show that Sullivan couldn't have seen the barn from where he clamed to be standing because there was another building that blocked the view entirely. Besides that, since Mr. Sullivan had lost his leg in the Civil War and had a wooden leg, he couldn't have hobbled nearly 200 feet to get to the barn and then release all the animals before the barn was completely engulfed in flames. He also claimed to have yelled, "Fire!" several times before he reached the barn, but no one was ever found who heard him.

The obvious conclusion is that Peg Leg must have been in the barn when the fire started. He had a reason to be there because his mother owned a cow that was kept there and he'd often be in charge of its care and feeding. It's very likely that he either accidentally started the fire or was there when the fire started, and lied about it to avoid any unpleasant consequences.

## WHERE'S THE FIRE?

The original investigators should have noted the inconsistencies in Peg Leg's story, but they were eager to bury the issue. The Chicago Fire Department's failure to respond quickly and deal effectively with the fire while it could have been easily managed was the primary reason that most of downtown Chicago was leveled.

## FROM THE ASHES

No one knows what happened to Peg Leg after he testified. He probably decided to leave town quietly. As for the O'Learys, their house survived the fire; they sold their property in 1879 and bought another home in Chicago. Catherine became a recluse, leaving her home only when she had to, until her death in 1895. In 1997, the Chicago City Council passed a resolution that officially exonerated her of any responsibility for the fire. Today, the Chicago Fire Academy now occupies the area where the fire started; a Maltese cross painted on the floor marks the spot where the O'Learys' barn once stood.

After Larry Fine's stroke in 1970 the Three Stooges never performed together again.

# A DYNAMITE GUY

*If anybody ever needed a major reputation makeover, it was the man they called the "merchant of death."*

When Alfred Nobel invented dynamite in 1863, he thought he'd created a highly useful compound for construction and mining. Instead, it made him one of the most hated men in the world.

Dynamite made acts of terrorism much too easy. An assassin used a dynamite-filled bomb to kill Czar Alexander II of Russia in 1881. Even Nobel's youngest brother, Emil, had been killed years before in an explosion at the Nobel plant in Stockholm. In the U.S., a death caused by the transport of Nobel's "blasting oil" was considered murder. In France, a newspaper called Nobel the "merchant of death."

## UPSTAIRS MEETS DOWNSTAIRS

Meanwhile, in Austria, a beautiful but impoverished countess (whose mother had squandered the family fortune at the gambling tables) was working as governess to the daughters of the wealthy Baroness von Suttner. The baroness's son, Arthur von Suttner, had fallen in love with the governess, who besides having a very long name—Countess Bertha Kinsky von Chinic und Tettau—and being penniless, was seven years Arthur's senior. The family despaired, until Arthur's mother found what looked like the perfect solution: a newspaper ad for a job in faraway Paris.

> Wealthy, highly educated, elderly gentleman seeks lady of mature age, versed in languages, as secretary and supervisor of household.

The baroness made it clear to Bertha that she'd better apply for the job or else. The "elderly gentleman" was Alfred Nobel. He was 43 years old.

## APRIL IN PARIS

Bertha and Alfred Nobel hit it off immediately; she brought out the charming, witty side of him. She spoke several languages, she

---

Bill Gates is richer than the poorest 114 million people in the U.S. combined.

was sophisticated—and it was springtime in Paris. Alfred fell for her with a thud. When he asked her if "her heart was taken," she admitted that she'd only come to Paris for the money, so that she and her beloved Arthur could run away and get married someday.

## PEN PALS
And even though she and Arthur did exactly that, Bertha and Nobel stayed in touch over the years. Besides writing letters to Nobel, Bertha wrote a best-selling novel, *Lay Down Your Arms!*, detailing the horrors of war. She lectured and wrote and organized peace congresses—and passionately debated her views in letters to Nobel, who didn't really believe that Bertha's methods would be effective in ending war. But she won him over eventually.

## WHERE THERE'S A WILL...
Nobel's revised, handwritten will not only transformed his reputation, but was a testament to his feelings for Bertha. He left a small percentage of his millions to friends and relatives, but the bulk of his estate went to a fund, the interest of which was to be divided into five equal parts. Annual prizes were to be awarded for physics, chemistry, medicine, literature, and peace.

On December 10, 1905, the ninth anniversary of Alfred Nobel's death, the Nobel Peace Prize (the fifth to be awarded) was given to Bertha von Suttner, the woman who had inspired it.

\* \* \*

## NOBEL MISCELLANY

The amount of each prize varies with the income from the fund and currently is worth over $1 million.

No Nobel prizes were awarded for 1940, 1941, and 1942.
Prizes for literature were not awarded for 1914, 1918, and 1943.

### Noble Refusal?
Jean-Paul Sartre was the only honoree to turn down the prize voluntarily. He refused the Nobel Prize for Literature in 1964 because he thought the honor might interfere with his responsibility to his readers.

Apollonia, the patron saint of dentists, had her teeth pulled for refusing to renounce Christianity.

# WHATEVER LOLA WANTS...

*Meet the original. When Lola cracked the whip, men jumped.*
*Including King Ludwig of Bavaria.*

Munich, 1846. The notorious adventuress Lola Montez was ushered into the presence of 60-year-old King Ludwig of Bavaria. No one knows for sure what went on at the private meeting, but the story goes that Ludwig took one look at the 25-year-old Lola's ample bosom and asked, "Nature or art?" meaning, "Are they real?" Lola reportedly grabbed a pair of scissors from the king's desk and slit open the front of her dress, revealing that her remarkable endowments were indeed the work of nature.

Needless to say, King Ludwig fell hopelessly in love. Bavaria would never be the same.

## A BRAZEN HUSSY IS BORN

Ireland, 1821. Miss "Montez" was christened Eliza Gilbert. Her father was a well-born ensign in the British Army; her mother was not Spanish (as some stories would have it), but Irish, from a prominent Protestant family.

Eliza grew to be a dark-haired, strong-willed beauty. At age 16, she married a British Army lieutenant and went with him to India. The marriage didn't last long. Claiming that she caught her husband cheating on her, Eliza decided to go back to Britain. While onboard the ship she met another lieutenant and they had an affair, which continued when she got back to London. Her lieutenant husband found out about the affair and divorced her. Eliza's lover soon dropped her, leaving the penniless, 19-year-old divorcée shamed as an adulteress in a scandalous divorce.

## WHAT'S A GIRL TO DO?

Eliza wasn't the kind of girl who'd sit around feeling sorry for herself. Ever resourceful, she decided to make her future on the stage. At the time, flamenco dancing was all the rage in London, so Eliza took some lessons and went off to Cadiz, Spain, for further instruction. Less than a year later she returned to London as Maria

---

**Leonardo da Vinci made a sketch for contact lenses in the 15th century.**

Dolores de Porris y Montez—Lola Montez for short. She claimed to be the daughter of a Spanish noble family that had fallen on hard times.

## HER NAME WAS LOLA, SHE WAS A SHOWGIRL

Lola Montez made her dancing debut at Her Majesty's Theatre, London's foremost theater, in 1843. By all accounts, Lola wasn't much of a dancer. One critic said: "Her dancing was no dancing at all, but a physical invitation." She caused a sensation. Unfortunately, a couple of her former lovers revealed her true identity, and her booking was canceled. What did Lola care? A whole continent lay across the English Channel, just waiting to be conquered.

## SO MANY MEN, SO LITTLE TIME

Here's where Lola began building her larger-than-life reputation. The Victorians delicately referred to her as "La Grande Horizontale," which had something to do with her being horizontal a lot of the time. Her most famous conquests—besides Ludwig—were pianist-composer Franz Liszt and author Alexandre Dumas (who wrote *The Three Musketeers*). Liszt had a reputation as a great lover, but our Miss Lola apparently so exhausted the poor guy that he left her by sneaking out of their hotel. At least he was enough of a gentleman to pay the hotel owner on the way out—for the furniture he knew the enraged Lola would break.

## WHIPPED INTO SHAPE

In fact, her terrible temper was part of her public persona. She once whipped a German policeman who got in her way at a parade. The story only added to her lurid reputation, and thereafter she almost always carried a horsewhip.

With or without the whip, Lola cut a truly striking figure. She was an expert horsewoman and a fine pistol shot (having learned in India), and she rolled and smoked her own cigarettes (a novelty for women at that time).

By 1846 Lola found her way to Munich, where she had her famous meeting with Ludwig. The king was a hard-working, conservative family man, but he had a weakness for the ladies that Lola exploited to the utmost.

Oliver Wendell Holmes, Sr., discovered the adrenal gland.

## THAT'S COUNTESS LOLA TO YOU, BUDDY

Ludwig was utterly besotted. He spent millions on her and even
made her a countess. But that didn't stop her from dallying with
other men. On one memorable occasion, Lola was knocked
unconscious when she hit her head on a chandelier while being
carried on the shoulders of a group of drunken young admirers at a
New Year's party.

## BAVARIAN CREAM

Poor Ludwig became a laughingstock. But that was only the
beginning. Lola convinced the king to fire his entire cabinet and
replace them with people loyal to her. Naturally, the Bavarian
people became increasingly hostile to both Lola and Ludwig.
Things came to a head when Munich's university students rioted
after Lola's large dog attacked one of their professors. Lola
demanded that Ludwig close down the university, which only
made things worse. Now everyone was rioting. Poor Ludwig was
forced to abdicate his throne, and Lola had to flee the country.

## THE LAND OF OPPORTUNITY

She married again—a kind of messy affair—and when it was over,
she set sail for the shores of America. In 1853 she arrived in San
Francisco and headed for the California gold fields, where the
miners—a crude lot—booed her off the stage.

She married yet again and settled in bucolic Grass Valley,
California, for a time, where she wrote her memoirs and a book
of beauty secrets. She also starred in a play about her time in
Bavaria. But she hadn't lost her edge. She threatened to horsewhip one newspaper editor who had given her a bad review, and
dared another critic to a duel.

## CURTAIN DOWN

There's no denying that Lola's two years in Bavaria marked the
zenith of her career. She died in New York, in 1861, of pneumonia
after suffering a stroke. She was 39 years old. A tombstone in
Brooklyn identifies her only as Eliza Gilbert.

---

Marian Anderson was the first African American to perform at the Metropolitan Opera.

# PIN MONEY

*Walter Hunt was a prolific inventor who wasn't in it for the money. What a concept!*

Pins are one of the earliest human artifacts. They were first made of thorns, bone, or wood, and later out of metals such as bronze and gold. The fibula, often called a prototype of the safety pin, was used as decorative clothing fastener throughout history and was especially popular with the ancient Greeks and Romans, who used it to hold their togas up.

## INVENTION BY ACCIDENT

Fast forward to 1849, New York City. Mechanic and amateur inventor Walter Hunt was sitting at his desk twisting a piece of brass wire around in his fingers, trying to come up with an idea that he could sell to pay off a $15 debt. He eventually twisted the wire into a loop with a point on one end and a clasp on the other. Voila! The humble safety pin was born. Hunt received a patent for what he called "a new and useful improvement in the make or form of dress-pins." He later sold the patent for $400.

## SEW WHAT?

In 1834, he'd invented a sewing machine, but he didn't patent it because he was afraid that it would put seamstresses out of work. Twenty years later, Elias Howe invented a sewing machine with a similar design and went for the patent. He became a millionaire after the courts settled a patent battle with Isaac Singer in his favor. Singer had argued that since Hunt had invented it first, Howe's patent wasn't valid, but the court sided with Howe.

## AND THAT'S NOT ALL

Hunt eventually patented over 100 inventions, including a fountain pen, a repeating rifle, a knife sharpener, a restaurant steam table, a streetcar bell, a coal-burning stove, artificial stone, road-sweeping machinery, a velocipede (an early bicycle), a tree-cutting saw... and much more. But he rarely cashed in on any of his inventions; he just enjoyed tinkering and inventing, and always sold his patents quickly and for very little money.

What have you been up to lately?

---

Freud pioneered the use of cocaine as a local anesthetic when he was a neurologist.

# SWEET REVENGE

*Pioneering "muckraker" Ida Tarbell brought down powerful monopoly Standard Oil at a time when women weren't even supposed to go to college.*

Ida Tarbell grew up in a Pennsylvania oil town where her father was a successful independent oil refiner (this was in 1857 when such things were possible). The family lived on easy street until a shady agreement between refiners associated with Standard Oil maven John D. Rockefeller and the railroads gave Standard Oil below-market transport rates. The Tarbell family business spiraled down as young Ida watched. But Ida would someday have her revenge.

The family still had enough to send career-minded Ida to school where, at Allegheny College, she was the only woman in her class of 1,880. After graduating, she tried teaching, but hated it so much she quit within two years.

### AU REVOIR, PENNSYLVANIA
Miss Tarbell moved to Paris and started writing articles for the magazines of the day, which is how she attracted the attention of fiery Irish-American magazine publisher, Sidney McClure. He lured her to New York where she began writing for *McClure's*.

### HELLO, NEW YORK
Tarbell had come to the right place. She finally had the opportunity to expose the wrongdoing she'd seen first-hand as a child. She spent two years putting together a series of articles on Standard Oil in which she painted a picture of a bullying corporation with a reckless, scheming leader, the same John D. Rockefeller who had ruined her father's business. The first installment was published in 1902; the entire 19-part series was collected into a book in 1904. The series was a smash hit, and it gave a new energy to the antitrust movement. The Supreme Court decided to break up Standard Oil and Congress passed a bill to guard against future monopolies. Ida Tarbell had her revenge.

But she also had her quirks—scads of them.

---

Freud's praise of cocaine to treat minor pains resulted in a wave of cocaine addiction in Europe.

## A WOMAN'S PLACE IS YOU-KNOW-WHERE

Tarbell was outraged when she found out that McClure was having an extramarital affair, so she quit *McClure's* in a huff, and started her own magazine, *The American Magazine*, which didn't sell as well as McClure's, but which would provide her with a new notoriety.

In a two-part series examining American women and the women's rights movement, she concluded that women were too emotional and fragile to either vote or work—career women were freaks and misfits, doomed to failure and dissatisfaction.

## YOU GET OUTTA HERE, GIRL!

Well, you can imagine the uproar. Feminists far and wide lambasted her. And although she went on to write books and articles and lecture all her life, her later career was tarnished by the anti-feminist views she continued to hold until her death from pneumonia in 1944.

In fact, when Tarbell described those pathetic career girls, she'd been talking about herself. She never married, never fell in love, never bore children, and had few close friends, male or female. And even though she's considered one of the top investigative journalists of all time, she tarnished her own image, so that even today, she doesn't have any friends or admirers among modern feminists.

\* \* \*

## THE LAST WORD ON EDUCATION

**H. L. Hunt:** The oil tycoon was home-schooled, but left home when he was a teenager. When he was interviewed many years later on *60 Minutes*, he said, "I didn't go to high school, and I didn't go to grade school, either. Education, I think, is for refinement and is probably a liability."

There really was a Dr. Scholl; William Scholl was a podiatrist who became a shoemaker.

# WHERE'S JIMMY?

*In a scenario straight out of* The Sopranos, *the powerful union boss in America made like a magician's assistant and disappeared, never to be seen again.*

At 17, James Riddle Hoffa quit school and went to work unloading produce from rail cars at a food warehouse. It proved to be a fertile field for a budding unionist. The shifts lasted 12 hours, the workers only got paid when they were actually loading or unloading, and the foreman was an abusive s.o.b. known to the workers as "Little Bastard."

In 1932, Hoffa helped organize a work stoppage just as a trainload of fresh strawberries arrived. Management buckled and Hoffa was on his way.

## HOFFA JOINS THE UNION

The Teamsters Union, which represents truck drivers and other workers in the trucking industry, was founded in 1899. In 1933, just a year after Hoffa's first successful strike, the union hired him as an organizer. Instead of a salary, he was paid a small percentage of the dues of all the new members he signed up. He was perfect for the job. All he had to do was enforce the innovative method the union had for recruiting new members—they'd go to the owner of a business and tell him to sign up all of his employees or they'd firebomb his trucks. After a few trucks were blasted to smithereens, word got around that the Teamsters meant business.

There were strikes to organize, too, a dangerous business in those days. Hoffa recalled: "If you went on strike, you got your head broken. I was hit so many times with nightsticks, clubs, and brass knuckles that I can't even remember where the bruises are. Every time I showed up on the picket line, I got thrown in jail. Every time they released me, I went back to the picket line." In one 24-hour period, he was arrested and jailed 18 times.

## MARRIED TO THE MOB

Hoffa worked his way up through the ranks. In 1952, he was elected one of the union's international vice presidents. Five years later— after the union president was sentenced to five years in prison for stealing union funds and tax evasion—Hoffa was elected president.

James H. Salisbury, a red-meat advocate, gave his name to Salisbury steak.

That same year, he became the subject of various government investigations into corruption. And what about the union's relationship with the Mafia?

Hoffa never denied those ties: "These organized crime figures are the people you should know if you're going to avoid having anyone interfere with your strike, and that's what we know them for...We make it our business, and the head of any union who didn't would be a fool."

## PRESIDENT FOR LIFE

The government nailed Hoffa in 1964, when he was convicted of misappropriating union funds, fraud, and jury tampering. He was sentenced to 13 years in prison. After exhausting all of his appeals, he started serving his sentence at the federal prison at Lewisburg, Pennsylvania. He refused to resign as union president, and his conviction didn't seem to hurt his popularity among most union members.

## THE OTHER PRESIDENT

Hoffa was paroled in 1971, thanks to President Richard Nixon, under the condition that he resign his office with the Teamsters and refrain from union activity till 1980. It was later revealed that the Teamsters had made quite a few illegal campaign contributions to the Nixon campaign. Tsk, tsk.

## BACK IN BUSINESS

Hoffa ignored the restrictions he'd agreed to and started a campaign to undermine the authority of Frank Fitzsimmons (his handpicked successor) and to get himself reelected. Very risky, because it wasn't just the government who didn't want him back in charge. The mobsters who controlled the union didn't want him back either. They were happy enough with Fitzsimmons and, wanting to keep their profile as low as possible, wanted no part of the attention that Hoffa's return would bring.

## STOOD UP BY THE MOB

Jimmy Hoffa told his wife he'd be home for dinner as he left for an afternoon meeting at a restaurant called the Machus Red Fox in Bloomfield Township, Michigan, on July 30, 1975. He was supposed to meet with Anthony (Tony Pro) Provenzano, a New

---

**Maya Ling Yin, a 21-year-old Yale architectural student, designed the Vietnam Veterans Memorial.**

Jersey Teamster official and reputed Mafia figure, and Anthony (Tony Jack) Giacalone, a Mafia enforcer from Detroit. When Hoffa arrived, neither Provenzano nor Giacalone were there, so he waited outside in the parking lot. He made two calls from a pay phone while he was waiting.

He disappeared sometime that afternoon. His car was found the next morning in the restaurant parking lot. Both Provenzano and Giacalone denied that they had seen Hoffa on that day or even that they'd scheduled a meeting with him. It was obvious that both men had made a point of creating airtight alibis for that entire day. Giacalone was reported to have told a Hoffa associate, "Maybe he took a little trip."

### RIDE OF CHUCKIE?
Hoffa's longtime friend Charles (Chuckie) O'Brien came under immediate suspicion because although Hoffa had treated him like a son for many years, their relationship had become increasingly strained, especially because Chuckie had recently started working for Frank Fitzsimmons.

Hoffa's family believed that Chuckie used some pretense to get him to accept a ride to another location, that in classic Mafia style, Hoffa had been set up by someone he trusted and "taken for a ride." Chuckie was the only person who could have persuaded Hoffa to get in his car—and there were plenty of holes in Chuckie's alibi for that day. A search of his car turned up a strand of hair and specks of skin and blood, but they couldn't be linked to Hoffa at the time.

Jimmy Hoffa's body was never found. He was declared legally dead in 1982.

### FBI, CSI, AND DNA
In September 2001, the FBI announced that DNA tests had been performed on the strand of hair that was found in Chuckie O'Brien's car. Those DNA tests confirmed that Hoffa had been in Chuckie's car, but it still wasn't sufficient evidence to charge O'Brien with murder. Chuckie O'Brien continues to deny any involvement in Hoffa's disappearance, and the FBI considers the Hoffa case still open and under investigation.

---

The almost 20-foot-tall female atop the U.S. Capitol is named the Statue of Freedom.

# PROBLEMS, PROBLEMS!

*Math is hard…just ask Galois.*

Galois's theory of algebraic equations would influence modern mathematics and assure his lasting fame. Too bad he was jinxed.

## MATH PROBLEMS

Evariste Galois, born on October 25, 1811, was an award-winning student when he began his studies at the Lycée Louis-le-Grand in 1823. But when he discovered mathematics he became so absorbed in geometry, algebra, and calculus that he neglected his other studies. His mind soared—and his grades crashed.

And math wasn't always such a cakewalk either. His teachers, confronted with a prodigy, tried to make him conform to standard practices. Galois defended his right to get the answers his own way, but all it got him was a reputation for insolence.

## RESPECT YOUR ELDERS

Impatient to study only mathematics, Galois took an entrance exam to the famous École Polytechnique for scientists and mathematicians. His professors pointed out that he needed to take some recommended courses first, but at the wise old age of 17, Galois decided to ignore their advice, and didn't take the classes. He failed the exam.

## LOST AND FOUNDERING

Galois stayed on at his old school and finally found a teacher who encouraged his brilliance by letting him create his own mathematical theories. Still only 17, Galois published his first mathematical paper, "Proof of a Theorem on Periodic Continued Fractions." That same year he created a theorem of equations that a respected mathematician, Augustin Cauchy, promised to submit to the prestigious Académie des Sciences. Galois thought this would at last begin his career in mathematics, but Cauchy never submitted Galois's paper, claiming that he lost it. Could things get worse?

The lights on the Las Vegas Strip were dimmed when Dean Martin and Frank Sinatra died.

## THINGS GET WORSE

If school wasn't bad enough, life at home turned tragic. A priest who hated Galois's father (who happened to be the mayor of Bourg-la-Reine) for his pro-democracy politics forged some nasty rhymes about the locals and signed the mayor's name to them. This caused a scandal that so unnerved Galois, Sr. that he committed suicide.

A month later, Galois, still mourning and distraught, tried to enter l'École Polytechnique for the second time. Quelle disaster! The legend goes that Galois impatiently threw an eraser at one obtuse professor. And when examiners asked the brilliant boy how he got his answers, he imperiously pointed out that his methods were obvious. The reaction of the examiners was just as obvious... they failed him.

## A DEAD END

The examination failures could be traced to Galois's abrasive personality, but other misfortunes were just, well...darned unfortunate. Galois submitted a paper directly to the Académie des Sciences through its secretary, Joseph Fourier. Math historians agree that Galois's brilliant work should have brought him the Grand Prize in Mathematics—if the paper hadn't been lost when Joseph Fourier inconveniently dropped dead!

## CAMPUS UNREST

Galois continued to publish papers, and was finally settling down in school when politics brought him new troubles. In July 1830, France experienced an anti-monarchy, republican uprising. King Charles X quit the throne and split the scene. Republican riots erupted throughout Paris, but the students in Galois's school were locked inside so they couldn't take part.

Galois tried to scale the wall to join the republican protests against bringing in a new monarch. When he couldn't get over the wall, he wrote a letter to the Gazette des Écoles protesting being locked in. Naturellement, he was expelled.

## FIGHTING MAD

Galois joined the battle against the monarchy as an officer in the republican Artillery of the National Guard. Nineteen of the

National Guards, including Galois (just his luck) were arrested for conspiracy to overthrow the government. Some months later, during a dinner to celebrate the officers' eventual acquittal, Galois raised his glass…and a dagger, making threats against the new king. He went straight from that celebration to prison.

Galois was acquitted on June 15, but within a month he was back in the pokey, this time for wearing the forbidden uniform of the now-disbanded National Guard. In prison, Galois received yet another rejection from the Académie des Sciences. They did encourage him to publish a more complete version of his theory, but that didn't exactly cheer the jailed genius. Galois tried to kill himself, but other prisoners intervened, so he failed at that, too.

## LOVE AND DEATH
In jail Galois discovered that there was more to life than math and politics. There was also l'amour. He fell for Stephanie, the daughter of the prison physician. She discouraged his affection, but that didn't stop him—hey, at this point he was used to rejection. On May 30, 1832, Galois agreed to a duel over Stephanie's honor. With typical bad luck, Galois was wounded in the duel and left to die, not only by his opponent, but also by his own assistants. A peasant found the boy and took him to the hospital, but it was too late to save his life. He died at the age of 20.

## PLAYING CATCH-UP
So what was Galois's theory, anyway? It's called "group theory," and it's used to analyze systems that have symmetrical elements. Galois used it to analyze polynomial equations, but it's since been used to solve such wide-ranging problems as Rubik's Cube, WWII's Enigma cipher, and Fermat's Last Theorem. It also has applications in genetics, nuclear physics, and quantum mechanics. It took until September, 1846, for someone to finally reread Galois's theory and understand it: Joseph Liouville, who published it and demonstrated its importance to the Académie. And about a century later an engineer named Murphy formed his own theory, which Galois would have had no trouble proving: if anything can go wrong…it will.

Wilbur and Orville Wright had two other brothers: Lorin and Reuchlin.

# PUTTING GERMS OUT TO PASTEUR

*Imagine that you're Louis Pasteur and you've just discovered the germ theory of disease. Now you know that germs are in the air and on everything you touch. They attack, they kill—and antibiotics won't be invented for another century. Wouldn't you be a little paranoid, too?*

Louis Pasteur (1822–1895) founded the science of microbiology. He's probably most famous for being the "Pasteur" in "pasteurization," the process he developed that removes bacteria from milk. Every day, he worked with invisible killers like streptococcus, staphylococcus, and the bacteria and viruses that cause diseases like anthrax, cholera, and rabies. Is it any wonder he became obsessed with contamination, contagion, and cleanliness?

## MISTER CLEAN

Pasteur's discovery that germs were everywhere haunted him. He spent a lot of time compulsively washing and rewashing his hands— he even washed the bar of soap!

He preferred to be considered rude rather than shake anyone's hand. The idea of having a stranger's—or even a friend's—germs on his hands repulsed him. If anyone managed to grab his hand to shake it, Pasteur immediately rushed to the sink.

His fear of contamination extended to the dining room. First he would examine the bread and remove any suspect particles. Then he would carefully examine the glasses he was going to drink from and wipe away any offending dirt with a napkin. During all this, his family respectfully waited to begin their own meals.

## BULLETS OVER BACTERIA

During the Franco-Prussian War, Pasteur's son, Jean-Baptiste, served in the French army. Jean-Baptiste was lucky enough to be stationed in an army hospital. But to his papa—*sacre bleu*, the germs! Louis actually wrote to his son's commanding officer requesting that Jean-Baptiste be sent to the front and away from the contagion in the hospital. In Pasteur's mind, flying bullets on the frontline were safer than all those germ-ridden sick and wounded men. Despite his father's concerns, Jean-Baptiste survived the war and lived to be 56 years old, a long life for that era.

---

William Blackstone invented a home washing machine in 1874 as a birthday gift for his wife.

# DAME OF DEATH

*Jessica Mitford's book,* The American Way of Death, *exposed the rampant corruption in America's funeral industry, but there was a lot of life in the "Dame of Death" herself.*

Someone once said that Jessica Mitford was born a communist. Maybe that's why most of the members of the large aristocratic family she was born in to in England in 1917 didn't understand her—and why she started saving money to run away from home before she was in her teens.

## YOU HAD ME AT "PERFECT SPECIMEN"

Political zeal ran in the family—Jessica and her sister Nancy discussed going to Germany and murdering Hitler, while their sisters Unity and Diana were ardent fascists and big fans of Der Fürher. When Unity hung swastikas on the walls of the girls' sitting room, Jessica scratched hammers and sickles into the window panes in retaliation. Unity went on to fall in love with Hitler and killed herself when she realized he wouldn't marry her—though he did call her a "perfect specimen of Aryan womanhood." More on the other fascist sister as our story unfolds...

## ADIOS, DAD!

Mitford met her romantic and political match, Edmond Romilly, her cousin and a nephew of Winston Churchill who had run off from England as a teenager to fight for the Loyalist cause in the Spanish Civil War. When the couple eloped in Spain in 1937, Jessica's father sent British agents to bring his rebellious daughter back. When she wouldn't return, she was disinherited. Did she give a hoot? Unlikely.

## BYE-BYE, EDMOND

Jessica and Edmond immigrated to northern California in 1939 and started a family. But WWII loomed, so the patriotic Edmond joined the Canadian Air Force. When the plane he was in went down over the North Sea, Mitford was so desperate to hear of his fate, she asked his Uncle Winston for help. He told her the sad news. Her husband was dead. And, he added, her sister Diana

---

**Before disposable diapers? Marion Donovan made the first diaper cover out of a shower curtain.**

(who'd married Oswald Mosley, England's facist party leader) had been thrown in jail for supporting the Nazis.

Mitford was now a 24-year-old widow, a mother, and a stranger in a strange land.

## TENNIS, ANYONE? NOT ME.

Two years later, Mitford married radical labor lawyer Robert Treuhaft. Together, they joined the Communist Party. When she— inevitably—was called before the California State Senate Hearings on Un-American Activities in 1952, Mitford refused to answer any questions about any of her associations. She wouldn't even admit to being a member of the Berkeley Tennis Club.

## THE WAY TO THE WAY

Treuhaft encouraged Mitford to write a book about American funeral practices. The resulting exposé—the sardonic, witty best-seller *The American Way of Death*—brought to light the exorbitant prices charged by funeral home directors who called themselves "grief counselors," and the high-priced coffins they foisted on the recently bereaved so that their "loved ones" (as corpses were sinisterly renamed) could rest in the utmost comfort while rotting underground. The huge best-seller was published in 1963 to furious criticism from the funeral industry and great interest from everywhere else.

Mitford followed it up with a string of books in the 1960s and 1970s: *The American Way of Birth, Kind and Unusual Punishment: The Prison Business, The Trial of Dr. Spock*, and an exposé of The Famous Writers School that drove the organization into bankruptcy.

## AND A ROCK STAR, TOO?

In her late 70s, Mitford surprised her family by taking up singing in a group she called Decca (her nickname) & the Dectones. The group opened for Cyndi Lauper at the Paradise Lounge, a nightclub in San Francisco, California, and released an album on which the 77-year-old Mitford let loose in such songs as "Maxwell's Silver Hammer."

Having done it all, she died a year later, in 1996, and was cremated in a cost-conscious $15.45 container.

---

The inventor of the diaper cover named them after herself: Marion Donovan's Boaters.

# MAN WITH A MISSION

*Albert Schweitzer, born in 1875 in Alsace when it was part of Germany, was a genius. He had degrees in theology and philosophy, and a great job teaching at the University of Strasbourg. He had written the definitive book on Bach and a religious text called* The Quest of the Historical Jesus—*all by the time he was 31. When Albert told his family that he wanted to join the Paris Missionary Society and go to work in the French colony of Gabon in darkest Africa, they were appalled.*

He meant well. Albert wanted to atone for the crimes committed by the white Europeans who had destroyed the African way of life. In 1913, with a degree in tropical medicine, he learned that the Paris Missionary Society considered him a dangerous "free thinker" who "could only disrupt the mission enterprise and confuse the natives with theological improvisations."

## ALBERT OF THE JUNGLE
Unfazed, Schweitzer managed to pull together enough resources to start building a hospital in Lambaréné, Gabon, in 1913. He and his wife, Helene, began seeing patients in a chicken coop, thereby providing the first modern medical care their African patients had ever had. But WWI broke out a year later and the Schweitzers, who were Germans living in a French colony, were confined to prisoner-of-war camps. Upon their release they went back to work, and over the years their once-tiny medical facility grew into an internationally renowned hospital.

## A NEW REVERENCE FOR LIFE
What made Albert Schweitzer a household name was a philosophy he called "reverence for life," the practically unheard-of moral code that the life and well-being of every living thing on earth was equally important. "Reverence for life is the ethic of love expanded to embrace the universe." Although this sounds like the lyrics of a 1960s folk song, at the time it was a radical theory, and very influential—not to mention controversial.

## THERE'S LIFE IN THE OLD GUY YET
Schweitzer's doctrine of reverence won him a the 1952 Nobel

---

Marie Antoinette's amusements included dressing up as a shepherdess and milkmaid.

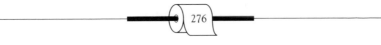

Peace Prize. He used the $33,000 prize money to expand his hospital and build a leper colony. In a 1956 Gallup poll of Americans, he was voted the fourth most admired man in the world.

By the late 1950s, he'd become a serious activist against nuclear testing, which didn't do much for his popularity with the U.S. government. He was branded a kook—or worse. America was in a serious arms race with the Russians and anyone who didn't follow suit was suspected of being on the wrong side.

However, the good doctor kept his day job and treated patients in Lambaréné until his death at age 90 in 1965. His daughter, Rhena, carried on his work and remains active in her father's interests and projects to this day.

**Epilogue:** During a trip to America, Albert Schweitzer was approached by two young girls who thought he was Albert Einstein and wanted his autograph. Schweitzer didn't want to let the girls down, so he signed: "Albert Einstein, by his friend Albert Schweitzer."

\* \* \*

## WHAT THEY HAVE TO SAY ABOUT THE REST OF US

"The great masses of the people will more easily fall victim to a big lie than to a small one." —Hitler

"You can fool all the people some of the time, and some of the people all the time, but you cannot fool all the people all the time." —Abraham Lincoln

"A single death is a tragedy, a million deaths is a statistic."
                                        —Joseph Stalin

"Three kinds—commonplace men, remarkable men, and lunatics." —Mark Twain

"I never met a man I didn't like." —Will Rogers

"Men are like wine—some turn to vinegar, but the best improve with age." —Pope John XXIII

---

President Wilson made Mother's Day a national holiday in 1914.

# THE FURTHER ADVENTURES OF MR. WATSON

*Thomas Watson was only 22 when he got that famous phone call from Alexander Graham Bell. He had his whole life in front of him and he spent it in a dizzying array of vocations. You could say that he was an inventor who couldn't stop reinventing himself.*

It's one of the most famous moments in the history of invention. Alexander Graham Bell has been struggling for weeks to get his telephone contraption to work. He suddenly spills some acid on his pants and yells: "Mr. Watson! Come here! I want to see you!" Watson, sitting in the next room behind a closed door, hears the scream over his crude telephone receiver. The first telephone call has been made—and the world will never be the same.

## THE MAN BEHIND THE MAN

Most historians doubt that the "spilled acid" incident ever occurred, but nobody doubts that Thomas Augustus Watson was an essential contributor to the invention of the telephone. He was only 22 on that momentous day in 1876, when he got that famous phone call, but Bell might never have made it if it hadn't been for Watson's knowledge of electrical devices, particularly wound-coil electrical devices, which were the key to Bell's big breakthrough.

Fifteen years after its invention in 1876, there were five million phones in America.

## COMPANY MAN

Watson worked for several years as the Bell Telephone Company's chief repairman, and testified for the company at patent infringement trials.

He also invented the telephone booth—his prototype was a tunnel of blankets used to insulate his voice so his landlady wouldn't complain about the noise. In 1883, he perfected the design using a wood frame, domed top, ventilator, windows, and a desk with a pen and ink.

By Susan B. Anthony's death, only four states (WY, CO, IA, UT) had allowed women to vote.

## THE MANY LIVES OF THOMAS WATSON

By the time he was 27, flush with patent royalties and eager to start new ventures, he quit Bell and tried farming for a while, but he didn't find it...um...fruitful. (Sorry.)

Next thing you know, he's got a machine shop, building marine engines, and the U.S. Navy ship *The Maine* is destroyed in Cuba (precipitating the Spanish-American War). Well, Watson's business took off, morphing into a Boston shipbuilding venture that managed the production of scads of ships, including two 400-ton torpedo boats and a 3,000-ton cruiser.

In Braintree, Massachusetts, he helped with the construction of schools—including the town's first night school and first kindergarten—and often paid teachers from his own pocket. He established the town's first electric plant and streetlights.

In 1903, he took up geology at MIT, then traveled to Alaska and California to prospect for precious ores.

In 1910, at the age of 56, Watson went to England to study acting, joined a Shakespeare company and eventually founded his own acting company. He returned to the U.S., gave public readings of the great Bard (as well as Browning, the Bible, and Greek drama) and adapted two Dickens novels for the stage.

## REACH OUT AND TOUCH SOMEONE

In 1915, as part of the launch of transatlantic telephone service, Watson and Bell reenacted their famous conversation, this time with Watson in San Francisco and Bell in New York. In response to Bell's "Mr. Watson! Come here! I want to see you!" Watson replied he would be glad to "but that it would take more than a week."

## HANGING UP

It's kind of ironic that a man whose fame was built on the spoken word would spend his final years enamored of an Indian mystic who had taken a vow of silence. At the age of 78, seeking spiritual knowledge, Watson traveled to England to meet the "Avatar of the Age," Meher Baba, an intense, enigmatic seer who communicated by using an alphabet board to spell out messages. At their first meeting at a country retreat, Baba placed his hand on Watson's head and the elderly inventor wept for 15 minutes. He later remarked, "Today is the first time I have experienced what divine love is." Three years later, in 1934, Thomas Watson had his last adventure; he died at his winter home in Pass-Grille Key, Florida.

# PUNOGRAPHY

*Did you know that the lowly pun goes all the way back to ancient Egypt? Surely you've heard of Cleopatra...the queen of denial. (Ouch.) To show you how sorry we are that we had to do that, we'd like to present a few puns that you'll like a lot better—or possibly hate a lot more, depending on your point of view.*

Brigham Young, the founder of the Mormon religion, had so many wives that someone was moved to say, "Pretty girls in Utah mostly marry Young."

The Emperor Nero was upset because the games at the Colosseum weren't making as much money as they used to. He called the manager into his august presence and demanded an explanation. "It's not my fault, sire," said the trembling manager, "It's because the lions are eating up the prophets."

Show me where Stalin is buried and I'll show you a communist plot.

Did Howard Johnson open his first drive-in restaurant for people who wanted to curb their appetites?

The Dalai Lama had to have a tooth pulled, but when he got to the dentist's office, he refused any sort of painkiller. It wasn't because of his religious beliefs—he just wanted to transcend dental medication.

Was Betty Crocker a flour child?

Does Emeril Lagasse correspond with pan pals?

Did Grace Kelly collect royalties?

Was Richard Nixon's downfall due to a staff infection?

Could you say that Jimmy and Rosalynn Carter are just Plains folk?

# ATTILA THE HEN

*We got to wondering: Where does someone like the outspoken, straight-backed Margaret Thatcher, a.k.a Britain's "Iron Lady," spring from? Full-grown from her father's head, like Athena? In a way, yes.*

Margaret Hilda Roberts was born over her parents' grocery store in Grantham—a town in eastern England—on October 13, 1925. She helped out in the store as a child, but she was way too clever to last long behind the counter. When she was nine, she won a poetry reading competition at school. The school principal told her that she was lucky to win, but little Maggie replied: "I wasn't lucky. I deserved it." Whoa. Where did she get all that chutzpah—enough, eventually, to take her to the highest nonroyal spot in the British government?

## A CHIP OFF THE GROCER'S BLOCK
Her dad, Alfred Roberts, was a grocer—but that's not all. He was also a local politician who held down a variety of jobs including mayor of Grantham. He and his daughter spent their time at the dinner table chewing over politics and finance. Mum and dad were staunch Conservatives—the English version of the U.S.'s Republican Party. Thatcher later proudly described her home as "practical, serious, and intensely religious."

## PARTY GIRL
She began studying chemistry at Oxford in 1943. But you can't keep a party girl down. Before you could say William F. Buckley, she'd joined the Oxford University Conservative Association. (Whooo-ee! Just imagine the hijinks that went on at those get-togethers!) And because she loved to be in charge of things, she soon became its president. Her life in politics had begun.

## THE PURSE COMES TO POWER
Fast forward to May 1979. Margaret Thatcher, the grocer's daughter, blondish coif straight from the hairdresser's and schoolmarm face almost—but not quite—smiling, stood chirpily on the steps of 10 Downing Street in London. She'd just become Britain's first—and

so far only—prime minister to carry a purse. In fact, that purse became her trademark, something for fans and foes alike to snicker about.

## INSIDE BRITISH POLITICS

She hadn't been elected, though. Here's the way it works in Britain. Thatcher had become leader of the Conservative Party in February 1975, so when her party won a big majority in the 1979 election, she was automatically named prime minister. She made it clear from the beginning who was in charge, too. "I don't mind how much my ministers talk, as long as they do what I say," she said in 1980. (Shades of little Maggie and the principal.)

## THE BITTER END

It was that unbending belief in her own opinions that did her in in the end—partly because of her fierce opposition to the European Community's inevitable move toward economic and monetary union. "They're a weak lot some of them in Europe you know. Weak, feeble," she once had the nerve to say.

But when, in 1990, her party began to oust her as party leader (what Thatcher called "treachery with a smile on its face"), she did notice that inevitability and, giving her greatest parliamentary performance, resigned in 1990.

## WHAT? NOT "MISS CONGENIALITY?"

A month later, Queen Elizabeth awarded her the Order of Merit as a consolation prize. In 1992, little Maggie became Baroness Thatcher of Kesteven and, in 1995, a member of the Most Noble Order of the Garter. In the years since her resignation, the baroness occasionally gives one of her trademark purses away to charity, to be auctioned off. And they invariably fetch thousands of dollars. That'll show 'em.

*Note:* The editors would love to take credit for the title of this article, but they admit to pilfering it from the very witty Clement Freud—British raconteur, serial womanizer, and grandson of Sigmund.

Oberlin College was the first U.S. college to admit women.

# WHO WAS THAT MASKED MAN?

*He's one of history's most intriguing mysteries. After three centuries, his legend lives on.*

In a high wig and pretty pumps to make him taller, Louis XIV lorded it over France. From 1643 to 1715, this height-challenged dandy was France's Sun King, the envy of the entire world. While Louis XIV presided over his glittering court at Versailles, any noble or commoner who failed to please him could land in that infamous French pokey—the Bastille.

On September 18, 1698, a new governor named Benigne d'Auvergue de Saint-Mars took over the Bastille. The Bastille's deputy wrote that Saint-Mars "brought with him, in a litter, a longtime prisoner, whom he had in custody in Pignerol and whom he kept always masked, and whose name has not been given to me or recorded." The deputy noted in his records that this prisoner was well treated (at least in the eyes of the authorities; nobody asked the prisoner) and allowed to attend Catholic mass on Sundays and holidays…where the prisoner always wore a black velvet mask.

## A KING'S IRON-FISTED RULE

Curiosity swirled around the prisoner who was not allowed to speak to anyone on pain of death. Who was this unlucky soul who had so upset the king? Was he a famous noble? Would friends try to free this prisoner if they knew his identity? Or was the prisoner kept hidden because his face would have resembled the country's most famous face—was the prisoner a relative of the Sun King? When the masked prisoner finally died in the Bastille in 1703, Saint-Mars buried him under the name "Marchioly," a name recorded in the parish church register along with the prisoner's age of 45. The authorities thought that would be the end of the prisoner's story. Wrong! Whoever Marchioly was, curiosity failed to die with him. Instead, the legend of "the Mask" grew.

## BEHIND THE MASK

The writer who most roused the public interest over the identity and plight of the Mask was Voltaire. Influential writers were always in danger of imprisonment in the Sun King's France. For Voltaire, who believed that all men were as noble as kings, spending time in the Bastille became as common as catching a cold. In 1717, while locked up in the Bastille, Voltaire decided to do some investigative journalism. Speaking to authorities and prisoners, he searched for the true story of the prisoner who'd worn the mask.

Though Voltaire's reports seem heavily doused with dramatic license, they fired the public imagination. Voltaire told his readers that during the early years of imprisonment, the Mask had dressed in the finest lace and linen. Tall and good-looking, the Mask enjoyed playing the guitar. And (this was the bombshell) this cultivated prisoner had been forced to wear a mask made of iron! Voltaire wrote that the Mask was riveted together around the prisoner's skull with a hinged lower jaw that made it possible to eat.

## ANYONE'S BEST GUESS

Voltaire also hinted that he knew the prisoner's true identity. But he wasn't the only guy with a theory. King Louis XIV made royal enemies as easily as he changed his royal wig and pumps. Among the famous of Louis's masked prisoner candidates:

• **Nicholas Fouquet:** The French Minister of Finance was arrested, supposedly for corruption, but more likely because Fouquet was just too stylish. Fouquet's glittering palace at Vaux-le-Vicomte not only inspired Versailles, but the jealous Sun King furnished Versailles with treasure confiscated from Fouquet's palace. Had the Sun King, in a jealous rage, forced Fouquet into a mask?

• **Molière:** This famous French playwright died in 1673 of tuberculosis. Or did he? Molière was an atheist who angered powerful Catholics. Some believed his satires—like *Tartuffe*, which poked fun at the establishment—so enraged authorities that they faked his death and sent him to prison.

• **The Duke of Monmouth:** The illegitimate son of Britain's King Charles II was at the center of another faked death/secret-imprisonment legend. Monmouth was supposedly executed in London in 1685 for leading a rebellion against his uncle, King James II. But some contended that he was actually sent to prison where his mask and silence hid his true identity.

• **Nabo:** A black dwarf who, as legend had it, had an affair with Louis XIV's queen, Maria-Theresa. Their illegitimate son was

---

**Tom Selleck lost out as a bachelor twice on *The Dating Game*.**

raised in secrecy and Nabo was imprisoned under a mask. Since the prisoner was said to be tall, this theory was problematic to say the least.

## THE EVIL TWIN
In the 1770s, Voltaire broadly hinted that the prisoner was an older half-brother of Louis XIV—which would have put the Sun King's claims to the throne in doubt. To his satisfaction, Voltaire's assertions stirred up anti-royal feelings and kept interest alive in the sufferings of the Mask.

In 1789, journalist Frederic-Melchior Grimm improved on Voltaire's story. Grimm claimed that the Mask had been Louis XIV's identical twin! The Sun King's father, Louis XIII, sent the twin brother away to avoid quarrels over who would be the heir to the throne. When the twin discovered his identity, Louis kept him imprisoned, disguised, and silent.

Though the prisoner was supposedly tall and the King was short, and though there'd never been any twin sightings, the theory gained wide popularity. There'd always been whispers and rumors about King Louis XIV's true heredity since his parents had been on the outs and hadn't been cuddly for quite a while before he was born. More important, the cruelty of a king imprisoning his twin, like the image of the iron mask, resonated with French anti-royalists.

## DOWN WITH IRON MASKS!
The sufferings of the Mask became a symbol. When the Bastille was stormed and liberated in 1789, the liberators claimed that the skeletal remains of a prisoner with an iron mask riveted around his head were found in a dungeon of the Bastille. Just three years later, the French dumped the monarchy and installed a republic—no more prisoners in iron masks! (That is, if there ever were any in the first place. It's likely all the reports of iron masks were simply rumors run wild. But iron is, let's face it, more dramatic than black velvet.)

Popular French author Alexandre Dumas immortalized the story in his novel *The Man in the Iron Mask*. Published in 1850, the book claimed that the Mask was indeed Louis XIV's identical twin; the novel was an immediate best-seller and translated into dozens of languages. It's been made into many movies, including the 1996 version that features a double dose of Leonardo DiCaprio as the Sun King and his masked twin.

## THREE CENTURIES LATER

So who was the prisoner? Modern historical detectives have combed through official letters and arrest, prison, and death records to come up with the two most likely suspects:

• **Antonio Matthioli:** A foreign minister of Italy serving the Duke of Mantua, he was in charge of a real-estate deal involving the sale of the duke's fortress of Casale. Matthioli swindled his boss and all potential buyers including Louis XIV, who had Matthioli kidnapped and sent to prison in Pignerol. Matthioli's name also closely resembles the "Marchioly" used on the death certificate. Both Louis XV and Louis XVI, the Sun King's son and grandson, believed that Matthioli was the Mask. Indeed it was an Italian custom to wear a mask to avoid sunlight and Matthioli may have voluntarily worn a velvet mask. Also Matthioli had powerful friends who might have helped him—hence the need for disguise and silence.

• **Eustace Dauger:** This was a prison name (with various spellings) given to a valet—possibly the valet of a traitor, Rous de Marsilly, who was executed. (And it's another name that "Marchioly" could have been a misspelling of.) Anyway, this poor guy was supposed to be fed only by Saint-Mars himself, who was commanded to "threaten him with death if he speaks one word except about his actual needs." Unlike Matthioli, Dauger accompanied Saint-Mars to each of his prison postings, helping him meet the Mask's description as Saint-Mars's "longtime prisoner," and he is known to have been transferred to one of those prisons in a covered sedan chair. Saint-Mars was told never to let anyone know what the Mask had done to deserve imprisonment; if the Mask was Dauger, no one knows his crime to this day. Which would mean Saint-Mars did a darn good job.

## REMEMBER THE MASK!

Although the Mask's identity is still debated, his significance is no mystery. He remains a symbol of all unknown prisoners suffering under tyranny.

# BORN A SLAVE

*"Slavery is one of those monsters of darkness to whom the light of truth is death." —Frederick Douglass*

Frederick Douglass, born Frederick Baily in 1818 in Easton, Maryland, only saw his mother a few times in his life. They'd been separated early and the little boy was raised by his grandmother, Betsy Baily. He never met his father, though it was rumored that his white owner, Aaron Anthony, was the sperm donor in question.

## HOOKED ON READING

When he was six, Frederick's grandmother brought him up to the "big house" to work. His engaging personality got him assigned to a cushy house position at the home of Hugh and Sophia Auld, relatives of his owners. The bright-eyed boy managed to charm his new mistress, too—seeing how excited Frederick got when she read the Bible to him, she impulsively taught him to read. Her husband put a stop to the lessons, but by then it was too late— Frederick was hooked. He used the little money he earned doing odd jobs to buy tracts that denounced slavery. By age 13, Frederick knew he had to fight for his freedom.

## BREAKING A SLAVE BREAKER

When Aaron Anthony died, his "property" was divided up, and that meant Frederick's entire family was split up. Worst of all, since the grandmother Frederick loved above anyone else was considered too old to work, the slave-masters pushed her out of her little cabin in front of Frederick's very eyes. They built her a tiny mud cabin in the woods and left her there to die, all alone. Witnessing his grandmother's banishment added more fuel to Frederick's anti-slavery fire; and as he became more and more rebellious, his masters became more and more determined to break his spirit.

They sent him to Edward Covey, who was known as a "slave breaker." On one hot August afternoon, after months of continual whippings, Frederick lost his patience. As Covey prepared to whip him after tying him to a post, Frederick grabbed the slave breaker by the throat. Two hours of hard fighting later, Covey gave up. At age 16, Frederick had discovered a great truth. "Men are whipped oftenist who are whipped easiest." Never again would he let himself be abused without a fight.

## ANNA VS. FREEDOM
Frederick was eventually sent back to work for Hugh Auld, when he began to meet secretly at night with free blacks to read and debate. It was here that he met Anna Murray and fell in love—experiencing his first moments of true happiness. But it wasn't enough; he'd already decided to run away. An earlier escape attempt had landed him in prison. If he was caught again, he'd surely be hanged or sold into what he called a "living death," as a slave in the Deep South.

## TRAVELING THE OVER-GROUND RAILROAD
No matter. He was determined to make it to the free state of Pennsylvania. Not an easy task—professional bounty hunters patrolled the free state borders, and free blacks had to carry official papers. Frederick charmed a friend into loaning him his documents and boldly bought a train ticket to Philadelphia. He boarded his train to freedom and quaked and quivered as a railroad official checked his documents. He didn't fit the description on the official papers, but all the same, he was allowed to cross over into Philadelphia and then New York City, in 1838.

## ALIAS FREDERICK DOUGLASS
A friend with the Underground Railroad gave him shelter in New York and helped Anna Murray travel east, where the pair was married. To make it more difficult for his former masters to find him, he took on a new last name—Douglass.

Frederick and Anna settled in the port city of New Bedford, Massachusetts, where Frederick immediately got involved in abolitionist causes. When the famed white abolitionist William Lloyd Garrison got to see Douglass speak at a meeting, he realized Douglass's potential and hired him. For the next 10 years Douglass toured for the American Anti-Slavery Society; transferring the magnetic power of his personality into passionate antislavery lectures that would sway thousand to his cause.

## $700 AND CHANGE

But Douglass wasn't convinced that his audiences truly understood the horror of slavery. He needed to tell people exactly what it was like, so—despite the near-certainty that it would result in his recapture—in 1845 he published his autobiography, *Narrative of the Life of Frederick Douglass*. The book was a huge success, and so was Douglass. He was invited to speak all over America and in England about abolition. He was so popular in England that a group of fans got together the necessary money to buy his freedom—$714. Frederick Douglass was free at last.

## PEACE, BUT NOT AT ANY PRICE

Among his most impressive exploits—and there were plenty—Douglass convinced President Lincoln to make emancipation a moral cause of the Civil War. Under his urging, Lincoln refused to sign a peace accord with the Confederacy during the Civil War that would leave slavery intact. Instead, Lincoln chose to continue the fight and to allow African American soldiers to fight for the Union Army—setting into motion a chain of events that would finally see slavery abolished in America.

## DOUGLASS OUTDOES HIMSELF

But nothing he did for the abolitionist cause would make him as famous as when he married his white former secretary, Helen Pitts, in 1884 after Anna died. The interracial marriage—not even 20 years after the Civil War—set off a storm of controversy, which Douglass shrugged off. He'd honored his mother's race by marrying Anna, he said. All he was doing by marrying Helen was paying homage to his father's race.

Frederick Douglass died of a heart attack in 1895, a great American writer, speaker, and thinker to the end.

\* \* \*

"I prayed for twenty years but received no answer until I prayed with my legs."

"I expose slavery in this country, because to expose it is to kill it. Slavery is one of those monsters of darkness to whom the light of truth is death. " —Frederick Douglass

# WORLD'S MOST PULCHRITUDINOUS EVANGELIST

*That's what they called her in the papers. The woman who put the "angel" in Los Angeles could have been likened to Mother Teresa... and Mae West. She was a self-promoter, innovator, and faith healer all rolled into one gorgeous package.*

Radio and television evangelists hardly ever fare well after being caught succumbing to the weaknesses of the flesh. But it didn't hurt Aimee Semple MacPherson one bit. In fact, the peccadilloes of her personal life outside the church only added to her fame and the strength of her mission.

## HEEDING THE CALL

Aimee was born in a small Ontario farmhouse. Her parents were God-fearing folk, but Christianity was a tough sell to Aimee. While only in her teens, she had a local reputation as a hard-nosed atheist orator. Then along came Robert Semple, an itinerant evangelist, just as handsome, glib, and gallant as an Irishman could be.

Aimee got "the call" and the pair was married in 1908. By 1910 they were preaching in Hong Kong where, unfortunately, Robert died, a victim of malaria and dysentery. Aimee moved to the U.S. to live with her mother in New York, where she met and married Harold McPherson (who would later divorce her because of her "holy hobo ways").

## THE CALL OF THE OPEN ROAD

By 1915, back in Canada, she was drawing 500 people to her evangelical meetings and from then until 1919, Aimee crisscrossed Canada and the U.S. spreading the good word. She traveled with a tent she called her "canvas cathedral" in a 1912 Packard she called her "gospelier."

## EVERYONE'S TWO CENTS WORTH

Her arrival in Los Angeles was the start of something big. Here,

---

"High Hopes" was U.S. democratic presidential candidate JFK's campaign song in the 1960s.

she decided, she would build a permanent facility, a platform from which to preach, that she would call the Church of the Foursquare Gospel. She managed to raise $1.2 million and, in 1923, opened her Angelus Temple. (She later calculated that the average donation toward the building fund was only two cents, which gives you some idea of the number of people she preached to over the three-year period from 1919 to 1922.)

## AIMEE GOES HOLLYWOOD

Staid local clergy were not impressed. Apart from her saving more souls than they did, her collection plates filled at the same rate that theirs emptied. Furthermore, Aimee was exhibiting all of the showbiz flair of a P. T. Barnum. She might roar onstage astride a motorcycle in a police uniform to call a stop to sin. Or appear in a nurse's uniform to "rebuke" illness. In one famous number, she had a dozen imperiled maidens cling to a storm-lashed "Rock of Ages" while the special-effects crew worked the thunder, lightning, and wind machines. And then, just when all seemed lost, Sister Aimee strode in wearing an admiral's uniform and ordered a squad of lady sailors to the rescue.

## AIMEE TAKES TO THE STREETS—AND THE AIRWAVES

She advertised her religious services in the newspapers, airdropped leaflets over the city, and even entered floats in the Tournament of Roses Parade. In 1923, her float—a miniature replica of the Angelus Temple covered with roses and carnations—won the Grand Marshal Award.

These attractions, along with the fact that she was a beautiful and charismatic woman, packed the house in 21 services each week.

In 1924 she established the harbinger of evangelism to come, the first radio station dedicated solely to spreading the gospel, KFSG in Los Angeles. No question about it, Aimee was on a roll.

## THE LADY VANISHES

Unfortunately, in 1926 the roll started downhill into a murky underworld of controversy.

On May 18, while supposedly swimming in Santa Monica, MacPherson was reported to have vanished in the surf. Headlines?

It became the biggest media story for its time. Thousands of devoted followers fell into mourning.

But five weeks later, Aimee reappeared in Arizona with a strange kidnapping tale. (It was later discovered that she'd really been in seclusion with a lover in the Hollywood Hills.) She was welcomed back to Los Angeles by an adoring throng of 100,000. The district attorney filed fraud charges against her, but they were dismissed before the case went to trial. Glimmerings of controversy persisted. Her lawyer died in a questionable car accident and another figure in the case committed suicide.

## AIMEE BOUNCES BACK (AND FORTH)

But ever resilient, Aimee labored on and her church thrived. In 1927 she opened the Commissary, providing food and clothing to thousands of needy Los Angelenos. During one month, 80,000 people were fed by the operation. That's the up side.

Over the next years, Aimee married and divorced again, had a nervous breakdown, and involved her church in a series of disastrous financial ventures. But through it all, the faithful stayed that way; she maintained her popularity to the bitter end.

## THE LEGACY CONTINUES

Aimee Semple MacPherson died in 1944 from an overdose of Seconal. Her death put an end to rumors she had pillaged millions of dollars from her ministry—her estate was valued at only $10,000. The International Church of the Foursquare Gospel is still doing business today, as is the radio station.

## SO DOES THE LEGEND

Aimee also found a place in American literature when she served as one of the inspirations for the famous Sinclair Lewis novel *Elmer Gantry*. On the other hand, her detractors persisted, too. Aimee's postscandal success aroused H. L. Mencken to write that "there are more morons per square mile in Los Angeles, California, than any other place on earth!" But then, Mencken was an Easterner unused to the glittering ways of Hollywood.

---

**The McIntosh apple is named for Canadian farmer John McIntosh who discovered it in 1796.**

# READ ALL ABOUT IT!

*He's hardly ever mentioned in Western history books, but you might not be reading this book if it weren't for him.*

Chances are you've never heard of T'sai Lun, but he was ranked number seven of the most influential people who ever lived in *The 100: A Ranking of the Most Influential Persons in History* by Michael H. Hart, all because, about 1,900 years ago, he invented paper.

## TIME ON HIS HANDS
T'sai Lun was an official in the Chinese Imperial court, c. A.D. 100. And because of the ancient (even then) custom of allowing only castrated males to serve within the walls of the Imperial Palace, he was also a eunuch. The practice had the additional advantage of freeing up a lot of time that a more…um…complete kind of guy would spend in other pursuits. So T'sai Lun tinkered.

## OUR CULTURE CAN BEAT UP YOUR CULTURE
At the time the Western world, thanks to the Egyptians, had papyrus to write on. But the Chinese were printing their books on bamboo, which made them (as you can imagine) very big and clunky. Silk was used for special occasions, but it was too expensive for everyday use. So T'sai Lun experimented and eventually came up with a process for making paper—boiling bark, silk, fishing-net, and hemp cloth all together—that's every similar to the one that's used today. He proudly presented his creation to his emperor, for which he was rewarded with a promotion.

The new paper was cheap, plentiful, easy to produce, and helped China speed ahead of the West—for a while, at least. Until Johann Gutenberg (who placed number eight on the most influential list) invented his printing process.

## PALACE POLITICS
T'sai Lun eventually came to a sad end. He got involved in palace intrigue, and ended his life by drinking poison. But you can make his life worthwhile. The next time you use paper—of any kind— save a thought for T'sai Lun. He gave his…you know, his all…so we could have paper party hats!

# FIRST CAPO
# DI TUTTI CAPI

*Vito Cascio Ferro was the greatest Mafia chieftain in Sicily, and the
first Sicilian to be considered capo di tutti capi.*

Back in Sicily, the Mafia offered protection against bandits,
foreign invaders, government repression, and even the local
police. Though these protectors would eventually morph
into ruthless thugs, Mafia "soldiers" were still seen as folk heroes
when young Vito Cascio Ferro was growing up in there.

### THE YOUNG "ASSOCIATE"
Vito was born near Palermo in 1862 to illiterate peasant parents,
but he attracted the attention of the "Men of Honor" early on.
He was handsome and smooth talking, but tough and hotheaded.
And he wasn't afraid to get his hands dirty—he racked up a string
of crimes starting with an assault charge in 1894, followed by
extortion, arson, and "menacing." But he was far from a thug. The
young Mafioso was valued for his diplomatic touch with bosses and
underlings. He was generous, doling out help to those who would
ask him for favors, much like Vito Corleone in *The Godfather*.

### THE WISEGUY
He never learned to read or write, but he was smart. He instituted
the practice of pizzu, or "wetting the beak," a system by which the
Mafia collects small sums from business as a tribute or for "protection." If the businesses didn't pay up, their shops and homes were
destroyed or their farms were burnt down. Other mobsters would
bleed small businesses dry, taking so much cash from them that
they couldn't survive, but Ferro took only small, regular payments
that kept the small businesses alive and the money flowing. Vito's
superiors were pleased with his success and awarded him more and
more power and prestige.

### POPPING AND SNATCHING FOR FUN AND PROFIT
After former Palermo mayor Emanuele Notarbatolo was stabbed to
death on a train trip in 1893, the Sicilian cops came sniffing

around Ferro, but they couldn't nail him for the murder. A few
years later, Vito was again the target of a serious investigation
when Palermo socialite the Baroness di Valpetrosa was kidnapped
for ransom. She turned up alive, but the cops again focused their
attention on Vito. This time, Ferro decided it would be best to
leave Sicily. He packed up the wife and kids and fled to New York
in 1900.

## NEW YAWK STORY

Ferro hid his criminal record from immigration officials and settled
his family into an apartment over a shop on 103rd Street. The city
was a lawless frontier at the time, particularly for Italians. In Sicily
the Mob's power structure was well established. In New York,
though, there were only street gangs, mostly Irish and Jewish
gangs, with no leaders, no traditions, and no rituals. So Ferro
started to put some into place.

He hired some young gangsters and established beats for
them, sending them out to set up "protection" payments from
storeowners. It would have all been perfect—if it hadn't been for
one nosy cop.

## SOME GUY GETS WHACKED

Officer Joseph Petrosino was a Sicilian himself, so he knew what
he was looking at when he was called to investigate a body found
stuffed into a barrel at Avenue A and 11th Street in 1903. The
victim had been stabbed, his throat slit, and his private parts had
been shoved into his mouth. That last little flourish meant only
one thing—the victim was a police informant, killed by the Mafia.
That same year, the *New York Herald* published a story about a
shopkeeper who'd received an extortion letter marked with an
imprint of a black hand, the symbol of Sicilian organized crime.
Petrosino made the solving of the murder his mission—to prove
that not all Italian-Americans were thugs.

## THE COP WHO WOULDN'T FUGGEDABOUDIT

It took him a year to do it, but Petrosino traced the victim through
the shadowy Mafia underworld. The dead man was identified as
Benedetto Maddonnia, a low-level mobster from upstate who'd
been trying to shake down the Morello brothers, a triumvirate of

New York City mobsters. Maddonnia—whose nickname should have been "the Idiot"—threatened to rat the Morellos out to the cops unless they paid him.

Petrosino started looking more closely at the Morellos and their compatriots—like Vito Ferro. Although it's not likely that Ferro murdered Maddonnia himself, he knew his record couldn't stand all that much scrutiny. Afraid that his criminal past would be exposed and he'd be deported, Vito skipped to New Orleans where the Mob had established a base in the late 1800s.

He moved into an apartment in the heart of the oldest Sicilian immigrant settlement in the U.S. But the Mafia situation in New Orleans was even worse than in New York—especially after a police chief had been murdered in 1890 and an angry mob had lynched 11 Sicilians suspected of involvement in the assassination. Afraid he'd meet a similar fate, Vito headed back to Sicily.

## THE BOSS COMES HOME
As an "American," Vito was accorded more respect than the Pope. He easily established himself as a powerful Mafia boss. He strode the streets of Palermo wearing a white frock coat, wide-brimmed fedora, and cravat. He hosted art exhibitions, attended high-society parties, and had coffee almost daily in the prestigious Palermo café, Birreria Italia, where underlings would actually kiss his hand. He was so popular with Palermo's women that at one point he had to scold his barber for selling his hair clippings to a man who made amulets with them.

As the "capo di tutti capi" (boss of bosses) he was involved in every crime committed on his turf. All criminals were "licensed" by him, could do nothing without his consent, or incidentally, without giving the Mafia a cut. Even beggars had to contribute a regular percentage of their daily collections, just like other businessmen.

Don Vito did all this without excessive violence. He worked hard—and he studied human nature. He gave away millions in loans, gifts, and charity. And he personally redressed wrongs. He reserved his brutality for the stupid. Again, those who didn't "wet the beak" had their shops or homes destroyed. In his long life, he may have killed only one man, and not for money, but for honor. He was on top of the world, ma, but he still harbored a burning resentment against Joseph Petrosino, the man he viewed as

chasing him out of America. He patiently waited for the chance
for vengeance.

## THE COP BUYS A ONE-WAY TICKET

Petrosino hadn't forgotten Vito either. Back in New York, he'd
convinced his superiors to let him form the Italian Squad, a small
group of plainclothes policemen who, by 1909 had arrested thousands of criminals and deported more than 500 to Italy.

Petrosino convinced his bosses to let him to travel to Italy to
investigate the links between Italian and New York criminals.
Sure, they said—and promptly leaked news of his "secret" mission
to the *New York Herald*. The Italian papers picked up the story,
giving Ferro and other mobsters plenty of warning before Petrosino
arrived.

## THERE WASN'T A RAT IN THE BUNCH

Though no witnesses ever came forward, this is what probably
happened (and we mean probably—we don't want any trouble) on
the night of March 12. Don Vito excused himself from a dinner
party at the home of a government official, stepped into a carriage
and was dropped off near the Piazza Marina.

Petrosino was sitting on a fence there, at a trolley stop; he
may have been waiting for an informant—or even just a trolley.
Here's where, they say, Vito walked up and shot him in the face.

Later, the American consul reported that two hired gunmen
fired the shots. Still others say there were three. In any event,
Petrosino was dead. The Don returned to the dinner party. When
he was arrested four days later, his politician friend insisted Don
Vito had been at his home when Petrosino was murdered. The
Don was released without having denied involvement in the
crime. Apparently, he had said nothing at all.

## THE DON GETS FRAMED

Ferro faced new, more powerful enemies in the 1920s. Fascist
leader Benito Mussolini vowed to crush the Mafia and rule
supreme. His Sicilian prefect of police started getting powerful
mobsters out of the way.

So Don Vito decided to diversify his power structure by

---

The term "ritzy" comes from the posh European hotels run by Swiss innkeeper César Ritz.

sending a steady stream of his most capable soldiers to New York to do business in his name, including Carlo Gambino, who would later form his own immensely powerful crime family, and Joseph "Joe Bananas" Bonanno.

## THE DON GETS PINCHED
Ferro's American Mafia branch flourished. But back in Sicily, Don Vito—who'd been arrested a total of 69 times but never convicted—was arrested for murder in 1929 on trumped-up charges and convicted of a crime he didn't commit.

## LIFE IN THE JOINT
Vito spent the rest of his life in jail. Of course, he was a little better off than other prisoners. His cell was luxurious by prison standards, and he was allowed privileges like good meals and fine cigars, smuggled in to him by visitors who also brought news and took away advice and instructions—the Don continued to conduct Mafia business from his cell. The American Mafia branch flourished under his control, pushed along by the profits made by bootlegging during Prohibition. Ferro would live to see the Mafia reach its greatest heights in the U.S.—and watch its tight structure fall apart in mob wars in the 1930s. But that's another story.

## DEATH IN THE JOINT
Don Vito Cascio Ferro died of natural causes in prison in 1945. His former cell, now something of a shrine at the Bourbon Ucciardone prison in Palermo, is used only to house prisoners of the highest distinction.

\* \* \*

## I MADE IT ALL UP
After the publication of *The Godfather*, Mario Puzo was approached by more than a few real-life underworld figures who were convinced that he was linked to organized crime. "I was introduced to a few gentlemen related to the material," Puzo once recalled. "They were flattering. They refused to believe that I had never had the confidence of a don." Not only did Puzo make it all up, he even coined the term "godfather" to refer to Mafia dons. Nowhere in the mob's history had the word been used before to refer to a *capo di tutti capi*.

The first Atlantic storm to carry a man's name was Hurricane Bob.

# STRANGER
# THAN FICTION

*Meet the real live people who inspired some familiar artistic creations.*

They're classic characters you've read about in books and/or seen at the movies or on TV. Maybe you didn't even know they were inspired by actual human beings, but they were. Step right up and say hello.

## DR. LIND: MACFRANKENSTEIN

Can you imagine Frankenstein with a Scottish accent, hobnobbing with the king?

**How the Story Got Started:** When Percy Shelley brought his 18-year-old girlfriend (and wife-to-be) Mary Wollstonecraft to Lake Geneva, Switzerland, in the summer of 1816, they planned to have fun in the sun. But the weather turned stormy and the pair wound up indoors in the rented villa of fellow tourist Lord Byron. Since Shelley and Byron were two of the greatest English poets of all time, it's not surprising that they came up with literary ways to pass the time. One dark and stormy night, Lord Byron challenged the group to a competition writing ghost stories.

Mary immediately got writer's block. But one night, after listening to Shelley and Byron pontificate about science until they made her yawn, Mary went to bed and had a waking nightmare about a scientist who tried to create a living man—and created a monster instead.

**The Fictional Story:** Mary's nightmare became the unforgettable novel *Frankenstein*. A German science student, Viktor Frankenstein, assembles a human body from parts of corpses, then brings his creation to life. Unfortunately, it's seen as a monster and rejected by everyone, and eventually takes revenge by killing everyone Frankenstein loves.

**The True Story:** A modern scholar, Chris Goulding, a post-

---

**Almost 20 percent of South Korea's residents are named Kim.**

graduate student at the University of Newcastle, discovered a real doctor who was a likely model for Dr. Frankenstein. He was Dr. James Lind, a semi-retired Scottish physician who lived in Windsor, England. Dr. Lind was a natural philosopher, an accomplished astronomer, and geologist. He also taught science to Mary's husband, when Percy was a student at Eton. Dr. Lind was deeply involved in scientific experimentation, and most people considered him eccentric. He believed life was connected to what he called "Animal Electricity," which he studied by carrying out experiments on dead frogs. The experiments, first begun by Italian scientist Luigi Galvani (from whom we get the word "galvanize"), used electricity to make dead frogs "jump like live ones." Lind was so fascinated with the power of electricity on the dead amphibians that he even demonstrated his creepy electro-medical frog experiments to King George III.

Dr. James Lind's scientific work was greatly admired by Percy Shelley, and Mary knew her husband's mentor. It's likely she knew all about Dr. Lind's attempts to make the dead move like the living, which are so reminiscent of the experiments conducted by that other eccentric scientist—Dr. Frankenstein.

## DR. SAM SHEPPARD: THE REAL FUGITIVE

The doctor was never really on the run, but his plight inspired good chase scenes.

**How the Story Got Started:** On September 17, 1963, Roy Huggins, creator of the popular Western TV series *Maverick*, launched a new series, *The Fugitive*. Dr. Richard Kimble (played by David Janssen) comes home one night to find his wife murdered. He had seen a one-armed man fleeing as he arrived, but no one believes his story that this one-armed intruder killed his wife. Kimble is wrongly convicted for his wife's murder and sentenced to die. However, the train carrying him to the death house derails, and Kimble escapes, becoming…the Fugitive (and spending four seasons being pursued by the indefatigable Lt. Gerard).

**The Reel Story:** In 1993, the story of the doc-on-the-run was recreated for a new generation of viewers in a film starring Harrison Ford as Richard Kimble and Tommy Lee Jones as Lt. Gerard. The

The most common surname initial is S; X is the least common.

movie was a huge success and nominated for six Academy Awards, including Best Picture. Tommy Lee Jones walked away with an Oscar as Best Supporting Actor.

**The Real Story:** Huggins denied that he based *The Fugitive* on a true story, but the events in the series are suspiciously close to a true-life murder trial that fascinated the American public for years.

Richard Kimble's life on the run is reminiscent of the 1954 Cleveland murder trial of Dr. Sam Sheppard. One July morning, Dr. Sheppard called police to tell them he'd been attacked by a large, bushy-haired intruder. The intruder had knocked the doctor unconscious and when Sheppard came to, he discovered his wife Marilyn (who was four months pregnant) had been brutally beaten and murdered.

The shocked public was sympathetic, but the cops were suspicious. They wondered why Sheppard couldn't find the T-shirt he'd worn that night. They said the crime scene didn't match a typical burglary crime scene—it was too tidy, too staged. And nobody found the murder weapon—or the bushy-haired intruder. Public feeling turned against Sheppard after he admitted to an adulterous affair that he'd previously denied.

The nation's press corps declared Sheppard guilty, and the jury agreed, sentencing him to life in prison. For a time, the case seemed solved. Or was it?

While Sheppard was serving time, police arrested a thief who had possession of Marilyn's wedding ring. The suspect, Richard Eberling, admitted that he'd burgled the home of Marilyn's sister-in-law, who'd inherited the ring after Marilyn's death. Eberling, a window-washer, also said he'd worked at Marilyn's home only days before her murder, and claimed he'd cut his finger while he was there. Still, the police let Eberling go after giving him a lie detector test.

Meanwhile, the U.S. Supreme Court was going over the prejudicial press coverage against the doctor—a "carnival" that the judge never tried to control or keep from the jury. In 1966 the high court granted the doc a new trial. At that second trial, Sheppard was acquitted, and many believed that the TV series *The Fugitive* had a lot to do with the acquittal.

**The Epilogue:** Unable to establish a successful medical practice, Sheppard performed as a professional wrestler under the name Killer Sheppard. The "Killer" drank heavily and died of liver failure at age 46, just four years after his release.

In 1996, Sam and Marilyn's son, Sam Reese Sheppard, who had slept through the murder all those years ago, tried to clear his father's name, by using DNA evidence to prove Richard Eberling was the bushy-haired intruder. Unfortunately, the DNA evidence was contaminated, but it showed that a third person could have been in the room on the night of the murder. Eberling had been convicted of murdering an elderly woman and was suspected of killing three other women as well. Eberling died in prison without ever publicly confessing to Marilyn's murder, though his cellmate claimed that Eberling confessed just before his death.

## CONSUELO DE SAINT-EXUPÉRY: THE NAME OF THE ROSE

Not all classics are about monsters or murder. Consuelo inspired a classic tale of love.

**How the Story Got Started:** In 1940 an unhappy, homesick French author, Antoine de Saint-Exupéry, was stranded in New York. A pilot in the French air force, Saint-Exupéry dueled with German planes, but had escaped France when the Nazi occupation began. He tried to enlist as a U.S. fighter pilot, but at age 40, he was rejected as too old.

"You can't fight fascism with a pen," Saint-Exupéry complained. But to console himself, he gave it a try anyway. The book was dedicated to a Jewish author, Leon Werth, who was in danger of being exterminated by the Nazis, and it celebrated spiritual values that the Nazis opposed. Saint-Exupéry called the book *The Little Prince*.

**The Fictional Story:** An aviator, forced down in the lonely Sahara desert, meets a child, a little prince who tells the aviator his story. The little prince's home is on an asteroid that has three volcanoes and one delicate rose that demands a lot of care. The lonely little prince traveled through the universe and down to Earth seeking friendship and solutions to his problems with the rose.

On Earth, he's disappointed to discover that roses are common flowers. (His own rose had assured him she was unique.) A friendly desert fox teaches the little prince an important secret: "Only with the heart can one see fully. Essential matters are invisible to the eyes." The little prince returns to his rose, and realizes that she is unique because she has the ability to touch his heart.

**The Real Story:** The aviator forced down in the desert was drawn from Saint-Exupéry's own experiences. A pioneer in aviation who would be decorated for heroism, Saint-Exupéry began his aviating career as an airmail pilot. At age 26, he took charge of a lonely North African refueling station and fell in love with the desert. No city ever appealed to him like that "vast sandy void." But the author also knew the dangers of the desert; he nearly died of thirst when he and a friend were lost in the Sahara.

If the Aviator was Saint-Exupéry as a pilot, soldier, and man of action, the little prince was drawn from the author's poetic side. The wandering little prince shared Antoine's philosophies and passions—including the passion for a "rose," who was inspired by Saint-Exupéry's wife.

In 1930, Saint-Exupéry had met a beautiful young widow, Consuelo Suncin Carillo from El Salvador. Although she was small in stature and delicate, Consuelo had a flamboyant, demanding personality, frequently making herself the dramatic center of fantastic stories. For example, she claimed she was born prematurely during a strong earthquake that turned the family home around on its foundation (though there was no earthquake recorded near the time of her birth).

Antoine and Consuelo's courtship was full of passionate break-ups and reunions, as was their marriage, Consuelo being a difficult flower who demanded more than her share of care and attention. It was while they were together in New York, during a period of reconciliation, that Antoine wrote *The Little Prince*.

**The Epilogue:** In 1943, Saint-Exupéry's wish to return to the air and fight the Germans was granted. Though he was only supposed to fly five missions, the aging author constantly volunteered for more, and took off on his ninth mission on July 31, 1944. He never returned, and his aircraft was never found. Historians believe his plane was shot down by the Germans; romantics like to think he disappeared from earth like the little prince.

---

Benazir Bhutto, prime minister of Pakistan, was the first woman to head an Islamic government.

# DR. DREW

*The virtually unknown African American doctor whose pioneering work in blood preservation has saved countless lives in every corner of the world.*

He was an all-American halfback and captain of his Amherst College team, but because his older sister died of tuberculosis when she was only 15, Charles Richard Drew chose to devote his life to medicine rather than sports.

### A BLOODHOUND IS BORN

Drew was born in 1904 in Washington, D.C. At age 24, he entered McGill University Medical School in Montreal, Canada, where he soon became interested in blood research. Later, at Columbia University Presbyterian Hospital (now Columbia Presbyterian Medical Center), he narrowed his field of research—to blood transfusions and the storing of blood.

### EUREKA!

In 1940, Dr. Drew documented a new technique for storing blood. He'd discovered that by separating the liquid red blood cells from the near-solid plasma and freezing the two separately, blood could be preserved and reconstituted at a later date—even a much later date. Blood banks had been around for decades by then, but Drew's work made it possible to preserve and store blood for the long-term. Just the thing that was needed in the war effort.

### BLOOD FOR BRITAIN

That same year he was asked to be the medical supervisor of "Blood for Britain." He took thousands of pints of dried plasma to England, where he organized a system of volunteer blood donors, centralized the collection of donated blood, and conceived of using a "blood mobile" to deliver the blood to where it was most needed.

When the project was taken over by the American Red Cross, Drew was named director of the Red Cross Blood Bank in New York. At the same time, he was assistant director of blood procurement for the National Research Council for the U.S. Army and

---

The architect of the attack on Pearl Harbor, Admiral Yamamoto, was a graduate of Harvard.

Navy. That was when and where—after all those years—the race issue reared its ugly head.

## DR. DREW MAKES A WITHDRAWAL

During WWII, the army, the navy, and even the Red Cross had separate blood banks for blacks and whites, which was not only costly and time-consuming but, to Dr. Drew, absolutely ridiculous. He denounced the policy as unscientific, but the military stood firm. So Drew returned to Howard University Medical School, where he'd taught pathology in the 1930s.

Dr. Drew died tragically in an automobile accident in 1950. Rumors that he could have been saved but was denied a blood transfusion at the nearest hospital because he was black were untrue.

## HONORABLE MENTIONS

In 1977, the American Red Cross headquarters in Washington, D.C., was renamed the Charles R. Drew Blood Center. In 1981, the U.S. Postal Service issued a stamp in his honor. Today every blood bank in the world is a living memorial to the genius and dedication of Dr. Charles Richard Drew.

\* \* \*

## HOW MANY JOHNS?

We've long been curious about the name "Johns Hopkins," as in Johns Hopkins famous hospital and school. Was there more than one John? Or were the hospital and school founded by someone whose last name was Johns and whose partner was someone named Hopkins?

Turns out the answer is one man named Johns Hopkins, a Quaker merchant from Maryland who, with profits from his investment in the B&O (that is, Baltimore and Ohio) Railroad, willed $7 million to found the university and hospital that still bear his name.

Hopkins died at 78 of pneumonia, some say because he was too cheap (he was a notorious skinflint) to buy a heavy overcoat, but the more likely story is that the winter of 1873 was exceptionally cold, and Hopkins insisted on walking to his office without a coat or overshoes (he was notoriously stubborn, too) on a day when the temperature plunged to 20 degrees below.

# COMPOSE YOURSELF

*Don't run away! You might actually like some of these guys.*

We live in an era in which most "composers" seem to make their living writing snippets of music that unspool underneath the movie image of a superhero duking it out with a guy in a hard plastic mask. Not that there's anything wrong with that (mmmm...superheroes), but sometimes it's nice to focus on the music without some guy in primary-colored tights filling your eyeballs. So here are four living, mostly nonfilm-related composers you might want to try out. To be fair, some of these guys have written music for films; just none of those films involved a central character with heat vision.

## JOHN ADAMS

What, the second president of the U.S. also composed avant-garde music on the side? Well, no. The John Adams we're talking about here was born in 1947, not 1735, although like the second president he is a graduate of Harvard. Adams once noted that he knew he wanted to be a composer by the time he was eight years old, and in his teens he had already written a number of orchestral pieces. However, Adams is also touchy about his early work; he regards his 1977 piano piece *Phrygian Gates* to be his first "mature work," leaving most of his early stuff unpublished. Adams hit the big time with his opera *Nixon in China*, which featured what many regard as a surprisingly balanced portrait of the disgraced president. The 1987 production featured a who's who of avant-garde theater, including director Peter Sellars and choreographer Mark Morris, and it was an instant smash with critics and art lovers.

### Touchy Subjects

Adams has also seen his share of controversy, most notably with his 1991 opera *The Death of Klinghoffer*, which is based on the hijacking of the *Achille Lauro* cruise ship and the murder of one of its passengers. Adams gave dimension to the terrorist characters, which caused some to call it anti-Israeli; its subject matter was enough to have a Boston performance of its choruses canceled in

November 2001, in the wake of the 9/11 attacks. Ironically, Adams was commissioned by the New York Philharmonic to write a work commemorating 9/11; the piece, *On the Transmigration of Souls*, was performed to wide critical acclaim a year later and was award the 2003 Pulitzer Prize for Music.

### Only Minimally Minimal
As a composer, Adams shares a number of traits with the "minimalist" set (you know, the people who write one measure of music, Xerox it 40,000 times, and call it a day). But unlike many of them, he also seems to like melody. This means that he's one modern composer most people can usually "get" the first time around. Probably for this reason, a 1996 survey of orchestras noted Adams was the modern composer whose music is most frequently performed.

**Suggested Spins:** 1999's *Naïve and Sentimental Music* is considered by many to be Adams's best orchestral work. For early Adams, you might try his 1978 Shaker Loops.

### GLENN BRANCA
You like guitars? You're gonna love Branca, whose forte is piling electric guitars on top of electric guitars until all those axes blasting together create unusual, amplified sonic mergers, dissonances, and augmentations (i.e., feedback and reverb aplenty!). Branca's usual touring ensemble features anywhere from four to eight guitars, along with a varying line up of drums, bass guitar, keyboards, and percussion. Sound like a rock band? It should—members of Branca's ensembles have included Lee Ranaldo and Thurston Moore, more famously known as the guitarists of art rock band Sonic Youth. More than one of Branca's symphonies involves guitar after guitar blasting out a single E chord with rising intensity.

### Rocking the Opera House
Loud? You bet. Controversial? Sure. No less a personage than John Cage, the godfather of modern avant-garde composition (or lack thereof), was heard to comment on Branca's music, "My feelings were disturbed.... I found in myself a willingness to connect the music with evil and with power. I don't want such a power in my life. If it was something political it would resemble fascism." In 1983, after a performance of Branca's *Fourth Symphony in Holland*,

members of the orchestra stood up and complained to the audience about the piece (and then went on play Wagner, which is some irony for you). Basically, Branca is as close as compositional music gets to a mosh pit, and that's not a bad thing.

**Suggested Spins:** Branca's *Symphonies 8 & 10 (The Mysteries)* are loads of amplified fun, with movements cheerfully titled "The Horror" and "Spiritual Anarchy." Otherwise, check out *Selections from the Symphonies*, which is sort of a "greatest hits" package featuring seven movements dispersed among Branca's ten symphonies.

## BRIAN ENO

Brian Eno does a lot of musical things really well—like, scary-not-quite-human-probably-an-alien-android well—and is best known to most people as a musician (he played keyboards for Roxy Music) and as producer of artists like David Bowie, Talking Heads, and U2. But he's also the founder of an entire genre of music—ambient music, with its subtle, minimally intrusive philosophy of sound. All Eno had to do to create it was nearly die in a car accident.

### Peace and Quiet

The 1975 accident laid Eno up, totally immobile, for a number of months. At one point, a pal visited, put on an album, and left, but the volume was so low that Eno could barely hear it. At the same time, there was a thunderstorm going on, and suddenly Eno had his lightning flash of inspiration—music that was embedded in its environment, not separated from it. He started experimenting with this new form, including using tape loops and letting the music "generate" itself rather than be directly composed, and he created several seminal albums, including 1978's *Music for Airports*, which was designed to soothe air travelers (and to keep them from freaking out about those occasional plane crashes).

### Insinuating Music

Eno's musical baby has since transmuted into or been incorporated into a number of different musical forms, from New Age (yeah, sorry about that) to Trance and Electronica. He's even been covered by classical artists. The hip Bang on a Can string quartet released a very good version of *Airports* in 1998.

**Suggested Spins:** *Music for Airports* is excellent and soothing, as is *Apollo, Atmospheres and Landscapes*, written by Eno (with his

---

A "Sweetheart" is better known today as a "Playmate."

brother Roger and musician/producer Daniel Lanois) for a documentary on the moon landings. On Land is a good choice if you want something darker and more complex. But to get right to the inspiration of ambient, try *Discreet Music*, which features odd variations on the "Pachelbel Canon," the composition Eno was not quite listening to when he was laid up during that thunderstorm.

## PHILIP GLASS
Sure, right now, Philip Glass is easily the best known of living modern composers, but don't think he didn't have to suffer for his art. Glass's revolutionary minimalist compositions met with huge resistance when Glass began as a young composer in the late 1960s, so much so that Glass, who studied philosophy at the University of Chicago and music at Juilliard, had to find work as a cab driver and a plumber. (So that's a warning—the guy snaking your sink trap could have a better education than you.)

### Is Philip Glass Half Full or Half Empty?
The resistance was not completely irrational, since Glass was working on some seriously out-there stuff. Early on, Glass tossed out traditional Western ideas about music composition and, heavily influenced by Ravi Shankar and Indian music, started picturing music as rhythmic themes rather than notes on a staff. This was immensely freeing to Glass, but to Western ears it resulted in music that sounded like some wahoo whacking at his keyboard over and over and over—whonk whonk whonk whonk, WHONK whonk whonk WHONK, to be repeated ad infinitum.

### Compose. Rinse. Repeat.
But Glass kept at it and eventually the cognoscenti came around. His rise to fame began with 1976's *Einstein on the Beach*, a five-hour opera that retained Glass's fascination with rhythm and repetition, but also threw Western audiences a bone with familiar harmonic elements. Glass composed several more operas and also branched out into film (scoring the zone-out classic *Koyaanisqatsi* and its two sequels, as well as more mainstream fare like 2002 Oscar contender *The Hours*) and even into pop music of sorts. His 1986 *Songs from Liquid Days* features actual songs, with lyrics by actual famous people like Paul Simon and Suzanne Vega. And that's a step up from snaking a sink trap for sure.

Alexander Graham Bell's father-in-law was the first president of the National Geographic Society.

**Suggested Spins:** Got three hours? The 1993 recording of *Einstein on the Beach* will give you the essential Glass, which will either make you a fan or make you lament that you've just lost three hours of your life that you will never get back. Less taxing but still quintessentially Glass: the *Koyaanisqatsi* soundtrack (which may be best experienced with the movie, finally available on DVD). If you'd prefer your Glass in single serving form, with familiar singers to soften the jagged minimalism, take a crack at *Songs from Liquid Days.* Or to explore Glass's roots, check out his 1990 collaboration with Ravi Shankar, *Passages.*

\* \* \*

Pete Townshend of rock's The Who titled his famous song "Baba O'Riley" in homage to his spiritual guru Meher Baba and to musical influence and California minimalist composer Terry Riley. Riley's *Rainbow in Curved Air* (1969) inspired Townshend to experiment with looped patterns and synthesizer sounds, and voilá—the song we always erroneously called "Teenage Wasteland" was born!

\* \* \*

What are the following: Zymo-Xyl, Quadrangularis Reversum, New Boo, Surrogate Kithara, and Chromelodion II?

One-of-a-kind musical instruments created by composer and visionary Harry Partch, who said: "I am not an instrument builder, but a philosophic music-man seduced into carpentry."

\* \* \*

Lev Termen invented one of the earliest electronic musical instruments, called the Theremin or Aetherophone. Designed to be played with little or no physical contact, it was used in the soundtrack of classic sci-fi film *The Day the Earth Stood Still* and in The Beach Boys song "Good Vibrations."

Termen was kidnapped from his New York apartment in 1938 and taken to a Russian labor camp in Siberia.

---

**Alexander Graham Bell was a private tutor to Helen Keller.**

# NOVEL STARTS

*Where you really just resting your eyes in high school lit class? Below are the first lines of classic works by famous authors. Go ahead, test yourself.*

1. "Whether I turn out to be the hero of my own life, or whether that station will be held by anybody else, these pages must show."

2. "Buck did not read the newspapers or he would have known that trouble was brewing, not along for himself, but for every tide-water dog, strong of muscle and with warm, long hair, from Puget Sound to San Diego."

3. "1801—I have just returned from a visit to my landlord—the solitary neighbor that I shall be troubled with."

4. "Well, Prince, so Genoa and Hucca are now just family estates of the Buonapartes..."

5. "Last night I dreamt I went to Manderly again."

6. "In my younger and more vulnerable years, my father gave me some advice that I've been turning over in my mind ever since."

7. "The cold passed reluctantly from the earth, and the retiring fogs revealed an army stretched out on the hills, resting."

8. "3 May. Bistritz. Left Munich at 8:35 P.M., on 1st May, arriving at Vienna early next morning; should have arrived at 6:46, but train was an hour late."

9. "You better not even tell nobody but God."

10. "It is a truth universally acknowledged, that a single man in possession of a good fortune, must be in want of a wife."

11. "Early in the spring of 1750, in the village of Juffure, four days upriver from the coast of Gambia, West Africa, a man-child was born to Omoro and Binta Kinte."

12. "He was an old man who fished alone in a skiff in the Gulf stream and he had gone 84 days now without taking a fish."

13. "When Mary Lennoz was sent to Misselthwaite Manor to live with her uncle, everybody said she was the most disagreeable-looking child ever seen."

14. "Who is John Galt?"

15. "It was a pleasure to burn."

16. "You will rejoice to hear that no disaster has accompanied the commencement of an enterprise which you have regarded with such evil forbodings."

17. "TOM!"

18. "It was a bright cold day in April, and the clocks were striking thirteen."

19. "As Gregor Samsa awoke one morning from uneasy dreams, he found himself transformed into a giant insect."

20. "Call me Ishmael."

Answers: 1. *David Copperfield* (Charles Dickens); 2. *White Fang* (Jack London); 3. *Wuthering Heights* (Emily Brontë); 4. *The Call of the Wild* (Jack London); 5. *Rebecca* (Daphne du Maurier); 6. *The Great Gatsby* (F. Scott Fitzgerald); 7. *The Red Badge of Courage* (Stephen Crane); 8. *Dracula* (Bram Stoker); 9. *The Color Purple* (Alice Walker); 10. *Pride and Prejudice* (Jane Austen); 11. *Roots* (Alex Haley); 12. *The Old Man and the Sea* (Ernest Hemingway); 13. *The Secret Garden* (Francis Hodgson Burnett); 14. *Atlas Shrugged* (Ayn Rand); 15. *Fahrenheit 451* (Ray Bradbury); 16. *Frankenstein* (Mary Shelley); 17. *The Adventures of Tom Sawyer* (Mark Twain); 18. *1984* (George Orwell); 19. *Metamorphosis* (Franz Kafka); 20. *Moby Dick* (Herman Melville)

Magician Harry Houdini died of peritonitis from a ruptured appendix on Halloween 1926.

# PLATINUM BLONDE

*Her name was only one letter away from "harlot." That's the kind of role that first earned her the public's attention. In her short life, she proved to the world that she was more than just a walking, talking sex bomb in a slinky dress.*

Jean Harlow had a weirdly close relationship with her mother. For instance, she thought her name was "the Baby" until she went to school. Once there, she discovered it was "Harlean," a blend of her mother's full maiden name, Jean Harlow. And when Harlean signed with Fox Studios at age 17 as an extra, she blurted out "Jean Harlow" when asked for her name. But to "Mother Jean," she would always be "the Baby."

### LOOKS THAT COULD KILL

Jean caused a commotion wherever she went. In addition to her ash blond hair, green eyes, flawless skin, and curvaceous body, she had that unexplainable quality that turned men into mush. She eloped to California with one of those men when she was 16, but when Mother Jean and her parasitic husband, Marino Bello, followed them to the coast, the young marriage disintegrated.

### GOING PLATINUM

Her acting may have been forgettable (the critics were less than kind), but her oozing sensuality left the public begging for more— maybe because she refused to wear bras or panties under those slinky 1930s dresses. Howard Hughes cast her in *Hell's Angels* and positioned her as "the Platinum Blonde," which hair colorists made happen by dousing her scalp every week with burning concoctions of peroxide, ammonia, bleach, and detergent.

### COMEDY AND TRAGEDY

A few films into her new hair color (which she hated), Jean found her acting niche as a sexy comedienne. She also found a new hubby in MGM executive Paul Bern. Two months into the marriage, Bern blew out his brains in their bedroom (his suicide note hinted at impotence). Jean wasn't there to see it—she was staying

---

Henry Ford was violently anti-Semitic and antiunion.

at her mother's that night. Ten days later, Dorothy Millette, Bern's common-law wife, washed up on the banks of the Sacramento River. She, too, had killed herself.

But the tragedies didn't have the slightest effect on Harlow's career. She went on to chalk up some great roles—*Bombshell* and *Dinner at Eight*—and a third husband, Hal Rosson, who'd been director of photography on some of her films. That marriage lasted a year. Jean moved back in with Mommy. She was 23 years old.

## CLEANING UP HER ACT
When the Catholic Church's Legion of Decency gained a foothold (their mission: to stop the production of movies that flaunted immorality), Jean was an easy target. So MGM transformed her into a "brownette" and cast her in movies that showed her intelligent side—yes, she had one—like *Wife vs. Secretary*. (In fact, Jean loved to read and wrote a novel called *Today Is Tonight*.) Her next film, *Libeled Lady*, was nominated for Best Picture.

## LOVE, HOLLYWOOD-STYLE
Everyone loved Jean (except Joan Crawford, who hated any kind of competition, especially of the female sort). Harlow was thoughtful, warm, and ingratiating, and she thought she'd finally found a soulmate in William Powell, the dapper star of *The Thin Man* series. But...

## HARLOW SLOWLY SLINKS AWAY...
Powell discovered that Jean's chronically unemployed stepfather had squandered most of her earnings on nonexistent business ventures, and she was in serious debt. And even though Powell and Harlow were engaged for three years, he seemed unwilling to legalize the union. Jean grew depressed and turned to booze. Her health started failing. Then, during the filming of *Saratoga* with Clark Gable, she was hospitalized with kidney failure.

With 42 movies behind her and a potentially great acting career in front of her, Jean Harlow died on June 7, 1937, at age 26. Mother Jean lamented the loss of the Baby until her own death at age 69. But in the end she managed to keep Jean to herself. The two Jeans rest in peace together (in a room paid for by William Powell) in Forest Lawn's Great Mausoleum.

---

Henry Ford introduced the 8-hour day, time clock, and a daily minimum wage (then $5).

# FOSSIL FEUD

*The story of a rivalry set in the old West and how it caused the brontosaurus to become extinct not once, but twice.*

You'd think the old West of the 1800s would be big enough to support the work of more than one dinosaur hunter. But it wasn't big enough for the likes of Marsh and Cope.

## A-HUNTING WE WILL GO
Our first player, Othniel Charles Marsh (1831–1899), had a rich uncle who bought Marsh a professorship in paleontology and a museum, both at Yale. In 1870, Marsh headed west to hunt fossils in places like the Dakota Badlands where, in 1871, his team found America's first pterodactyl.

In the other corner was Edward Drinker Cope (1840–1897), who funded his digs with the sale of a farm he'd inherited. He'd scored a college professorship at age 24, but gave it up three years later to spend the next 22 years exploring the western states. He only returned to teaching when his expeditions used up his cash.

Cope was more of a scientist; Marsh was more a politician. Both were excessively possessive and ambitious. Even though they started out as friends, it didn't take long for them to figure out that only one of them could be the biggest name in paleontology.

## DIGGING UP DIRT
Who started it? Cope claimed that, after introducing Marsh to some fertile digs in New Jersey, Marsh paid to have the area closed to everyone but himself. Marsh also bribed Cope's workmen to send him some of the fossils they dug up. Both men had spies in the other's camp, and even dynamited good fossil sites so the other wouldn't be able to work on them. As they hammered away at each other's reputations, their peers began to call it "the great bone wars." It was a race to see who could tote up the most discoveries, and their haste to win led to some sloppy science.

## GOING THE WAY OF THE DINOSAUR
When Cope hastily restored a skeleton of a plesiosaur (a marine reptile), Marsh pointed out correctly—and in print—that Cope

had put the head on the wrong end. Then it was Marsh's turn. He'd been the first to describe and name the apatosaurus, based on the discovery of a few bones in Colorado. A few years later, one of his teams found an almost complete (and what seemed like a distinctively new) skeleton in Wyoming. In his eagerness to outscore his rival, Marsh plunked a random head on his headless skeleton and named it brontosaurus. This conveniently got him credit for two discoveries. Eventually, though, other paleontologists figured out that the two skeletons were from the same dinosaur and that Marsh's brontosaurus had just been an adult version of the apatosaurus. Since paleontology has strict rules, the older name beat out the more familiar one, and the name "brontosaurus" was formally discarded in 1974. Thus making the brontosaurus the only dinosaur we know of to become extinct twice.

## TILL DEATH DO THEY PART

The feud ended in 1897 when Cope died—penniless, by the way, having spent his entire fortune hunting dinosaurs. Marsh ended up with the highest score, but in his haste to beat out Cope, he neglected his paperwork, so a lot of inside knowledge died with him in 1899 and had to be restudied and rewritten by the scientists who followed in his footsteps. All the same, many of the most awe-inspiring dinosaur displays in the world can be traced back to the feud that drove two men to occasional superhuman efforts and, despite their all-too-human frailties, provided a solid base for future investigation.

\* \* \*

## FEUDING WITH A DEAD WOMAN

Five years after Margaret Mead died, a rival anthropologist, Derek Freeman, published a book challenging all the findings in Mead's *Coming of Age in Samoa,* especially the ones having to do with the "dating" habits of young girls. He claimed that her surviving informants told him they hadn't engaged in casual sex as Mead had reported. Of course, the original informants were now old women who'd converted to Christianity (and had possibly adopted some new puritanical sexual standards). Not to mention the possibility that these women wouldn't be as honest about sex when speaking to an older man as they would've been speaking to a young woman.

# BUT ENOUGH ABOUT ME

*What did you think of my last movie? Or so goes the joke. Match the autobiography (1–12) to its author (a–l), then check out the answers.*

1. And the Beat Goes On
2. Africa in My Blood
3. The Art of the Comeback
4. Dirty Jokes and Beer
5. I Ain't Got Time to Bleed
6. I Can't Wait Until Tomorrow... 'Cause I Get Better-Looking Every Day
7. Landing on My Feet: A Diary of Dreams
8. Little Girl Lost
9. My Point—And I Do Have One
10. Private Parts
11. Rewrites: A Memoir
12. Under Fire: An American Story

a. **Drew Barrymore** (member of the illustrious acting family who appeared in *ET: The Extra-Terrestrial* at age six)
b. **Sonny Bono** (one-time husband of Cher, mayor of Palm Springs, and congressman from California)
c. **Drew Carey** (star of *The Drew Carey Show* and host of *Whose Line Is It Anyway?*)
d. **Ellen Degeneres** (stand-up comic and lesbian who "came out" on her own TV show in 1997)
e. **Jane Goodall** (famous animal researcher and friend to chimpanzees everywhere)
f. **Joe Namath** (former New York Jets quarterback)
g. **Oliver North** (Marine lieutenant colonel who starred in the Iran-Contra scandal)
h. **Neil Simon** (playwright who created *The Odd Couple*, *The Sunshine Boys*, and so on)
i. **Howard Stern** (New York City–based radio shock jock)
j. **Kerri Strug** (U.S. Olympic gymnast and heroine of the 1996 Games)
k. **Donald Trump** (real estate mogul, one-time owner of the Empire State building, and general all-around rich person)
l. **Jesse Ventura** (former pro wrestler who was elected governor of Minnesota in 2000)

Answers: 1-b; 2-e; 3-k; 4-c; 5-l; 6-f; 7-j; 8-a; 9-d; 10-i; 11-h; 12-g

**Pope John Paul II is the first non-Italian pope in over 450 years.**

# WHEN HE WAS A SHI

*Not all magicians pull rabbits out of hats; some create illusions. Meet Shi Pei Pu, the Chinese master (or was it mistress?) of illusion.*

The play and movie M. *Butterfly* tell the incredible tale of a Chinese opera star who had such a passionate affair with a French diplomat that he betrayed his own country for her. But all the time, the femme fatale was a fake! The glamorous opera star was a man. And her French lover never knew it! How did playwright David H. Hwang ever come up with such a bizarre idea? Well, actually, he read about it in the newspaper.

## WHEN THE REAL IS MORE BIZARRE THAN THE REEL

Bernard Boursicot went to Beijing as an accountant for the French foreign service when he was only 20 years old. He'd been born into a Catholic working class family and had dropped out of high school—but he managed to lie his way into a job with the French Embassy.

In the play and movie the opera star first appeared to her French lover as a woman wearing the beautiful robes of a Chinese opera diva. But in reality, when Boursicot met 26-year-old Shi Pei Pu, the former singer was dressed as a man.

Shi told his new friend about how, as a teenage opera star, he'd performed as a woman (a common tradition in Chinese opera). Shi confided in the young Frenchman a family secret—he really was a woman!

## BOY, GIRL, BOY, GIRL...

Shi confessed that he was actually his mother's third daughter. Because boy children were so much more desirable in China, Shi's father would have been forced to take another wife if Shi's mother couldn't give him a son and heir. So Mom pretended that Shi was a boy and all his life Shi had kept the secret. Boursicot fell for the story and he fell for Shi. In 1965, the two began an affair. Boursicot had no prior experience with women and chalked up Shi's shy behavior to Oriental modesty.

## PREGGERS!?!

Boursicot left Beijing in December 1965 to fulfill a dream of

---

**President Nixon, raised a pacifist Quaker, advocated a strong military.**

exploring the Amazon. After some months, he received a letter from Shi, telling him that he was the father of a child, a son named Bertrand. (Of course Shi, being a he, couldn't have been pregnant! But that slight detail wasn't mentioned to the proud papa.) Boursicot tried to reunite with his son and his son's "mother" as soon as possible, but it took him four years to get back into Communist China.

## BUSTED!?!

By 1969 Mao's Cultural Revolution had made life dangerous for China's artists, many of whom were killed or sent off to do hard labor. Shi Pei Pu had lost his comfortable life in Beijing; he now lived in cramped quarters writing government-approved plays that praised Mao's loyal workers. When Boursicot finally made it, there was no patter of little feet in Shi's apartment. Shi told Boursicot that the little fella was living in the country as a safety precaution in these dangerous times. Boursicot was disappointed, but the worst was to come! Someone told police that a foreigner was meeting a Chinese citizen without permission. And Boursicot was arrested by the Red Guard.

## A SPY IS BORN

Over the years, Boursicot had worked his way up in the French diplomatic corps. He was now a minor diplomat who personally transported French official papers in a diplomatic pouch. Now, hoping to protect Shi and Bertrand, Boursicot promised Chinese officials that he'd bring them secret information.

In 1973 and again in 1977 Boursicot was able to visit Shi and their son—and meet his Chinese contact, Mr. Kang. Even though Boursicot gave Shi money, TV sets, tape decks, and other capitalist treasures, it was never enough. Fortunately, Kang was easier to please. He seemed content with the French government secrets that Boursicot handed over.

## SHI COMES TO GAY PAREE

In 1982 Boursicot brought his little family—Bertrand (now in his teens) and his "uncle," Monsieur Shi—to Paris. They moved in with Boursicot, who was now living an openly gay life with a Frenchman, Thierry Toulet. But Shi was so jealous that Toulet finally moved out.

Brezhnev's body fell out of the bottom of his coffin when he was being laid to rest.

But at least Boursicot had his adored Bertrand! He showed his son off to his entire family, who loved the child, but—being practical people—couldn't understand why Boursicot wouldn't talk about the child's mother. And why was this strange Uncle Shi always coming along with Bertrand? Something seemed wacky.

## BERNARD TELLS HIS STORY
The family grew even more mystified when, in July 1983, French counterintelligence called Boursicot in to ask him why he had a Communist Chinese national staying at his place. Boursicot told the authorities the truth, and as a reward for his honesty, he was placed under arrest. International headlines screamed the story of a French diplomat seduced by a Chinese Mata Hari. Shi was arrested, too, and counterintelligence accused Boursicot of lying: Shi Pei Pu wasn't the mother of his child! C'est impossible! Shi was no she!

## UNANSWERED QUESTIONS
Blood tests revealed that Bertrand wasn't related to Shi or Boursicot, but had probably been sold to Shi by his Chinese Turkoman family. Boursicot refused to believe the police. At last, forced to admit Shi Pei Pu's masculinity and his own blindness, he slashed his throat in despair. The suicide attempt failed and Boursicot served time (as did Shi) for espionage. Meanwhile the story spread around the world and became the basis for M. *Butterfly*.

## HE SAID, SHI SAID
So how did Shi keep Boursicot believing he was a woman? Boursicot still can't explain why sex with Shi seemed "just like being with a woman." He thinks his lover might have "put cream between his thighs," and that he penetrated Shi's tightly closed legs. But Shi says he kept himself covered with a blanket in a darkened room and never allowed Boursicot to touch his "private area."

Either way, it's probably better not to think about it.

# AIDS ERA NOTABLES

*Four men who mattered in the early days of AIDS.*

I n the early 1980s, a mysterious new disease began to appear
among gay men, a disease that would eventually become
known as AIDS—Acquired Immune Deficiency Syndrome.
Today, although AIDS is still without a cure, it has become a disease
most people are familiar with, and one that, thanks to innovative
treatments, no longer threatens a quick death to those who carry
the virus that causes it. Let's take a look at four men who made an
impact on the AIDS crisis as it developed in the early 1980s—one
who spread the virus, one who identified it, one who fought
against it, and one who helped change people's minds about those
who were its victims.

## GAETAN DUGAS

Generally speaking, the perception is that the AIDS virus first got
its hold in humans sometime in the late 1970s or early 1980s, but
that perception is not exactly right. AIDS researchers now think
that the HIV virus, which causes AIDS, crossed over into human
populations as early as the 1930s or even before. The first verifiable
instance of the HIV virus in human blood comes from a 1959
blood sample from a man who lived in what is now the Democratic
Republic of Congo; other evidence of the virus has been found
from the 1960s and 1970s, not only in Africa but also in Europe
and the U.S.

### Following the Trail

For all that, it wasn't until the 1980s that AIDS started appearing
in a great number of people here in North America. Scientists
who initially grappled with this unknown killer—first called a
"Gay Cancer" or "GRID (Gay-Related Immune Deficiency)"
because its victims were largely gay men—cast about looking for
connections among the infected men. Eventually a pattern
emerged. Nearly all the patients had sexual histories that pointed
back to a "cluster" of about 40 gay men. In turn, this "cluster" also
had something in common—each man in it either had sex with,

or had sex with someone who had sex with, a French-Canadian flight attendant named Gaetan Dugas. Dugas was "Patient Zero"—the first major vector of AIDS infection in North America.

### Mad, Bad, and Dangerous to Know

What made Dugas the perfect infection vector for AIDS? To begin with, Dugas was incredibly promiscuous, claiming to have more then 250 sex partners a year. He was also highly mobile. His job as a flight attendant allowed him to travel to major cities worldwide and throughout North America. (It also took him to Africa, where it is likely he was first exposed to the virus.) Finally, he was a self-absorbed hedonist who didn't care that he was spreading a disease that was killing people. In a 1992 interview, AIDS researcher Dr. Selma Dritz recalled telling Dugas he was infected and that he should stop having sex. "[He said], 'Don't be silly, I won't cut it out. It's my life. I'll do what I want.' I said, 'Yes, but you're infecting other people.' [He said], 'I got it. Let them get it.'… He walked out. I never saw him again." Gaetan Dugas himself died of AIDS in 1984.

## DR. ROBERT GALLO

Dr. Gallo, who first identified the virus that causes AIDS, was very nearly a victim of it himself—not through infection, but because accusations about his scientific methods infected his research.

### External Evidence

In the early 1980s, scientists didn't know what caused AIDS; what they saw were the opportunistic diseases that took root because of them. Some of these opportunistic diseases were cancers, such as Kaposi's Sarcoma, which causes large purple lesions on the victim's skin, one of the earliest recorded symptoms of the disease. Dr. Gallo, who was the head of the Laboratory of Tumor Cell Biology at the National Cancer Institute, was one of the first to suggest that the cause of the disease might be viral in nature.

### Forward Thinking About Retroviruses

Gallo had made the connection between viruses and cancer before. In 1981 Gallo had published his findings linking a "retrovirus" (a kind of virus that hijacks living cells and splices its own

DNA into them) with the development of leukemia. This discovery had more than the usual scientific satisfaction for Gallo, since as a child Gallo had seen his own sister perish because of childhood leukemia. Gallo's virus hunch was correct, and in 1984, he and his team isolated the HIV virus and helped develop the blood test to detect it in patients.

## A Strained Situation

So everyone's happy, right? Not quite. Gallo became enmeshed in a debate as to whether his research stole from earlier research by Luc Montagnier at the Pasteur Institute; Montagnier discovered a virus in 1983 but didn't definitively link it to AIDS. Montagnier and Gallo eventually agreed to share credit for the discovery of the HIV virus, but in 1989 reporter John Crewdson of the *Chicago Tribune* implied that Gallo had stolen Montagnier's virus and labeled it as a new strain. Aside from the career-threatening implications of the allegation for Gallo, there was also (of course) money involved, thanks to the blood test Gallo developed. This led to a lawsuit so the Pasteur Institute could get a share of the profits from the test manufacturer. The good news (for Gallo, not for the Pasteur Institute) is that after several years of inquiries, Gallo and his researchers were exonerated of all wrongdoing.

## LARRY KRAMER

The AIDS crisis' angriest man, Larry Kramer was (and is) famously nasty and mean-tempered against anyone he perceived as not doing enough to stop AIDS in its tracks, whether they be politicians, drug companies, or even gay men themselves. This is a man who once stopped then–New York City mayor Ed Koch (whom Kramer accused of not doing enough to arrest the AIDS crisis) from petting his dog Molly by pulling back on the dog's leash and saying, "Molly, meet the man who murdered so many of your daddy's friends."

## The Write Stuff

Pre-AIDS, Kramer was best known as a movie producer and screenwriter with a mixed bag of credits. He produced and wrote 1969's *Women in Love*, which nabbed an Oscar award for Glenda Jackson and a screenwriting nomination for Kramer, but then he

Rodrigo Diaz is better known by the name of El Cid.

also produced and wrote a really awful remake of *Lost Horizon* (which Kramer called "the one thing I've ever done that I'm ashamed of"). But in 1981, Kramer jumped into the AIDS crisis feet first by cofounding the Gay Men's Health Crisis, an organization to promote awareness of AIDS within the gay community of New York. But frustrated by what he saw as the organization's increasingly timid behavior (he called it "a sad organization of sissies"), Kramer left the organization, wrote a landmark play about his frustrations (*The Normal Heart*), and in 1987, after a stem-winding speech in which he dared gay men and women to become angry at the slow pace of AIDS research and treatment, founded ACT-UP: The AIDS Coalition to Unleash Power.

## Active Activism
This rather more feisty group quickly became known for dramatic and (pun intended) arresting displays of civil disobedience, including a polarizing 1989 "Stop the Church" event, in which ACT-UP members continually disrupted a mass led by New York Cardinal John O'Connor to protest his opposition to distributing condoms. More moderate AIDS campaigners believed that ACT-UP's extreme acts were more trouble than they were worth; Kramer's response was that it was ACT-UP, not more moderate groups, that caused the FDA to accelerate drug-testing schedules to get more treatment alternatives for people dying of AIDS.

## The Power of Positive Thinking
Kramer, who is HIV-positive himself, continues to be a polarizing figure, often in unusual ways. His liver transplant, performed in 2001, stirred up controversy about whether HIV-positive men and women should even be considered for organ transplants. As of this writing, Kramer is alive, cranky, and busily writing his magnum opus, a 2,000-plus page novel of the AIDS era called *The American People*.

## RYAN WHITE
In North America and Europe, the primary victims of AIDS were (and are) gay men and drug users, but another population that experienced disproportionately high numbers of early AIDS cases were hemophiliacs: People with a disease that prohibits blood

clotting. Hemophiliacs often require blood transfusions, and in the early days of the AIDS epidemic, before blood testing, tainted blood products sometimes passed on the virus to unknowing recipients.

## Blaming the Victim

One of these was young Ryan White. The day after Christmas in 1984, he was told he'd contracted the virus through a transfusion. He was 13 years old at the time. The news of his infection spread through his hometown of Kokomo, Indiana, and the response was not very good at all. People avoided the family at church, Ryan was heckled by other children at his school, and school administrators eventually blocked Ryan from attending school at all; he took classes over the telephone. Someone even shot at the White's home. Ryan and his family didn't take the discrimination lying down. They fought to get Ryan allowed back into school, and in doing so made Ryan a household name across the U.S. He appeared on morning talk shows and in national magazines and caused mainstream America to confront its assumptions about what so many people up until that time dismissed as a "gay disease."

## A New Home

Ryan eventually won the right to return to school, but continued to feel discriminated against; he moved to Cicero, Indiana, where, in contrast to his previous experience, the locals went out of their way to make him feel he belonged, including having each student at his new high school attend a seminar on AIDS. Ryan's fight turned him into a national celebrity; his story became the basis for an autobiographical book as well as a made-for-TV movie (in which Ryan had a cameo). He also met and became friends with celebrities Michael Jackson and Elton John, the latter of whom was with Ryan, along with Ryan's mother, when he passed away in April 1990, at age 18. That same year Congress passed the Ryan White Comprehensive AIDS Resources Emergency (CARE) Act, to help those living with AIDS get the medical care they need.

\* \* \*

"The first casualty when war comes is truth."
—Senator Hiram Johnson, 1917

**Virginia Dare was the first child of English parents born in America.**

# SIX DEGREES OF KEVIN BACON

*In which we explore who—among all the actors in the world—deserves the title "Center of the Hollywood Universe."*

S ix Degrees of Kevin Bacon was someone's playful turn on the phrase "six degrees of separation," based on the idea that everyone in the world can be linked to anyone else in the world in just six steps—that your Aunt Betty's dentist's son's teacher lives next door to the guy who was the president of your high school senior class way back when. And so on.

## FOUR DEGREES

For the uninitiated, the object of Six Degrees of Kevin Bacon is to link any actor or actress, through the movies they've appeared in, to Kevin Bacon in less than six steps. For example, O. J. Simpson was in *Naked Gun* with Priscilla Presley, who was in *The Adventures of Ford Fairlane* with Gilbert Gottfried, who was in *Beverly Hills Cop II* with Paul Reiser, who was in the movie *Diner* with Kevin Bacon. That's four steps.

And it works with most actors you can name.

## THE LAW OF AVERAGES

A computer scientist, Brett Tjaden at the University of Virginia, was curious about what the average "Bacon number" would be for the nearly 500,000 or so actors and actresses listed in IMDb, the Internet Movie Database, so he applied a theorem to the database and found that the average number came out to an amazing 2.917 steps. In other words, anyone who has ever acted professionally can be linked to Bacon in an average of under three steps.

## THE CENTER OF THE UNIVERSE

It's the nature of science (and scientists) to try to take things one or more steps further. Tjaden then wondered who, if anyone, was more "linkable" than Bacon; who—he asked himself—was closer

---

**Franco adopted the nickname El Caudillo ("the Leader").**

to the center of the Hollywood Universe? When he did the math, he found that there were 1,160 other actors who were even better centers than Kevin Bacon, that is, who could be linked to the largest number of actors in fewer steps. Bacon is still in the 99th percentile, but he was beaten out by Shelley Winters, for instance, who can be linked to every other actor in the world in an average of 2.69 steps.

## THE TOP 20

By now you might be wondering who among all the actors in the world is the center of the Hollywood Universe. Here's the list of the top 20, followed by the average number of steps it takes to link them with all the other actors in the known universe.

1. Lee, Christopher (2.622940)
2. Steiger, Rod (2.627270)
3. Pleasence, Donald (2.651306)
4. Welles, Orson (2.661389)
5. Sutherland, Donald (2.662426)
6. von Sydow, Max (2.662549)
7. Hopper, Dennis (2.665564)
8. Quinn, Anthony (2.667077)
9. Heston, Charlton (2.670193)
10. Hackman, Gene (2.675916)
11. Keitel, Harvey (2.677892)
12. Connery, Sean (2.681795)
13. Caine, Michael (2.682431)
14. Mitchum, Robert (2.682564)
15. Stanton, Harry Dean (2.683768)
16. Sheen, Martin (2.684875)
17. Winters, Shelley (2.696842)
18. Plummer, Christopher (2.698008)
19. Gould, Elliott (2.699126)
20. Borgnine, Ernest (2.702159)

The complete list of the top 1,000 can be viewed at the Oracle of Bacon website: http://oracleofbacon.org/, where you can also play Six Degrees of Kevin Bacon the easy way, by letting your computer do the work.

---

**Sideburns are named after Civil War General Ambrose Burnsides.**

# DR. J

*The dictionary is so familiar that we don't give much thought to how it's put together. But how would you go about writing one from scratch?*

Samuel Johnson's *Dictionary of the English Language* took nearly 10 years to write, but when it was finished in 1755, it was the definitive English dictionary until the *Oxford English Dictionary* was compiled at the start of the 20th century. Not bad for someone who claimed he never got out of bed before noon.

## DEFINE AND DANDY

Johnson's was not the first English dictionary. There was, for example, a dictionary of Shakespearean words (yes, they needed Shakespeare explained, even in the 1700s!). But the idea that dictionaries should include all words, not just obscure ones, was new. And without other dictionaries to start from, Johnson had to collect most of the entries himself.

So how do you write a dictionary? Johnson's method was this: He read books, pamphlets, poetry, and anything else he could get his hands on. He marked any words he hadn't yet collected and wrote his definition in the margin. Then he passed the marked books and papers to his assistants (he had six), who copied each defined word and the sentence it came from onto their own sheet of paper. To put the book together, the papers were assembled into alphabetical order and copied into a manuscript—by hand.

The same technique of reading, marking, and keeping card-files was used by lexicographers until very recently. (Nowadays they don't seem to want to make pencil marks on their computer screens.)

## IN HIS OWN WORDS

Unlike modern dictionaries, Johnson's work contains plenty of his own opinions and wit in the definitions. For example:

> **gallery:** the seats in the playhouse above the pit, in which the meaner people sit.

> **novel:** a small tale, generally of love.

Of course, one reason Johnson had the freedom to write his definitions however he liked was because he was writing his

---

**Genghis Khan was Kublai Khan's grandfather.**

dictionary practically single-handedly. So it's probably good he found a way to amuse himself, given that one of his definitions of the word "dull" read: "To make dictionaries is dull work."

## FROM LEXICOGRAPHY TO BIOGRAPHY

So what did Johnson do with the rest of his life? Dr. Johnson is remembered today as the original 18th-century man of letters, drinking with actors and trading witty remarks with writers. But his fame has little to do with his dictionary. Instead, it comes from one of the most famous biographies ever written: James Boswell's *The Life of Samuel Johnson, LL.D.* (1791).

Johnson had been well-known and well-liked in literary London in his day, but Boswell's book made him into an international celebrity after his death. Although Johnson was a prolific author, his prose style was mostly dull and lacked the wit and sparkle of his conversation. Johnson's humor and personality and Boswell's ability to capture those traits made for a biography so popular and entertaining, it is still widely read today.

## JOHNSON FROM A TO Z

Overall, Johnson had a pretty hard life. His father was nearly bankrupt when he died, leaving young Samuel to struggle through university and scratch out a living as a writer. Although known as Dr. Johnson, he was not a medical doctor but a doctor of letters, a title he received from Oxford University in later life.

Johnson was troubled by depression and poor health all his life. This didn't help his poverty, nor did his generally lazy character or his generous tendency to support other people on his meager income.

Several years after his dictionary was complete, some influential friends helped to get him a government pension for his services to literature. Perhaps they hoped this would give him plenty of time to write great literature. But with his money worries over, Johnson just indulged his sociable and lazy nature. He never produced another major work.

So now we know how to write a dictionary and a little about a man who wrote one. But none of this explains *why* someone would want to write one. Perhaps the question is best answered with Johnson's own words: "No man but a blockhead ever wrote except for money."

# MONOGRAMS

*From Uncle John's bottomless bag of wordplay tricks.*

By some delicious quirk of fate, the initials of famous names sometimes lend themselves to self-descriptive phrases. Take child care expert Dr. Benjamin Spock, for instance, who, in this case, can be described as "Baby Specialist."

See if you can figure out who the rest of these monograms refer to.

1. Plays Bond

2. Chicken Sultan

3. Action Superstar

4. Classic Couturier

5. Media Warhorse

6. "Girls'" Spokesperson

7. Prince O'Thespians

8. Surrealism Dynamo

9. Mrs. Schwarzenegger

10. Home-run Ace

11. Ripa's Partner

12. Married Bancroft

13. Notable Astronaut

14. Quintessential English-woman

15. Major Jumper

16. Acted "Hannibal"

17. Madame Tory

Answers: 1. Pierce Brosnan; 2. Colonel Sanders; 3. Arnold Schwarzenegger; 4. Coco Chanel; 5. Mike Wallace; 6. Gloria Steinem; 7. Peter O'Toole; 8. Salvador Dali; 9. Maria Shriver; 10. Hank Aaron; 11. Regis Philbin; 12. Mel Brooks; 13. Neil Armstrong; 14. Queen Elizabeth; 15. Michael Jordan; 16. Anthony Hopkins; 17. Margaret Thatcher

**Beethoven's "Eroica" symphony was originally dedicated to Napoleon.**

# HISS-TORY'S A LIE

*One was a spy and the other a patriot—but which was which?*

What do all the following have in common: a pumpkin patch, a Woodstock manual typewriter, Richard Nixon, an old Ford Roadster automobile, a prothonotary warbler bird, the House Un-American Activities Committee, and microfilms of secret State Department documents?

Answer: They were all key elements in one of the best-known espionage cases in U.S. history—the Alger Hiss case.

## IN THE CHAMBERS OF POWER

Whittaker Chambers was an admitted former communist who claimed that Hiss spied for the Soviet Union while he held a high-ranking position in the U.S. State Department. Hiss denied everything, claiming that he had been unjustly accused and framed by Chambers and the U.S. government. One of them was lying. But which one?

The question ignited a debate that lasted for almost 50 years.

## THE WELL-BRED AND THE EX-RED

Like Lewis and Clark, Antony and Cleopatra, and other historic duos, Alger Hiss and Whittaker Chambers will always be thought of together. But they were as different as Laurel and Hardy.

Hiss was tall, slender, elegantly dressed, and aristocratic—a pillar of the liberal establishment. A graduate of Harvard Law School, he clerked for the legendary Supreme Court Justice Oliver Wendell Holmes and worked for a Wall Street law firm. He joined the Franklin Roosevelt administration in 1933 and rose steadily. By 1945, he was a high-ranking State Department official who accompanied FDR to the Yalta Conference with Churchill and Stalin—a vital WWII meeting in which crucial decisions about the post-war world were made. In 1946, he left the State Department to become head of the prestigious Carnegie Endowment for International Peace.

Whittaker Chambers was short, plump, and shabbily dressed. A brilliant but deeply troubled man, he attended Columbia

University, but never graduated. He worked at various jobs, including as a translator. (He translated the German children's novel *Bambi* into English.) He was fired from a job at the New York Public Library when he was accused of stealing books. His abiding interest was the Communist Party. He joined the party in 1925 and wrote quite a few articles for its publications. In 1932 he started working as a full-time espionage agent for the Soviet Union. But he grew disenchanted in the late 1930s, abandoned communism, and became a devout Christian and fervent anti-communist. At the same time his life took a turn for the better; professionally, when he was hired by *Time* magazine (eventually becoming one of its senior editors), and personally, when he married happily.

## J'ACCUSE!

Chambers accused Alger Hiss of being a communist in 1948 in testimony before the House Un-American Activities Committee (HUAC) (whose most forceful member was the young congressman Richard Nixon). When Hiss learned of the accusation, he demanded a chance to testify before the committee, where he adamantly denied ever being a communist and claimed that he'd never even met Whittaker Chambers. Most people believed what Hiss said, but not Richard Nixon, who persuaded the other committee members to appoint him as the head of a subcommittee to investigate further.

Chambers began to give Nixon more information. It appeared that he'd known both Hiss and his wife quite well—he said he had lived for a time in Hiss's home in Washington, D.C., that Hiss had given him an old Ford Roadster, and that the Hisses were amateur ornithologists who became quite excited when they spotted a rare prothonotary warbler.

Who but a friend would let you tell him about your boring bird-watching hobby?

## PUMPKIN SPY

Later, while being interviewed on a radio show, Chambers claimed that Hiss was not only a communist, but had been a member of the same spy ring to which Chambers had belonged. Hiss promptly

---

**Benito Mussolini was a newspaper editor before he came to power.**

sued Chambers for libel, and both were called to testify before a federal grand jury.

Then came the real bombshell. Chambers claimed to have microfilm copies of secret State Department documents that had been given to him by Hiss. For safekeeping, he had placed these inside a hollowed out pumpkin shell on his Maryland farm (and there he kept them very well). These "Pumpkin Papers" were confirmed to be authentic and caused a sensation. The government was now convinced that Hiss was a spy, but he could not be charged with espionage because the Pumpkin Papers dated from 1937 and the statute of limitations had run out. Hiss was charged with perjury—the government claiming he had lied under oath when he testified before the grand jury and HUAC.

## A TRYING TIME

Hiss was first tried for perjury in 1949. The trial turned on, of all things, an old Woodstock manual typewriter. In this era, long before the invention of photocopy machines, copying voluminous secret documents wasn't easy. Chambers said that Hiss took the documents home with him from the State Department and had his wife type copies on the Woodstock typewriter. Hiss gave the typewritten copies to Chambers, who had them photographed. The actual Woodstock typewriter that Hiss admitted he had owned in the 1930s was never found, but letters Hiss and his wife typed on the typewriter in the 1930s apparently matched the typed copies of the State Department documents.

Hiss's first trial ended in a hung jury. He was tried again, convicted, and sentenced to five years in prison.

## THE END OF DAYS

Released after 44 months, his career over, Hiss worked as a salesman and proclaimed his innocence until his dying day—in 1996 at age 92.

Chambers, vindicated by Hiss's conviction, became a conservative icon and wrote a best-selling book about his life called *Witness*. He died of a heart attack in 1961.

Richard Nixon, the obscure freshman congressman whose investigation led to Hiss's trial and conviction, became a national figure. The Hiss case directly led to his meteoric rise in national

---

Janet Guthrie was the first woman to compete in the Indy 500 in 1977.

politics. He entered the Senate in 1950 and was elected vice president in 1952—and you know how that turned out.

## THE ENEMY WITHIN

Hiss always claimed he was the victim of a right-wing conspiracy designed to discredit the Roosevelt administration, and lots of people believed him. In fact, his innocence was an article of faith for many leftists for decades. But today most people believe he was guilty because of a particularly damning piece of evidence that came to light in the 1990s when the FBI released copies of secret cables it had intercepted from the Soviet consulate in the 1940s. These "Venona Cables" contained a document stating that an unnamed Soviet agent who worked in the State Department had flown from the Yalta Conference to Moscow in 1945. Only four people who were at Yalta matched this description—Alger Hiss was one of them.

But whatever spying Hiss may have done for the Soviets caused much less damage to the U.S. than the effect of his trial on the body politic. A few months after his conviction, a relatively unknown senator named Joseph McCarthy declared that there were hundreds of communists in the State Department. It wasn't true, of course, but, because of the Hiss case, millions believed him. McCarthyism and the red hysteria of the 1950s were unleashed.

\* \* \*

## THE MOST HOLY FELLA

We have it straight from Carl Bernstein and Marco Politi, the authors of *His Holiness*. Not only did Pope John Paul II's parents meet in a church, all the windows in the apartment he was born in faced a church. And at the moment of his birth, hymns to the Blessed Virgin were being sung across the street.

John L. Sullivan, the "Boston Strong Boy," was the last bare-knuckle fighting champion.

# INGENIOUS INSULTS

*Ever wish you had a witty put-down when you needed it?*

Okay, we admit it. We're like Alice Longsworth Roosevelt who once said, "If you haven't got a good word to say about anyone, come and sit by me." In our book, flattery will get you nowhere.

**Insulting General MacArthur (and generals in general):**
"I fired him because he wouldn't accept the authority of the president. I didn't fire him because he was a dumb s.o.b. although he was. But that's not against the law for generals. If it was half of them would be in jail."
**Put-down artist:** Harry Truman

**Insulting William Gladstone (19th-century prime minister of England):**
"If Gladstone fell into the Thames, it would be a misfortune. But if someone pulled him out, it would be a calamity."
**Put-down artist:** Benjamin Disraeli (19th-century prime minister of England)

**Insulting former First Lady Rosalyn Carter:**
"I'm often tempted to drown my troubles. But I can't get my wife to go swimming."
**Put-down artist:** former president Jimmy Carter

**A Presidential Insult Threefer:**
"History buffs probably noted the reunion at a Washington party a few weeks ago of three ex-presidents: Carter, Ford, and Nixon—See No Evil, Hear No Evil, and Evil."
**Put-down artist:** former senator and presidential candidate Bob Dole

**Insulting Calvin Coolidge:**
"Calvin Coolidge didn't say much, and when he did he didn't say much."
**Put-down artist:** Will Rodgers

# BEHIND EVERY SUCCESSFUL MAN...

*Was Einstein the greatest mind of the 20th century or a selfish egotist who stole credit for his most famous theory?*

Einstein was devoted to physics...Einstein was accepted to the University of Zurich as a Ph.D. candidate against great odds...Einstein worked on the theory of relativity....Okay, quit snoring! We aren't talking about that brainy dude with the frizzy hair, Albert Einstein. The above facts all refer to Mileva Maric Einstein—Albert's brilliant first wife—and possibly the brains behind the world's most famous genius.

### I ENJOY BEING A GIRL GENIUS

Mileva Maric was born on December 19, 1875, near Vojvodinae, a village in what is now Serbia. Although little is known about her, even as a young girl, Mileva's brilliant mind and hunger for knowledge made her seem destined for great things. Mileva was one of the first women in the Austro-Hungarian Empire to go to high school. She studied physics and math and graduated with top grades, then went on to study science at the university level. And she was the only woman in her class at the elite Swiss Federal Institute of Technology (ETH) where she was training to be a teacher. She was respected as a gifted and brilliant student. But the professors had less admiration for her fellow classmate, Albert Einstein.

### A RISING AND FALLING STAR

When Mileva and Albert met at ETH in 1896, she was a star science and math student. He had a reputation for being lazy, and no professor would hire him as a teaching assistant. But by the time they parted, Albert was on his way to becoming the world's most revered scientist, while Mileva was strained, overworked, and suffered from psychological problems. What caused his rise and her fall? Was it simply his brilliance—or did Maric give her all to her husband only to be discarded once he made it to the top of the heap? In 1986, Albert's private letters to Mileva surfaced. The letters provided

---

Notorious pirates Anne Bonny and Mary Read were reputed to be lovers.

glimpses of a woman who might have been a scientific as well as marriage partner, and they revealed that Einstein—that humorous, lovable genius—had a troubling side.

## PHYSICS AND...CHEMISTRY

At ETH, Einstein and Maric were taking the same classes and love bloomed as they studied together and chatted about such lighthearted subjects as double integrals and electromagnetic light theory. "My dear kitten," Albert wrote, "I just read a wonderful paper by Lenard on the generation of cathode rays by ultraviolet light." Einstein may have benefited from working with Maric; he'd never done so well before at ETH. Maric, the more respected student, failed her ETH exam in 1900. Oddly, her grade was pulled down by mathematics scores, one of her strongest subjects.

Was Maric distracted by romantic overtures from passionate Albert? The two students were certainly growing close. In 1901 they took a lovebird's excursion to Italy, and the next time Mileva Maric took the ETH exam, she had a good excuse for failing—she was single and three months pregnant, a condition considered shameful in those days. Einstein passed his exam, but his professors wouldn't recommend him for a teaching degree. Since Maric's illegitimate child would be his very own, Einstein promised to take a low-paying job and marry Maric right away. It didn't happen.

## MUM'S THE WORD

In 1902, Maric was staying with her parents in Serbia when Maric and Einstein's daughter Lieserl was born. The infant girl may have been cared for in Maric's family or given up for adoption. Nothing certain is known about the little girl's fate. His daughter's birth was kept so secret that none of Einstein's many biographers knew of the child's existence until Mileva's letters came to light. For the first time, scholars realized how secretive Einstein could be.

He did eventually marry Maric. She was a woman that Einstein could talk to—who else would understand the latest news on electrons? When they finally wed in 1903, he was working at the patent office in Bern, Switzerland. To help support them, Maric worked, too. Collaborating with another physicist, she invented a machine to measure small electric currents. Interestingly, the machine was patented under her husband's name, not hers.

---

British scientist Thomas Huxley coined the term "agnosticism."

## RELATIVE COMFORT

In 1904, the couple's first son, Hans Albert, arrived. Maric continued to help support the family while she also cared for the house and their child—and Einstein bragged that she did math calculations for him, too! In the early days of their marriage Einstein seemed very satisfied. He wrote to a friend: "Well, now I'm a thoroughly married husband and lead a nice comfortable life with my wife. She takes excellent care of everything, cooks well, and is always in a good mood." Perhaps because Maric worked so hard to make Einstein comfortable, his years with her were his most productive.

In 1905, the comfortable Einstein published three of his most important papers in physics: The first on the motion of particles suspended in liquid, the second on the photoelectric effect, and last and most famous the paper on the special theory of relativity.

## SCIENCE AFFAIR

Einstein started to move up in the scientific world. He was finally a professor in Zurich in 1910 when his second son, Eduard, was born. Einstein was doing well, but Maric was showing signs of strain. Einstein would later complain that she became brooding and suspicious. But perhaps Maric had reason to be suspicious. In 1912 Einstein began an affair with his second cousin Elsa—it was likely not his first flirtation. In 1914 the couple separated and never reunited; by 1919 the divorce was final, and Einstein married Elsa.

## IS IT ALL RELATIVE?

When it came to marriage, it's clear that Albert was no Einstein. When times got tough for his wife, the famous absentminded professor was just plain absent. But was Einstein also a rogue who never gave Maric due credit for her work? Could it be that Maric was the brains behind the greatest mind of the 20th century? Speculation grew when it became known that the divorce papers promised Maric the prize money if Albert won the Nobel Prize. Was that just a strange alimony settlement or proof that Maric felt she deserved something for her contributions to the scientific theories published by her husband?

Maric's supporters point out that after their divorce, Einstein had access to great scientific resources and the best minds of his generation. So why didn't his work ever again reach the same

Henri Becquerel discovered radioactivity, not the Curies, who got a prize for their research.

brilliance that it did when he and Maric lived together? Some scholars speculate that Maric allowed her husband to take credit for the physics papers for the same reason she let him put his name on her invention's patent. The financially struggling couple knew that inventions and scientific theories published under a woman's name would make acceptance (and Albert's professorship) much harder to achieve. A Russian physicist who saw the original papers Einstein submitted claimed that Maric's name was on them. Unfortunately, those original papers no longer exist.

The private letters of Maric and Einstein hint at a working collaboration. In 1901, for example, Einstein writes to Maric, "How happy and proud I will be when both of us together will have brought our work on relative motion to a successful end." But the letters also support the arguments of those who say Maric's contributions were minimal at best. Aside from mentioning a scientific book she's reading, Maric never writes about physics to Einstein. Her letters concentrate only on their deepening relationship. It's Albert who's always tossing off ideas about physics in his love letters to his "sweet witch." Nor did Maric ever complain to Einstein or anyone else when he failed to publicly acknowledge any help with the development of his physics theories.

### AN (IG)NOBEL PRIZEWINNER?
In 1922, Einstein received the Nobel Prize, and Maric received the prize money. Einstein became an international icon while his ex-wife struggled to raise the icon's sons. Her job was all the more difficult because Eduard was tragically ill with schizophrenia. In 1948, suffering mentally and physically, Maric died. We'll never know if Maric was a true collaborator in Einstein's early work, but without her personal sacrifices, surely Einstein wouldn't have been able to produce those revolutionary scientific theories of 1905. Maric dedicated herself to Einstein's career and well-being. Sadly, that dedication never allowed her to fulfill her own promise. Einstein, who had troubles with his second marriage, too, probably summed up Maric's situation best: "When it comes to close relationships I failed twice, disgracefully...marriages are dangerous."

# THE MAN WHO CAME TO HOLLYWOOD

*He was only 5'2", but Carl Laemmle was a giant in the movie industry, boss to the likes of Bette Davis, Bela Lugosi, Rudolph Valentino—and even Zasu Pitts. He's the man who invented movie stars, publicity stunts, and a lot of other Hollywood shenanigans we couldn't live without.*

Born in Germany in 1867, Carl Laemmle immigrated to New York to seek his fortune when he was just 17. Ten years later, he was in Chicago, working at a department store and earning $18 a week. Always ambitious, and now with a family to support, Laemmle decided to open his own store. After an extensive search, he found the perfect building. It was long—just right for the long counters needed to hold his dry goods, and perfect for his night job.

After hours, Laemmle hung a large white sheet at one end of his long store and put a projector at the other end. He charged five cents admission and showed the latest "flickers"—what movies were called back then. Before long he was drawing a standing-room-only crowd, but they thoughtlessly leaned on his merchandise, which irritated him no end. So Laemmle found another long store, put in some seats and—voilá!—he had a movie theater, or, in the parlance of the day, a "nickelodeon."

## THE TRUST

The logical, and more lucrative, next step was to rent movies to other theaters. As the flickers increased in popularity, Laemmle Film Service became the country's largest film distributor. This ticked off the early production companies—including Edison, Vitagraph, and Biograph—known as "The Trust," or the Motion Picture Patents Company. The conglomerate monopolized the early film industry by buying up "film exchanges" (distribution companies that bought short films and rented them to exhibitors at lower rates). Laemmle refused to kowtow to The Trust—he not only held on to his exchange, but he started making his own movies, which ticked The Trust off even more. The big guns took him to court, but ended up losing their case after a three-year feud.

---

Lyndon Johnson was the only U.S. president to be sworn in on an airplane.

## THE LITTLE IMP

By then, Laemmle's first film company, The Independent Moving Pictures Company of America—or, as he affectionately called it, IMP—was firmly entrenched in New York, where he'd moved with his family in 1912. Always the clever businessman, Laemmle listened as his patrons raved over their favorite actors. He realized that a successful movie company needed a "star."

## THE FIRST MOVIE STAR

At the time, Biograph Films featured a 20-year-old actress who was dazzling audiences. Fans of the Biograph Girl demanded to know her name, but Biograph, believing unidentified actors meant low-paid actors, refused to tell. Laemmle knew better. He not only hatched a plan to bring young Florence Lawrence (the Biograph Girl) to IMP, he did it with theatrical flair. In the world's first publicity stunt, Laemmle leaked a story to the press. A streetcar had killed the Biograph Girl! The shocked public flew into a frenzy, but was relieved when Laemmle announced that it was all a hoax. He swore that jealous competitors made up the whole thing. To prove she had not yet met her maker, Miss Lawrence appeared in St. Louis, Missouri, where Laemmle hired "fans" to mob her and tear off her clothes. Florence Lawrence became a household name. Her movies made big box office. A star was born. That same year, Laemmle also lured future superstar Mary Pickford away from Biograph, advertising his coup as "Little Mary is an IMP now."

## THE MASTER OF THE UNIVERSAL

As IMP grew, Laemmle decided it was time for a new corporate name—something big. When he saw a truck with the name "Universal Pipe Fittings," he found what he was looking for. The Independent Moving Pictures Company of America was replaced by the Universal Film Manufacturing Company, the precursor of Universal Pictures. Soon after, Laemmle purchased one of the first film studios in California. A studio was a fine thing, but a city would be even better—a city with one sole purpose: to make movies. So, in 1914, Laemmle paid $165,000 for a 230-acre site in the San Fernando Valley, just 10 miles from Los Angeles. A year later in front of thousands of movie fans, 48-year-old Laemmle presided over the opening of Universal City.

---

Q: What was Eleanor Roosevelt's maiden name? A: Roosevelt.

In addition to its six-mile-long main street, Universal City boasted its own police department, fire brigade, and school. Two restaurants served 1,000 customers daily. Blacksmiths, tailors, and mechanics coexisted with leather shops, mills, and apothecaries. Buildings varied from English colonials to Italian villas with French provincials and Japanese teahouses in between. Laemmle knew that people were curious about the making of motion pictures, so he opened the gates and charged the curious 25 cents to take a tour. Sometimes a lucky few even got cast as extras!

## A REAL HORROR SHOW
Over the next 20 years, Universal built its success on classics like *Phantom of the Opera* (1925), *Dracula* (1931), *Frankenstein* (1931), *The Mummy* (1932), *The Invisible Man* (1933), and *The Bride of Frankenstein* (1935).

## BEHIND THE SCENERY
Laemmle was a soft touch. In addition to the 70 relatives he'd given jobs to, Laemmle put his son, Carl Laemmle, Jr., in charge of production when he turned 21. The kid wasn't up to it; he was too extravagant during the Depression years, so by March 1935, the studio was in debt and Laemmle was forced to sell his city to a group of financiers for a little more than $5 five million. The new owners were in for a surprise. They found two dead men still on the payroll, employees who showed up just to collect paychecks, and others who came to work every day, but had no real jobs. Some of Laemmle's relatives even lived on the lot. They were all evicted. The last to leave were Laemmle's widowed sister-in-law and her daughter; the ladies had been living in one of Universal City's three-bedroom bungalows—their furniture compliments of the prop department.

## UNIVERSAL SUCCESS
Carl Laemmle died in 1939, but not before he saw his former company bounce back to financial health thanks to the acquisition in 1936 of singing teenage superstar Deanna Durbin. Today, Universal is still one of the most successful studios in Hollywood and produced two of the highest-grossing movies of all time, *E.T.: The Extra-Terrestrial* and *Jurassic Park*.

Dieu et Mon Droit ("God and My Right") is Queen Elizabeth II's motto.

# LIGHTS! CAMERA! CONTROVERSY!

*They can't all be Steven Spielberg. Here's a quartet of filmmakers who are as controversial as their films.*

## LENI RIEFENSTAHL

Here's what's good about Leni: A former movie star herself, she was working as a director in the 1930s when few other woman were. And boy, did she have an eye for the epic. She had a distinct, clear, and stunning visual style, the elements of which are studied and shamelessly imitated even now. Here's what's bad about Leni: She did all of that while working for the Nazis, and not as some mere rank-and-file Nazi stooge, but as Hitler's personal filmmaker. Der Führer enjoyed her 1932 mountaineering melodrama *The Blue Light* so much (it was romantically volkish) that he recruited her to film the Nazis' Sixth Party Congress in Nuremberg, giving her the money and control needed to do it up right.

**When Your Benefactor Is a Malefactor**
The resulting film was 1935's *Triumph des Willens* (*Triumph of the Will*), which is as visually compelling as its content is repellent. Riefenstahl's cinematic compositions of rows and rows of Nazi faithful are basic elements of the filmmaking toolbox—you can see them replicated in films as far-flung as George Lucas's *Attack of the Clones* or even in Disney's *The Lion King* (in the "Be Prepared" musical sequence). After *Triumph*, Riefenstahl was back behind the lens, documenting the 1936 Berlin Olympics in the two-part film *Olympia*. Then came WWII and in the aftermath it suddenly wasn't such a great thing to be Hitler's favorite director.

Riefenstahl maintained that she never bought into the whole Nazi thing (a point augmented by her sole post-WWII feature film, *Tiefland*, which can be seen as an oblique protest of Nazi tyranny), but you can't spend that much time snuggling up to evil without reeking of brimstone.

**A Hard Act to Follow**
After the war, Riefenstahl spent four years in detention before being released. (No war crimes charges were filed against her by

the Allies.) Unable to find anyone to hire her as a director, she headed to Africa. She found some fame and notoriety as a still photographer and continued to work well into her 90s. *Tiefland,* which she had begun during the war, was eventually cobbled together and released in 1954. In 2002, the 100-year-old Riefenstahl released *Impressionen unter Wasser* (*Impressions Under Water*), a 45-minute film focused on undersea life. It's unlikely Riefenstahl will ever live down her Nazi associations (which is understandable), but by any estimation, she was a formidable filmmaker.

## JOHN WATERS

To say John Waters reveled in bad taste would be to understate the case; as Waters himself once said, "If someone threw up at one of my screenings, it would be like a standing ovation." Not to mention that Waters might then use the scene for his next film. Growing up in Baltimore in the 1950s and 1960s, as a teen Waters began creating outrageous short films designed primarily to annoy and horrify. His earliest short film, 1964's *Hag in a Black Leather Jacket,* featured an interracial couple married by a Ku Klux Klansman. By the early 1970s, Waters was making full-length films that were booked as "midnight shows" in art film theaters.

### To Gross Out Is Divine

It was there that audiences met the film that would make Waters infamous: 1972's *Pink Flamingos,* which featured two trailer trash women (one of them being the massive transvestite Divine) slugging it out to claim the title of "the Filthiest Person in the World." The contest was eventually settled when Divine ingested some animal byproduct, fresh from the animal. The fact that it's clear that this particular byproduct is the genuine article made *Pink Flamingos* notorious, and Waters spent the 1970s making similar, viscerally disgusting films.

### Cool Waters

Then a funny thing happened: Waters became respectable. His 1988 movie *Hairspray* still starred Divine (his last film before his death) but was—gasp!—rated PG, and, was a hit with mainstream audiences. (It also became the inspiration for the smash 2002 Broadway musical of the same name.) Since then Waters has worked exclusively in mainstream film with varying success. He's become a camp celebrity in his own right, guest-starring on a classic episode of *The Simpsons* in which Homer finds out that his new friend John is, like, totally gay. (John Waters is openly gay in real life.) It's proof that people mellow with age, although in Waters's case, it could be argued that there was nowhere to go.

## KENNETH ANGER
Some people have always known where they were going in life, and Kenneth Anger was one. Born in 1930 as Kenneth Wilbur Anglemyer, Anger is said to have taken his stage name at age five. In his teens he began creating the graphic and disturbing short films he would be known for. The first, 1947's *Fireworks*, was a 20-minute film in which Anger is sexually assaulted—not the sort of film typically made in 1947 Hollywood, but one now regarded as a classic of sorts in gay cinema circles.

### The Angry Young Man
Other disjointed, bizarre short films followed over the next few decades, with intriguing titles like *Inauguration of the Pleasure Dome*, *Invocation of My Demon Brother*, and *Lucifer Rising*. These films are frequently derided by critics as incomprehensible mishmashes of quick-cut editing, chaotic layered images, and confounding demonic and/or homoerotic imagery, but others see them as legitimate predecessors of the most common film short done today—music videos. Anger often made music integral to his films: 1969's *Invocation of My Demon Brother* features the Rolling Stones and a soundtrack by Mick Jagger, and 1973's *Lucifer Rising* has a score written by Bobby Beausoleil, a member of the Manson family.

### Making Gold from Dirt
Ironically, Anger's true fame comes not from his films, seen by a relatively small number of people, but from his authorship of the lurid Hollywood Babylon books, in which he airs the movie industry's dirty laundry. One book features a photo of Nancy Reagan in her modeling days; Anger sent her a copy of the book while she lived in the White House. Two weeks later (or so Anger has maintained in interviews) he was audited by the IRS.

## MICHAEL CIMINO
Michael Cimino is the second greatest example of "Hollywood giveth and Hollywood taketh away" (the greatest example being

portly wine seller and total freakin' genius Orson Welles). In the early 1970s, Cimino was a reasonably successful screenwriter with a *Dirty Harry* screenplay (*Magnum Force*) to his credit when Clint Eastwood tapped him to write and direct his next film, 1974's *Thunderbolt and Lightfoot*. The robbery caper was a big hit, inspiring Universal to bankroll the young director's next project, *The Deer Hunter*, a harrowing tale of friends who go off to Vietnam. The film, a major success in 1978, rang up Oscars for Best Picture, Best Director, and a Best Supporting Actor award for Christopher Walken. Cimino, for the moment, was the toast of the town.

## Burnt Toast

Then came *Heaven's Gate*. United Artists gave Cimino a blank check to create the Western, and Cimino ended up making the studio pay for it. He ran up the film's budget to $50 million (in 1980 dollars) by creating meticulous-to-the-point-of-obsessive re-creations of the Western era he was portraying. He also became notoriously controlling and had his actors do some very strange things, such as star Isabelle Huppert decamping to a bordello to "research" her role. (She was strictly an observer.) As detailed in the insider tome, *The Final Cut*, United Artists executives became increasingly concerned with mounting costs and realized that if the film failed, their company would go under as well.

## Heaven and Hell

*Heaven's Gate* not only failed, the three-and-a-half hour epic was hailed as the biggest flop in movie history. It was so critically reviled that the film was withdrawn from theaters after just three days. United Artists did indeed go under and was folded into rival Metro-Goldwyn-Mayer, where it exists (sort of) today. "It was really a great trauma, as everyone knows," said Cimino in 1996 of the experience. "Since then, I've been unable to make any movie that I've wanted to make." No kidding. After *Heaven's Gate*, Cimino's career nearly dropped off the radar screen entirely, which is not unreasonable. While directors make failed films all the time, it takes some special effort to bring down an entire studio. Still, he directed four more films, the last in 1996. Unfortunately for Cimino, none found any commercial success.

# DONUTS TO DOLLARS

*Tim Horton wasn't happy enough being a Canadian pro hockey player. Noooooo. He had to go out and build a coffee empire that rivals America's Starbucks.*

Today's hockey elite have minions (like managers) to make sure they get their millions, but back in the 1950s it was pretty tough-going for your average NHL player with a wife and family.

And so it was for Maple Leaf player Tim Horton when a hard body-check in a 1955 game broke his jaw and leg. Horton was off the ice for a year—no play, no pay. But he stayed with the game.

## KISS YOUR MONEY TROUBLES GOOD-BYE

Horton he struck the pot of gold (or maybe deep-fryer of fat) in 1964 when he went into partnership with an ex-cop named Ron Joyce in a chain of coffee and donut shops that still bear his name today. Serving nothing but those two commodities, Tim Hortons became synonymous with Canada, right alongside beavers and maple syrup. The menu, including Horton's own personal creations— the dutchie and apple fritter—had customers flocking in to pay a quarter for a coffee and a donut.

The single shop grew into a chain, and by his mid-40s Horton didn't really need to keep playing hockey. But he did anyway, winning MVP for the Buffalo Sabres in 1973.

## KILLED IN THE LINE OF DUTY

The coffee-and-donut man died in a car accident in 1974 on the way home from a game, behind the wheel of a sports car he'd gotten as a bonus. The widow Horton sold her interests in the chain the following year for $1 million. Today Tim Hortons has over 1,500 shops in Canada, with gross sales of more than $1 billion a year.

Incidentally, that same cup of coffee (small) and a donut, would cost you $1.81 (Canadian) today, tax included.

---

The first African American to publish a volume of poetry was Phillis Wheatley.

# GUDRID THORBJARNARDOTTIR

*The winner of our Longest Name in the Book award was also an adventuress to whom a pleasure cruise meant crossing the Atlantic Ocean in an open boat.*

Born around A.D. 985, Gudrid Thorbjarnardottir lived in a time when Viking women were generally considered good enough to procreate, cook, clean, and not much else. She burst these role boundaries to become the first Caucasian woman to set foot on North American soil, and (it is believed) the most well-traveled female of her time.

## I TOLD YOU TO STOP AND ASK FOR DIRECTIONS

Gudrid, described in Icelandic sagas as "the most attractive of women and one to be reckoned with in all her dealings," began her adult life in the typical manner of Viking women—she married. But instead of staying by the hearth, she persuaded her husband, Thorir, to follow her father to the newly discovered Greenland— and to take her with him.

He agreed, and off they went. Long story short, they ended up stranded on a tiny island north of Greenland. Death seemed unavoidable until they were rescued by none other than Leif Erikson, whose father, Erik "the Red" Thorvaldson, had discovered Green-land (so presumably his family knew their way around it pretty well). The couple stayed in Erik's home for the winter, but Thorir became ill and died the following spring.

## HUSBANDS AND MORE HUSBANDS

Thorir's death didn't cause too much heartbreak for Gudrid. She stayed in Greenland with her father and married again, this time to Thorstein Erikson, another son of Erik the Red. But it seems Gudrid was destined to be a widow. A contagious disease swept the small settlement, and Thorstein died.

Gudrid was distraught. She took the loss of her second hus-band hard. Since her father, meanwhile, had also died, she had no

---

**Pearl Buck was the first American woman to win the Nobel Prize in Literature.**

one to act as her protector. Leif took on the task to act as her surrogate father. While living in his home, Gudrid met the man who would become husband number three.

## SWF, LOVES TO TRAVEL...

Thorfinn Karlsefni was a wealthy man with a good reputation as a merchant. Gudrid married him, and their travels brought them to a place the Vikings called Vinland, which is now Newfoundland, Canada. And that's where Gudrid and her husband began the first European colony in North America.

In the fall of 1007, Gudrid gave birth to Snorri Thorfinnson, the first European born in the New World. Their second son, Thorbjorn (named after Gudrid's father), was also born in Vinland. Three years later, tensions with the natives, known to the Vikings as Skraelings ("pagans"), forced Gudrid and her family to leave Vinland and set sail for Norway.

## ONE LAST OUTING

Once there, Thorfinn bought land and promptly died. Okay, well, maybe not promptly, but he did die before his children reached adulthood. Gudrid took over management of the estate, but as soon as Snorri married, she was off traveling again. This time she sailed to Rome to visit the Vatican.

When Gudrid returned from Rome, she discovered her son had built a small monastery. It was there that Gudrid died after—finally!—settling down and living her last years in quiet seclusion.

\* \* \*

The tourist sights have nothing like Stonehenge,
The literature is all about revenge.
And yet I like it if only because this nation
Enjoys a scarcity of population.
—W. H. Auden, Louis MacNeice, in *Letters From Iceland*, 1937

There are to date no female Nobel laureates in economics.

# HOCKEY HIJINKS

*Our goal is to tell you about some sportsmen who've been the icing on professional hockey's cake.*

Hockey is more than just a bunch of guys hitting each other with sticks. They're hitting each other with sticks *while standing on ice.* You think that's easy? Also, some of them were pretty memorable athletes.

### JACQUES PLANTE

Jacques Plante, goalie extraordinaire for the Montreal Canadiens, was playing against the New York Rangers at Madison Square Garden on November 1, 1959, when he took a puck to the face that rearranged his nose. In the dressing room, Plante informed his coach he would not go out and play any more unless he was permitted to wear a special facemask he'd developed and had been practicing with.

Now, if Plante didn't return to the ice, the Canadiens would be forced to play with a spare goalie...supplied by the Rangers. (In that day and age, teams carried only one goalie; the rules at that time required that the home team provide a replacement.) And since they had only one goalie of their own, it might be a minor leaguer, or, if the visitors were out of luck, a trainer or equipment handler.

### The Man in the Fiberglass Mask

Coach Toe Blake gave in, and the goalie mask eventually became a fixture in the NHL, although Plante took a lot of ribbing at first. But he was already being ribbed for other things, like the way he celebrated victories by kissing the ice. When playing in other rinks, he often fussed that the nets were nonstandard and demanded measurements. (He was often right.) Plante also had a not-traditionally-seen-as-macho habit taught him by his mother—knitting. He'd knit shirts to wear under his uniform and hats for his friends. Plante won six Vezina Trophies (the NHL award for best goalkeeper) and one MVP award during his tenure with the Canadiens, but in 1963, they traded Plante for the New York Rangers' Lorne "Gump" Worsley. Ironically, Worsley was the last goalie in the NHL to play barefaced. He retired soon after league expansion, because it required traveling by plane and Gump was afraid to fly.

---

**Arthur Ashe was the first black male tennis player to win at Wimbledon.**

## JOHNNY BOWER

It was getting close to Christmas, 1965, when songwriter Chip Young wandered into Maple Leaf Gardens in Toronto looking for someone to sing a children's song for charity. Most of the practicing hockey players escaped to the showers, but Young managed to corner goalie Johnny Bower.

### Goosed By a Goalie

The soft-hearted Bower wound up on the hit list of Toronto radio stations warbling "Honky, the Christmas Goose" (Honky evaded his destiny as a holiday entrée by getting hired by Santa to help clear traffic in the upper atmosphere). It was a gratifying musical debut for the 42-year-old goaltender, who would be the last Leaf goalie to win a Stanley Cup ring. But he was knocked off the charts the next week by teammate Eddie Shack who'd recorded his personal motto as music: "Clear the Track, Here Comes Shack."

## MARTIN BIRON

Little did Quebec-born Martin Biron realize that when he stepped on the ice in 1995 for his NHL debut with the Buffalo Sabres, his number was almost up.

### Agent 00

Biron's sweater was numbered 00, and he wore it for the first three games he played as the new kid on the block. But when he next hit NHL ice, a rule had been enacted stating that no number could be more than two digits, or a decimal, a fraction, or 00. But wait, it didn't say anything about exponents and factorials! Hey, Martin!

## LIONEL CONACHER

There wasn't a sport he tried that he didn't leave a mark on. Toronto-born Lionel Conacher (1901–1964), younger brother of hockey great Charlie Conacher, excelled in everything. His cleats covered the 100-yard dash in 10 seconds flat, only two-tenths of a second off the world record. He reigned as Canada's heavyweight boxing champion and swung a mean bat in baseball's International League, the breeding tank for the majors. In the 1921 Grey Cup game, he passed the pigskin for 15 points as his Toronto Argonauts trounced the Edmonton Eskimos to win the coveted national championship. By 1925, he'd joined the NHL, where he'd be known as "Big Train," a twist on his first name.

### A Sport to the End
Conacher retired from professional sports in 1937, but won a different kind of race to become a member of the Canadian Parliament. He died of a heart attack in 1964—after hitting a triple in a sandlot ball game. He holds a place in both the Hockey Hall of Fame and the Canadian Football Hall of Fame, and was voted Canada's Athlete of the Half Century.

## PETE MAHOVLICH
Things were getting stressful for the Canadian team in 1972's infamous Summit Series between Canada and the Russian hockey elite. After four games in Canada and two in Moscow, the Canadians trailed three games to two, with one game tied. The Russians started harassing the team: Mysterious voices crackled on their hotel intercoms, and team members would get phone calls in the middle of the night with no one on the other end of the line. It's no wonder the players felt a tad nervous. Pete Mahovlich, center for the Montreal Canadiens, decided to defuse the tension.

### Don't Bug Me
All the teammates were looking for bugs in their room, and Pete spread the story that his brother (and Canadien teammate) Frank had found one—a metal disk attached to the floor under his rug. But when he unscrewed the disk (so Pete said), there was a crash from below; he had detached the anchor for the chandelier in the suite below.

Pete also turned up before the crucial final game of the series on crutches, with one leg bandaged. As the Canadian sportswriters gasped and hurried to report the bad news, he tossed the crutches aside and peeled off the bandages, laughing.

In the end, the Russian's tactics backfired, and Canada's team, fighting mad, came from behind to win the series.

## TED GREEN AND WAYNE MAKI
Professional hockey is a rough-and-tumble world, with some touchy tempers and plenty of sweater grabbing, but rarely does it

**Cassius Clay, Jr.'s middle name was Marcellus.**

come to the question of assault, which is sort of surprising considering the litigious nature of people in general. In 1969, the first case of criminal assault in a hockey game was prosecuted after an Ontario exhibition game between the St. Louis Blues and Boston Bruins. Ted Green, playing for Boston, swung his glove at Blues player Wayne Maki, striking him in the head. Maki then retaliated with his stick, and in the ensuing brawl, Green was speared in the head by Maki and landed hard on the ice. At the hospital, Green's fractured skull required the insertion of a steel plate. Charges were filed against both players, with two different courts hearing the cases.

**From the Rink to the Court**
Both cases ended in acquittal and both focused on the issue of consent. The judge in *Regina* (*the Queen, that is*) v. *Green* noted that fighting was part of the game and that players consented to the risk and came prepared for it. The argument couldn't be used to excuse a clearly criminal assault, but the judge in *Regina* v. *Maki* decided there was reasonable doubt as to the claim that Maki used more force than necessary in self-defense.

Surprisingly, Green, who was not expected to live, eventually returned to a productive hockey career. Wayne Maki was sent down to the AHL, with only a brief return to the big leagues from 1970 to 1972. He was diagnosed with brain cancer in December 1972 and never played again. He died in May 1974.

**HOWIE MORENZ**
The Montreal Canadiens' Howie Morenz is considered to be hockey's first superstar, bursting onto the scene almost a half century before Wayne Gretzky learned to skate. Morenz played 14 NHL seasons, 12 with the "Habs" (for Les Habitants), winning three Hart trophies for MVP and three Stanley Cups. But the "breaks" were not all good ones. In 1937, in a game at the Montreal Forum, his skate caught in a crack in the boards, and his leg twisted and then snapped.

**A Superstar Nova**
After weeks in the hospital, Morenz collapsed and died from a pulmonary embolism. He was 35. His last appearance at the Forum was his funeral; 10,000 fans crowded the arena and as many lined the streets outside. The last game ever played at the Forum took place March 11, 1996, exactly 59 years after his death.

# FAMOUS PET TRICKS

*Celebrity animals and the famous people they've owned.*

## JACK WAS NO TURKEY

In 1863 a live turkey was sent to the White House for the Lincoln family's holiday dinner. Tad Lincoln, age 10, named the turkey Jack. Soon Jack was eating from Tad's hand and following him everywhere. When the time came for the cook to talk turkey, Tad burst into one of his father's cabinet meetings and pleaded for Jack's life. Lincoln halted the nation's business to write Jack a special pardon to give to the cook.

On Election Day 1864, a booth was placed on the White House grounds so that nearby Union troops could vote. President Lincoln and Tad were watching from an upstairs window when they noticed Jack standing in line behind some soldiers. "Why is your turkey at the polls? Does he vote?" Lincoln asked his son. "No," Tad answered. "He's not of age yet."

## GERTIE'S MACHO POODLE

In 1928 Gertrude Stein brought home a white poodle puppy. Her companion Alice B. Toklas named him Basket because he looked like "he should carry a basket of flowers in his mouth." That's something Basket never learned to do, but Stein taught him a better trick. She'd flap a handkerchief in front of his face and command: "Be fierce! Play Hemingway!" At which, Basket would jump up and bark his little head off. All the great and near great of Paris knew about Basket's macho Hemingway trick, including Pablo Picasso—but he mustn't have been all that impressed because after Basket died, he suggested to Stein that she get an Afghan.

## A NAG IN THE WHITE HOUSE

In 1901, when Theodore Roosevelt's family moved in, so did countless of his six children's pets: kittens, guinea pigs, dogs, snakes, rabbits, turtles, squirrels, etc. When one of the kids, Archie, came down with the measles, his brother Quentin thought he might recover more quickly if he could spend some time with one of his pets—like his pony, Algonquin. So when no one was looking

---

Babe Ruth allegedly wore a cabbage leaf under his cap to keep cool on hot days.

Quentin snuck the pony into the basement and up the elevator of the White House to his brother's room. But Algonquin was so fascinated by his reflection in the elevator mirrors that they had trouble getting him out again.

## DON'T BLAME BLONDI
Blondi was Adolf Hitler's German Shepherd. Despite his cruelty to people, Hitler treated Blondi well, though his morning routine often consisted of ordering the dog to jump through hoops, leap over a six-foot wall, climb to the top of a ladder, and beg.

On April 28, 1945, when the Allies were closing in, Hitler tested the cyanide capsules he'd been saving on Blondi. They worked.

## JFK'S DOGGY SPACE CASE
Soviet premier Nikita Khruschev gave a Siberian Husky puppy named Pushinka ("fluffy" in Russian) to First Lady Jacqueline Kennedy in 1961. The dog came from good stock: Her mother, Strelka, had traveled on *Sputnik 5*, and was one of the two first animals (with her copilot, Belka) to survive orbital space flight. Meanwhile, back at the White House, Pushinka's favorite sport was playing on the Kennedy kids' slide, climbing the ladder, then sliding down. When she grew up and had puppies of her own, JFK called them "pupniks."

## MY LITTLE MARMOSET
In 1935, when Gerald Durrell (brother of the famous author Lawrence Durrell) was about 10 years old, his family went to live on the Greek island of Corfu, where little Gerald started collecting the local wild animals, one of them being Pavlo, the marmoset.

Pavlo lived in Gerry's mother's dresser dresser (much to her dismay) and would never go to bed unless Gerald gave him a hot water bottle. Pavlo ate what the family ate—porridge or cornflakes with warm milk and sugar for breakfast; green vegetables, potatoes, and dessert for lunch. "At teatime he had to be kept off the table by force, or he would dive into the jam-pot." Understandably the family hoped Gerald would outgrow his zookeeping habits. But he didn't. Instead he became a famous naturalist, using his best-sellers, TV shows, and the famous Jersey Zoo that he founded to save endangered species.

# LOOKING GOOD

*"Every woman has the right to be beautiful."*

Cosmetics queen Elizabeth Arden coined the above phrase for an ad promotion, and with single-minded ambition, hard work, and the business philosophy/acumen of a robber baron, devoted more than 60 years to producing the consumer products to make it possible.

## SUCH A GOOD GIRL

Childhood was anything but glamorous. The third of five children, she was born in 1884 to a tenant farmer and his wife near Woodbridge, Ontario, just outside Toronto. She was six when her mother died, and Elizabeth, like her siblings, took up the household chores to help fill the void.

She got some early experience in business, accompanying her father when he'd go to Toronto to sell their produce. At home, she took care of the family's livestock, notably the horses. Years later her love of horses would leave a mark on history, too.

She was also the family's nurse, tending to their colds and scrapes, aches and bruises. She enrolled in nursing school in her early teens.

## GLAMOUR WILL OUT

To the eventual benefit of many women, Florence's heart was not in nursing. In her own words, she "didn't like looking at sick people." Instead she took a different approach. She decided to help people stay beautiful and healthy—call it the practice of preventive cosmetic medicine.

## I'LL TAKE NEW YORK

Florence opened her first beauty salon on New York's Fifth Avenue in 1909. A partner, Elizabeth Hubbard, departed the business within a year, leaving only her first name behind. Florence added "Arden" from Tennyson's poem, *Enoch Arden*. To go with her new business, Florence adopted the same name for herself.

---

**"Nerd" was invented by Dr. Seuss and first used in *If I Ran the Zoo*.**

## THEN I'LL TAKE PARIS

By 1913 Arden was searching out new products in the renowned beauty salons of Paris, at the time a hotbed of the booming cosmetics industry. Her products were already selling fairly well in New York, but she wanted to get ahead of the game—not an easy task when the competition included household names like Helena Rubinstein and Max Factor.

On the way back home on the *Lusitania*, she bumped into Thomas Jenkins Lewis, whom she'd met before in New York. Romance would blossom in 1915 when news that the *Lusitania* had been sunk by a German sub brought them back together. But for now, as soon as she returned to New York, Arden had the good fortune to collaborate with a chemist who developed Venetian Cream Amoretta, a lightly textured face cream that was much more pleasant to use than the heavy cold creams then available. Business exploded.

## AND FINALLY, I'LL TAKE THE WORLD

With her sister Gladys handling the wholesale marketing and now-husband Tom Lewis keeping the books, Arden was free to develop new products and establish an international chain of full-service beauty salons. Along with makeup, she introduced exercise classes in her salons and even sold exercise phonograph records. By 1947, a banner year for her, Arden had 300 products on the shelves of her 100 salons.

Arden introduced American women to the spa experience, the epitome of luxurious pampering (which was crassly described by a biographer as helping "the fatties to slim, the drunkards to dry, and the skeletons to put on flesh.") She also dabbled in high fashion, working with designers like Oscar de la Renta. Artistic and temperamental differences eventually scotched that endeavor, but the spas thrived.

## AND I'LL DO IT ALONE

Arden's marriage to Tom ended in 1933. She not only divorced him, but also fired him from the firm—it seems he'd given one of his girlfriends a job there. And even though he'd been instrumental in building the multimillion dollar company in the first place, Arden gave him a settlement of $25,000 along with his walking papers.

**Napoleon Bonaparte was afraid of cats.**

## FROM FACIALS TO FILLIES

In 1947 Arden was ready to pursue a second passion—no, not another husband—her passion for the ponies. As surely as she knew the right makeup for every skin tone, she knew horses. The raising and care of horses was a part of her childhood she had never forgotten. In 1931, when her marriage to Tom was faltering as it came around the home stretch, Arden focused her interest on racing and raising thoroughbred horses, a preoccupation that brought her a Kentucky Derby winner in 1947.

Her approach to racing was as single-minded as her approach to the cosmetics business. She approved every aspect of training regimens for her horses. And sometimes the two interests overlapped—her Ardena Skin Tonic was used as a horse liniment and her famous Eight Hour Cream was used to treat equine bruises. In fact, according to the official Elizabeth Arden website, the Eight Hour Cream was originally developed to treat horses.

## THE MEDIA GETS THE MESSAGE

Until the day she died in 1966, Elizabeth Arden remained involved with the operation of her company and her horse farm. In 1946 she made the cover of *Time*. In 1990, *Life* magazine named her one of America's top 100 VIPs of the 20th century.

\* \* \*

## WAR PAINT

Helena Rubinstein and Elizabeth Arden never met, but that didn't stop them from detesting each another. Once, "Madame" Rubinstein spotted her gingery-blonde rival across the expanse of a chic restaurant, and remarked: "Ha! Too much hair color for a woman of her age." She remained blithely unselfconscious of her own implausibly black tresses.

While they were feuding, Estee Lauder sneaked ahead. She was the only woman on *Time* magazine's Top 20 Builders and Titans of the 20th Century list.

# MORE
# INGENIOUS INSULTS

*Famous critics take on the famous, and everyone else in sight.*
*Is nothing sacred? Not to these famous critics.*

**Insulting Richard Wagner:**
"Wagner's music is better than it sounds."
**Put-down artist:** Mark Twain

**Insulting Mark Twain:**
"A hack writer who would have been considered fourth rate in Europe, who tried out a few of the old proven 'sure-fire' literary skeletons with sufficient local color to intrigue the superficial and the lazy."
**Put-down artist:** William Faulkner

**Insulting Freud:**
"Fifty years spent analyzing women. And he still can't find out what they want. So this makes him the world's greatest expert on female psychology?"
**Put-down artist:** Clare Booth Luce

**Insulting Princess Anne of England:**
"Such an active lass. So outdoorsy. She loves nature in spite of what it did to her."
**Put-down artist:** Bette Midler

**Insulting Dante Rossetti:**
"Rossetti is not a painter; Rossetti is a ladies' maid."
**Put-down artist:** James Whistler

**Insulting James Whistler:**
"With our James, vulgarity begins at home, and should be allowed to stay there."
**Put-down artist:** Oscar Wilde

Real people on Pez dispensers: Betsy Ross, Daniel Boone, and Paul Revere.

# FROM WAR TO INNER PEACE

*What did Tolstoy and L. Ron Hubbard have in common?*

Both Leo Tolstoy and L. Ron Hubbard were novelists, as you probably already know…but both also formed their own religions. Except Tolstoy's religion didn't involve aliens named Xenu (and, of course, Tolstoy was a good novelist).

### AH, YOUTH
Leo Tolstoy was born into a wealthy family of Russian aristocrats on September 9, 1828, and raised by aunts (both his parents died before he turned 10). Never a particularly enthusiastic student in his youth, Tolstoy dropped out of Kazan University at age 18, leaving him plenty of time to pursue a life of debauchery.

Self-conscious about his looks and unsuccessful with girls, Tolstoy lost his virginity at a brothel (and later contracted venereal disease, probably at one of his return visits). He drank heavily, and gambled so much that he was forced to sell part of his estate to pay his debts.

### A LOVER AND A FIGHTER
Tolstoy was plagued with moral qualms about the emptiness of his lifestyle and decided to clean up his act. At 23, he joined one of his brothers in the Russian military, where he began writing…and, you know, fighting in the Crimean War and whatnot. He stayed with the army for five years (and two novels).

After his stint as a soldier, Tolstoy briefly founded an experimental school for peasant children and married at age 34, eventually finding time between writing *War and Peace* and *Anna Karenina* (among other works) to father 13 children.

### WHAT'S UP, ORTHODOX?
After finishing *Anna Karenina*, Tolstoy became obsessed with death and fell into a deep depression. At first, he sought comfort in the Russian Orthodox Church, but soon came to feel that it was corrupt—along with all other churches, which, in his opinion, no

---

Beethoven dipped his head in cold water before he composed—maybe to stay awake!

longer promulgated Christ's teachings as Christ had intended. Tolstoy didn't see how Christ's statement, "Ye resist not evil," could be carried out except through nonviolence, which didn't jibe with church support of the military. (It was Tolstoy's opinions on nonviolence that eventually led to a correspondence with a young Mahatma Gandhi, who had read an article of Tolstoy's and been strongly inspired by it.)

Tolstoy essentially created his own version of Christianity from scratch and devoted himself to telling others about it. He gave up writing fiction and instead produced works such as *The Kingdom of God Is Within You*, which denounced the Russian military, money, owning property, smoking, and eating meat. (He even published his own vegetarian cookbook, *I Eat Nobody*.) These writings, while unlikely to provide any juicy movie roles for Greta Garbo, were very influential, especially in the growing anarchist movement.

## TOLSTOY VS. EVERYBODY

Tolstoy may have found inner peace, but it ended up leading to outer turmoil. The Russian government considered him a menace, putting him under police surveillance and banning his "treasonable" books. He was excommunicated from the Russian Orthodox Church, and his family relationships deteriorated seriously (his family wasn't so keen on his desire—thwarted by his wife—to give away all their possessions). Only his youngest daughter, Alexandra, supported his conversion.

On October 28, 1910, Tolstoy left his troubled home behind, heading off with no particular destination. He was accompanied by Alexandra and one of his followers, a doctor. But the doctor couldn't help when Tolstoy caught pneumonia and died on November 20 while resting at the home of a train stationmaster.

## EVER GREEN

When Tolstoy was a young boy, one of his brothers had jokingly announced that the secret to happiness was written on a green stick, which he had buried near a ravine on their estate. Two years before his death, Tolstoy, who had spent so much time searching for the secret to happiness, tearfully asked to be buried by that same ravine, "at the place of the green stick."

# BATTLEFIELD ANGEL

*Most know her as a Civil War nurse, some know her as the founder of the Red Cross, but few know she was responsible for the U.S. signing the Geneva Convention.*

C larissa Harlowe Barton, born 1821, was the youngest of five children. She was shy and timid, but events would soon draw her out. Her aptitude for nursing emerged early, when at 11, one of her brothers was seriously injured in a fall and she devoted two years to his care and recovery. Since most of Clara's education came from her older siblings, it must have seemed natural to her at age 15 to start a school at her father's Massachusetts mill and teach the worker's children. Over the next fifteen years, Clara taught in many schools throughout the Northeast.

## ITS THE PRINCIPAL OF THE THING

In 1851, some businessmen persuaded Clara to open a school in New Jersey. When enrollment topped 600, the city fathers decided to hire a man as principal because it was too much for a woman to handle. Clara quit in disgust, but shortly thereafter suffered a nervous breakdown. She soon recovered and moved to Washington, D.C., where she was hired as a recording clerk in the U.S. Patent Office. Clara was the first woman hired by the Patent Office, and she received the same salary as the men working there.

## CLARA GETS HER WINGS

When the Civil War began in 1861, the first major confrontation between the Confederate and Union armies took place at Bull Run, just outside Washington. The battered Union army was forced into a headlong retreat. Casualties began arriving in Washington hospitals and it became clear that the Union army hadn't allocated adequate resources to treat them; they hadn't planned on being routed.

Clara decided to help alleviate the shortages by advertising for donations of food, clothing, and medical supplies. The response was overwhelming, so Clara set up a warehouse and began distributing the supplies. Although women were not allowed anywhere near the battlefields, a year into the conflict Clara received

**Anne Bradstreet was the first published American woman writer, in 1604.**

permission from the surgeon general to travel wherever the troops went, which made her the first woman on the front lines of battle in a major conflict. She was granted a general pass "for the purpose of distributing comforts for the sick and wounded, and nursing them." Clara often rendered assistance to wounded soldiers during the heat of battle. Once, while giving water to a wounded soldier, a bullet passed through her sleeve and killed him. Doctors were overwhelmed by the number of casualties, and the wounded had to wait hours, sometimes days for treatment. Clara helped wherever she could; once she removed a bullet from a soldier's face using only her pocketknife.

## CIVIL SERVANT EXTRAORDINAIRE
In 1864, Clara was made superintendent of nursing for the Union Army. Clara helped care for the wounded from both sides though and even visited Confederate field hospitals and provided them with supplies and assistance. One newspaper called her, "The true heroine of the age, the angel of the battlefield"—a phrase that was used to describe her for the rest of her life.

After the war, President Lincoln asked Clara to set up an office to help locate missing soldiers. She was the first woman to head a government bureau and ran The Missing Soldier's Office for four years, answering over 63,000 letters and determining the fate of over 22,000 men. She interviewed returning soldiers to obtain information about the missing and succeeded in reuniting many soldiers with their families. She compiled lists of the killed, wounded, and missing, and had those lists published in newspapers. She even traveled to the infamous Confederate prison at Andersonville to identify and mark the locations of buried soldiers. Nearly 13,000 graves were identified and the prison was transformed into a national cemetery.

The sign and files from Clara's office recently were found in the attic of a building scheduled for demolition. The artifacts now reside in the Ford Theater Museum.

## HOW I SPENT MY SUMMER VACATION
Clara had worked very hard during and after the Civil War and her health was failing. In 1868, she suffered another nervous

breakdown. Her doctor advised her to rest, so she went to Europe in 1869 for a vacation. While in Geneva, she was contacted by the International Red Cross, who wanted her to help persuade the United States to sign the Geneva Conventions of 1864, which, among other things, provided protection to those who cared for the sick and wounded during wartime.

Clara was also asked to aid in the Franco-Prussian war. She distributed supplies and provided relief in war-torn areas of France and Germany, and was awarded the Iron Cross by Kaiser Wilhelm. By the time she returned home, she was more exhausted than she had been before her departure. She suffered a third nervous breakdown, and this time she temporarily lost her eyesight.

## CRUSADES AND CROSSES

By 1877 she was able to begin the fight to have the Geneva Conventions signed by the president and ratified by the Senate. She wrote articles, made speeches, and lobbied Congress. It was an uphill battle because of the Monroe Doctrine, which prohibited treaties and alliances with Europe. President James Garfield promised to sign it, but he died before he got the chance.

In 1881, Clara created the American Red Cross. She organized a national office and local chapters in cities across the U.S. President Chester A. Arthur finally signed the Geneva Conventions in 1882, and the United States officially became a member of the International Red Cross.

Clara ran the Red Cross for 23 years duirng which time she expanded its role to help civilians in war as well as victims of natural disasters. She was often at the forefront of relief efforts throughout the U.S. during epidemics, tornadoes, droughts, floods, fires, and hurricanes. She also stressed the importance of educating victims to look after themselves. This evolved into what became known as "First Aid" and the original first-aid kits. She established first-aid training one of the core responsibilities of the Red Cross.

## CLARA STARTS TO SLOW DOWN

Clara was 77 when she went to Havana, Cuba, at the start of the Spanish-American War to care for sick and wounded soldiers and to provide relief to the civilian population. She worked 16-hour

**St. Peter is regarded as the first Pope.**

days delivering supplies by mule wagon and providing medical care to soldiers living in camps rife with dysentery, typhoid, malaria, and yellow fever.

She wrote several books including, *History of the Red Cross* (1882) and *The Red Cross in Peace and War* (1899) as well as a famous poetic tribute to Civil War nurses, *The Women Who Went to the Field*.

## RED CROSS REBEL

Clara was outspoken and self-reliant. She refused government funding for the American Red Cross because she didn't want to relinquish any control to bureaucrats. Many of her subordinates criticized her authoritarian management style and a accused her of mismanaging Red Cross funds.

Finally, after the attacks became too much to bear, Clara Barton resigned as president of the Red Cross in 1904. She was quite bitter about her treatment, saying: "The government I thought I loved and loyally tried to serve has shut every door in my face." She died of pneumonia at the age of 91 in 1912. It's not surprising that her last words were purported to be: "Let me go! Let me go!" Her home in Glen Echo, Maryland, is a National Historic Site.

## EPILOGUE

The American Red Cross currently has eight regional centers, 1,000 local chapters, and 36 blood services regions that collect, process, and distribute blood and blood products to hospitals and medical centers. The American Red Cross supplies nearly 50 percent of the blood and blood products used in the U.S.

Quite a legacy for a shy young girl from Massachusetts.

\* \* \*

The mission of her life summed up in her own words:
"You must never so much as think whether you like it or not, whether it is bearable or not you must never think of anything except the need, and how to meet it." —Clara Barton

---

**A spinal injury at age 15 left Elizabeth Barrett Browning an invalid.**

# COOL COMMUNICATIONS

*Ever wish you could read celebrity mail? Here's your chance!*

After delving into famous correspondence, we agree with Christopher Morley who believed "there are some people who should hurry up and die so you can read their letters."

When George Bernard Shaw's *Pygmalion* opened, he sent Churchill tickets with a twist.

> Have enclosed two tickets to premiere. Come and bring a friend—if you have one.

Churchill replied:

> Impossible to attend opening night. Will attend second night—if there is one.

Abraham Lincoln was unfailingly courteous—even in 1862 when, concerned about the slow pace of Union troops under the less-than-speedy General McClellan, he fired him.

> Dear McClellan,
>
> If you don't want to use the army, I should like to borrow it for awhile.
>
> Abraham Lincoln

Most people, when invited to a banquet, are happy to get a free meal. Not Mark Twain, who found them more "fatiguing" than ditch digging. Here's how he refused one invitation:

> Dear Lee,
>
> Can't. I am in a family way with three weeks undigested dinners in my system, and shall just roost here and diet and purge until I am delivered. Shall I name it after you?
>
> Mark Twain

---

Napoleon's last words were purported to be: "France, the army, Josephine."

# A BIRD-BRAINED GUY

*The National Audubon Society's namesake wasn't a conservationist or a trained scientist. Just a man who was good with a gun and a paintbrush.*

John James Audubon, the son of a French sea captain and his Creole mistress, was born in what is now Haiti in 1785. His father made a fortune as a merchant and slave trader; his mother died soon after her son's birth. His early years were spent in France where he was educated like the well-off youth that he was. But he had no interest in school—he wanted to be outdoors.

He studied art in Paris for a while, but he didn't like the restrictions of the life or the classes, so his father sent him to America where he finally felt free to indulge in his hobbies of fishing, hunting, and drawing birds.

### READY, AIM...DRAW

Audubon said that he preferred to draw his subjects from life. And he did study birds, but only before he shot them. In fact, Audubon killed thousands of birds, both for sport and for investigation. After he'd killed them, he stuck wires in them and arranged them into everyday-looking positions. This is how he created his amazingly lifelike depictions.

### BIRDS ON THE BRAIN

At 35, he turned his spare-time hobby into a professional obsession. He was determined to draw every last bird in America. He set out to find (and shoot) and draw new birds. After five years of wandering and drawing, he couldn't find a publisher in the U.S. A few years later, he tried again in Europe, and in 1827 *Birds of America* began to appear. It took 11 years to complete the 435 life-size engravings.

### A MAN AMONG BIRDS

Just as he'd hoped, the drawings made him famous. By 1831, without any formal training, he was recognized as America's leading naturalist. Eventually, he took on the role of advisor for young scientists. Today, we might question his methods—after all, he killed at least one of every bird in America, something the society that's named for him might frown upon.

Charlemagne didn't object to his daughters having illegitimate offspring.

# LITTLE GUY WITH BIG IDEAS

*Uncle John introduces you to the most amazing and controversial inventor you've never heard of.*

In 1958, Jerome Lemelson quit his engineering job to become a full-time inventor. His wife Dorothy recalled the decisive moment. "One day it was snowing, and Jerry didn't want to go to work." That snowy day began a career that spawned more than 500 patented inventions, most of which touch your life every day.

## THE FEISTY GENIUS

Born in Staten Island, New York, in 1928, Jerome Lemelson showed two remarkable traits as a kid. First, he had a genius for inventing things (like a lighted tongue depressor for his dad to use in his medical practice). Second, even though he was scrawny, he was a scrapper. He went after any bully who dared to pick on him—or his younger brothers.

## LEAN YEARS

The first years of Lemelson's life as an inventor were pretty abysmal. Dorothy helped support the family while Jerry patented his inventions and approached companies in the hope they'd pay to license his patents. They kept showing Lemelson the door, but in between rejections he churned out inventions and piled up patents, at the rate of about one per month.

## MA-MA!

Lemelson invented everything from crying baby dolls to illuminated highway signs. He created futuristic technologies, too, including "machine vision," which connected a video camera to a computer and would one day be used for bar-code scanning. He conceived the basic technology for computer-controlled fax machines, camcorders, robots, and compact discs.

---

**Karen Horney challenged Freud's theories and suggested that men suffered from "womb envy."**

## THE SERIAL INVENTOR MEETS THE CEREAL MASK

Early on, Jerry got a patent for a "constructional mask," a face mask kit that could be printed on the back of cereal boxes, and approached Kellogg's with the idea. No thanks, they told him. So when he saw toy masks printed on Kellogg's cereal boxes three years later, he sued for patent infringement—and lost. He pursued his case against Battle Creek for 20 years until he'd exhausted his appeals, during which time he became better known for aggressively protecting his patents than for inventing.

## PATENTLY WEALTHY

In 1964, he sold exclusive rights to his automated warehousing system, a technology that used computer-control systems to direct equipment that automatically stacked and loaded merchandise. A deal with Triax, an Ohio company, put Lemelson closer to becoming that lucky one in a million—an inventor living off his royalties. But Jerry also plowed his profits into legal expenses when he and Triax jointly sued other companies for unlicensed use of their automated system.

The big corporations started to take notice of Lemelson. Sony licensed his patent for an audiocassette drive mechanism in the Sony Walkman, and IBM paid $1 million for his data and word processing systems.

In all, Lemelson filed more than 20 infringement lawsuits. Though in court he lost far more often than he won, he wouldn't quit suing. Eventually persistence paid off—big time. When companies began using bar-coding systems, Lemelson sued them for royalties on his machine vision patents. Settlements from those and other cases brought Jerry and his heirs more than a billion dollars.

## UP FROM THE DEPTHS

Jerry and Dorothy moved from New Jersey to a fancier home in Lake Tahoe, California. Big bucks didn't change the inventor's hard-working lifestyle; he still spent his days writing ideas in his notebooks, and he kept on patenting inventions. And he spent a lot of his money to help his fellow inventors. The Jerome and Dorothy Lemelson Foundation has given away millions of dollars in programs and awards that nurture American invention.

As Lemelson grew richer though, his detractors grew more vocal. They insisted he never invented anything useful at all—except the "submarine patent," which covers a secret invention that lurks in the oceans of paper at the patent office, then when an industry unknowingly develops a similar product, the submarine patent surfaces and its owner sues a surprised company for infringement.

Critics claimed Lemelson was more of a brilliant futurist than an inventor. He'd write up vague versions of a product or technology, but he never made models to demonstrate that his invention actually worked. Then he'd delay his patents with changes and amendments until industry developed something similar that did work. At that point, he'd let his submarine patent surface to claim his royalties—and torpedo his target with lawsuits.

## PATENTLY RIDICULOUS!

Lemelson and his supporters scoffed at the accusations that he delayed his own patents. It was true that he didn't manufacture working models for most of his inventions, but hey, he was a true inventor, not a corporate mogul. He didn't want to run a company to manufacture his inventions—he wanted to invent.

Jerry's own death in 1997 bolstered his claim that bureaucracy (rather than his own foot dragging) slowed his work. Years after his funeral (and obviously too late to do him any good) new Lemelson patents kept popping out of the clogged, patent office pipeline.

## LEMELSON LIVES!

Jerry's court cases dragged on after his death, too; part of his legacy is an ongoing legislative battle over how to reform patent law. Meanwhile, the Lemelson Foundation keeps donating millions of dollars every year to individual inventors—the little guys and gals with the big ideas.

\* \* \*

"I just invent, then wait until man comes around to needing what I've invented." —R. Buckminster Fuller

"An inventor is simply a fellow who doesn't take his education too seriously." —Charles Kettering

---

**Malcolm X named his first daughter, Attilah, after Attila the Hun.**

# BATTLE OF THE BRANS

*One brother wanted to fill your bowl, the other wanted to empty your bowel.*

Most people think of bowls—not bowels—when they think of Kellogg's. Well, think again. Those GRRRRREAT sugar-frosted corn flakes you eat every morning were not what the good Dr. Kellogg had in mind. It was his younger, more entrepreneurial brother who had the better idea.

## THE DOCTOR AS A YOUNG MAN
One of America's first health gurus, Dr. John Harvey Kellogg was raised with the healthy living tenets advocated by his church, the Seventh-Day Adventists. Some church members helped finance John's medical school and upon graduation he became a staff physician and then superintendent of his hometown's Battle Creek Sanitarium. As his influence and ideas rose to national prominence, it was renamed the Kellogg Sanitarium.

## A CHARITY CASE
John wasn't the least bit interested in riches; his focus was on sharing his health reform ideas with his colleagues and the public. He didn't accept a salary for his work at the sanitarium and instead derived his income from royalties on the numerous books and treatises he published in his lifetime. His "rejuvenation" clinic was an elegant hotel, hospital, and spa in one and attracted wealthy health seekers.

## NO SEX PLEASE, WE'RE MICHIGANDERS
Dr. John had lots of good ideas, including the benefits of a healthy diet, exercise, fresh air, and rest. And he was way ahead of his time in suggesting the link between smoking and lung cancer. But he had some pretty drastic ideas—like extolling the benefits of excessive chewing of food and opposing any sexual activity—and also practiced some quack cures involving various treatments with extremely cold water, electric shocks, and mechanical manipulation.

## HAPPY ENTRAILS TO YOU
But nothing fascinated him as much as his obsession with the

bowel. He believed that 90 percent of all illnesses could be traced to unclean bowels, and his views became, for a time, a national obsession. He emphasized a regimen that would promote colon cleansing and regularity (and we don't mean being on time for spa classes).

It was his attempts to provide clients with a palatable and healthful vegetarian diet that leads to our story's next chapter.

## THE DARK AGES, CEREAL-WISE

In Kellogg's day, there were not a lot of breakfast options. Believe it or not, there were no cold breakfast cereals. Most people ate dry toast or crackers. That is, until Kellogg invented Granola. (What's that? You thought the hippies invented it in the 1960s? Oh, no, it was created way back in 1881.) Actually, Dr. Kellogg stole another man's invention (and name) of a clustered graham flour product called Granula, and modified the ingredients. When the other inventor sued him, Dr. John renamed his oatmeal-based product Granola. Within a decade, Kellogg was selling two tons of the stuff a week.

Meanwhile, business at the sanitarium was booming, and by 1888 it had been expanded to include a medical college and accommodate up to 700 patients. (After a fire in 1902, it was rebuilt to accommodate 1,000 guests annually, attended by an even larger staff.)

## SERIAL CEREAL INVENTOR

Inspired by this success, the good doctor created yet another hit— wheat flakes. Again, he "borrowed" someone else's idea. A Denver man had created a product he called Shredded Wheat, little square wheat biscuits. Dr. Kellogg's innovation was the flaking and toasting process. (For now, the corn flakes are still a twinkle in the good doctor's eye, but not far off—give him time.)

## KELLOGG VS. KELLOGG

Meanwhile, he gave his younger brother William a job as the clinic's accountant. Unfortunately, as is so frequently the case with siblings, they did not always see eye to eye. By this time, Battle Creek had been transformed into cereal central and new manufacturers were appearing overnight to cash in on the new breakfast fad. Competitors were jumping into the cereal market left and right, but Dr. John was only interested in the sanitarium and his medical theories. As for his precious whole-grain foods, he was more interested in playing with it than selling it. His brother, Will, on the other hand, was interested in the bottom line.

Will was particularly annoyed when the corn flake followed the wheat flake and his brother John wanted to name the product Sanitas. Will thought this sounded a little too sterile and unappealing. When his brother took a business trip, Will boldly added some sweeteners to the corn flakes. We don't know what inspired this treasonous behavior, but we imagine he was pretty fed up with the whole health regimen of the clinic and his brother's fuddy-duddy ways.

Before you know it, Will was managing The Battle Creek Toasted Corn Flake Company (founded in 1906) and selling Kellogg's Toasted Corn Flakes under his own name. The two brothers went to court and ultimately Will was the winner.

William K. Kellogg built a successful business based on a cereal that tasted better and had a more appealing name than his brother's brands (like the unappetizing Kellogg's Sterilized Bran). Ultimately Will won the right to use the Kellogg's brand name exclusively. Dr. John tried to make a go of the sanitarium, but after the stock market crash, his wealthy clientele couldn't afford the luxury of a week or two at a spa.

## SOMETHING IN COMMON AFTER ALL

Both brothers lived to be 91. But they'd stopped speaking to each other years earlier. To this day, every box of Kellogg's cereal bears W. K.'s signature.

But Dr. John earned a place in history, too, and is credited with helping foster the development or popularity of such diverse products as the electric blanket, peanut butter, granola (with an "o"), and a menthol nasal inhaler. His sanitarium later served as one of the army's largest medical installations before it was eventually converted into federal office space.

**Epilogue:** If you want to enjoy a send-up of the Kellogg story, T. Coraghessan Boyle penned a funny book called *The Road to Wellville* that was later made into a not-as-funny movie.

---

Rachel Carson's book, *Silent Spring*, inspired measures to curb the use of DDT.

# MORE COOL COMMUNICATIONS

*Another peek at letters and telegrams from the famous.*

Lord Byron liked letters as a way of talking to people without them talking back. "Letter writing is the only device for combining solitude with good company." Here's how some other famous people spent their letter-writing time.

We wonder how Nathaniel Hawthorne's mom felt about this letter where he gave up on all the occupations she'd likely suggested.

> Dear Mother,
>
> I don't want to be a doctor, and live by men's diseases; nor a minister to live by their sins; nor a lawyer to live by their quarrels. So I don't think there's anything left for me but to be an author.
>
> Nathaniel

Igor Stravinsky composed music for a Broadway musical produced by Billy Rose. After the opening, Rose sent the classical composer a cable.

> Stravinsky,
>
> Your music great success stop could be sensational if you would authorize Robert Russell Bennett retouch orchestration stop Bennett orchestrates even the works of Cole Porter stop
>
> Rose

The great Stravinsky cabled back:

> Rose
>
> Satisfied with great success stop
>
> Stravinsky

---

**The Wright brothers were practically inseparable and neither ever married.**

A magazine editor sent a telegram asking Cary Grant's agent about the star's age.

> How old Cary Grant stop

Grant answered the telegram himself:

> Old me fine stop how you stop
>
> Cary Grant

A young woman who'd been in love for years with a fellow worker at the *New Yorker* magazine went off to England on a long vacation, and surprised everyone with an announcement that she'd given birth to a baby. The young lady received a cable of congratulation from one of the *New Yorker*'s most famous writers.

> Well done, we didn't know you had it in you stop
>
> Dorothy Parker

Groucho Marx wasn't the best correspondent—but at least he was honest about it.

> Excuse me for not answering your letter sooner. I have been so busy not answering letters lately that I couldn't get around to yours.
>
> Groucho

M. F. K. Fisher's books helped make the joys of French cooking internationally famous…but an excerpt from her private letters could make you think twice about entering a bistro.

> French people eat the most intricate entrails of everything from the horse to the snail; they have perfectly awful table manners, mop up their plates after each course with a piece of bread, change napkins once a week…

---

**Charles Lindbergh won a Pulitzer for *The Spirit of St. Louis*, his autobiography.**

# MY NAME'S JOHN FORD—I MAKE WESTERNS

*But he must have had something more going for him. When Orson Welles was asked which American film directors appealed to him most, he answered "The old masters...by which I mean John Ford, John Ford, and John Ford."*

John Ford was one of Hollywood's most demanding and ornery directors. Lots of film people considered him cruel and sadistic and refused to have anything to do with him.

But even his worst critics admit that he was the preeminent director of American Westerns, guiding the evolution of the Western from a black-hats-versus-white-hats stereotype into a quintessential American story.

During a career that spanned over 50 years and 200 films, he won seven Oscars; four for directing, one for best picture and two for best documentary.

## HOLLYWOOD NEPOTISM, EVEN THEN

His real name was Sean Aloysius O'Feeney, and he was born in Maine in 1895, the youngest of 13 children of Irish immigrants. He went to Hollywood at age 16, following after his brother Francis who'd gone 10 years earlier and become a successful actor and director. John began as an assistant to his older brother and later worked as a stuntman and actor before becoming a director.

## COWBOYS ARE PEOPLE, TOO

He directed his first feature film for Universal in 1917—a Western called *Straight Shooting*.

Most films of the era used flat lighting and mundane settings, but Ford was heavily influenced by the German style of filmmaking of the 1920s, which pioneered the use of artistic light and shadow. Ford shot most of the exteriors for his Westerns in Monument Valley in Arizona and Utah (known in Hollywood as "Ford country"),

---

Nineteen years elapsed between the first and second women in space—both were Russians.

the perfect backdrop for his striking visuals. And the characters who moved across his screen had actual personalities, in a genre where one-dimensional characters were the norm.

## DON'T THINK YOU'RE SPECIAL
John Ford was tough on all of his actors, often ridiculing them endlessly—and that was if he liked them. Being ignored by Ford was even worse because that meant he probably wouldn't work with you again. During the filming of *Stagecoach*, Ford constantly ridiculed John Wayne, telling him he was a bad actor and making fun of the way he talked and walked (even though, in his biography of Ford, Peter Bogdanovich insists that Wayne learned his signature walk from Ford himself). Finally the other actors came to Wayne's defense and told Ford to lay off. Later Ford revealed that he'd intentionally created the problem so that the experienced actors on the set, who would normally be jealous of a newcomer in a starring role, would come to Wayne's defense.

Ford's mistreatment of Wayne didn't end with *Stagecoach*. They made 21 films together and Ford taunted Wayne during the filming of all of them. Ford treated all of his favorite actors that way and on several occasions an actor got so fed up he challenged Ford to a fistfight.

## THAT'S MISTER ROBERTS, TO YOU, BUDDY!
He made a few propaganda films for the navy during WWII, and retired as a rear admiral.

After the war, Ford's confrontational methods backfired on him during the filming of *Mister Roberts*, which starred Henry Fonda (who'd also starred in the stage version). Fonda had worked with Ford before, most notably on *The Grapes of Wrath*, and had bristled at Ford's mistreatment in the past.

This time around, Fonda had more clout with the studio heads and refused to put up with the abuse. Ford wouldn't compromise, so Fonda had Ford replaced by Mervyn LeRoy.

## A LITTLE SCARED BY THE RED SCARE
Ford actively participated in the witch-hunting in the entertainment industry during the McCarthy era of the 1950s, when anyone suspected of being a communist was blacklisted.

The last astronaut to walk on the moon was Eugene Cernan in 1972.

He took part in an attempted takeover of the Director's Guild of America by legendary director Cecil B. DeMille, who believed that the guild was being run by communists. But Ford somewhat redeemed himself when he became so appalled by De Mille's red-baiting tactics that he publicly broke with him during a guild meeting.

First he stood up and introduced himself: "My name's John Ford," he said. "I make Westerns." Then, to DeMille, he said: "I don't like you and I don't like what has been happening here tonight." Ford then called for a vote on retaining the current leadership. The vote passed and DeMille's challenge was defeated.

## MORE THAN A COWBOY

Ford's Westerns express a deep understanding of America's past and the spirit of the frontier. And though he's best known for them—movies like *My Darling Clementine* and the cavalry trilogy (*Fort Apache*, *She Wore a Yellow Ribbon*, and *Rio Grande*)—Ford won his four directing Oscars for non-Westerns: *The Informer*, *The Grapes of Wrath*, *How Green Was My Valley*, and *The Quiet Man*.

His last feature film was *7 Women* (1966), a critical and box-office disappointment that many critics thought was a throwback to Ford's 1930's techniques. There was talk that he had "lost it" and didn't know how to direct anymore. Stung by the criticism and plagued by ill health, Ford retired. In 1973, he was awarded the American Film Institute's first-ever Life Achievement Award, as well as the Presidential Medal of Freedom a few months before he died of cancer.

\* \* \*

**A few of our favorite lines from John Ford movies:**
Tom Joad (Henry Fonda) in *The Grapes of Wrath*:
"Seems like the government's got more interest in a dead man than a live one."

Reverend Rosenkrantz (Arthur Shields) in *Drums Along the Mohawk*:
"Any man failing to report to duty will be promptly hanged. Amen."

Eloise Kelly (Ava Gardner) in *Mogambo*:
"Look, Buster, don't you get overstimulated with me!"

Captain Flagg (James Cagney) in *What Price Glory*:
"It's a lousy war, kid...but it's the only one we've got."

So far the longest reign of any British monarch was Queen Victoria's—64 years.

# JOHNNY CANUCK, EH?

*Is it a bird? A plane? A candied duck? No! It's a Canadian!*

Johnny Canuck isn't a real live Canadian—he started life in 1869 as the Canadian counterpart to America's Uncle Sam or England's John Bull.

And how did he get the name Canuck? Almost every dictionary you consult will have a different origin for the word, including:

• **Connaught:** a French nickname given to Irish immigrants who moved to Quebec in the early 1800s, over the objections of the resident Quebecois.

• **Canuchsa:** an Iroquois word for anyone living in a kanata (village), the word from which "Canada" was derived.

• **Kanaka:** a Hawaiian word for South Sea islanders. In Canada? Strange as it may seem, French Canadians and Hawaiians were both involved in the Pacific Northwest fur trade.

Some dictionaries are honest and just say "origin unknown." In any case, it's the sort of word that Canadians use freely about themselves, but gets them hot under the collar of their Mountie uniforms when it comes out of the mouth of an unwitting Yank.

## O CANADA, HE STANDS ON GUARD FOR THEE

When Johnny Canuck first appeared in 1869, he was the wholesome image of Mr. Average Canadian, often portrayed as a farmer, logger, or rancher, but generally also depicted as being a little slow-witted—which doesn't say a lot for Canadians or the people who created him. A product of editorial cartoonists, he was generally seen standing up for himself against his pushy neighbor to the south... whoever that was.

He reemerged in 1942, when a cartoonist resurrected him as a crusader fighting stolidly against the Nazis; your average run-of-the-mill one-man fighting machine. Another blow was struck for the Canucks in 1975, when comics superhero Captain Canuck—in his red and white tights—hit the stands. One of his sidekicks was a French Canadian, Kébec, demonstrating, we guess, that Quebec really could cooperate with the rest of Canada. The Captain was quite the upstanding citizen, prone to leading his troops in prayer before a big mission. Johnny would have been proud.

The only English king to die on the battlefield was Richard III at Bosworth Field.

# OF ALL THE GIN JOINTS IN THE WORLD...

*Carry Nation's life was so hard it could have driven her to drink. Instead, her troubles drove her to become the famous hatchet-wielding bar smasher of the temperance movement.*

A few years after Carry's birth in 1846, her mother, Mary Moore, announced to the family that she wasn't Mary Moore anymore. No, she was Queen Victoria. From that time on, Mrs. Moore wore a crystal crown to breakfast, saw family members by appointment only, and toured the Kentucky countryside in her ornate carriage. Slaves in scarlet uniforms announced her arrival by blasting horns. She even knighted several (no doubt confused) local farmers.

That's right. Carry Nation's mother was bonkers.

Carry, poor child, escaped into religious visions. Her father was falling into debt (in part due to supporting "the queen's" fancy carriage) and kept selling land and moving farther west. By the end of the Civil War, their Missouri farm was in ruins and Carry had to leave school to care for her younger brothers and sisters and her unstable mother.

## PUNCH DRUNK LOVE

At 20, Carry fell for Dr. Charles Gloyd, a handsome, ex-Union officer and medical doctor who was well educated, spoke several languages, and drank like a fish. He came to their wedding drunk. Five days after that, he stayed out all night—drinking with his mason buddies. His attempt to establish a medical practice in a nearby town failed; all his patients left. A few months after the wedding, Carry was penniless and pregnant with a husband who was sloshed more than he was sober. Carry's father came and took her back home. Six months later, Charles Gloyd died of acute and chronic alcoholism. Carry's daughter, Charlien, was born moderately mentally handicapped. In Carry's mind, her husband's alcoholism was to blame.

King George III's diary entry on July 4, 1776, was: "Nothing of consequence happened today."

## MORE TROUBLE BREWING
For four years, Carry supported herself, her daughter, and Gloyd's
mother, who had lived with them and whom Carry refused to
abandon. Carry prayed for a husband to rescue her. For some reason,
the good Lord sent ne'er-do-well David Nation as the answer to
her prayers. At least he didn't drink. The couple bought a farm in
south Texas, but the stock died and the crops failed. Then they
moved to Columbia, Texas, where Carry got a job managing the
rat-infested Columbia Hotel. Carry worked from before dawn until
after midnight. Eventually, Carry saved enough to buy a hotel in
Richmond, Texas. But David had been writing newspaper articles
and editorials supporting voting rights for blacks, which wasn't a
very popular stance with some of the neighbors, and one night he
was shot at and attacked. Carry and family packed up once more
and moved to Kansas.

## ONE NATION UNDER GOD
Throughout all her troubles, Carry never lost her faith, even after
she was refused admission to the Methodist and Episcopalian
churches (for being too religious—can you believe it?). Thus
spurned, she held her own Sunday school classes in her hotel's
dining room. (And she was still having those darn religious
visions.) When her daughter became a heavy drinker, Carry found
a new and personal reason to hate alcohol. At age 53, Carry
Nation knew that her mission in life was to rid the world of alcohol.

## I'M SHOCKED, SHOCKED TO LEARN LIQUOR IS
## BEING SOLD HERE
Kansas had supposedly been a "dry" state since 1880. The sale of
liquor was permitted only for scientific, mechanical, or "medicinal"
purposes. This last loophole was big enough to drive a beer wagon
through. Drugstores sold alcohol as medicine; saloons sold it, too,
without any excuse. After joining the Women's Christian Temperance
Union, Carry raided a drugstore and confiscated some illegal brandy.
    At her next stop, Kiowa, Kansas, officials refused to enforce
the law. Carry was a large woman, about six feet tall, and strong
from years of hard work. She was now at the formidable weight of
180 pounds, and she knew how to throw her weight around. On
June 6, 1900, using bricks and rocks, Carry smashed everything—

Sunglasses became popular in the 1920s; movie stars wore them to minimize bright camera lights.

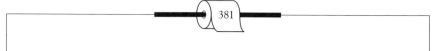

bottles, mirrors, and windows—in three bars in Kiowa in the space of a few minutes. She wasn't prosecuted because the establishments were illegal. The bar owners were found guilty and their establishments were shut down.

On December 27, 1900, Carry descended on Wichita and using an iron rod and more rocks demolished the elegant bar at the Hotel Carey. She spent two weeks in jail before the charges were dropped. It wasn't until January 21, 1901 that Carry picked up the hatchet that became the symbol of her crusade. She and three assistants wrecked another bar in Wichita. On February 27, 1901, crowds led by Carry smashed bars all over Topeka, all day long.

## HATCHET JOB

Carry Nation was suddenly a national celebrity, going on speaking tours and publishing a newsletter called *The Smasher's Mail.* She was arrested 30 times over the course of her campaign against alcohol. She sold miniature hatchets to pay her legal bills. Children around the country played at bar smashing, and "hatchetatio" became a new word. Carry's smashing and lecturing kept her away from home so much that David filed for divorce on the grounds of desertion—and Carry was glad to be rid of him.

## LAST CALL

Public sentiment was with Carry until the assassination of President William McKinley on September 6, 1901. Carry hated McKinley, calling him "the Brewer's President." As he lay dying, she said that she shed no tears for him. The statement was misquoted; it turned into Carry saying that she hoped he would die. The outrage almost ended her mission. She became the butt of endless jokes. For a time, she was reduced to delivering her temperance message on the burlesque circuit.

The unstoppable Carry persevered. She continued lecturing against alcohol throughout the U.S., Canada, and Europe, supporting herself with the sales of little hatchet pins, donations, and speaking fees. After having to place her daughter in an institution for the insane (we told you she had a tough life), she retired to Arkansas where she opened a center for women abused by alcoholic husbands. She died on June 9, 1911.

**Chuck Berry's biggest hit was "My Ding-a-Ling."**

# PAIGE PAGES

*I ain't ever had a job, I just always played baseball.*

Professional baseball in the U.S. was segregated until 1947, when Jackie Robinson broke the color barrier in the major leagues. In the years prior, there were several very successful Negro leagues in which Leroy "Satchel" Paige was considered the greatest pitcher. He was known as much for his charisma and longevity as for his legendary pitching skills. Satchel was a colorful and engaging character who had a great talent for entertaining the crowds from the mound with his own version of a vaudeville act.

## CURTAIN UP!

Paige was born in Alabama, the sixth of 12 children to John, a gardener, and Lula Coleman, a domestic. His actual birthdate is unknown, but as he often joked: "Age is a question of mind over matter. If you don't mind, it doesn't matter."

As a boy, he earned money carrying suitcases at the Mobile train depot. He was paid by the number of bags he moved, so he rigged a pole and some rope to carry three or four additional bags at a time. His friends thought he looked like a "walking satchel tree" so they called him Satchel.

At 12, he was sent to reform school for shoplifting and truancy. While he was there, he developed his pitching skills and after his release he joined the semipro baseball team, the Mobile Tigers.

## MR. SHOWMANSHIP

In 1926, Satchel Paige made his debut in professional baseball with the Negro Southern League, pitching Chattanooga to a 5–4 win over Birmingham. From then on, he played baseball year round—in the U.S. in the summer and in South America during the winter. He often pitched two games a day in two different cities.

Paige made a habit of striking out the first nine batters he faced in exhibition games, and on quite a few occasions he sent the infield to the dugout or called the outfield in to sit behind the mound while he faced the best hitters in the opposition lineup. When he wasn't playing league games, he barnstormed around the

---

**Don McLean's "American Pie" was written in remembrance of Buddy Holly's plane crash.**

country playing against all takers. To this day you can bet there are still some old duffers who reminisce about "the day Satchel Paige came to town." The word went out. All of a sudden the stands were filling up with white folks who'd come to watch ol' Satch strut his stuff.

## LIFE'S A PITCH

He nicknamed his pitches: the "bee-ball," the "barber," the "two-hump blooper," the "jump-ball," the "trouble-ball," the "long-ball," the "bat dodger," and his fastball, which he called "Long Tom." His most unusual throw was called the "hesitation pitch," because he stopped his arm for a second right before he released the ball to throw the batter's timing off.

He once told a sportswriter, "I use my single windup, my double windup, my triple windup, my hesitation windup, my no windup. I also use my step-n-pitch-it, my submariner, and my sidearmer. Man's got to do what he's got to do."

Satch took the Kansas City Monarchs to four consecutive Negro American League pennants from 1939 to 1942 and then again in 1946. During the 1930s and 1940s, he was baseball's greatest gate attraction. It's estimated that he pitched in more than 2,000 baseball games in the Negro leagues. He had a string of 64 consecutive scoreless innings, and a stretch of 21 straight wins.

## THAT DAMNED OLD MAN

He'd been playing baseball for more than 20 years when, in 1948, the Cleveland Indians provided him with his first opportunity to play in the major leagues. That first year, he registered a 6–1 record with a 2.48 ERA to help pitch the Indians to the pennant and a World Series victory.

He joined the St. Louis Browns in 1951 as a full-time reliever and routinely arrived for games around the fifth inning. He would sneak drinks into the bullpen and relax between innings in a plush rocking chair provided by the coach. New York Yankees manager Casey Stengel once remarked: "If the Yanks don't get ahead in the first six innings, the Browns bring in that damned old man and then we're sunk."

Twelve years after playing in the All-Star games of 1952–53, in his late 50s, Satchel pitched three innings for the Kansas City

Athletics to become the oldest man to pitch in a major league game. He retired when his two-month contract for $4,000 expired. In 1968, the Atlanta Braves signed him as a coach because he needed 158 days on a major league payroll to qualify for a pension.

## GOING TO THAT ALL-STAR TEAM IN THE SKY

Paige was elected to the National Baseball Hall of Fame in 1971, becoming the first player elected from the Negro Leagues. He remarked: "The only change is that baseball has turned Paige from a second-class citizen to a second-class immortal."

In 1982, suffering from advanced emphysema, ol' Satch made his last public appearance at the dedication of Satchel Paige Memorial Stadium in Kansas City, Missouri. He died three days later.

## SATCHEL'S WIT AND WISDOM

Work like you don't need the money. Love like you've never been hurt. Dance like nobody's watching.

Mother always told me, if you tell a lie, always rehearse it. If it don't sound good to you, it won't sound good to no one else.

I don't generally like running. I believe in training by rising gently up and down from the bench.

Ain't no man can avoid being born average, but there ain't no man got to be common.

I never threw an illegal pitch. The trouble is, once in a while I would toss one that ain't never been seen by this generation.

Just take the ball and throw it where you want to. Throw strikes. Home plate don't move.

Don't look back. Something might be gaining on you.

Money and women. They're two of the strongest things in the world. The things you do for a woman you wouldn't do for anything else. Same with money.

You win a few, you lose a few. Some get rained out. But you got to dress for all of them.

My pitching philosophy is simple; you gotta keep the ball off the fat part of the bat.

Custer was court-martialed for an unauthorized leave he took to visit his wife.

# NOTABLE NICKNAMES IN BASEBALL

*What is it about the sport of baseball that inspires so many nicknames?*
*Maybe it has something to do with the leisurely pace—and all those*
*extra minutes that announcers have to fill.*

Here are some of the nicer names that have been yelled from the stands over the last century or so.

### The Sultan of Swat—George Herman "Babe" Ruth (1895–1948)
During his career in baseball, the Babe hit 714 home runs (including 60 in one season). He may hold the world's record for number of nicknames, too, including "the Home Run King," "Herman the Great," "the Colossus of Clout," and "Bambino."

### The Yankee Clipper—"Joltin Joe" Joseph Paul DiMaggio (1914–1999)
His 56-game hitting streak has never been equaled. He won two batting championships, was named MVP three times, and always carried himself with grace and a quiet dignity.

### The Georgia Peach—Tyrus "Ty" Raymond Cobb (1886–1961)
During his 24-year career Cobb amassed 4,191 hits, 892 stolen bases, and batted .367. His "win at any cost" attitude gave him a reputation as a "dirty" player by most opponents. Most of his teammates despised him, too, because of his obnoxious personality.

### Shoeless Joe—Joseph Jefferson Jackson (1887–1951)
Acquitted in court, but banned from baseball for life for his involvement in the "Black Sox" scandal of the 1919 World Series, Jackson was nicknamed Shoeless Joe after he played a game in his stockings because a new set of baseball shoes were hurting his feet.

### Charlie Hustle—Pete Rose (1941– )
Rose holds the records for most hits, singles, at-bats, and games

---

Only Baseball Hall of Fame member in three countries: Martin Dihigo.

played. Accused of betting on baseball and his own team, he was banned from baseball for life for "conduct detrimental to baseball." Whitey Ford nicknamed him "Charlie Hustle" because of his work ethic.

### Stan the Man—Stanley Frank Musial (1920– )
Musial won seven batting titles, played in 24 All-Star Games, won three World Series, and was named MVP three times. He played for the St. Louis Cardinals but was nicknamed "Stan the Man" by Brooklyn Dodger fans who respected his batting prowess.

### Oil Can—Dennis Ray Boyd (1959– )
This pitcher with a volatile temper is most famous for the tantrum he threw in 1986 after learning he didn't make the All-Star squad. He was suspended from the Reds and landed in a hospital for emotional exhaustion. His nickname is a slang term for beer in his hometown in Mississippi.

### Donnie Baseball—Donald Arthur Mattingly (1961– )
Mattingly won nine Golden Glove awards, was named to All-Star teams six times, and set the record for the most grand slams in a season. Kirby Puckett of the Minnesota Twins dubbed him "Donnie Baseball."

### The Splendid Splinter—Theodore "Ted" Samuel Williams (1918–2002)
Also known as "Teddy Ballgame," he had a lifetime average of .344, played in 17 All-Star games, and won six AL batting championships. His tempestuous relationship with the sportswriters in Boston made him famous, too.

### The Wizard of Oz—Osborne "Ozzie" Earl Smith (1954– )
One of the greatest shortstops of all time, Smith won 13 Golden Glove awards, had more than 2,500 hits and 500 stolen bases, and was named to the All-Star team 12 times.

### Mr. October—Reginald "Reggie" Martínez Jackson (1946– )
They called him "Mr. October" because he played his best in postseason games; he had a .357 average in World Series games. He hit 563 home runs—but is also the all-time strikeout leader with 2,597.

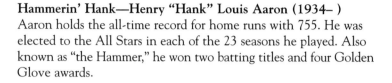

**Hammerin' Hank—Henry "Hank" Louis Aaron (1934– )**
Aaron holds the all-time record for home runs with 755. He was elected to the All Stars in each of the 23 seasons he played. Also known as "the Hammer," he won two batting titles and four Golden Glove awards.

**Tom Terrific—George Thomas "Tom" Seaver (1944– )**
In 20 seasons with the Mets, Seaver won 311 games, struck out 3,640 batters, and won the Cy Young Award three times.

**Iron Horse—Ludwig "Lou" Heinrich Gehrig (1903–1941)**
"The Pride of the Yankees" had a lifetime batting average of .340 and had played in 2,130 consecutive games until he was forced to retire in 1939 because of the illness (a.k.a. ALS) that now bears his name. Also known as "Larrupin' Lou" ("larrup" being an old-fashioned word for "whip" or "beat").

**Yogi—Lawrence Peter Berra (1925– )**
Universally loved by players and fans alike, Yogi was elected to the All-Star team in 14 out of the 18 seasons he played. He played 148 consecutive games without an error and was selected MVP three times. He is most famous for Yogi-isms like "It ain't over till it's over," "It's déjà vu all over again," and "The future ain't what it used to be."

**Other great baseball nicknames:**
Luis "Little Looey" Aparicio
Luke "Ol' Aches and Pains" Appling
Richie "Whitey" Ashburn
Jim "Sunny Jim" Bottomley
Roger "the Duke of Tralee" Bresnahan
Mordecai "Three Finger" Brown
Frank "the Peerless Leader" Chance
Mickey "Black Mike" Cochrane
Earle "the Kentucky Colonel" Combs
Johnny "Crab" Evers
Carlton "Pudge" Fisk
Whitey "Chairman of the Board" Ford
Jimmie "Beast" Foxx (also known as "Double-X")

---

Butch Cassidy, a Mormon, said he never killed anyone during any of his many bank holdups.

Frankie "the Fordham Flash" Frisch
Charlie "the Mechanical Man" Gehringer
Lefty "Goofy" Gomez
Hank "Hammerin' Hank" Greenberg
Rogers "Rajah" Hornsby
Jim "Catfish" Hunter
Walter "Big Train" Johnson
Al "the Line" Kaline
Willie "Wee Willie" Keeler
George "Highpockets" Kelly
Harmon "Killer" Killebrew
Napoleon "Larry" Lajoie
Mickey "the Commerce Comet" Mantle
Christy "Big Six" Mathewson
Willie "Stretch" McCovey
Joe "the Little General" Morgan (also known as "Little Joe")
Tony "Big Dog" Perez
Eddie "Gettysburg Eddie" Plank
Frank "the Judge" Robinson
Nolan "Express" Ryan
Al "Bucketfoot" Simmons
George "Gorgeous George" Sisler
Tris "the Grey Eagle" Speaker (also known as "Spoke")
Honus "the Flying Dutchman" Wagner
Ed "Big Ed" Walsh
Zack "Buck" Wheat
Carl "Yaz" Yastrzemski
Cy "the Cyclone" Young

\* \* \*

## EVERYBODY'S A FAN

Mickey Mantle loved to tell a story about a dream in which St. Peter turns him away from the Pearly Gates. "But before you go," says St. Peter, "God has six dozen baseballs he'd like you to sign."

"Baseball players are smarter than football players. How often do you see a baseball team penalized for too many men on the field?"
—Jim Bouton

Butch Cassidy got his nickname because he worked as a butcher.

# RENAISSANCE WOMAN

*Artemisia's depiction of traditional stories of vengeance—from a woman's viewpoint—marked a breakthrough in the history of art.*

Artemisia Gentileschi was born in Rome in 1593 and was taught to paint by her father, a well-known artist himself. Rome had a vibrant art scene and Artemisia met all the famous painters of her day, including Caravaggio, whose style of contrasting light influenced her work.

## A SERIOUS TURNING POINT

Not all of the artists her father knew and worked with were interested in Artemisia's artistic skill. When Artemisia was 19 she was raped by Florentine artist Agostino Tassi. At the trial, Tassi denied it and accused Artemisia of not having been a virgin at the time of the rape, and of already having had many lovers. He called her an "insatiable whore." She was examined by midwives to determine whether she'd been "deflowered" recently or a long time ago.

Tassi also told the court that Artemisia was such an unskilled painter that he'd been giving her a lesson on the day of the alleged rape, which is why he was in her bedroom. But Tassi had boasted to a former friend about the rape. That and the facts that he'd been imprisoned previously for incest with his sister-in-law and was charged with arranging his wife's murder was enough to convict him. He served less than a year in prison. Artemisia married a month after the trial ended to quiet public speculation about her morals, and perhaps to protect herself from further attacks.

## BLOODY MURDER

Tassi had tried to convince the court that Artemisia lacked talent, but she'd been painting mature works since age 17. The whole ordeal inspired her to reach new heights as an artist—and to plumb the depths. During and after the trial, Artemisia worked on one of her most famous paintings, *Judith Beheading Holofernes*, a

---

**Michelangelo spent four years painting the Sistine Chapel.**

bloody and disturbing depiction of the Biblical story in which an Israelite widow seduces the general who is besieging her city, and while he's in a drunken sleep, beheads him. (See "Seduced and Beheaded" on page 66 for all the gory details.)

Judith was a popular subject for painters but few ever depicted her the way Artemisia did. Holofernes, huge and muscular, is struggling helplessly on his bed, blood spurting from his wound, as Judith and her maid hold him down to finish the job. It is such a disturbing picture that even now it hangs in an out-of-the-way part of the Uffizi gallery in Florence.

Artemisia went on to paint other heroic and tragic women—Cleopatra, Bathsheba, and Jael, another Biblical heroine, pictured in the act of driving a metal tent peg through a sleeping foe's head. Her subject matter made the critics of the day a little uneasy, but her style wowed them; she was the only female painter of the Renaissance known to have influenced her male peers.

## SHE GOT AROUND

Most successful artists made their money from church commissions—not an option for a woman. Instead, Artemisia took on private commissions from the wealthy of Rome and Florence (including the powerful Medicis). In time, she was famous throughout Europe. She painted works for the king of Spain and went to England for three years to paint for Charles I. When war broke out in 1641, she returned to Italy and settled in Naples.

## LIFE AFTER DEATH

After her death in 1653 at 60 years old, Artemisia was forgotten. Since she was no longer able to defend her talent, critics and art historians began to doubt that a woman could have painted so well and so powerfully. Her works were attributed to her father or to other painters. Artemisia stayed anonymous until she was redis-covered about 25 years ago. Interest in her life and art have been increasing ever since, with numerous books, exhibitions of her work, and even a film of her life. (It should come as no surprise that 1998's *Artemisia* is wildly inaccurate.) The critics and historians have made her famous again. And new works by Artemisia, previously attributed to other painters, are still being discovered.

Michelangelo's father didn't want him to become an artist.

# THE MOON ALSO RISES

*Though he's best known for the giant "Moonie" weddings that have married as many as 30,000 couples in one ceremony, Sun Myung Moon is so much more than just a modern-day millionaire guru.*

For a guy who would proclaim himself rightful ruler of the whole world, Sun Myung Moon was born in humble circumstances to a family of poverty-stricken Korean farmers in 1920. His early life consisted of farm work and farm life, broken up by interludes at the local Confucian school whenever his family could spare him.

His life changed dramatically when his family converted to Christianity when he was 10. They had to be careful spreading the word about their newfound faith because Japan, which had taken control of Korea 40 years before, only permitted Shinto religious practices. Religious fervor overtook the whole family in spite of it and by the time he turned 12, Moon was teaching Sunday school.

## MOONSHINE

He turned out to be an exceptionally charismatic teacher. His renown only grew when, on Easter of 1935, he announced that Jesus had appeared to him and asked him to continue Christ's work on earth. Fellow Christian preachers in Korea snubbed him and said he was imagining things. But a few were drawn to the mystical boy who seemed to have a direct line to God.

## MOON OVER KOREA

For the next 10 years, Moon threw himself into religious studies. He participated in political activities as well, advocating for Korea's independence from Japan during WWII; at one point he was briefly jailed for his rabble-rousing activities. Then, taking advantage of Japan's WWII defeat, he started to publicly preach in Korea's Communist north.

The Commies didn't any more take kindly to Christian preaching than the Japanese had—particularly not Moon's strange brand of Christianity, which he called "the Divine Principle," mixing teaching from Christianity, Confucianism, and Buddhism with a giant dollop of Moon-worship mixed in. The communists threw Moon in jail in 1946 and again in 1948, when he was sentenced to five years hard labor along with other Christian ministers. Moon only ended up serving two years, though, because UN and American troops liberated the prison after the Korean War.

## FULL MOON

Moon moved to Pusan, Korea, and there he built his church—the very first Unification Church (in his official biography he says he built it out of old army ration boxes, but that may be an exaggeration). The tiny church would prove to be the first of many. Unification churches started popping up like mushrooms. By 1957 there were 30 of them in Korea and by 1959 missionaries were racking up converts in America. Moon was seen as an all-knowing father of hundreds of followers, who genuflected for hours-long lectures about God—and Moon's exalted place in uniting the world's Christians.

## MR. AND MRS. MOON

In 1960 Moon took a wife, who was installed as his coleader. Together, they were "the True Parents," the first couple who could bring forth children with no original sin. This is where their habit of "blessing" marriages started. By 1997 they were presiding over a union of 30,000 couples at RFK Stadium in Washington, D.C., while an estimated 3.6 million other couples participated via satellite linkup from 84 countries. To this day Moon puts couples together (he claims "matchmaking" as a special gift) by picking their images from a pile of photos.

## NOT JUST MOONING AROUND

During the 1960s and 1970s, Moon was also consolidating a business empire, founding churches, schools, construction companies, tourist resorts, hotels, newspapers, real estate brokerages, and on and on and on. Moon even founded *The Washington Times*, a paper intended to compete with the "liberal" *Washington Post*.

## NEW MOONIES

The Moonies were a million-dollar business by the time Moon brought his ministry to America in 1971, where he was met with wild acclaim. A generation of young people coming down off the sexual revolution and flower power were a ready audience. By the time of the Unification Church's peak in the mid 1970s, Moon

---

On his first night hosting the *Tonight Show*, Johnny Carson was introduced by Groucho Marx.

made claim to 4.6 million members who lived in communal groups in Korea, China, and the U.S. The reverend was so famous he was invited to the White House to hang out with Richard Nixon. In airports across the the U.S., robed Moonie converts sold flowers to anyone who wasn't annoyed by their presence.

## THE MOON GOES DOWN

But Moon wouldn't be on top for long. The U.S. government was carefully watching his growing business empire, suspicious that he was funneling profits from his various enterprises into his tax-free church. In 1981 they charged him with tax evasion. Moon only served a little more than a year in prison, but the crunch was out of his cookie. His Church, now tainted, began to lose members. Accusations of money laundering followed Moon wherever he went. He settled down quietly in his Irvington, New York, mansion and began directing Unification activities more covertly.

## THE DARK SIDE OF THE MOON

Moon also suffered from family problems. One of his 12 children, 17-year-old son Heung Jin was killed in a car accident in 1984. Daughter Ye Jin, 37, moved to Boston in 1993 and cut off family contact. Daughter Un Jin, who'd been married to a Unification Church member in an arranged union at age 18, abandoned the family in 1996. And most scandalous of all, oldest son Hyo Jin, the apple of Moon's eye, divorced his wife in 1997; she wrote a tell-all book claiming that Hyo Jin spent millions of church money on cocaine and punched her in the face when she was seven months pregnant. Finally, in 1999, 21-year-old son Young Jin leaped out of a window on the 17th floor of a Reno hotel.

## SAME OLD MOON?

Moon still lives in Irvington and directs the worldwide operations of the Unification Church and its business industries. The church continues to actively recruit members—there are said to be about 30,000 members left in the U.S. Most recently the Unification Church has been buying newspapers and banks in Uruguay and giant tracts of land in South America with plans to set up foundations dedicated to Unification principles. But it looks like Moon may be up to his old tricks again. At press time, Brazilian federal police were investigating Moon for tax evasion.

**Groucho Marx's trademark moustache was often painted on.**

# UNDRESSED FOR SUCCESS

*Josephine Baker was a spy, a civil rights hero, and a mother to twelve adopted children. But what everyone remembers is the night she danced wearing flamingo feathers—and nothing else.*

As Freda Josephine Carson was growing up in the slums of St. Louis, Missouri, she spent her free time learning the dopiest dances of 1919, like the Shake, the Mess Around, and the Itch. And she dreamed of dancing her way to stardom—instead of doing white folks' laundry.

At 13, she left home to become (in rapid succession) a waitress, a wife, a separated wife, and a chorus girl touring with an African American musical. Since she was too young and too "dark and skinny" to be glamorous, Josephine started out as the comedic "end girl"—the goofy dancer who couldn't get things right. She clowned around while she danced, crossing her eyes, giving a nutty grin, and tripping over her feet. Audiences loved her. So did her husbands.

## ONE MORE TIME

She married again, in 1921. This time the lucky man was Willie Baker, whose last name she kept. But she never depended on a man for financial support, so she never hesitated to leave when a relationship soured.

## CROSSING THE POND

By 1925, Baker was dancing at the Plantation Club in Harlem. She'd moved up from the St. Louis slums, but she was still a clown, dancing with her eyes crossed. So at 19, she crossed her fingers as well as her eyes, and took a risky job offer to join La Revue Negre, in Paris, France.

## THE CITY OF LIGHT...AND DARK

Paris introduced her to a new experience: integration. In Paris, no one kept her out of cafés or clubs, nor did she have to go on

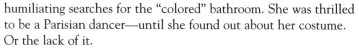

humiliating searches for the "colored" bathroom. She was thrilled to be a Parisian dancer—until she found out about her costume. Or the lack of it.

Parisians adored black dancers, believing they were naturally sexy, with pure jungle souls that shouldn't be tamed. (It was a friendlier version of American racism, but racism just the same.) Baker had dreamed of dancing in Parisian silks and furs. Instead she was to star with Joe Alex, wearing a skimpy feather skirt. She wept. She tried to quit, but the hard truth was that she was stranded in a foreign country. She'd have to dance as a bare-breasted native in front of la crème de Parisian society.

## A FEATHER IN HER CAP...OR AT LEAST SOMEWHERE
On opening night, Josephine and Joe performed the "Danse Sauvage." As one journalist described it, Baker "made her entry entirely nude except for a pink flamingo feather between her limbs." (Actually, the dancer also had feathers around her ankles and neck, but they didn't exactly keep out the cold.)

Joe and Josephine performed what Parisians saw as an exotic African mating dance. (But as Josephine twined around Joe and moved her body sensually, any kid from St. Louis or Harlem would have recognized the Shimmy, the Shake, and the Mess Around.) Stunned, the audience stood to either boo or applaud wildly. Baker had done just what the producers had prayed for—she'd shocked Paris.

## THE ORIGINAL EDIBLE UNDIES
When La Revue Negre closed, Baker moved to the Folies-Bergère. She became the highest-paid entertainer in Europe, which helped cure her aversion to skimpy costumes—of which her most famous was 16 bananas strung into a skirt.

In 1936, the Parisian star was ready to conquer New York as the lead in the Ziegfeld Follies. Quelle disaster! *The New York Times* mocked her success in Paris, claiming that in matters of "sex appeal to jaded Europeans, a Negro wench always has a head start."

Josephine returned to Europe. She became a French citizen the next year when she married Frenchman Jean Lion.

---

Mao's body is preserved in Tiananmen Square.

## GLAMOUR AS A WEAPON

New York's loss was France's gain. Baker went on to become a chevalier in the Legion of Honor for her work in the French Resistance. When the Nazis occupied France, she hid Resistance leaders on her country estate. To smuggle them out of the country, she went on tour and made them her "entourage." Starstruck border guards paid no attention to the men with the great Josephine Baker (who was also smuggling secret information written in invisible ink on her sheet music).

## SHE HAD A DREAM

Josephine visited the U.S. again in the 1950s, hoping to perform. The Stork Club refused her services, so the media-savvy diva turned her humiliation into a public battle against segregation. The idealistic Josephine also adopted 12 children of different races. She raised a rainbow tribe (with the help of her fourth husband, French orchestra leader Jo Bouillon) that proved that love, not race, mattered. And she continued to wow her audiences— performing well into in her sixties. Of course, in her later years she wore sequins and satin.

But no more bananas.

\* \* \*

## NOW YOU'RE COOKING!

During WWII—and decades before becoming a famous chef— Julia Child worked for the Office of Strategic Services (the prede- cessor to the CIA).

One of her assignments was to solve a problem for U.S. naval forces. The navy was placing explosives underwater, but sharks were bumping into them and setting them off, not only using up some perfectly good booby traps, but warning the German U-boats for whom they'd been intended. So Child and a few of her male compatriots got together and literally cooked up a shark repellent that was used to coat the explosives.

# PLASTIC MAN

*If you've ever wondered who put the Tupper in Tupperware, sit right down and meet the man...no, the genius...who created an iconic kitchen staple from a hunk of oil refinery waste.*

After high school graduation, Earl Tupper resolved to earn a million dollars by age 30. He started out as a mail clerk, then worked on a railroad labor crew. Not a lot of money in either, he found out, so in 1928, he decided that he could fulfill his mission in life by becoming a tree surgeon. After taking a course, he started a company called "The Tupper Tree Doctors." He did pretty well for a time until, in 1936, he was forced into bankruptcy—a far cry from the million he'd set out to make.

### THE CHICKEN PLUCKER'S FRIEND
He'd been born in 1907 on a farm in New Hampshire. Even as a boy, Tupper was interested in inventing and making money. One of his gadgets—a frame to simplify the cleaning of chickens—even earned a patent. He also sold poultry and produce door-to-door, which helped out the family and introduced him to the perks of client contact.

### BETTER LIVING THROUGH CHEMISTRY
After that darn bankruptcy in 1936, he went to work for DuPont. He only spent one year there before he struck out on his own, determined to use his newly acquired skills in plastic design and manufacturing. In time he started to concentrate on producing plastic consumer goods—a formidable market since plastic was fragile, slimy, and foul smelling.

### THE PROMISE OF PLASTIC
The invention that catapulted Tupper's ingenuity into every American kitchen started with "slag," a dark lump of oil refinery waste. He transformed that grim mass of debris into a plastic that was heat-resistant, odorless, affordable, and translucent. Then, to top it all off, he created an air- and watertight seal based on the design of an upside-down paint can lid.

Che Guevera suffered from severe asthma, a factor in his move to Argentina to study medicine.

Finally in 1946 he introduced his shatterproof and colorful creations—cigarette cases, kitchen containers, and the oxymoronic "plastic" glasses (which he called "tumblers")—to hardware and department stores. But his intended customers weren't convinced. Plus, quite a few of them were confused as to how to operate the lids.

## A WISE MOVE
One of his salespeople, a divorced mother named Brownie Wise, was more successful than anyone else on his staff; she was selling his plastic doodads at home to 1950s housewives who were longing for adult companionship as much as new housewares. In one fell swoop, Earl Tupper promoted Wise to vice president in charge of sales and distribution. He also helped launch a new distribution plan—the Tupperware party was born, and within the decade, would be a national phenomenon.

## TUPPER, WHERE?
In 1958, Tupper sold the company for $16 million, clinching his boyhood dream of affluence. He remained on the board of directors until 1973, when he retired. He then moved his family to Costa Rica, where he became a citizen and lived until his death in 1982.

## TUPPERWARE UPDATE
Today, there's a Tupperware party every 2.2 seconds, but about 85 percent of them take place outside the U.S. in one of the more than 100 countries across the world where Earl Tupper's wares are sold. There are even such culturally distinct items as the Kimchi Keeper, the Kimono Keeper, and the Japanese Bento Box.

## TUPPERWARE FASHION THROUGH THE DECADES
**1940s:** Containers from that era are utilitarian but drab—opaque white cylinders "more laboratorylike than luxurious."
**1960s:** The use of color expands and we have the beginning of light greens and yellows.
**1970s:** Earth tones were in so consumers got browns and dark greens—remember that avocado refrigerator?
**1980s:** Practically a color riot with a profusion of reds, blues, and purples.
**2000+:** The sky's the limit with a panoply of colors and safari, floral and other patterns.

Shortly after his exile from Russia, Leon Trotsky stayed with Diego Rivera and Frida Kahlo.

# "THE LAW IS AN ASS"

*So said Mr. Bumble in Dickens's* Oliver Twist. *Does anybody like them?*

"Lawyer: One skilled in the circumvention of the law."
—**Ambrose Bierce**

"A jury consists of twelve persons chosen to decide who has the better lawyer."
—**Robert Frost**

"A lawyer is a person who writes a 10,000-word document and calls it a 'brief.'"
—**Franz Kafka**

"A town that cannot support one lawyer can always support two."
—**Lyndon Baines Johnson**

"There is never a deed so foul that something couldn't be said for the guy; that's why there are lawyers."
—**Melvin Belli**

"I told you all lawyers are worthless. After all it takes won [sic] to know one."
—**Former Vice President Dan Quayle**

"A countryman between two lawyers is like a fish between two cats."
—**Benjamin Franklin**

"I don't know as I want a lawyer to tell me what I cannot do. I hire him to tell me how to do what I want to do."
—**J. P. Morgan**

"I think we may class the lawyer in the natural history of monsters."
—**John Keats**

"Lawyers are just like physicians: what one says, the other contradicts."
—**Sholom Aleichem**

"He is no lawyer who cannot take two sides."
—**Charles Lamb**

"He saw a lawyer killing a viper on a dunghill hard by his own stable; And the Devil smiled, for it put him in mind of Cain and his brother Abel."
—**Samuel Taylor Coleridge**

"It is the trade of lawyers to question everything, yield nothing, and to talk by the hour."
—**Thomas Jefferson**

Sam Walton of Wal*Mart was an army intelligence officer during WWII.

"I don't think you can make a lawyer honest by an act of legislature. You've got to work on his conscience. And his lack of conscience is what makes him a lawyer."
—**Will Rogers**

"Litigation is the basic legal right which guarantees every corporation its decade in court."
—**David Porter**

"When there is a rift in the lute, the business of the lawyer is to widen the rift and gather the loot."
—**Arthur Garfield Hayes**

"Lawyer: One who helps you get what is coming to him."
—**Anonymous**

"Lawyers are the only persons in whom ignorance of the law is not punished."
—**Jeremy Bentham**

## LAWYERS WHO GOT FAMOUS FOR SOMETHING ELSE
Here's a list of famous people who practiced law at one time—but found a better way to make their mothers proud.

**Hoagy Carmichael:** Songwriter ("Stardust" and "Georgia On My Mind")
**John Cleese:** Comic actor and member of Monty Python's Flying Circus
**Howard Cosell:** Sports commentator
**Mahatma Gandhi:** Leader of the movement for India's independence from Britain
**Erle Stanley Gardner:** Author of 82 Perry Mason novels
**Julio Iglesias:** Singer
**Franz Kafka:** Writer (*The Metamorphosis*)
**Francis Scott Key:** Author of "The Star Spangled Banner"
**Tony LaRussa:** Major league baseball manager
**V. I. Lenin:** Leader of the Russian Revolution and the first leader of the Soviet Socialist Republic
**Ozzie Nelson:** TV star
**Otto Preminger:** Movie director/producer (*Anatomy of a Murder*) and actor (*Stalag 17*)
**Geraldo Rivera:** TV personality
**Scott Turow:** Author (*Presumed Innocent*)

---

Draftee John D. Rockefeller paid someone to fight in his place in the Civil War.

## LAWYERS WITHOUT LICENSE

None of the following men had a law degree, but that didn't stop them from practicing law. This, of course, was back in the old days— Uncle John doesn't recommend trying it today. Or even tomorrow.

**Patrick Henry (1736–1799):** Member of the Continental Congress, Virginia governor
**John Jay (1745–1829):** First chief justice of the Supreme Court
**John Marshall (1755–1835):** Chief justice of the Supreme Court
**Daniel Webster (1782–1852):** U.S. secretary of state
**Abraham Lincoln (1809–1865):** 16th U.S. president
**Stephen Douglas (1813–1861):** U.S. representative and senator from Illinois

## ENTIRELY LEGAL: LAWYERLY STORIES LACED WITH A LITTLE AMERICANA...

Ulysses S. Grant was not a man who took a great deal of care with his appearance. Thus, he often passed unrecognized in a crowd. One stormy night he entered an inn in his hometown of Galena, Illinois. Court was in session, so a number of lawyers were in town. The lawyers clustered around the fire looked up upon Grant's arrival and the following exchange ensued: "Here's a stranger, gentlemen, and by the looks of him he's traveled through hell itself to get here." "That's right," said Grant cheerfully. "And how did you find things down there?" "Just like here," replied Grant, "lawyers all closest to the fire."

At a dinner party, Mark Twain was called upon to give one of his customary speeches. When Twain concluded, a prominent lawyer stood up, shoved both of his hands into his pockets and said: "Does't it strike this company as unusual that a professional humorist should be so funny?" Twain shot back: "Doesn't it strike this company as unusual that a lawyer should have both hands in his own pockets?"

A Windham, Connecticut, tradesman had just finished boiling some cattle's feet. He threw the bones at the back of the courthouse. An attorney who happened to be passing by queried: "What bones are those?" A bystander replied: "I believe they are the client's bones, as they are well picked."

# OH NO, MR. BILL!

*A world without computers and cell phones? It might exist if it weren't for scientists like William Bradford . But scientists, as we know, can have their quirks. In true weirdo fashion, Bill did something else to shock the world after he invented the transistor.*

Technology was in a serious slump in the 1930s, as if it were waiting for William Shockley, born in 1910, to complete his education in physics. An undergrad science degree from California Institute of Technology, followed by a Ph.D. in physics from MIT set him up.

### LAB RATS AT WORK

At Bell Telephone Laboratories, which later became AT&T, Shockley headed a team of scientists trying to find a replacement for vacuum tubes—glass cylinders with filaments used to generate and process electric signals in early electronic devices such as radios and TVs. (Scientists considered vacuum tubes inefficient because of their relatively large size and inability to withstand high temperatures.)

### YOU WIN!

Two of Shockley's coworkers accidentally created the lab's ultimate goal, the transistor, and Shockley modified the design of the early model (called "point-contact") to come up with the "junction" transistors that are still used today. Their invention caused an explosion in the advancement of electronics, earning Shockley, along with the other two scientists—Bardeen and Brattain—the 1956 Nobel Prize in Physics.

### SHOCKLEY MISSES THE BOAT

Shockley formed his own company in 1955 to concentrate on using silicon for transistors instead of the usual germanium, but that might have been his last intelligent decision. He was brilliant, but his lack of managerial and people skills made him rude, paranoid, and controlling—those were his good traits. He made things so uncomfortable that the scientists who worked for him left his floundering company and started their own business making silicon transistors. The new lab led to a series of companies that created the billion-dollar industry now known as  Silicon Valley. Shockley

**Gandhi observed a day of silence on Mondays.**

was left behind. Instead of becoming a billionaire, he taught physics at Stanford University.

## IN HIS SPARE TIME
He was kind of an all-around kook. He liked doing magic tricks, and he once pulled out a bunch of roses from nowhere after a speech he'd made to a professional science group. He loved rock climbing and often scaled the stone façade of his lab building during lunch hours. He kept ant colonies in large glass containers and used mini-straws to train them to move in circular patterns.

## SHOCKLEY SHOCKS SOCIETY
He also took pleasure in driving fast. While recovering from a serious auto accident in 1961, he read about a teenager with a low IQ who was hired to throw acid in someone's face. This started Shockley's obsession with what he termed "dysgenics"—the alleged downhill slide in American genetic traits, especially intelligence.

Using data that modern science has disproven, Shockley claimed that poor Caucasians and African Americans inherited low IQs and reproduced at a much higher rate than "intelligent" people, thereby reducing the national IQ average.

He shockingly declared that social service programs, which he called "humanitarianism gone berserk" and "Dark Ages dogma," prevented evolution from allowing only the "fittest," that is, the "highly intelligent," to survive. He suggested that genetically disadvantaged people should be offered money to undergo sterilization.

He repeatedly tried to present his views through articles and lectures. Instead, he was labeled a racist, booed off the podium, and hung in effigy.

## OH, THAT SMARTS!
At age 70, in an attempt to raise the national IQ, Shockley kept busy by donating his sperm to a sperm bank that only solicited donations from "highly intelligent, creative" men. While most sperm donators remained anonymous, Shockley proudly announced his offerings to the press.

And what about his own kids, you ask? Well, in his older years he referred to his three adult children as examples of a "very significant regression" in terms of his intellectual powers.

Excuse us if we say "nyah-nyah," Mr. Bill.

---

**Duke Ellington's first job was selling peanuts at Washington Senators baseball games.**

# PAUPER PRINCESS

*Madam C. J. Walker, a woman born into poverty, used her head to become one of the wealthiest African Americans of her time.*

As the old proverb says, "When life hands you hair loss, make some lemonade." Or something like that. And something like that is exactly what one woman did at the turn of the last century.

### FROM RAGS...
Born two days before Christmas 1867, Madam C. J. Walker began life as Sarah Breedlove. She was the sixth child of freed slaves Owen and Minerva Breedlove, and had four brothers and one sister. The family lived in Delta, Louisiana, where a yellow fever epidemic in 1874 killed both Sarah's parents and left her an orphan at the age of seven. A few years later, she left her home to live with her sister and brother-in-law.

The brother-in-law turned out to be a cruel man who made Sarah's life miserable. To escape his abuse, she ran away at 14 and married Moses McWilliams. Moses was the first of Sarah's three husbands, and the only one she had a child with. Two years after the birth of their daughter, Moses died. (Some people believe he was lynched, but there's no actual evidence of how he died.) Sarah was suddenly a 21-year-old single mother with no means of support for herself or her daughter, Lelia.

### TO MISSOURI
Sarah packed up their belongings and moved to St. Louis, Missouri, to be near her four brothers. The next 18 years were busy ones. Besides going to night school, working as a cook and housecleaner, and paying for her daughter's education, Sarah found the time to snag herself a second husband, John Davis. That marriage, reportedly abusive, lasted just under ten years.

Maybe it was because those years were so stressful that Sarah began to lose her hair. A lot of other women had the same problem, though so it probably had more to do with the scarcity of indoor plumbing and the difficulty of maintaining good scalp hygiene.

---

**Miles Davis was once married to actress Cicely Tyson.**

There were, of course, many products available to stop hair loss, and Sarah tried lots of them. But none of them worked. Then, in 1905, according to legend, Sarah had a dream in which a black man revealed the recipe for a scalp-conditioning formula that would help hair grow and keep it soft and lustrous. Not wanting to compete with a local hair-care company, Sarah moved to Denver where, a year later, she married newspaperman Charles Joseph Walker, adopting his name for her merchandise.

## TO RICHES

Sarah—now Madam C. J. Walker—first sold her "Madam Walker's Wonderful Hair Grower" door-to-door and at churches. It was wildly successful. Before long she had her own sales force, who received a commission on sales. Since her products sold so well, her workers earned wages that were remarkably high for the time. In 1908, she founded a college (named after her daughter) to train hair stylists who would, of course, use her products in their treatments, creating further sales.

Around 1910, Madam Walker decided she'd rather run her business—and her life—by herself. She and her husband divorced, although he continued to work for her. That same year she built her first factory, along with a hair and manicure salon.

Walker had a very forceful and persuasive personality. When she wasn't recognized at a 1912 business conference (presided over by Booker T. Washington), she made an impassioned speech from the floor that made such an impression she was invited back the next year as the main speaker.

Physicians at the Kellogg Clinic warned her to reduce her activities because she suffered from hypertension, but she continued her busy schedule. Madam Walker died in May 1919 in her upstate New York mansion. She left an estate worth approximately $700,000 at the time and remains an inspiration to entrepreneurs everywhere.

Madame Walker was an extremely generous donor to black charities. When she gave $5,000 to the NAACP's antilynching campaign, it was the largest donation the organization had received up to that time. She also made the single largest donation to the National Association of Colored Women for the purchase and preservation of Frederick Douglass's home.

Miles Davis had a cameo as a street performer in the Bill Murray movie *Scrooged*.

# THERE'S GOLD IN THEM THAR POEMS

*The man who wrote* The Shooting of Dan McGrew *earned the international acclaim usually reserved for rock stars and movie idols.*

Countries distinguish themselves by bragging—oh, excuse us, praising—the fame of their citizens. England has Shakespeare; France has Zola; Greece has Plato; and so it goes. But Robert Service is unique. He's been claimed by no fewer than five countries. This testifies to his fame and, of course, to the fact he traveled a lot. And we mean a lot.

## THIS GUY'S ALL OVER THE PLACE
Service was born in England in 1874 and educated in Scotland. But Europe was too tame to hold him. In 1896 he moved to Canada and spent his next years traveling up and down the western seaboard of that vast continent, as far south as Mexico and, in 1904, as far north as the Yukon, where he worked as a bank clerk in Whitehorse. He lived the later years of his life in France (with a sojourn during WWII in California and British Columbia). Accordingly, England, Scotland, Canada, the U.S., and France have all claimed him as their own.

## WILL WORK FOR FOOD
Robert Service found his fortune in the Klondike, but his mother lode turned out not to be gold. In his autobiography, he admitted to a lifelong dislike of hard work; but in his early vagabond years before he headed north, he was no stranger to it. He worked at farm labor, dishwashing, road building—whatever he came across. He wasn't particularly choosy, either; for a while he worked as a handyman in a bordello.

## THE CAREER PATH LEADS NORTH
Creeping up on 30 years old, Service decided the life of a near-destitute tramp was perhaps not the most secure. That's when he

**Albert Einstein was an accomplished violinist.**

went to work as a bank clerk in Victoria, British Columbia. Within a year the bank had transferred him to the Yukon. The rest is history.

The Klondike Gold Rush may have been over and thousands of prospectors long gone in search of other El Dorados, but enough old-timers remained to recount the adventures that Service would transform into legends.

For example, the "lady known as Lou," made famous in the poem *The Shooting of Dan McGrew* had been a Dawson cabaret singer named Lulu Johnson. Sam McGee, of "Cremation of Sam McGee" fame was a name Service plucked from Whitehorse bank records.

## STRIKING GOLD

His first book of poems, *Songs of a Sourdough*, was a private press run in 1906 of only 100 copies, meant for distribution to his friends and acquaintances. A friend helped Service market his book more widely and by the end of 1907 the book had gone through 15 printings. By 1940 more than three million copies had been sold.

Although in 1907 Service still hadn't made it to the Klondike, the royalties from his supposed first-hand experiences far exceeded his bank wages. But he stuck it out with the bank. Finally, in 1908, the bank transferred him to its Dawson branch—at least he was within sight of the Klondike River. (Even though by then the population of Dawson had shrunk from the 40,000-plus of its gold rush days to less than 4,000.)

In 1909 he published *Ballads of a Cheechako*, another instant best-seller. His fame and fortune were secure. Now he could indulge his love of travel and adventure in style.

## ON THE ROAD AGAIN

In 1912 Service left the Yukon and traveled to France as the correspondent for the *Toronto Daily Star*, covering the second Balkan War. He married in France in 1913 and bought a small villa in Brittany, which he named Dream Haven. This would be his home base until he died in 1958.

Service kept writing and traveling. He was among the few Western writers who visited Russia. In 1940 he returned to North

America to get away from the Nazi occupation of France. Although he spent the next five years splitting his time between Hollywood and Vancouver, he didn't really settle anywhere. He managed at least one trip to Tahiti, a 2000-mile freight barge-canoe trek to the Arctic and then south, following the arduous former overland route to the Klondike gold fields.

## ALL THAT GLITTERS...
By now he was considered the authority on the Klondike, so he was enlisted to work on the Hollywood version of *The Shooting of Dan McGrew*. In 1942 he had a cameo appearance in *The Spoilers*, working alongside Randolph Scott, Marlene Dietrich, and John Wayne. But he was impatiently marking time until the war in Europe ended.

## LIFE IS BUT A DREAM HAVEN
As soon as France was liberated, Service packed up his family and moved back to Dream Haven. He continued to write until he was 80, publishing *Carols of a Codger*, his last book, in 1954.

## WHAT A SLACKER!
Shortly before his death at 84, Service estimated that he'd written 2,000 pages of poetry and 30,000 couplets of verse. (Not to mention three novels, two autobiographies, screenplays, and articles.) A remarkable output for a man who talked about how much he hated hard work!

## THAT WASN'T SO HARD AFTER ALL
He would have been first to chuckle at the seeming honesty of his lines from the poem, *Spell of the Yukon*: "I wanted the gold, and I sought it / I scrabbled and mucked like a slave,"

He did no such scrabbling and mucking. But further into the poem, he may have revealed feelings much closer to his personal truth when he wrote: "Yet somehow life's not what I thought it / And somehow the gold isn't all."

**Darwin suffered from seasickness.**

# IMPRESARIO EXTRAORDINAIRE

*That's what Flo Ziegfeld's business card read. And it wasn't an exaggeration.*

Florenz Ziegfeld, Jr., had an innate talent for promotion. As a child he sold tickets to the neighborhood kids to see his school of "invisible fish," which turned out to be nothing more than a glass bowl filled with water.

### IN OLD CHICAGO
Ziegfeld was born in Chicago in 1869, into a well-to-do family. His German immigrant father owned the very successful College of Music and a nightclub called the Trocadero. The club wasn't doing that well untill junior offered to manage the talent.

### STARTING STRONG
Ziegfeld, Jr.'s, first showbiz success came when he booked 23-year-old strongman Eugene "The Great" Sandow. Flo invited several ladies from the audience backstage to examine Sandow's extraordinary physique—which created quite a stir and a lot of favorable press coverage. The Trocadero was soon the most popular club in town.

### FLO MEETS HIS MATCH
While in London scouting for talent, Ziegfeld met a beautiful café singer named Anna Held. Anna had a sexy French accent and a fantastic figure, and Ziegfeld was so enchanted by her that he married her, planning to bring her back to America and serve as her manager. He organized a publicity blitz and by the time they returned from Europe, she was already a celebrity.

### NOT A FOLLY
It was Anna who suggested that he create a show like the famous Folies-Bergère of Paris; a variety show with lots of scantily clad women. Anna said: "Your American girls are so beautiful, the most beautiful girls in the world. If you dress them up chic, you'd have a better show than the Folies-Bergère."

To raise money for the project, Ziegfeld had to sell his ownership in it and settle for a salary as a producer. The *Follies of 1907* opened at the New York Theatre and was an instant smash hit. In it, Anna was backed with a chorus line of 50 beauties in extravagant costumes; they were called "the Anna Held Girls."

## ZIEGFELD'S GIRLS
Ziegfeld's shows emphasized glamour and beauty. Flo called himself the "glorifier of the American girl" and he had a great talent for finding beautiful and talented women. He auditioned girls for his shows by first watching them walk in high heels. "Before I see their faces, I want to see how they walk. There's more sex in a walk than in a face or even in a figure."

His "Ziegfeld girls" were soon regarded as the standard of beauty. And no wonder, since they always appeared in scanty costumes and were often partially or completely nude.

## ANNA AND THE KING OF BALLYHOO
Ziegfeld featured Anna in seven Broadway musicals over the next 12 years and she became one of the first big stars of the era—thanks to her husband's mastery of publicity.

Anna once fell off her bike while riding through Brooklyn and Ziegfeld planted the story that she had leaped off her bike to stop a runaway carriage that was headed straight for a retired judge.

On another occasion, Ziegfeld told the press that Anna took a milk bath every day and claimed that once he had to send the milk back to the dairy because it was sour. The dairy sued him for libel and he lost, but what did he care? The publicity that the incident generated was priceless.

## BIG CHANCE
In the *Follies of 1910*, Ziegfeld risked alienating his white audience by featuring Bert Williams, making him the first black man to costar on Broadway with white performers. Other stars who got their start or were featured with the Ziegfeld Follies included Sophie Tucker, Fannie Brice, Eddie Cantor, Ruth Etting, Will Rogers, W. C. Fields, Marion Davies, Enrico Caruso, and Ed Wynn.

## PERSONAL STYLE
He was a demanding producer, but he drove himself harder than anyone else. A perfectionist, he often revised his shows during their run to keep them fresh for returning audiences. "Details are

what makes a show's personality. I hunt for chances of putting in a 'laugh or taking out a slow bit. I keep my shows combed, polished and groomed."

Ziegfeld was flamboyant, a big spender, and a womanizer. His constant dalliances with showgirls finally led to his divorce from Anna in 1912. He married actress Billie Burke (who played the good witch "Glenda" in 1939's *Wizard of Oz*) in 1914.

## THE ORIGINAL GLASS CEILING

He produced some nightclub shows, too. One of his most famous shows included a glass walkway, so that chorus girls could dance right over the audience's heads. And he thoughtfully provided little wooden hammers so that the audience could bang out their approval and not hurt their hands from clapping so much.

## SHOWBOATING ON BROADWAY

In the 1920s he started producing Broadway musicals, among them the fabulously successful *Show Boat*, which opened in 1927. The musical, based on Edna Ferber's sprawling novel (music by Jerome Kern, book and lyrics by Oscar Hammerstein II), included hits like "Make Believe," "Bill," and "Old Man River." The story is about the inhabitants of a Mississippi showboat from the 1880s to the 1920s—an incredibly brave venture at the time, because the show had a multiracial cast and dealt with taboo subjects like as racism, miscegenation, and broken marriages.

## DEATH BY DROWNING?

Ziegfeld made a lot of money, but he also lost a lot of it by gambling. As if that wasn't bad enough, he lost his entire fortune in the stock market crash of 1929. The Depression dried up the box office receipts because people couldn't afford to attend Broadway shows, and the high production costs of his lavish shows had to draw in large audiences to make money.

Meanwhile a recurring lung infection had progressed from pneumonia to pleurisy. His health was failing, and he knew he didn't have much time left. Ziegfeld spent the last few months of his life hosting an endless stream of gin-soaked orgies. He died on October 22, 1932.

John Gotti could quote long passages of Machiavelli's *The Prince* from memory.

# PHILOSOPHIZED TO DEATH

*Sometimes, thinking can hurt.*

As far as the risk of horrifying death goes, being a philosopher has nothing on, say, the guy who feeds branches into a wood chipper all day long. Be that as it may, over the course of history, quite a few deep thinkers met bad ends, and mostly because they were philosophers. Come with us now as we explore the final moments of some of the biggest names in thought—and wonder with us just how philosophical they were about that whole death thing when it was actually happening to them.

**SOCRATES:** Might as well get this one out of the way. Socrates was accused by Athens of corrupting the youth of the city (a charge that had an entirely different meaning in ancient Athens than it does today, incidentally) and was condemned to death in 399 B.C. He was offed by ingesting hemlock. Plato, who recorded Socrates's death in the *Phaedo*, gives the impression that the philosopher died peacefully and nobly, but since the typical symptoms of hemlock ingestion are vomiting, violent convulsions and delirium, many historians believe Plato was cleaning up the death scene for dramatic purposes. However, there is more than one type of hemlock plant, and one of them, *Conium maculatum*, does not cause the same awful symptoms as other varieties (although it still causes death, quite obviously). So maybe Socrates had his noble, dramatic death after all.

**LUCRETIUS:** We know almost nothing of the life of the Latin philosopher/poet who wrote *On the Nature of Things*, but we have a tantalizing rumor of how he died. He supposedly drank a love potion, that, rather than driving him toward love, drove him insane. Depending on the historical source, he either died quickly, or lived for a long time, wrote books during his brief flashes of coherence, then killed himself. Either way, he died sometime around 55 B.C., and it's clear any love potion stronger than a box of chocolates is a bad idea for anyone.

---

As a teenager, Mafia boss Joe Bonanno fought against Mussolini's fascists.

**SENECA:** This famed Roman statesman, orator, and philosopher was a great pal and tutor of Emperor Nero. This wasn't such a bad thing when Nero was just starting out and leaned on Seneca's wisdom to help him run things. Wouldn't you know, though—sooner or later those emperors start getting big heads and begin forgetting their friends. Or worse, since in Seneca's case Nero ordered him to kill himself in A.D. 65. And that's just what Seneca did, by opening up his veins while in the bath. Yes, just like that guy in *The Godfather Part II*.

**HYPATIA:** She was a top-flight neoplatonist philosopher, a brilliant mathematician (the first woman mathematician known to history), and a fair astronomer to boot. Sadly, she was also known as a pagan—and that wasn't such a great thing to be known as in fifth century Alexandria, which was filled with some very nasty Christian mobs who went about burning libraries and pagan temples and such. One such mob caught up with Hypatia in 415, dragged her from her classroom, and murdered her by peeling her skin from her body with oyster shells—which is probably even more painful than it sounds, and it sounds pretty painful.

**BOETHIUS:** The original example of "You have to suffer for your work," Boethius was a high muckety-muck in the court of the Ostrogothic king Theodoric. But around 520 or so, Theodoric stopped liking him so much, there was a charge of treason, and Boethius was sent to the slammer. There he wrote *The Consolation of Philosophy*, a keystone work for Scholasticism, the philosophy of the medieval Christian church. Hopefully Boethius did indeed receive consolation from philosophy, because Theodoric didn't give him any; Boethius was tortured over a period of several months before finally being executed in 524.

**THOMAS MORE:** Henry VIII of England wanted a divorce; the Pope wouldn't grant him one. Fine, said Henry, I'll start my own church, so there. And that's what he did, forming the Church of England in the process. This rubbed philosopher Thomas More the wrong way, so in protest he resigned his position as Lord Chancellor. In 1535, Henry called on More to make a loyalty oath to him and acknowledge the legitimacy of any children of Henry and his new wife, Anne Boleyn. More refused, so Henry had him thrown into the Tower of London and then beheaded (which is exactly what he ended up doing with Anne, as it happens). He then stuck More's head on a stick as a warning to anyone else who was getting any big philosophical ideas. For his trouble, More was sainted by the Catholic Church in 1935.

**GIORDANO BRUNO:** Bruno was ahead of his time. A philosopher and astronomer, he believed the universe was infinite and that it was filled with a nearly infinite number of worlds (and he was right). Alas, it doesn't pay to be ahead of your time when your time is the 16th century and the Catholic Church thinks the universe is finite and the stars are stuck in the firmament like glowing pushpins. The Church grabbed him in 1593 and let him marinate in prison for six years before providing him a trial by inquisition, at which he refused to recant his views. He was burned at the stake as a heretic in February 1600. But he's remembered fondly by scientists, who named a moon crater for him. So that's something.

**RENE DESCARTES:** The famed philosopher who gave us the concept of mind-body duality got a nasty lesson about just how intimately the two are connected when he expired of pneumonia in 1650 in Sweden. There's some reason that the indirect cause of his death may have been his job at the time. Tutor to Queen Christina of Sweden, who made poor Rene get up in the early morning, to some detriment to his health. So the next time a philosopher you know wants to sleep in late, for goodness sake, let him!

**BARUCH SPINOZA:** This Dutch philosopher died in 1677 not because of his philosophical views (which makes him rare in our little collection, doesn't it?), but because of his day job as a lensmaker. All those years of grinding lenses had caused Spinoza to suck in a lot of glass dust, leading to a severe case of lung disease. Proof that you can be smart enough to be a major figure in philosophy and still not smart enough to, oh, invent a filter for your face.

**KURT GÖDEL:** Gödel was a brilliant mathematic mind, but that doesn't mean he couldn't be wrong about some things. For example, near the end of his life, he fervently believed that his food was being poisoned. So to avoid being poisoned, he stopped eating. A logically elegant solution, to be sure, although it was ironically not brilliant, since not ingesting food had the unfortunate side effect of causing Gödel to starve to death in 1978.

# AMERICAN PRINCESS

*You'd think that having a princess with you on a cross-country trek might slow you down. In this case, you'd be wrong.*

When French-Canadian fur trapper Toussaint Charbonneau agreed to go on one of the world's greatest road trips, he had every intention of bringing his 16-year-old wife Sacagawea along. And she wasn't going anywhere without her newborn baby boy.

As a child, the young Shoshone princess was kidnapped by the Hidatsa, a rival tribe, and taken hundreds of miles from her home. She was raised by her captors and either sold to Charbonneau or won by him in a gambling game. Either way, according to Indian custom, he claimed Sacagawea as his wife sometime in 1804 just before Lewis and Clark came along. Since Charbonneau lived among the Indians and spoke their language, the Corps of Discovery hired him as an interpreter and reluctantly accepted his wife and infant son as part of the package.

### FORTY MEN AND A BABY

The men, the princess, and the baby set out in spring of 1805, Sacagawea carrying eight-week-old Jean Baptiste, nicknamed Pomp, on her back. Within the first month, the Corps of Discovery discovered one important thing: their princess was not a wimp. She not only gathered wild roots and berries for everyone to eat, but became a bona fide hero when Charbonneau's canoe tipped over during a sudden gale. Charbonneau, along with their supplies, fell out. Sacagawea, still inside the canoe with Pomp on her back, calmly righted the canoe, at the same time saving such critical items as compasses, books, clothes, a sextant, and a microscope. The men were dazzled by her quick thinking and level head.

As the Corps of Discovery trekked westward, Sacagawea recognized the countryside. She even remembered the exact place where she was captured as a child. On August 8, Sacagawea saw a high point on the plain not far from the Shoshone summer camp. She knew her people were nearby. Lewis and Clark arranged a critical meeting with Cameahwait, the Shoshone Indian chief. To continue

---

Captain Cook tried to prevent scurvy by feeding his men sauerkraut.

west, the expedition needed horses, and the Shoshones had them. Sacagawea was called in to translate the chief's Shoshone words into Hidatsu for Charbonneau, who would relay the conversation in French to François Labiche, who spoke both French and English. Labiche, in turn, would give the final English version to Lewis and Clark. As Sacagawea entered the tent where the conference was being held, she recognized Cameahwait as her brother and rushed to him, weeping for joy. Even the chief lost his composure as he embraced his long-lost sister. Their dramatic reunion visibly moved everyone present—even the tough guys. The princess convinced her brother to give the Corps the horses they needed. How could he say no? He threw in a few Indian guides for good measure.

The Corps continued westward, following the Columbia River to Oregon before—4,100 miles later—they found what they were looking for: the vast Pacific Ocean. Now they had to settle in for the winter before the long journey home. They chose a spot and built eight cabins surrounded by a stockade.

Winter turned to spring. On March 23, 1806, the Corps headed home. Sacagawea continued gathering food and caring for the sick as they traveled eastward. Nine miles beyond the Continental Divide, they were forced to make a crucial choice between three different passes. Once again Sacagawea saved the day. She recommended Bozeman Pass and Clark wisely listened. As a result, the Corps covered an amazing 48 miles in just three days, ending up in Yellowstone Valley close to what is now Livingston, Montana. By mid-August, the group was back at Fort Mandan where they originally met Toussaint Charbonneau and his remarkable wife 16 months earlier. Charbonneau received $500.33 for his services. Sacagawea? Hey, what would a princess do with money, anyway?

## THE END OF THE TRAIL

After the trip, Sacagawea's fate remains a mystery. It's believed that she had another baby—a girl. Court records in St. Louis report that on August 12, 1813, Clark formally became the guardian of both Pomp and the girl, Lizette. Clark's notes from 1825–26 list Sacagawea as dead, but Shoshone oral legend has it that Sacagawea returned to the Shoshones and died with them in 1884. We hope, of course, that the latter is true.

# MAN OF HIGH FIDELITY

*What do Hendrix and Edwin Armstrong have in common? Feedback.*

Edwin Armstrong's crowning achievement was the invention of wide-band frequency modulation (FM). His inventions are so significant that even today your radios or televisions include one or more of his breakthrough discoveries. In the process he became a millionaire. He was honored by his fellow scientists. What then would drive him to take his own life?

## BACKGROUND BUZZ

Radio's story has three elements and begins with Edison's light bulb. A bulb's filament emits light and heat when a current passes through it. Edison knew electrons were being boiled off of the fila-ment, so he devised a plate to collect them. He sent an electrical current from the filament through space to the plate. He'd invented the first vacuum tube, without a clue to what end. In 1904, John Fleming found that purpose. Alternating current (AC) flows in both directions. Fleming created a valve to control the current and let it to pass in one direction. His discovery converted alternating into direct current (DC). (Marconi used Fleming's valve in the first wireless telegraph receiver.) Lee de Forest added a third element to the tube, a grid between the emitter and the plate. When a current flowed between the emitter and the plate, a small signal applied to the grid was boosted at the plate. The "valve" had become an amplifier; de Forest called his invention the Audion. The Audion made it possible to receive sound. Until then radio had been used as a wireless telegraph to communicate from point-to-point—one transmitter to one receiver. De Forest realized that one transmitter could broadcast information and entertainment to many receivers. The big problem with early broadcasts was weak signals—people could barely hear them through headphones.

## RADIO'S BIG BREAK

Enter Edward Armstrong (born 1890), who, fired by reading about Marconi's exploits, resolved to become an inventor. While a student at Columbia, he studied the three-element Audion vacuum tube and developed its full potential. He noticed that if a small portion of the amplified signal was fed back to the grid (feedback), it would pass through the grid again and again, each time being amplified further. He boosted weak signals a thousandfold with his invention—the regenerative or feedback circuit. At its highest amplification, Armstrong boosted the feedback signal to a point where the circuit began oscillating rapidly and generating strong electromagnetic waves. Now the Audion could be used as a radio transmitter and an amplifier in a receiver.

WWI interceded and the Army hired Armstrong to develop devices to detect enemy radio signals. He invented an eight-stage amplifier (the superheterodyne circuit) that could reliably tune in very weak signals. After the war, he sold the rights to two of his inventions to Westinghouse for over a quarter million dollars and an amplifier design to RCA for a large amount of stock.

## A PATENT RIP-OFF

Armstrong was riding high when things took a turn for the worse. Although he had patented his regenerative circuit in 1914, de Forest applied for a patent on the same concept in 1915. While not much of a scientist or businessman, de Forest was an opportunist. He never really understood how his Audion worked. Colleagues described his "research" as putting things together in different combinations, applying for patents, and hoping something of value would result. De Forest was embarrassed that a young college student had figured out and made important discoveries with the Audion. He convinced himself that he'd discovered feedback and Armstrong had stolen his idea. Determined to claim the honor and profits he felt he deserved, he filed a patent infringement lawsuit against Armstrong. In addition, de Forest sold his patent to AT&T, who despite ample evidence to the contrary, cynically chose to support de Forrest's claim for its own gain. The patent battle lasted from 1922 to 1934. Armstrong won the first case, lost on appeal and lost again in the Supreme Court. The scientific community never accepted the verdict, but de Forest reaped the rewards.

While the patent battle raged, Armstrong continued his research on radio's last major problem—static—background noise inaudible unless amplified. Because atmospheric conditions could worsen static, newspapers printed the weather reports next to the radio schedule so people would know if a broadcast might be affected. Radio transmissions used a method called amplitude modulation (AM). Armstrong tried to design AM circuits to filter out the noise. After many unsuccessful attempts, he tried an entirely new concept and found a solution using frequency modulation (FM). Reception was clear and the overall sound quality was much better. FM was superior to AM in every way, but one problem remained before Armstrong could cash in on his idea.

A switch to FM would render millions of radios and the transmitters that broadcast to them worthless. RCA was already making lots of money with the old technology, so it conspired to keep FM off the market and used its influence with politicians and Federal Communications Commission (FCC) bureaucrats to pass regulations that prevented Armstrong from going public with FM. But by the 1940s Armstrong had started an FM station, licensed manufacturers to make FM radios, and begun to build an audience.

## STRONG ARMED
Meanwhile, the FCC was working out the specifications for television and had decided to use FM because of its superior sound quality. Armstrong was set to make millions from licensing deals. Now RCA wanted FM, but offered Armstrong a paltry million dollars instead of royalties. Armstrong refused. So RCA got the FCC to change the frequencies allocated to FM. All preexisting FM sets were rendered useless. RCA then developed and patented its own FM specification using Armstrong's idea. Armstrong sued, but RCA kept the case tied up in the courts for years.

Though Armstrong made millions from earlier inventions, he spent most of it on legal fees and developing FM. The court battles also took a toll on his marriage. Having sold most of his assets and facing bankruptcy, he desperately needed money to continue his legal fights. When he begged his wife for some money set aside for their retirement and she refused, he took a swing at her. She left him. Now he'd lost everything, his wife included. Armstrong was a broken man. One day he dressed in a nice suit, put on his scarf, overcoat, and hat, and walked out of his 13th floor apartment window. Though Armstrong was never able to reach a compromise with those who had stolen from him, his widow settled with RCA for a million dollars—the amount he'd turned down in 1940. Settlements with other corporations who'd infringed on her husband's patents ultimately netted her close to 10 million dollars.

---

**Walt Disney named names in his testimony before the House Un-American Activities Committee.**

# THE RIEL DEAL

*Despite having been hung for treason over a century ago, the jury is still out on Louis Riel.*

The actions of some politicians, sometimes just the mention of their names, can rouse controversy and angry exchanges even long after they are dead. In Canada, one such is Louis Riel. In November 15, 1885, Louis Riel, convicted of treason, was hanged. His career and the events leading up to his trial and execution continue to be the subject of much debate.

Riel, a Metis of French-Indian descent, was born in 1844 at the Red River Settlement, part of the future Province of Manitoba. At the time the Metis were a significant part of the population of Canada's three prairie provinces: Alberta, Saskatchewan, and Manitoba.

## HIGH HOPES AND HISTORIC TIMES
In his lifetime, Riel was involved in the shaping of the Dominion of Canada. In 1867 when the British North America Act was signed (signaling independence from direct English rule), Riel was living in Montreal and training for the priesthood. He dropped out to study law. By 1868 he was back in Red River, getting involved in politics on behalf of local Metis, whose rights he feared might be ignored in a Canadian confederation.

In 1870, Riel and his followers formed a provisional government, with Riel as its leader. His action filled a vacuum created when the Hudson Bay Company withdrew its control from western Canada and before the new Canadian government could assert its sovereignty. Riel was actively courting American involvement; not so surprising, considering that the area's best trade route was south to St. Paul, Minnesota, rather than eastward. The Canadian government negotiated with the provisional government and the province of Manitoba was formed and joined Canada. Riel also secured concessions regarding French language rights in Manitoba.

## ALWAYS A BRIDESMAID
Subsequently Riel was elected three times to Canada's House of Commons but was destined never to take his seat. During his provisional government, Riel had court-martialed and executed a

prisoner, Thomas Scott. In English Canada this was viewed as plain old-fashioned murder. No warrant was sworn out for him, primarily because of political pressure from Quebec, but he wasn't allowed to take his elected seat in parliament. Instead, Riel was exiled for five years. Apart from Metis and French-language Quebeckers, Riel had few friends in Canadian politics. During his exile he maintained contact with the Metis, including Gabriel Dumont, a former Riel lieutenant in 1870 and now a Saskatchewan leader. He made at least one trip to Washington to persuade the Americans to invade western Canada, and for a time, settled in the U.S.

## LAST TRIP TO THE WELL

Riel's success in Manitoba made him the de facto leader of French Metis. He was a hero. It was not surprisingly when in 1884 some Saskatchewan Metis, including Dumont, traveled to Montana to meet with Riel, then teaching at a Jesuit mission. They wanted him to represent their grievances to the Canadian government. Principal among these was loss of land to new settlers from a major push by the government to populate the West and, thus, to affirm sovereignty. Canada was still fearful that western Canada's geography lent itself far better to north-south alliances than east-west. Riel traveled to Saskatchewan and set to work, becoming de facto political leader for the Metis cause. Metis grievances continued to be ignored. In 1885 Riel repeated the tactic that worked so well in Manitoba—he formed a provisional government.

But a lot can change in 15 years. One change was the railroad, construction of which had been underway for some time. Compared to 1870, the government now had a relatively easy time moving troops to Saskatchewan to put down what it perceived as a rebellion by a minority of the population. Unlike the 1870 rebellion, which was relatively peaceful, this time nearly 100 lives were lost before the end of the Metis' last stand at Batoche. Riel surrendered shortly thereafter and was taken to Regina, Saskatchewan's capital, to face a charge of treason.

His lawyers wanted to use an insanity defense because of Riel's history of breakdowns. And, based on his previous writings and on his testimony at his trial, he appeared to have a Moses-like fervor to lead the Metis. Riel rejected the defense because he believed in the rightness of his cause. He was found guilty. The judge ignored the jury's recommendation for mercy and sentenced

JFK was the first 20th-century president born in the 20th century.

Riel to hang. The verdict and sentence caused an immediate political storm in predominately French Catholic Quebec, in part because the jury had been comprised of six English-speaking Protestants. To Quebec, the verdict had nothing to do with justice; it was all politics. The federal government appointed doctors to determine Riel's mental health and declared him legally sane. On November 16, 1885, Riel was hung at the Regina Jail.

## THE NATIONAL DREAM

For Saskatchewan Metis, Riel had offered a vision of an independent Metis state within Canada, but one having nation-state prerogatives. Unfortunately, the government and a majority of Saskatchewan's citizens had a different vision. The immediate fallout from the Northwest Rebellion of 1885 was of immense political benefit for the government. Efforts to complete the national railway had stalled, but now its strategic importance was clear. Construction became a national priority. As it pushed westward, the influx of immigrants to the prairie provinces increased dramatically, further undermining the Metis' political hopes and economic well-being.

Issues around exclusive legislated language rights are still hotly debated in Canada. Dreams of a Metis nation also persist. Many efforts have been made to repatriate Louis Riel as a Father of Canadian Confederation. So far they've resulted in small victories. Parliament has proclaimed an annual Louis Riel Day each November 16—a date far removed from the Metis' annual Back to Batoche Days commemorating the last battle of the Northwest Rebellion. In Winnipeg, Metis representatives also succeeded in having a nude statue of Riel in front of the Manitoba Legislature replaced with a clothed version.

## CONTROVERSY RAGES ON

In October 2002, revisionist history and real-time TV merged in a national program that retried Riel using modern law. A majority of voters on the Internet acquitted Riel, but that didn't stop Ontario's Metis Association from threatening to sue the network for biased programming. Riel is still remembered and revered as a Metis leader. His actions speeded the development of Canada, if indirectly. Had he been less precipitous, he may have become one of Canada's great political leaders. He was only 41 when he died.

**Gloria Swanson and Joseph Kennedy, Sr., had an affair.**

# BARFLY BUZZ

*Charles Bukowski, the man that* Time *magazine once called "the laureate of American lowlife," drank his way into becoming possibly the most popular "underground" writer in the English language.*

It's 1936. Sixteen-year-old Charles Bukowski rides a streetcar into the seedy underbelly of downtown Los Angeles, searching for a bar detestable enough that his pockmarked, downtrodden appearance will go unnoticed—or at least unacknowledged. It's here, among the lowlifes, drunken degenerates, and generally doomed, that he finds the comfort that enables him to later discover his ability to translate the details of his disturbing life into profoundly honest works of what millions of loyal fans consider literary genius.

## HOME IS WHERE THE HARM IS
Henry Charles Bukowski, Jr., was born in Andernach on the Rhine River in Germany on August 16, 1920. His father, a serviceman from Los Angeles, was discharged two years later and returned to California with his wife, Katherine, and their son, Charles.

Bukowski's childhood wasn't exactly of the fairytale variety. Henry Senior had a fierce temper and an obvious disdain for pretty much everyone. He unleashed his anger on both Katherine and Charles, but while Katherine sustained only verbal lashings—which she returned with equal force—Charles also endured regular beatings for offenses as insignificant as missing a patch of grass with the lawnmower. His mother said nothing about his frequent encounters with the dreaded razor strop, which often bloodied his backside, except that it was for his own good. As a 60-year-old man, Bukowski said of his parents: "I had some pretty terrible parents, and your parents are pretty much your world."

## JUST IN CASE HE WASN'T SELF-CONSCIOUS ENOUGH
At 14, Bukowski's world went from terrible to nearly intolerable. He developed what he and his parents initially dismissed as a bad case of typical adolescent acne. But it quickly worsened, escalating to boils the size of marbles that covered his face and upper body. His father had recently lost his job as a milk cart driver because of the Depression, and his unemployment enabled Charles to get free

---

Kris Kristofferson, Janis Joplin's former lover, penned her hit single "Me and Bobby McGee."

treatment at L.A. County Hospital. Under ultraviolet light, doctors and nurses drilled at the boils while they exchanged insensitive observations about the severity of Bukowski's disfigurement. "Geez, it's incredible, huh? Have you ever seen anything this bad, doctor?" the nurse asked while Bukowski listened in astonished humiliation. "Never. Imagine having to walk around like that."

Bukowski's condition kept him on the periphery of a normal teenage social life. As an adult he recalled that only the "poor and the lost and the idiots" were drawn to him. Weary of the alienation and generally discontent with what he viewed as the mundane world around him, he dropped out of high school at 16 and shortly thereafter discovered the only two places on earth that made life tolerable for him: the bars and the public library.

## NIGHT SCHOOL

At night Bukowski went to dingy bars, where no one ever bothered to inquire about his age, and nurtured his new love for whiskey. During the day, in the quiet rows of the library, he'd casually scan the shelves for titles that caught his attention, then peruse the pages hoping to find something that even remotely related to the world he knew. He dismissed book after book as "fake," feeling like the words on the pages offered little more than ordinary depictions of bland topics. In one interview, Bukowski discussed the impact that most contemporary American writers of the time had on him:

> I'd see these people in the libraries with their heads down on the tables, asleep, with the books open in front of them and flies buzzing around their heads.... I guess that about summed up what I thought of most of the writing.

Then he came across *Ask the Dust* by John Fante. In Fante, whose writing Bukowski described as "simple, honest, and full of passion," Bukowski found the literary hero he was looking for. Fante wrote about poverty, sex, paternal hatred, Catholic guilt, misplaced pride, hard drinking, and fighting, and he did so in a way that Bukowski respected, admired, and understood. Bukowski went on to discover the works of D. H. Lawrence, Upton Sinclair, Carson McCullers, and Knut Hamson, who all wrote with emotional intensity about unconventional ideas and the less finer things in life.

**Richard Byrd was the first man to fly over both the North and South Poles.**

## BAD-TIME STORY

Bukowski returned to high school just one semester after leaving, and graduated in 1939, determined to become a writer. Over the next several years, he would submit countless short pieces to what he called "the littles," small publications that had a reputation for publishing material that the larger publishers wouldn't dream of touching. Although one day millions of people would hang on every word of his raw and shocking (but usually humorous) tales of poverty, hookers, hangovers, failing, and feeling bad, back then he couldn't sell anything. When he was 24, a frustrated Bukowski wrote *Aftermath of a Lengthy Rejection Slip*, a short story about his reaction to the worst of the many letters politely rejecting his submissions. To his amazement, *Story Magazine* published the piece.

His elation at being published turned sour though. The story was printed on the back page (with a somewhat condescending bio); Bukowski was insulted and humiliated. Feeling like his work would never be taken seriously, Bukowski gave up writing and spent the next 10 years on a drinking binge that landed him in the hospital for a bleeding ulcer. He was told that if he had another drink it would probably kill him. To calm his nerves after such disturbing news, he went to the nearest bar to suck down a few beers.

## THE (TYPEWRITER) KEYS TO SUCCESS

He spent his recovery getting reacquainted with his typewriter, which he affectionately referred to as his "typer," and working a myriad of menial jobs—including truck driver, security guard, gas station attendant, and mail clerk—to maintain his substandard living situation of skid row apartments and cheap rooming houses.

In 1970, at the urging of his primary publisher at Black Sparrow Press, John Martin, who promised him a stipend of $100 per month for the rest of his life, Bukowski finally abandoned the security of his job at the post office, where he'd spent the last 12 years of his life hunched over a table sorting mail, and started writing full time.

Faced with the realization that his writing was now more than just a hobby, that his livelihood was now directly linked with his success—or failure—at it, Bukowski wrote his first novel in just three weeks. *Post Office* was an instant success, as was each subsequent book over the next two decades. At 50-something, the shy outcast Charles Bukowski had finally lurched his way into the literary world, hailed as a genius and antitraditionalist. He also had a wholly justified reputation as a womanizing boozer.

Benito Mussolini was named after Benito Juarez, a Mexican revolutionary.

## WINE, WOMEN, AND THE TRACK

As a young adult, Bukowski's sexual exploits were restricted (mostly because of his scarred appearance) to the indiscriminate halls of whorehouses and the anonymity of dark bars. But as he got older, and especially after he achieved literary success, Bukowski managed to maintain long-term, albeit dysfunctional, relationships with a few different women. Most notable among the women who played a significant role in his life were a drunk with an insatiable appetite for sex and a love for the track that Bukowski soon shared; an editor with a trust fund that he married on a whim and who divorced him amicably shortly thereafter; and an aspiring writer (with a volatile temper and jealous nature that both drove Bukowski away and kept him coming back for more), who became his second wife and stayed with him until he died.

## THE BARFLY'S LAST FLIGHT

Over the course of his life, Bukowski published more than 50 books of poetry and mostly autobiographical prose, although in his mind he was first and foremost a poet. Between books and poetry readings, he even managed to write one Hollywood screenplay about a five-year stretch he spent in the same bar getting into fist-fights with the bartender and drinking heavily with his first steady girlfriend (for lack of a better word), Jane Cooney Baker (who eventually drank herself literally to death). *Barfly* was produced by Francis Ford Coppola and starred Mickey Rourke and Faye Dunaway.

Despite the popularity and influence that Bukowski's work commanded once he'd been taken under Black Sparrow's wing, it wasn't until after his death that his work was truly recognized by scholars of American literature as possessing more than shock value. He's now featured in such college-level anthologies as *The Norton Anthology of Poetry* and *A Geography of Poets*. But his largest following is in Europe; his books have sold millions in Germany alone.

Charles Bukowski died of leukemia on March 9, 1994. His gravestone in Green Hills Memorial Park in San Pedro bears his philosophy in life: "Don't Try."

**Epilogue:** Actor Sean Penn was Bukowski's best friend during the last years of his life. At the end of Penn's movie *The Crossing Guard* is a dedication to "my friend, Charles Bukowski. I miss you, S.P."

# WE HATE HOUSE-KEEPING AWARDS

*Uncle John celebrates these heroes; they didn't just hate housework, they darn well did something about it!*

Here at Uncle John's place, where we keep everything spotless...oh drat! (Excuse us, we just tripped on that stack of books that someone left by the toilet.) Yes, at Uncle John's we're so neat and tidy, we feel it's our duty to honor the folks who give us more time to sit and read.

### GIANT SUCKING SOUND AWARD

Before the invention of vacuum cleaners, cleaning the house was literally heavy duty. You hauled your carpet to the backyard, hung it over a line, and swatted it with a carpet beater until it was clean—or your back gave out. The more energy you used, the bigger the clouds of dust and grime you sent into the air to make you sneeze and cough. Good thing that in 1871 Hubert Cecil Booth was born in Gloucester, England, to change all that.

Cecil Booth designed everything from Ferris wheels to battleships for the Royal Navy. Cecil was definitely an upper-class fellow. So, on an evening in 1900, his fellow diners at a London restaurant were shocked to see Cecil suddenly stand, place his hanky on the upholstered arm of his chair, and suck loudly on it. Those proper Brits stared through their monocles at Cecil, who coughed and choked because the chair's dirt was now in his mouth. But Cecil smiled while he coughed, because his experiment was a success. His handkerchief sported dirt and dust from the upholstery. He'd proven his theory: Suction was a good way to clean up dirt.

In 1901 he received a patent for Booth's Original Vacuum Cleaner, nicknamed the Puffing Billie. The Puffing Billie was a suction pump driven by a gasoline engine mounted on a horse-drawn cart. When a carpet needed cleaning, a troop of men dressed in white would ride up to the house, start the engine, bring long hoses through the windows, and vacuum the carpet dirt into a hollow container.

The Puffing Billie had its problems (for instance, the motor was so loud that carriage owners sued Booth for scaring their horses), but it did the job. Booth's invention became famous when he successfully cleaned a blue carpet in Westminster Abbey after the coronation of Edward VII and Queen Alexandra in 1902. The royals loved it and asked Cecil to install one in Buckingham Palace and one in Windsor Castle. Unfortunately, the average homemaker couldn't afford to buy a Puffing Billie for their smaller palaces.

## DIRTY PILLOW CASE AND LOUSY JINGLE AWARD

James Murray Spangler picked up on Booth's idea of cleaning with suction and brought it to the common folk. In 1907, James was working as a janitor for a department store in Canton, Ohio. Part of his job was to clean the carpeted floors with a broom and a carpet sweeper. James was allergic to dust—he had an asthmatic cough, and the more he cleaned, the more he hacked. He needed the job, and since he didn't want to make a choice between breathing and eating, he decided to try inventing. His idea was a carpet sweeper with a bag to catch all the dirt and dust.

He assembled his vacuum from odds and ends. He made a roller brush from stiff goat bristles, stapling the bristles to a piece of broom handle. He powered the rotating brush with an electric fan motor. He made a dust bag from a pillowcase. The vacuum case was a wooden soapbox sealed with adhesive tape to make it airtight. The contraption may have been chintzy compared to the Puffing Billie, but it only weighed 40 pounds—and it worked.

James was so proud of his invention that he founded the Electric Suction Sweeper Company. One of his first customers was his cousin. (Let's face it, who besides a relative would buy a goat-whiskered broom handle attached to a pillowcase?) His cousin showed it to her hubby, William Hoover, who was in the saddle business at the time. Hoover was so impressed that he bought the patent and James's company—renaming it the Hoover Company. James became a superintendent of the company, and he never had to do janitorial work again.

James Spangler gets a dirty pillowcase tribute, not only for bringing us the Hoover vacuum, but for inspiring the jingle: "All the dirt, all the grit, Hoover gets it every bit."

Immigrant Russian songsmith Irving Berlin wrote over a thousand tunes.

## PRINCESS AND THE PEE AWARD

The bathroom is, of course, Uncle John's favorite room in the house, and cleaning the bathroom is a treat to look forward to...just like root canals and tax audits. Toilet scrubbing isn't high on anyone's fun list, but even the bewst of us have to do dirty work sometimes. Like anything worth doing, toilet cleaning is worth doing well. That's what Park Avenue's Dorothy Feiner Rodgers discovered—and we're very grateful that she did.

Born to wealth, Dorothy seemed the last person who'd invent a better way to clean toilets. To illustrate how pampered young Dorothy was, you need only hear the story of her underwear. Her French slips, petticoats, and handkerchiefs were all sharply knife-pleated. The pleats came out once the lingerie was washed and New York laundries wouldn't bother with the time-consuming repleating. Nevah mind dahling, on her many trips to Paris, Dorothy packed her dirty underwear, where French laundresses hand washed and pleated them to her fastidious satisfaction.

Dorothy's princesslike existence continued when she married her prince, Richard Rodgers, the most successful composer on Broadway. Richard was the composing half of Rodgers and Hart (*Babes in Arms*, etc.)—and later—Rodgers and Hammerstein (*South Pacific*, *The Sound of Music*, etc.). Dorothy was a leader in New York society. But along with her talents for decorating, enter-taining, art collecting, and charity work, Dorothy demonstrated ingenuity and business smarts.

When the Rodgers family retreated to their country house in Connecticut during World War II, Dorothy found it harder than usual to get good help. She sometimes (*gasp!*) had to do her own housework. Obviously the fastidiously elegant Ms. Rodgers needed something better than dirty, germ-filled brushes for scrubbing out her toilet bowls. So Dorothy invented the Jonny-Mop.

The Jonny-Mop—still in use today—had a detergent-filled, flushable pad on the end of a handle, and it worked simply fabu-lously, dahling. But should the fashionable Mrs. Rodgers keep her new invention to herself? It was one thing for a society leader to have to clean the bathroom, quite another to become the possible "butt" of high-society toilet jokes. Instead of being snobbish, the noble inventor shared her good idea with the world and sold her invention to a manufacturer in 1950. Sure, she was teased as the "toilet queen," but she had the last laugh when, flushed with success, she framed her royalty check and hung it in her bathroom.

## HOME SWEET CAR WASH AWARD

The trophy of honor goes to Frances Bateson Gabe, who decided to end housekeeping once and for all. While other inventors concentrated on making vacuuming, dusting, or dishwashing easier, Frances did away with the whole rotten job. She invented the self-cleaning house!

Born in 1915, the daughter of an architect and building constructor, Frances learned a lot about home construction by tagging along with Daddy. She was no slouch in the academic department either, finishing her four-year program at Portland's Girl's Polytechnic College in just two years. After World War II, she opened a building repair business but she found it increasingly difficult to manage a business, children, and a house. Something had to go…why not housework? What if a house cleaned itself, not only the walls and the floors but the dishes in the cupboard and the clothes in the closet? All at the touch of a button!

Frances drafted plans. It took her 30 years, but she engineered her home in Newburg, Oregon, to be completely self-cleaning. Each room has a ceiling unit that contains revolving showerheads that spray soapy water over the room, followed by water to rinse it. Floors and walls are coated with waterproof resin and sloped to drain the water. Industrial-sized blowers dry the room. Vulnerable items are under glass, but most of the furniture is waterproof. The kitchen has cabinets that double as dishwasher units. Dirty dishes are returned to the cabinet and washed right there. Clothes are cleaned and dried while hanging in a closet that's also a washing machine. Add sinks, bathtubs, and toilets that clean themselves, bookshelves that dust themselves, and the toil of housekeeping is—whoosh—vanished!

Frances once hoped that there would be neighborhoods filled with self-cleaning homes, but so far her house is unique. Not everyone loves her idea of home life, which has been compared to living inside an automated car wash. As of this writing, the inventor (now in her late 80s) is still living independently in her self-cleaning house. She's had plenty of time to relax and enjoy her long, dirt-free life. It seems like there are worse things than living inside a car wash…and maybe one of those things is housework.

# TOUCHED BY ANGELS

*They could have turned away. Instead, they faced death to help strangers. Uncle John honors a few heroes who helped save their fellow men (and women and children) during the Holocaust.*

In Jerusalem, at a site called Yad Vashem, an eternal flame burns in memory of the 6,000,000 victims of the Holocaust. The avenue leading to the flame is lined with hundreds of carob trees marked with the names of heroes who rescued Jews from certain death. As individuals they seemed to have nothing in common—so what transformed them into saviors?

## RAOUL WALLENBERG

Raoul Wallenberg's father was a naval officer, his grandfather had been an ambassador, and his cousins were powerful bankers and industrialists. Well educated, well traveled, and well off, Wallenberg could have comfortably lived out the war in neutral Sweden. Instead, he launched a battle against Hitler's death machine.

### Hungary: Germans In, Jews Out

In March 1944, when WWII was entering its last phase, the Germans invaded Hungary. Hitler dispatched General Adolf Eichmann to ship the Hungarian Jews (the last large Jewish population in occupied Europe) to Auschwitz in southern Poland. The U.S. War Refugee Board (WRB) held a meeting in Sweden to consider ways to help Hungary's Jews.

That summer Wallenberg had become the first secretary of the Swedish diplomatic mission in Budapest, Hungary. His real mission—with the backing of the Swedish government—was to save people from certain death. By the time Wallenberg arrived on the job, Eichmann had already deported 400,000 men, women, and children to Auschwitz. Wallenberg had to act fast.

### Passport, Please

Far from being a traditional diplomat, Wallenberg was a con artist who bribed, bullied, bluffed, and blackmailed Hungarian and German officials to save Jews. He designed "protective" Swedish passports in blue and yellow (Sweden's national colors) that had no real authority—but low-level Nazi bureaucrats were intimidated by "official" documents. He'd jump on top of freight train boxcars—where Jews were packed in by the hundreds—and hand the "passports" through the window. Then he would jump down, approach the soldiers, and demand that all those under the "protection of Sweden" be released immediately. His aristocratic and authoritative manner prevailed as he led Jews away from the Auschwitz-bound trains. He did all this unarmed.

### Outfoxing the Foxes

Wallenberg used every trick he could think of to foil Eichmann's extermination plans. He had a "staff" of hundreds—all Jews who had protected status as Swedish employees. He helped his embassy establish a Swedish territory in Budapest; this "territory" was just a group of buildings labeled with Swedish signs and draped with Swedish flags, but the Gestapo couldn't arrest Jews on Swedish turf. Fifteen thousand Jews were eventually crammed into these buildings—and saved. When a frustrated Eichmann ordered a massacre in a Jewish ghetto, Wallenberg personally delivered a note to the German threatening to declare him a war criminal if the massacre took place. It didn't.

### Wallenberg's Nine Lives

An infuriated Eichmann was determined to get rid of Wallenberg. Germans fired on his car, but he survived. Another time Wallenberg walked along the tops of boxcars handing out passes (by now his protective passes were just mimeographed sheets bearing his signature). German soldiers were ordered to shoot and kill Wallenberg, but even the soldiers must have admired his courage on some level since they aimed high and spared his life.

### A Mysterious Ending

When the Soviets marched into Hungary in 1945, 120,000 Jews were still alive. Most of these people felt they owed their lives to Wallenberg. They wanted to honor their hero, but where was he?

Witnesses say that Wallenberg was arrested at the Soviet military headquarters in Debrecen, Hungary, in January 1945, and taken to Moscow. The Soviets might have considered him a spy

---

**Tiddles, Horatio Nelson's cat, was with him at Trafalgar.**

because he'd worked with the WRB. Or maybe Stalin feared
Wallenberg's power as a liberator. Sweden's attempts to free
Wallenberg—which many claimed were not aggressive enough—
failed. The Soviets declared that the great man died in his cell in
1947. However, witnesses released from Soviet prisons in the
1950s and 1960s said that Wallenberg was still alive. Even after
the Soviet Union collapsed and its secret documents became public,
no answers were ever found.

### Raoul Remembered
Raoul Wallenberg would now be in his 90s, so there's little hope
that he's alive. He was made an honorary citizen of the U.S.,
Canada, and Israel. A tree stands in his honor at Yad Vashem. A
memorial was established in Hungary. Those who owe Wallenberg
their lives continue to testify that he renewed their faith in humanity.

## CHINUE SUGIHARA
On the first day of the 20th century, Chinue Sugihara was born in
a rural village in Japan. Raised in a samurai family, he was taught
samurai virtues including loyalty, duty, and responsibility. Sugihara
also took to heart a Samurai moral proverb: "Even a hunter cannot
kill a bird that flies to him for refuge."

### A Man Who Knew His Own Mind
As a young man, Sugihara's grades were so good that his father insisted
he go to medical school. Sugihara's academic love was literature,
and his dream was to see the world, so he paid his way through
college and after graduation signed on with the Japanese foreign ministry. When he was promoted to vice minister of foreign affairs in
Japanese-controlled Manchuria, he was shocked at his government's
cruel treatment of the Manchurian Chinese. He resigned in protest
in 1934.

### East Meets Eastern Europe
In 1939, Sugihara was installed as Japanese consul general in Kaunas,
Lithuania, a prosperous city of over 120,000 people—about a
quarter of them Jewish. Sugihara and his wife, Yukiko, befriended
many Jewish families, even attending Hanukkah celebrations at
their homes.

## A Cry for Help
Meanwhile, Hitler invaded Poland, and thousands of terrified Jewish refugees poured into Kaunas. They'd fled without possessions or money, and they were telling unbelievable tales of humiliation, forced labor, and mass executions.

By 1940, the Nazis were advancing toward Lithuania. On a sunny July morning that year, the Sugiharas awoke to find that their house was surrounded by around 100 Jewish refugees from Poland begging for transit visas to get them out of Europe and into Japan. Sugihara wanted to help, but his government didn't. He pleaded—the answer was no.

## Sugihara's Choice
Knowing his diplomatic career—and possibly his life—were on the line, Sugihara ignored Japan's orders and began issuing visas. He barely paused to eat, and his hands became so stiff with writing that Yukiko had to massage them.

When the Soviets annexed Lithuania and ordered him to desert his consulate, Sugihara ignored that order, too. For a total of 29 days, he and Yukiko spent every possible moment issuing visas. When he finally had to leave Lithuania for Berlin, Sugihara handed out visas though the window of his train compartment. By his own estimate, the diplomat saved 4,500 lives. Others estimated the number of "Sugihara survivors" as closer to 10,000.

## A Good Deed Punished, Then Remembered
In 1947, the Japanese government dismissed Sugihara from the diplomatic service—possibly for insubordination. He found low-paying work, but the family never recovered financially.

In 1969, some of the people he'd saved started looking for their hero. Sugihara was honored that they had remembered him. Despite the hardship in their lives, Yukiko claimed she and her husband never regretted their actions. In 1985, Israel recognized Sugihara as "Righteous Among the Nations."

# AMAZING SURVIVORS

*Three men who've accomplished amazing things in the 20th century—
one from the Ukraine, one from Austria, one from Romania.
None of them was meant to survive.*

They were sent off to certain death in Hitler's concentration camps in WWII. All three came out alive, and each turned a terrifying experience with evil into a force for good.

## SIMON WIESENTHAL
Like a heroic homicide detective in a movie thriller, the man known as the "Nazi hunter" pursued justice with a vengeance. He never forgot a crime or its victim; he wouldn't rest until he got his man. Simon Wiesenthal made it his mission that "no Nazi murderer however old he may be will ever be allowed to die in peace."

### Surviving
Before the war came to Lvov in the Ukraine, Wiesenthal was an architectural engineer, happily married to his blond, blue-eyed wife, Cyla. But by 1941, the Germans had taken over. Because they were Jewish, Cyla and Simon were sent to a nearby Janwska's concentration camp, which few people survived.

Aided by the Polish Resistance, Wiesenthal obtained false papers and a hiding place for Cyla. The Resistance spirited her out of the camp in autumn 1942; her fair coloring helped her pass for a non-Jewish Pole for the rest of the war. But Wiesenthal (except for a brief period as a Resistance fighter after he'd escaped from a labor camp) was in and out of 13 death camps.

### A Reason for Living
He was nearly executed several times, only to be saved at the last minute. Once his executors were about to shoot him, but church bells rang out and they left to attend services. Another time he was pulled away from an execution so that he could make a poster for Hitler's 54th birthday. (The Nazis made use of Wiesenthal's drawing and architectural drafting talents.) He was sent to the Auschwitz gas chamber, only to be turned away because the overworked crematoriums had broken down.

## Finding Justice

By the time Wiesenthal was liberated from Mauthausen in 1945, the once-strong young man weighed only 99 pounds. He stumbled outside to rejoice at the sight of American tanks, then collapsed and fainted. But only a few days after liberation, Wiesenthal watched an event that gave him new strength. The U.S. army had recognized that many of the SS were criminal killers, not soldiers; Wiesenthal saw SS officers arrested and interrogated.

Drawing on his formidable memory, which has been called photographic, Wiesenthal gave the Americans a list of the camps he'd been in and the names of Nazis who'd murdered hundreds, thousands, even millions of civilians. He also gave the army a list of those Nazis who had treated people humanely and should not be treated as criminals. Eighteen months later, reunited with Cyla, Wiesenthal opened the Jewish Historical Documentation Center in Linz, Austria, and staffed it with other survivors of camps. The institute tracked down more than 1,000 Nazi criminals and helped bring them to trial.

## Trial by Television

Wiesenthal's most famous work was instrumental in the capture of Adolf Eichmann, whose trial in 1961 was televised worldwide. Eichmann had been hiding out in Argentina. One of Wiesenthal's men even cozied up to Eichmann's former girlfriends in order to obtain a photograph of him.

Television viewers saw a man who resembled an ordinary bureaucrat and learned how he'd tried to murder millions of people as efficiently as possible. The trial brought international attention to the Holocaust and new interest to avenging Nazi crimes. Encouraged, Wiesenthal continued his pursuit of justice for the next three decades. He only stopped his work in his 90s, after he'd outlived most of the Nazis.

## Who Would Believe it?

In 1994, an SS corporal told Wiesenthal that even if a concentration camp prisoner lived, no one would believe his story. "They'd say you were mad. Might even put you in an asylum. How can anyone believe this terrible business?" Wiesenthal made the worst Nazis pay for the "terrible business" and taught the rest of us to believe that the genocide happened and that it must never be repeated.

## VIKTOR FRANKL

In 1909, at the tender age of four, Viktor Frankl decided he would be a doctor—and he never changed his mind. By 1937, Frankl ran a successful private practice in neuropsychiatry based on his own brand of psychotherapy. Sigmund Freud had claimed that sexual desire motivated human behavior, but Frankl believed people were motivated to find meaning and purpose in life. He started work on a manuscript he called *The Doctor and the Soul*.

Everything changed in 1938 when Hitler's troops conquered Austria. Because Frankl was Jewish his practice was closed. He became the head of the neurological department of Rothschild Hospital, the only hospital in Vienna where Jews were allowed. Frankl gave many false diagnoses—if he admitted that his patients were mentally ill, the Nazis would "euthanize" them.

### Surviving

In 1942, Frankl and his wife Tilly were arrested and forced to move into a Jewish ghetto north of Prague. In 1944, Frankl was separated from Tilly, his mother, and his brother when they were deported to death camps. Arriving at Auschwitz, Frankl was given the number 119104. He watched while a smiling guard destroyed his most prized possession—the manuscript of *The Doctor and the Soul*. The former doctor was now a starving laborer who dug tunnels and laid railway tracks.

Even in Auschwitz, the doctor/scientist in Frankl kept track of his psychological state. He noted how upon entering the death camp he experienced what he called the "first stage" of shock and revulsion. Then, as he became entrenched in camp routine, Frankl entered a second stage in which human emotions and feelings died. He had encased himself in a "protective shell of apathy." His most important observation was that when men lost hope they gave up and died.

Frankl started testing his theories in the most terrible of circumstances. For himself, he found that his love for his wife and his determination to rewrite *The Doctor and the Soul* helped him through some of the worst times. Could there be meaning and purpose to a life even in a concentration camp?

### Finding Inspiration

In their grim barracks Frankl told fellow prisoners not to despair. Though everything meaningful in life was stolen from them—no one could deny them the freedom to choose their own attitudes. Frankl asserted that even inmates in their terrible circumstances could find something to live for. They could choose to grow as human beings so their sacrifice and suffering wouldn't be meaningless. His fellow prisoners took comfort from Frankl's insights.

### Postwar Mission
After liberation back in Vienna, in the space of a few days he learned that his wife, his mother, and his brother had all died in Auschwitz. Frankl threw himself into his work. Now a free man and determined to rediscover what it was like to live as a human being—not a number, Frankl became the director of the Vienna Neurological Policlinic and used his spare hours to rewrite the manuscript that had been destroyed in Auschwitz. He also spent nine days dictating another book, a slender volume about his experiences in the camp, *Man's Search for Meaning*.

### Little Book With Big Ideas
*Man's Search for Meaning* was written in simple—not scientific—language. It described Frankl's psychological observations and his struggle to find reasons to live. Knowing that most of us would never experience anything so horrible as Auschwitz, Frankl used it as a symbol—if freedom and humanity were possible in a death camp, they were possible anywhere. He was surprised when one of his greatest successes was his little book. By the time he died in 1997, *Man's Search for Meaning* had sold over nine million copies. Many consider it the most important work of psychiatric literature since Freud, and it was voted one of America's 10 most influential books by the Library of Congress.

### ELIE WIESEL
Eliezer "Elie" Wiesel grew up in the provincial town of Sighet, Romania. He enjoyed a happy childhood surrounded by a loving family until the Nazis came to Sighet when Elie was 15. As he later wrote: "Everything changed overnight. A few words were uttered by a man in uniform, and the order of Creation collapsed."

### Surviving
In 1944 Wiesel's family was rounded up with the other Jewish townspeople and forced into cattle cars on freight trains that rolled from Romania into Poland. On the journey, in Birkenau,

**James Cook was the first person to cross the Antarctic Circle.**

the reception center for Auschwitz, they saw smoke rising from the chimneys and realized that Hitler's men had delivered them to certain death.

"Men to the left! Women to the right!" the Germans ordered, and Wiesel never saw his mother or younger sister again, but he managed to stay close to his father. It was his constant concern for his father's well-being that helped Wiesel stay alive. Three months before the Americans would arrive, the elder Wiesel caught dysentery and died. Elie was 16 years old.

## The Terrible Secret

Wiesel was sent to France with a group of other Jewish orphans. After his schooling, he became a journalist for French and Israeli newspapers. For 10 years, he kept silent about what he'd undergone during the war, afraid of what might happen if he revealed his memories, which he said "which I bear within me like a poison." Not many other survivors spoke about the death camps either. Finally, he broke his silence.

## Publish or Perish

Wiesel's first version of his camp experience was titled *And the World Remained Silent*. In 1958 a second version of the book, called *Night*, was published first in French, then in English. It took readers into hell with an anguished 15-year-old as their guide.

> Never shall I forget that night, the first night in
> camp, which has turned my life into one long night,
> seven times cursed and seven times sealed. Never
> shall I forget that smoke. Never shall I forget the
> little faces of the children, whose bodies I saw turned
> into wreaths of smoke beneath a silent blue sky.
> Never shall I forget those flames, which consumed
> my faith forever.

*Night* told terrifying truths that most people wanted to forget, but acclaim for the author grew. And Wiesel continued to chronicle the Holocaust in over 30 books bearing witness and giving a voice to the victims and survivors of what he called "history's first crime." Wiesel explained that, "I have tried to fight those who would forget. Because if we forget, we are guilty, we are accomplices."

In 1986 he used the money from his Nobel Peace Prize to found the Elie Wiesel Foundation for Humanity.

---

Former heavyweight champion George Foreman has five sons—all named George.

# I HAVE A DREAM...

*Jose Rizal's life was one of the shortest in this book, but it wasn't short on interesting legends, including a rumor he'd fathered Adolf Hitler.*

As Philippine patriot, doctor, and man of letters Dr. Jose Rizal sat in his prison cell awaiting execution, he penned "Ultimo Adios" ("Last Goodbye"), about his love for his homeland, even though his writing was what got him into trouble in the first place. Rizal was imprisoned for allegedly fomenting rebellion through his works of literature. Although he never advocated independence, his words inspired the Filipino sovereignty movement and helped usher in the end Spain's occupation. Filipinos revere Rizal as Americans do Dr. Martin Luther King, Jr.—as a man who could ignite a revolution through nonviolent means.

## A WAY WITH WORDS

Jose Rizal was born in 1861, the seventh of 11 children of a prosperous landowner. He displayed an early affinity for language. At age eight he penned "Sa Aking Mga Kabata," a poem about his native tongue, significant because Tagalog was being fused into a Spanish hybrid. Besides Tagalog and Spanish, Rizal would master 22 languages, including Arabic, Catalan, Russian, Hebrew, Malayan, and Sanskrit.

Because there was not much public education in the Philippines, many sons of the wealthy went abroad to study. Rizal began his medical studies in the Philippines but dropped out because he felt the Spanish professors discriminated against Filipino students. He sailed to Spain in 1882, where he earned his medical license. He also became involved with Filipinos who were carrying out a literary campaign known as the Propaganda Movement, so-called because of the nationalistic and reform-minded poetry and pamphlets they generated. Inspired, Rizal wrote two political novels with the hope of securing social and political reform for his homeland. Jose became the movement's most brilliant figure.

*Noli Me Tangere* (*The Social Cancer*) exposed the evils of Spanish rule in the Philippines. *Noli* and its sequel, *El Filibusterismo* (*The Reign of Greed*), were banned in the Philippines because of their diatribes against the country's Spanish government and clergy. A

contemporary of Rizal said: "In writing *Noli*, Rizal has signed his
own death warrant," which wasn't far from the truth. Rizal's writings
created a furor among both Filipinos and the Spanish authorities.
For over 200 years, the Spanish had controlled the Philippines.
Their stranglehold affected every aspect of Filipino life—language,
religion, dress, and cuisine—nearly eradicating any native cultural
traditions. Although rebellion had been percolating among the
native Filipinos before publication of Rizal's groundbreaking
works, his words sparked a groundswell of cultural pride.

## PRISONER OF MINDANAO
Rizal was still living abroad, but that didn't prevent Spanish
authorities from harassing his family and friends. When Rizal
returned to the Philippines in 1892, he established a nonviolent
reform society, Liga Filipina. The society was modest in scope and
didn't advocate independence, but the Spaniards viewed Rizal as a
threat and arrested and exiled him to Fort Santiago on the island
of Mindanao. His four years there proved to be some of his most
productive—he built several houses, started a school, and studied
the island's flora and fauna. With his students, he also built a dam
and the first relief map of Mindanao. And he fell in love.

## A LOVER, NOT A FIGHTER
Rizal had many companions during his short 35-year life and has
been romantically linked to nine women from five different countries. There is even a persistent rumor that the Filipino "Don
Juan" fathered Adolph Hitler! The allegations follow the logic
that the short, dark haired, dark-eyed Hitler was not the "blue-
print" of the super race he was trying to create, but rather had
some vague characteristics of a Filipino. Although Rizal did spend
time in Berlin, there is no evidence of an affair with Hitler's mom.

In 1885, an Irish woman named Josephine Bracken brought
her father to Dr. Rizal for treatment of his eyes. Bracken was the
woman that finally captured Rizal's heart. Rizal asked Father
Orbach to marry them. The priest agreed under one condition,
that Rizal retract his comments about the Spanish clergy. Rizal
refused and married Josephine without the church's blessings.
They remained happily married until the day of his execution.

# CLERIHEWS

*The clerihew is the brainchild of mystery writer Edmund Clerihew Bentley,*
*whose* Trent's Last Case *is considered the first contemporary detective*
*novel. Bentley published the first clerihews 1905.*

The clerihew is related to the limerick, but it operates under its own unconventional rules: The first line is always the name of a famous person, but the meter is intentionally (and often ridiculously) irregular, as you'll see. Here are a couple of Bentley's own concoctions.

Sir Christopher Wren
Said, "I'm going to dine with some men.
If anyone calls,
Say I'm designing St. Paul's."

George the Third
Ought never to have occurred.
One can only wonder
At so grotesque a blunder.

In the 1990s *The Atlantic Monthly* magazine updated the clerihew to include some more contemporary subjects. To wit:

Michael Jackson
Is not Anglo-Saxon,
No matter how many surgeons plastically tweak
His beak.
      —Emily Cox & Henry Rathvon

Warren Beatty
Loved to date, he
Fooled around with every girl he
Met except of course for Shirley.
      —Ann Chester

**Timothy Leary is the godfather of actresses Uma Thurman and Winona Ryder.**

# Extended Sitting Section

# MORE ROYAL BAD ENDS

*Hot poker, mineshaft, guillotine, poison—there's more than one way to kill a king. Here are some of the more colorful episodes in which his royal highness became his royal deadness.*

Being king sounds like a pretty good gig, what with beautiful palaces, toadying servants, and frilly clothes. It's certainly heaps better than being a peasant. Yet many a king has found himself on the wrong end of a rebellion, plot, or revolution. Then suddenly he's on the wrong end of something else—say, a tapered metal implement. To bring this point home, here are five kings from five countries who found their exalted positions meant diddly in the end. It'll make you feel good to be part of the rabble.

## KING LOUIS XVI

Take Louis XVI of France. To be fair, Louis never had a chance. The two prior kings (Louis XIV and XV) spent most of France's savings on big shiny palaces and home furnishings, leaving the royal treasury in a cash crunch by the time Louis was crowned in 1774. Although heir to the throne, Louis's education in things kingly was spotty. While Louis was book smart (good at history, geography, and English), he was unschooled in dealing with aristocrats, who eventually spun the poor king in tight political circles.

### Buddy, Can You Spare a Franc?

Finally, it was the late 18th century and the French were getting restless, and rightfully so. In 1788, half of Paris was out of work, crops were failing, and food prices were soaring. Revolution was around the corner, along with its shiny new toy, the guillotine. Then there was Louis's wife, Marie Antoinette, who in addition to her famous cake-eating disregard (don't write, we know this is a misquote) for the lower classes, was also a foreigner (Austrian). We all know how jittery the French can get about foreigners.

The term "Third World" was coined in 1956 by G. Balandier.

## Heading Out

Long story short, Louis was a bad king, although not entirely under his own steam. Revolution ensued and France became a republic. The National Convention condemned him, death on January 19, 1793, for crimes against the people of France, which you may read as "being a weak and confused king at exactly the wrong time." The vote was actually pretty close—387 to 334—but the "guilty"s won and on January 20, he was escorted to the guillotine.

## Louis, Louis

At least Louis did death well—he calmly read psalms as he was paraded through the streets of France, scolded the guards who tried to bind his hands, and walked to his death under his own power. There he declared: "I die innocent of all the crimes laid to my charge; I pardon those who have occasioned my death; and I pray to God that the blood you are going to shed may never be visited on France." Louis's last wish went unheeded, since guillo-tining enemies of the revolution is apparently much like eating potato chips—you can't stop at just one.

## KING EDWARD II

Edward II of England, who ascended the English throne in 1307, had a problem. That problem's name was Piers Gaveston, Earl of Cornwall. Edward and Piers were close—in a "love that dare not speak its name" kind of way that made Edward's barons a little twitchy (it was the 14th century, not a very enlightened age). If that had been the extent of it and Piers and Ed had just kept it behind the tapestries, everyone probably could have lived with it.

But Gaveston wasn't that discreet, and Edward wasn't that smart. In addition to being Edward's special friend, Gaveston was Edward's chief advisor. Gaveston had no problem getting in the barons' snouts about it. The barons were incensed, and in 1311 they drew up "The Ordinances"—which among other things exiled Gaveston and curtailed Edward's power. Edward was forced to sign those Ordinances, like it or not. But after only a few months, Gaveston was back in court, the barons were rebelling again, and Gaveston ended up losing something of relative impor-tance to him—his head—in 1312.

Moe Howard of *Three Stooges*'s fame married a cousin of Harry Houdini.

## A Royal Pain

Hell hath no fury like a king without his special friend. After a few years of patient plotting, Edward (now sharper) played his nobles against one another, killed off some of the more annoying ones, and revoked the Ordinances in 1322. Unfortunately, relations between Edward and his wife, Isabella, soured along the way. In 1325, she took a lover named Roger Mortimer, who happened to be one of those barons on Edward's bad side (in fact, Mortimer had been imprisoned but had escaped to France). In 1326, Isabella joined him and they invaded England, deposed Edward, and put his son (Edward III), a mere child, on the throne. Edward the deuce was imprisoned, and in September 1327, he met a bad end—literally. Legend has it he died from a red hot poker shoved into a certain body orifice. You know, the one at the end of the digestive tract. Stop squirming, it was more than 700 years ago.

## CZAR NICHOLAS II

The reign of Czar Nicholas II got off to a bad start. At the 1896 coronation celebration, people rioted because they were afraid the gifts would run out before they got any. And things didn't improve much from there. Nicholas was a stubborn autocrat who believed his imperial powers came directly from God. Nick had a tendency to dislike advisors, of which, alas, there were many who were smarter than him. Nicholas was largely responsible for getting Russia involved in a losing war with Japan in 1904, which in turn paved the way for the 1905 revolution. The new Russia called on Nicholas to share power with the more-or-less democratically elected Duma. That didn't go very well (see above for Nick's opinion on the divine transfer of authority), and that led to the 1917 revolution with Lenin and the Soviets. Seeing the writing on the wall, Nicholas abdicated the throne within the year.

## Getting the (Mine) Shaft

Though Nick had stepped down, the Glorious Worker's Revolution wasn't done with him. The imperial family was supposed to head for exile in England. (Nick's cousin just happened to be King George V.) Instead, they were herded off to Siberia and, in April

1918, landed in the Ural city of Yekaterinburg. There, on the night of July 16, most of the family was murdered—in part to forestall a rescue attempt by approaching loyalist forces. The bodies were burned, tossed down an abandoned mine shaft, and haphazardly buried.

### Hey Sergei, Look What I Found!

For decades, the whereabouts of the bodies remained a mystery (leading to the "Anastasia" myth, in which one of the czar's daughters escaped and went to live in Europe). In 1976, the bodies were found, although their discovery was a state secret until the fall of the USSR. Genetic tests in 1994 showed that the bodies were, in fact, the czar and his clan (likely the famous Anastasia, too). The remains got a state burial in 1998, and in 2000, the czar and his family were canonized by the Russian Orthodox Church. One suspects that given the choice between being tossed down a mine shaft then sainted vs. dying comfortably in bed as a plain old czar, Nicholas would have chosen the latter.

## EMPEROR KUANG-HSÜ

You have to feel sorry for Kuang-hsü. He was crowned Emperor of China in 1875 at the tender age of four, under highly irregular circumstances. As a mere cousin of the previous emperor, he wasn't in line to the throne. So who was ruling the empire? The infamous and scary Empress Dowager, that's who. She was the mother of the recently deceased emperor (and was rumored to have had a hand in his death). She announced that she was adopting little Kuang-hsü and that he was the new emperor. Everyone at the court said, basically, "Fabulous. Emperor he is." And emperor he was—in name only, of course, since the Empress Dowager went on running things, even after Kuang-hsü nominally came to power in 1889.

### That's a Hundred Days of Nothing to You, Buddy

In 1898, Kuang-hsü decided he'd had enough—he was emperor, after all. He boldly instituted the "Hundred Days of Reform," a broad series of reform edicts. There was reform, alright. The Empress Dowager teamed up with the Chinese military to take over the government and kick poor Kuang-hsü off his throne.

### Timing Is Everything

Officially, the emperor had taken ill. Unofficially (and truthfully), he was confined to palace quarters, where he proceeded to do a whole lot of nothing for the next 10 years. The Empress Dowager died in November 1908. After her death, it was announced that coincidentally, the "ailing" Kuang-hsü had died the day before the Empress Dowager. The poison he was fed at the Empress Dowager's command probably sped things along.

### KING TUT

Tutankhamen of Egypt looked great in eyeliner, but that only gets you so far. Another child monarch, King Tut became pharaoh at age nine (around 1347 B.C.). Tut's advisors used him to undo the monotheistic edicts of the previous pharaoh, Akhenaton, and to return Egypt to its traditional bevy of gods. That done, Tutankhamen died mysteriously at the age of 18, before he could effectively start messing with the plans of his advisors (one of which, Ay, married his widow and subsequently became pharaoh himself).

### Tut, Tut

For years, historians speculated that Tutankhamen was poisoned—possibly by his wife, Ankhespaton. In 1968, analysis suggested that Tut could have been killed by a head injury. More recent analysis of the actual skull suggests that the injury was neither accidental (it was on a place on the back of the head that is difficult to strike unless you're planning to) nor entirely successful. Bone thickening indicates that the poor kid survived the initial attack and stayed alive (but probably incapacitated) for as long as two months. The most likely culprit: Ay, of course. Proof that good help was hard to find, even in ancient Egypt.

\* \* \*

### GOLDEN GUY

Jack Kelly, father of actress/princess Grace Kelly, won three Olympic gold medals in rowing at the 1920 and 1924 Olympic Games.

---

**In 1968 Barbara Streisand became the first female composer to win an Academy Award.**

# DID THEY DIE WITH THEIR BOOTS ON?

*Did those gunslingers of the old West die in bed or at the wrong end of a Colt .45?*

**BILLY THE KID AND PAT GARRETT**

The Kid—christened Patrick Henry McCarty in New York City—was a kid, just 21 when he died. It's said that he was a "nice boy" and a good dancer. Unfortunately, he fell under the influence of a young man known only as "Sombrero Jack," which led to Billy's first crime, at age 16—stealing clothes from a Chinese laundry in Silver City, New Mexico. He was arrested, but escaped two days later. He worked as a cowhand for the next two years, until the day when he shot his first victim, a blacksmith who had called him a "pimp." There was no turning back. Going by "Billy the Kid," "William H. Bonney," and a few other aliases, Billy spent the rest of his short life stealing horses, rustling cattle, robbing stagecoaches, and killing the occasional lawman here and there.

In 1880, acting on a tip, Sheriff Pat Garrett found Billy and arrested him and some of his gang. The Kid was convicted for the murder of Sheriff William Brady some three years before. He was scheduled to be hanged but escaped, killing two deputies in the process.

**Boots On:** Garrett tracked Billy down a few months later and, before the Kid had a chance to go for his gun, shot him right through the heart. After he killed Billy, Garrett spent the next 28 or so years as a sheriff, a rancher, a tax collector, and, for a time, as captain in the Texas Rangers. He bought himself a ranch around 1905, and proceeded to run it into the ground.

**Boots On:** When Garrett made plans to sell the ranch to get out of debt in 1908, he was shot to death by a disgruntled tenant.

## BAT MASTERSON

William Barclay ("Bat") Masterson began his career as a buffalo hunter and a living story. He killed only three people in his career,

---

Itzhok Ben-Zvi, Israel's second president, founded the first Hebrew high school in Israel.

two of them being the men who shot and killed the Dodge City
marshal who was Bat's older brother, Ed. At the time, Bat was the
sheriff of Ford Country (which contained Dodge City). This was
in 1878.

Even as a sheriff, Bat spent most of his free hours in the local
gambling halls, which is probably why he was not reelected when
his term ended. He was on the right side of the law for most of his
life, but he really wasn't cut out to be a lawman. Later in his
checkered career he managed a burlesque troupe and a saloon for
a while, but he was fired for drinking too much. In general, he was
considered a troublemaker whether he was wearing a badge or not.

In 1905 he was appointed U.S. marshal of southern New York
by no less than President Teddy Roosevelt. Two years later he
resigned and took a job as sports editor at the *Morning Telegraph*.
He made money on the side by buying guns, notching them, and
selling them as his own legendary gun.

**Boots Off:** He died at his news desk on October 25, 1921, in
his 60s.

## WYATT EARP

Wyatt and his brothers, Morgan and Virgil, survived the famous
1881 gunfight at the O.K. Corral in Tombstone, Arizona, but the
bad blood between the good guys and the bad guys hadn't been
completely spilled. Three months later, Virgil was gunned down
on the street; he didn't die, but he was crippled for life. Less than
three months later, Morgan was shot in the back while playing
pool in a saloon—but he wasn't as lucky. Wyatt went on the
warpath. He shot dead at least three of the men involved, and
when the Tombstone sheriff tried to arrest him, he crossed the
border into Colorado with his friend, Doc Holliday.

By all accounts, Wyatt didn't use his gun again. He had met
a Jewish girl, Josephine Marcus, in Tombstone around 1880. After
he'd hung up his holster, he joined her in San Francisco, California,
and together they managed to acquire some lucrative oil and mining
properties, dividing the rest of their lives shuttling between homes
in Oakland, California, and Los Angeles, California. There is no
evidence of an official marriage, though Josephine took Earp as
her last name.

**Boots Off:** When he was 80 years old, Earp visited Tombstone again for one last look—he was greeted by Coca-Cola signs and a souvenir stand outside the famous Tombstone cemetery. He died a natural death soon after, survived by Josephine. Cowboy actors Tom Mix and William Hart were among his pallbearers.

## WILD BILL HICKOK

James Butler Hickok was "Jim" until his early 20 and is thought to have gotten the "Bill" as a shortened form of "Duckbill," given the size of his nose and his protruding upper lip. His exploits as a scout and spy for the North during the Civil War earned him the "Wild."

**Boots On:** Hickok was holding two pair—aces and eights— at the time of his demise. He was sitting at a gaming table in the Number Ten Saloon in Deadwood, Dakota Territory, when Jack McCall walked up behind him and shot him in the head. To this day, aces and eights (technically, the two *black* aces and eights) are called a "deadman's hand." It's believed that McCall was hired by John Varnes, who, the previous month, had argued with Hickok over a card game. Varnes was never brought to justice.

McCall claimed that Wild Bill had killed his brother—a nonexistent person—so he was let off by the unofficial court that tried him. He moved to Laramie where he regaled folks with the story of how he'd shot Wild Bill and got off on a phony defense. A deputy marshal arrested him. He was tried, found guilty, and hanged.

## DOC HOLLIDAY

If John Henry "Doc" Holliday hadn't had the consumption (what tuberculosis was called at the time) he might have stayed in Atlanta, Georgia, built up a thriving dentistry practice, and never seen a six-gun or the O.K. Corral. In seeking better climes for his illness, he moved to Dallas, Texas, where, unable to find work in his chosen profession, he became a gambler. To protect himself— because he cheated a lot—he learned how to shoot. He killed a man in Dallas and fled to a small town where, two years later, he killed a cavalry trooper. Then he fled to Denver, Colorado, where this time he almost killed a fellow gambler...you get the picture.

He met Wyatt Earp around 1876 and followed the straight-and-narrow for a while, but he was too fast on the trigger (and with a knife) to lead a life completely inside the law.

**Boots Off:** Eventually, Doc's TB became what they called

The Marquis De Sade was imprisoned for most of his life for illegal sexual perversions.

"galloping" consumption, so he checked himself into a sanitarium in Colorado, where, six months later, his short but eventful life ended. He was 35 years old.

## THE JAMES GANG

They robbed banks. The gang evolved around Frank and Jesse James and Cole Younger, but numbered as many as 12 during any given job—many were former members of the famous Confederate Army's guerrilla band known as Quantrill's Raiders. Their first bank robbery, in early 1866, netted them $57,000 and left one innocent bystander dead. Thus encouraged, they targeted more banks and the occasional train or stagecoach—from Kansas to Texas, from Arkansas to Iowa, the James gang got around. Their biggest success, more than $100,000 taken from a Missouri-Pacific express train in 1876, was followed by an abortive attempt to rob the First National Bank of Northfield, Minnesota.

The Youngers were captured by a posse, but Frank and Jesse escaped. Disconcerted by the public outrage they'd engendered, the James boys laid low for three years, during which time Jesse started using the alias "Howard." They picked up their guns again for a few more robberies, the last of which took place on September 7, 1881. Jesse had seven months to live.

**Boots On:** The James clan was close-knit. Jesse married his cousin Zerelda Mimms in 1875, and in 1882 was shot to death by his cousin, Bob Ford, who's known in old cowboy ballads as "the dirty rotten coward who shot Mr. Howard." Jesse was shot at home in his own parlor. Zerelda heard the shot and rushed into the room. Ford told the new widow, "It went off accidentally." Ford was tried, convicted, and immediately pardoned by the governor, who also bestowed on Bob and his brother Charley the $10,000 reward for killing Jesse James. Charley killed himself two years later (because of remorse, if rumors are correct).

**Boots Off:** After Jesse died, Frank surrendered to the governor of Missouri. He stood trial for the murder of a passenger who'd been killed during a Chicago and Rock Island train robbery. The prosecution trotted out a parade of eyewitnesses—and Frank was acquitted. He spent the next three decades of his life at various jobs, including farmer and shoe salesman. He died at the family home in 1915.

## THE DALTON GANG

The three brothers, Robert (the undisputed leader), Emmett, and Grattan (known as "Grat") had all been deputy U.S. marshals in Arkansas before they took up the outlaw life. The gang swelled in number on occasion, but the brothers were the hard core, concentrating mostly on train robberies that netted them, on at least one occasion, as much as $17,000. They robbed banks, too, and it was a double bank job in Coffeyville, Kansas, that proved to be their last.

At 9:30 A.M. on October 5, 1892, the Dalton brothers and two friends rode into town. By chance, the hitching rails outside the banks had been temporarily removed by a construction gang who was working on the streets. Instead of taking this as an ill omen, the boys parked their horses in an alley that was a block away from the banks. At 9:42, Robert and Emmett entered one bank; Grat and the two others went into another bank a mere 50 yards away. Despite the false whiskers that the latter were wearing, they'd already been recognized. The alarm was sounded and the residents of Coffeyville—hey, it was their money—grabbed their guns and a bloody shoot-out commenced.

**Boots On, Mostly:** The final score: Daltons 4, Coffeyville 4. Dead, that is, including the Coffeyville marshal. Emmett Dalton was the only one of the gang to survive, and he was given a life sentence in the Kansas State Prison.

## THE CLANTON GANG

N. H. "Old Man" Clanton was his name, and cattle rustling was his game (along with the occasional stagecoach or train robbery). He was more like a Mafia chieftain than your typical outlaw. He ran his vast enterprise (an amalgam of gangs whose combined strength sometimes numbered more than 300 men) from his Arizona ranch. Clanton raised three sons: Ike, Phin, and Billy. Ike was a loudmouth braggart, Finn was a slacker, but Billy was a son a man could be proud of. But...

**Boots On:** Billy died in his teens at the O.K. Corral.

**Boots On:** His paw didn't live to hear about Billy's death, having been killed himself a few years earlier by Mexican vaqueros (cowboys) as a payback for a mule-train robbery that had left 19 of their *compadres* dead.

**Boots On:** Ike survived the O.K. Corral. Reports on his death

---

Chaim Weizmann, first president of Israel, discovered a method to mass-produce acetone.

vary. Near as we can tell, he was ambushed while cattle rustling by a man named Jonas V. Brighton, who may have been a hired killer.

**Boots Off:** Phin not only survived the O.K. Corral, he outlived them all; he died at 61 in 1905, of what we do not know. His partner Pete Spence married Phin's widow a few years later, so foul play is not out of the question.

## JOHN WESLEY HARDIN

By all accounts a nasty piece of work, Hardin has been called the most sadistic killer ever to come out of the Texas. He killed his first man at age 15 for no good reason and so became a fugitive, leaving scores of dead bodies in his wake. While celebrating his 21st birthday in Comanche, Texas, he killed a deputy and was saved from a lynch mob by the sheriff. He hotfooted it to Florida, then Alabama, with various lawmen on his trail. The sheriff who'd prevented the lynching tracked him down. Hardin was sentenced to 25 years in jail but was released after serving 16. He studied law and hung out his shingle in El Paso, Texas. (If you're beginning to think that Wes must have died with his boots off, think again.)

**Boots On:** When a lady friend was arrested for being drunk and disorderly, Hardin complained to the arresting officer's father, John Selman, who was one of those men who straddled that thin line between gunslinger and lawman. A few days later, John Wesley Hardin lay dead on the floor of the Acme Saloon, courtesy of the 60-year-old Selman. Some say he was shot in the back, but Selman denied it.

## BLACK BART

Charles E. Boles (or Bolton) was one of the most successful "road agents" in California history. A master at his chosen profession, he managed to rob 27 Wells Fargo stagecoaches between 1875 and 1883. He wore a long white duster coat and a flour sack with eyeholes over his head. His weapon of choice was a large, threatening double-barreled shotgun, but he never killed a single soul. He is said to have pulled in an annual average "salary" of $6,000—a lot of money in those days.

During his last job, he dropped a white handkerchief, which a Wells Fargo detective traced back to him via a San Francisco

---

Ulysses Grant suffered from intense migraines that were sometimes reported as bouts of drunkeness.

laundry. Based on the detective's report of Bart's sterling qualities—proper, polite, and witty—the judge gave the highwayman six years at San Quentin. He was released four years later at age 60 or so.

**Boots Off:** Mr. Boles declared to the press that he had given up his life of crime. He disappeared soon after. So far as we know, he was telling the truth.

## JOHNNY RINGO

John Ringgold (Ringo, to those who knew him) may have been educated (he'd attended some college and knew how to tell people off in classical Greek and Latin), but he wasn't smart—he ran with the Clanton gang. He was present at the attempted murder of Virgil Earp and acted as lookout when Morgan Earp was gunned down. He had a run-in with Doc Holliday in Tombstone and—lucky man!—survived almost certain death by the arrival of the law. Six months later his luck ran out.

**Boots On/Boots Off:** Johnny Ringo's body was found propped against a tree out in a lonely canyon. He'd been shot through the right temple with his own Colt .45, which was clutched in his right hand. Even though he'd been shot, he literally died with his boots off, that is, his boots were missing; the cloth wrapped around his feet showed that he'd walked a little ways without boots. There were no powder burns around the bullet hole (which there would have been if the gun had been fired at close range). All the same, the judge ruled it a suicide.

Hours after Johnny's death, the missing boots turned up—attached to the saddle of his horse, which had been found wandering the range of a local cattle company. There were quite a few suspects at the time—Ringo being one of the less popular figures in his neighborhood—but it wasn't until 47 years after the fact that Wyatt Earp confessed to the slaying, which some think may just have been a case of wishful thinking.

\* \* \*

**Boot yard:** A cemetery, especially for those who died with their boots on; also called a bone yard, bone orchard, grave patch, still yard, and boot hill. (Source: *Dictionary of the American West*)

Churchill called Gandhi "a seditious lawyer...posing as a half-dressed fakir."

# PUBLIC ENEMY #1

*John Dillinger once said, "Never trust a woman or an automatic weapon." He should have taken his own advice, because it was a woman—the legendary "Woman in Red"—who betrayed him.*

The Depression of the 1930s was a sad time. People who couldn't pay their mortgages had their homes and farms taken away, and the government didn't seem to be doing anything to help. Your average Joe and Josephine hated banks and distrusted their government. So it was only natural that they'd idolize some of the more colorful criminals, especially the notorious John Dillinger.

## MORE LIKE A ROBBIN' HOOD

The Dillinger gang's crime spree only lasted from September 1933 to July 1934, but during that time they robbed ten banks, killed ten men and wounded seven, and staged three jailbreaks. FBI director J. Edgar Hoover named John Dillinger "public enemy #1," which automatically made him a romantic figure—almost like Robin Hood, except for the fact that Johnnie Dillinger took from the rich, period.

## THE KID

John Herbert Dillinger was born in 1903 in Indianapolis, Indiana. His mother died when he was three. His father was strict but inconsistent about it, and his stepmother was evil—at least in Johnnie's eyes.

He had a lot of charisma and personal charm, but he was always getting into trouble. He was the leader of a neighborhood gang called the "Dirty Dozen." The gang's "criminal" activities were pretty tame: vandalism, stealing coal from a railroad yard.

Johnnie dropped out of school when he was 16 and went to work in a machine shop. He was a hard worker but he liked to stay out late at night. Johnnie's father worried about the corrupting influence of the city on his son, so in 1920 he moved the family from Indianapolis to a farm in Mooresville, Indiana.

## HOW YOU GONNA KEEP HIM DOWN ON THE FARM?

Johnnie hadn't the slightest interest in farming. He kept his job in Indianapolis and continued to enjoy the city's nightlife. By this time, he was committing petty crimes—in 1923 he was caught stealing a car. He joined the navy to escape punishment, but after only five months, Johnnie went AWOL and returned to Indianapolis.

## CRIME TIME

The next year, Dillinger got his first lesson in the vagaries of justice, the results of which put him on the road to serious criminality. He and a friend robbed a grocery store, netting $555, and were caught almost immediately. Before the trial, the prosecutor convinced Johnnie that the judge would be lenient if he pleaded guilty. Johnnie went along and the judge handed him a harsh 10 to 20 years. His partner in crime, who didn't plead guilty, served less than two years despite the fact that he was older and had already done time for assault. After serving two years, Dillinger was denied parole. His bitterness grew.

In October 1933, Johnnie wrote his father a letter from jail:

> I know I have been a big disappointment to you but I
> guess I did too much time, for where I went in a carefree
> boy, I came out bitter toward everything in general…
> If I had gotten off more leniently when I made my
> first mistake this would never have happened.

## NO TURNING BACK NOW

In jail, Johnnie met Harry Pierpont and Homer Van Meter. Pierpont had been convicted of bank robbery and Van Meter was doing time for robbing passengers on a train. Under their tutelage, Johnnie began his education in the basics of career criminality. The three graduated to advanced bank robbery, as taught by the very experienced Walter Dietrich, a smooth operator who taught them a method that relied on military-style precision—how to plan out every movement to the second, determine how long it would take for the police to respond, and, in case of trouble, to have alternate escape routes already mapped out.

## JAILBREAK?

As the time approached for Dillinger's parole, the gang came up with a plan for a jailbreak. After his release, Johnnie would rob a couple of banks, the proceeds of which would be used to bribe prison guards so that guns could be smuggled into jail for his friends. He was paroled on May 22, 1933, and went right to work. Everything was in place, but as luck would have it, Johnnie was arrested and jailed for bank robbery just four days before the planned breakout.

## JAILBREAK!

His pals escaped anyway, and they didn't forget him. Pierpont and a few others arrived at the prison in Lima, Ohio, where Dillinger was being held, claiming to be marshals sent to transfer Johnnie to another prison. When the sheriff got suspicious and demanded to see their identification, they opened fire. They left the sheriff to die, freed Johnnie, and made their escape.

## THE PROFESSIONALS

After that, they stuck together. Dillinger, Pierpont, Van Meter, and several of the inmates who had escaped with them formed what would later be known as "the Dillinger gang." Pierpont ran the gang, though. He brought a sense of professionalism to their ventures—not allowing any of them to drink alcohol, for instance, because they had to be prepared—at all times—to avoid capture.

## A MEDIA STAR IS BORN

But it was John Dillinger who fascinated the press and the public because of his good looks, friendly banter, dapper clothes, and penchant for athletic leaps over bank counters. People regularly followed the gang's exploits in the newspapers. John Dillinger was a folk hero. With a status like that, he could justify anything. After killing a cop during a bank robbery on January 10, 1934, Dillinger said, "He stood right in the way and kept throwing slugs at me. What else could I do?"

## A LOSE-LOSE SITUATION

All the same, Dillinger knew it was just a matter of time before he'd be caught. He told a friend, "I'm traveling a one-way road,

---

**Cleo and Caesar were the early stage names of Cher and Sonny Bono.**

and I'm not fooling myself as to what the end will be. If I surrender, I know it means the electric chair. If I go on, it's just a question of how much time I have left." He was right, his days were numbered. But there was still time to offer the crowd a few more thrills.

## JAILBREAK!

On January 25, 1934, Dillinger and a couple of his partners were captured in Tucson, Arizona, and transported to jail in Crown Point, Indiana, to await trial for the cop killing two weeks earlier. Johnnie had sworn that no jail could hold him, but the warden at Crown Point boasted that his jail was escape-proof. At first glance, it sure looked it. Inside, the jail was full of machine gun–toting police; outside, it was surrounded by National Guardsmen. It took Johnnie nearly two months, but he eventually escaped by using a wooden gun he'd carved out of a washboard.

That would have been enough of a coup, but on his way out he stole the local sheriff's brand new car and drove it to Chicago, Illinois. It was a flashy, headline-grabbing stunt, but a mistake that would seal his fate, because driving a stolen car across a state line was a federal crime that brought in the FBI.

## A MAN NAMED MELVIN

J. Edgar Hoover put Special Agent Melvin Purvis in charge of a task force whose mission was to get Dillinger—dead or alive. Purvis had his first try a couple of weeks later, when his team tracked Dillinger and his girlfriend to an apartment in St. Paul, Minnesota. Van Meter was the first to spot the agents and start shooting. Dillinger heard the noise and sprayed the hallway with machine gun fire. Then he and his girlfriend escaped out the back.

## ANOTHER CLOSE ONE

It was probably frustration at having come so close to capturing Dillinger that made Purvis and company a little overzealous the next time. At a famous encounter at the Little Bohemia Lodge in Rhinelander, Wisconsin, the agents shot three innocent men they'd mistaken for gang members, killing one of them. The noise alerted the gang, who shot their way out. All of them managed to escape—even Lester Gillis (better known as "Baby Face Nelson"),

U.S. General George Patton's hobby was writing poetry.

who'd recently joined the gang. During this confrontation, Nelson killed one lawman and wounded two others. The incident was a huge embarrassment to the FBI. Hoover was more determined than ever to get the Dillinger gang.

## BREAKING UP THAT OLD GANG OF MINE
With the FBI hot on their trail, Dillinger and his gang (which now also included Charles Arthur "Pretty Boy" Floyd) continued to rob banks and shoot their way out of even more FBI-laid traps. Dillinger was declared America's first public enemy number one, and a reward of $10,000 was offered for his capture. At this point, the "heat" was too much—the gang had to split up.

## ARMED AND DANGEROUS
Under Hoover's orders, Special Agent Purvis began to systematically eliminate them one by one. Pierpont was the only one who was captured and survived long enough to be executed in the electric chair. Most of the others, including Van Meter, Pretty Boy Floyd, and Baby Face Nelson, were cornered and gunned down by Purvis's team.

## NEW FACES OF 1934
Because his increasing notoriety made it more and more difficult for him to avoid the same fate, Dillinger underwent plastic surgery on May 27, 1934. Maybe he should have taken the doctor's name (Loeser, pronounced "loser") as a bad omen. He nearly died on the operating table from suffocation after his tongue swelled up when the doctor used too much ether, but Loeser was able to revive him and continue the operation. Johnnie's friends said they didn't see much difference, except that he now looked like he had the mumps. A few days later, Dr. Loeser went to work on Johnnie's fingertips in an attempt to change them, but (as later fingerprinting by the police would show) that was a failure as well.

## THE FINAL NAIL IN THE COFFIN
Enter Anna Sage, who would later become infamous as "the Woman in Red." Sage had immigrated from Romania and was trying to avoid deportation after arrests for operating several

brothels. Johnnie moved into Sage's Chicago apartment in July; within three weeks, Sage sold him out. She contacted the authorities and told them that Dillinger would be at the Biograph Theatre that night to see *Manhattan Melodrama*. She promised to wear a red dress so she would be easily identified. FBI agents gunned down Dillinger after Melvin Purvis identified him as he left the theater with a girl on each arm—one of whom was Anna Sage.

## AFTERMATH

Johnnie was only 31 when he died. Nearly 10,000 people showed up to view his body at the funeral home in Mooresville, Indiana. Anna Sage was double-crossed by the FBI; they retracted their promises and Sage was deported to Romania soon after the ambush she helped set up.

Melvin Purvis became a national hero—to everyone but J. Edgar Hoover, who was so jealous of the agent's popularity that he made Purvis's life at the FBI a living hell. The agent was eventually forced to resign from the FBI, but Hoover continued to harass him even after he left. Purvis committed suicide in 1960 and, even though he himself had never fired a shot during his war with the Dillinger gang, he shot himself with the same gun he carried the night John Dillinger was killed.

\* \* \*

## IT'S ALL DOWNHILL FROM HERE

When Olympic skier Bill Johnson was 17, he stole a car. The judge found out that he was excellent skier, so sent him to a ski academy instead of jail. Johnson never stole another car…and went on to win the 1984 Downhill race at Sarajevo, the first American male to win a gold medal in an Alpine skiing event.

*The Joy of Cooking* was first self-published by Irma Rombauer in 1931.

# BOBBY GOES A-COURTIN'

*An aging tennis pro named Bobby Riggs proclaimed himself the world's biggest "male chauvinist pig," and boasted that "Even an old man like me with one foot in the grave could beat any woman player." Here's what happened when two women champs took him up on his dare.*

I n 1973, when the women's movement was picking up some serious steam, 55-year-old Bobby Rigs bellowed into every media microphone he could find that women should stay in the kitchen and the bedroom, and off the tennis court.

For all his public woman-bashing, few men wound up doing more for feminism, and few people knew that Riggs was actually proud of his part in feminism's success.

## TENNIS WAS HIS RACQUET

By the time he was 12, Bobby was both a brilliant tennis player and a sharpie, eager to take a sucker's buck. Wearing street clothes, Bobby, a self-described "runt," would walk awkwardly on to Los Angeles's public tennis courts, challenging older, more powerful opponents to a game. His older brother John would find people to bet against poor little Bobby—and the Riggs brothers would go home richer.

Bobby was discovered by Dr. Esther Bartosh, a women's tennis champ who noticed his quick footwork, perfect balance, and smooth racquet control. She took over Bobby's tennis instruction, and believed Riggs could make a name for himself.

Bobby started on the junior circuit in 1934, when tennis was a gentleman's game dominated by the wealthy. Fiercely competitive and money hungry, Bobby was no gentleman. The powerful men who made the rules in the tennis establishment discouraged Bobby; they told him he'd never make it to the top. But although Riggs had a crass side, he also had a reverence for his sport. The humble preacher's son practiced long hours until his game was what he called airtight and what fans called perfect.

---

**Henry and Richard Bloch founded H&R Block in 1956.**

## GOING FOR THE GOLD, BOBBY-STYLE

By 1936, at only 18 years old, Bobby was ranked number four in
U.S. tennis. By 1939, he was the best in the world. He won at the
U.S. National Championship and at Wimbledon. True to form, he
also scandalized the aristocratic purists who didn't want gambling
polluting the courts of Wimbledon.

On the eve of Wimbledon, Bobby went to a London betting
parlor and bet every dime he had that he'd win the singles, doubles,
and mixed doubles titles. No one debuting in Wimbledon had
ever won a triple title, so the odds were about 200 to one. The
bookies smiled when Bobby made his bets; they looked a lot sadder
when he won the triple title and collected the equivalent of $108,000.

## MAN IN A RAINCOAT

Fast forward to 1973. The women's movement is at its zenith,
shaking up the status quo. By now, Bobby has had a brilliant
amateur and pro career, and has refused to retire. To hustle up
interest—and some decent prize money—for his matches, the guy
did just about anything—even playing tennis while wearing a
raincoat and carrying an umbrella, or holding a lion cub on a
leash. Obviously worried about losing his place in the limelight,
Bobby was thrilled when he thought up his coolest hustle yet. A
battle of the sexes!

## THE LOBBER TAKES ON THE LIBBERS

At the time, a lot of Americans believed that females couldn't
cope with high-pressure situations. It was a standard excuse for not
letting "ladies" venture into the military, the world of business, or
professional sports. Capitalizing on American unease about the
changing role of women in society, Bobby announced (to any
reporter who'd listen) that he could prove women were the less
capable and weaker sex. Declaring himself an old has-been, he
challenged all the reigning women champions of tennis to a game.
Australian-born Margaret Court, three-time Wimbledon champion,
and the number one female tennis player at the time, took the bait.

## BATTLE OF THE SEXES I

On Mother's Day 1973, in Ramona, California, Bobby and Margaret
had a winner-take-all match for $10,000. Three thousand spectators

watched as Bobby played his woman-baiting role to the hilt.
Court, usually so comfortable on the court, was obviously out of
her element. Riggs psyched her out again and again, and overwhelmed her with shots that he'd perfected over years of play.
(Riggs was especially famous for his lob, a high-rising shot that
sent opponents scrambling to the back of the court.) That Mother's
Day, Riggs demolished Margaret 6–2, 6–1. Then he not-so-humbly
declared himself the greatest female tennis player in the world.

After his "Mother's Day Massacre," Bobby knew he could
attract a big audience. He immediately upped the stakes to
$100,000. In full macho mode, he challenged the top five women
in tennis to exhibition matches. Was there anyone out there who
could save the reputation of women tennis players, someone who
couldn't be intimidated?

### A DIRTY JOB, BUT SOMEBODY HAD TO DO IT

Bobby may have been seeing dollar signs after his match with
Margaret, but a 29-year-old tennis pro named Billie Jean King was
seeing red. Like Riggs, Billie Jean King had worked hard to prove
herself in tennis and had also been disdained by the tennis establishment. In King's case it was because she was attempting to get
the same pay and prize money as the men—a radical idea at the
time. The gentlemen who ran the tennis associations didn't think
women would ever be taken seriously or pull in big audiences.

King had watched in horror when Riggs trounced Court in
the first Battle of the Sexes, seriously worried that he'd destroyed
any chance of women achieving equality in tennis—or anywhere
else. King didn't know if she could beat Riggs, but she knew she
had to try. She challenged Bobby to another battle of the sexes.

### BOY TOYS AND BOSOM BUDDIES

The match was a highly publicized winner-take-all for the best of
five sets. The prize was $100,000. Millions of folks who'd never
seen tennis before were suddenly fascinated by the fine points of
the game. Bookmakers gave the odds to Bobby, and nearly everyone (even some of her fellow women tennis players) bet against
King. While Bobby kept himself busy with commercial endorsements,
Billie Jean focused on her game.

## BATTLE OF THE SEXES II

On September 20, 1973, at the Houston Astrodome, before 30,000 spectators and 50 million television viewers, the second battle of the sexes took place. The hype made professional wrestling look highbrow. King wore a mint-green sequined tennis dress designed by Ted Tinling, couturier to the (tennis) stars. She entered the arena like Cleopatra, resting on an Egyptian litter held aloft by four University of Houston football players in togas. Bespectacled Bobby rode onto the court in a rickshaw pulled by his "bosom buddies," six sexy showgirls. Riggs gave King a gigantic Sugar Daddy sucker, and she gave him a live baby pig.

Finally, an actual game of tennis began.

## "ROBERTA" GETS SLAMMED

While Billie Jean playfully called Riggs "Roberta" out on the court, the fans were going wild. The King fans screamed: "Atta Boy, Billie!" The Riggs fans yelled: "Kill, Kill!" Billie Jean's father, Bill Moffitt, leaped out of his seat hollering: "Go, baby go!" at every point his little girl made. So did George Foreman, the heavyweight champion at the time.

King later admitted she neither saw nor heard the fans that day because she was so focused on her play. She tired Bobby out with long rallies, smashing his best shots back at him. She dominated the game completely, running an exhausted Riggs from one side of the court to the other. She slammed him 6-4, 6-3, 6-3. When the game was over, viewers suddenly realized that Billie Jean had withstood the pressure that was supposed to annihilate her sex. She'd proved that women could play for high stakes and win. It was a moment that affected the attitude of a nation. It even touched the hustling heart of Bobby Riggs.

Bobby immediately dropped his macho bluster and jumped the net to pump Billie Jean's hand and praise her game. For all his conning ways, Bobby loved great tennis. And he knew an airtight game when he saw one.

## MAKING A DIFFERENCE

Billie Jean's win put women's tennis on the map. It also brought her fight for equality into the spotlight—a favorable light. As he

In 1994 George Foreman reclaimed the heavyweight title he lost 20 years earlier to Ali.

pocketed his endorsement cash, even Bobby realized he'd been part of something revolutionary.

For a supposed male chauvinist, Bobby was surprisingly comfortable with his defeat at the hands of a woman; he and Billie Jean became close friends. Even though his loss sent him back to obscurity, friends say he remained proud of his defeat. Proud that he'd boosted women's success in sports as well as in the workplace. In 1995, not long before his death, Bobby shared that pride with his one-time opponent, Billie Jean, saying, "We really made a difference didn't we?"

\* \* \*

## RAQUETY-YAK
*Billie Jean looks back on the Battle.*

"The Battle of the Sexes triggered everybody's emotions. I felt so much pressure. I thought it was life and death. The height of the women's movement was 1973, you had *Roe* v. *Wade*, Vietnam cooling down, Watergate heating up. Things were crazy. People questioned their own gender, the opposite gender, the relationship between the two. Everybody thought Bobby was going to win."

"The...Ted Tinling dress is in the Smithsonian. They took it right away. They didn't have security [on the courts] at the Astrodome, and after the match George Foreman ran out of the stands to escort me off the court."

"Men who saw that match as boys come up to me daily. I call them the first generation of men of the women's movement. They're the ones who insist their daughters have equal opportunities—a huge phenomenon that people haven't paid much attention to."

### Battle of the Broads
"Ladies, here's a hint; if you're playing against a friend who has big boobs, bring her to the net and make her hit backhand volleys. That's the hardest shot for the well-endowed." —Billie Jean King

---

*Star Trek* creator Gene Roddenberry's ashes were scattered in space by the shuttle *Columbia*.

# BIG BANG BOOMERS

*The Manhattan Project had nothing to do with low-income housing in New York City. It was a much more dangerous enterprise than that.*

In February 1940, prodded by a letter from Albert Einstein that warned of German research in the field, the U.S. government grudgingly allocated $6,000 to research the feasibility of nuclear fission. Five and a half years and $2.2 billion dollars later, the scientists they'd hired detonated what they called their "gadget," the world's first nuclear bomb, at the Alamogordo air base in New Mexico. It created an explosion with the equivalent power of more than 15,000 tons of TNT—enough power to fuse desert sand into glass for 800 yards in every direction from the blast point.

"I am become Death, destroyer of worlds," said Manhattan Project leader Robert Oppenheimer, in the aftermath of that first detonation. That intonation has proved to be thankfully overdramatic (knock on wood), but the work of the scientists who gave the world the bomb has had a mighty influence on how the world is shaped today. So it's not a bad idea to get to know a few of the top minds inside the Manhattan Project.

## LEO SZILARD

Szilard kept some pretty interesting company. When this Hungarian native went to Berlin to study physics in 1921, his teachers included Albert Einstein and Max Planck. Szilard and Einstein also collaborated to invent a refrigeration device with no moving parts. If it wasn't for the discovery of freon, your fridge might have an Einstein-Szilard pump in it right now. In 1933, Szilard found living in Berlin a little uncomfortable (it had something to do with him being Jewish), so he went to England.

### Epiphanies and an Epistle

It's there, later that year, that Szilard had the first of three important epiphanies. As he was standing, waiting for the light to change, he suddenly visualized a neutron chain reaction. This doesn't make for a good joke ("Why did Leo Szilard cross the road?" "To get to the other side of nuclear physics!"), but it did make for exciting

---

Charles Lindbergh was *Time* magazine's first man of the year in 1927.

scientific advancements. The implications of his discovery led to his second epiphany: In 1939, living in the U.S., he heard news that German scientists had induced fusion and he feared that the information might be used by the Nazis to create a weapon.

Together with Einstein Szilard drafted the aforementioned letter describing the need for the U.S. to get moving on nuclear research before the Nazis got the bomb. The letter, sent on August 2, 1939, didn't cause a great rush on U.S. President Roosevelt's part. Aside from the initial $6,000, serious research wasn't approved until December 6, 1941 (by strange coincidence the day before the Japanese attack on Pearl Harbor).

### Birth of a Peacenik

The Germans never did develop the nuclear bomb, and after V-E day in May 1945, Szilard's enthusiasm for a U.S. bomb—and particularly its practical application against the Japanese—waned considerably, setting the stage for his third nuclear epiphany: the use of the bomb in Japan might trigger an arms race with a newly resurgent Russia. Szilard circulated a petition among the project scientists urging a demonstration of the bomb's power. The idea was shot down, in part because the U.S. government had only two nuclear bombs at the time and didn't want to waste one in exhibition (just in case the Japanese weren't convinced). After the end of the war, Szilard campaigned for international control of nuclear weapons, and for the peaceful use of nuclear power.

### ENRICO FERMI

Szilard was the first person to imagine how a chain reaction might happen, but it was Italian scientist Enrico Fermi who first made it happen. In the mid-1930s, while working on an experiment to induce artificial radioactivity, Fermi caused uranium atoms to split, but the significance escaped even Fermi until 1939, when German scientists did the same thing and figured out what had happened (the news that had panicked Szilard).

Fermi and family got permission from Italy's Fascist government to pick up his Nobel Prize in Sweden, and in all the excitement somehow forgot to go back. Safe in the U.S., Fermi replicated the German experiment and finally connected all the dots. Nuclear fission was possible.

---

**It took Tolstoy nearly 10 years to write *War and Peace* and was originally published in 6 volumes.**

## A Whole New World

Once the Manhattan Project got into full swing, Fermi was given the job of creating a controlled, self-sustaining nuclear reaction—because while splitting atoms was all very nice, if they couldn't control the reactions in some way, they weren't going to be of much use. With Szilard assisting, Fermi went to work on the campus of the University of Chicago, constructing the "atomic pile" in a squash court underneath the stands of the football stadium. On December 2, 1942, Fermi's crew pulled a cadmium control rod out of the atomic pile, and with that safety removed, the uranium in the pile began fissioning and creating energy. News of the successful event was sent in code.

"The Italian Navigator has landed in the new world," said one of Fermi's crew to colleagues at Harvard. "How are the natives?" was the response, to which came the reply "Very friendly."

## Loads of Energy

The principles behind the construction of the pile are the basis for the design of nuclear energy plants worldwide. As for Fermi, he and his wife became U.S. citizens in 1944. Fermi stayed at the University of Chicago and was awarded the Congressional Medal of Merit for his work.

The location of the self-contained nuclear reaction Fermi created is now marked by a bulbous sculpture (near tennis courts as opposed to squash courts), which unintentionally but unmistakably looks like a mushroom cloud.

## GLENN SEABORG

Glenn Seaborg's job was to make plutonium, and lots of it—enough, at the very least, for the bomb that would eventually be used on Nagasaki. (The bomb dropped on Hiroshima featured uranium as its fissionable material.) Seaborg was a natural because he was the guy who discovered plutonium in 1940. More important, he also created plutonium 239 in 1941, an isotope of the radioactive element that fissions when struck by neutrons.

Between 1940 and 1958, Seaborg codiscovered plutonium, americium, curium, berkelium, californium, einsteinium, fermium, mendelevium, and nobelium. (It's worth noting that Seaborg made his discoveries at the University of California at Berkeley, which explains the named of elements berkelium and californium.) Another element Seaborg discovered was named seaborgian—because, really, how many people discover 10 elements?

### Discovered Any Good Elements Lately?
Elemental discoveries are usually announced officially, but in 1944, while a guest on the radio show *Quiz Kids*, Seaborg was asked by one of the kids on the show if he'd discovered any new elements. Yes, he said, he had—elements with the atomic numbers 95 and 96. (The official announcement had been scheduled for the next day.) Interestingly, history notes that that particular episode of *Quiz Kids* was sponsored by Alka-Seltzer; considering that the elements in question (americium and curium) are both radioactive, this brings a whole new meaning to the catch-phrase "plop, plop, fizz, fizz."

Seaborg was also granted patents on both of these elements, becoming the only person to actually patent fundamental building blocks of the universe. Way to go, Glenn!

Like many scientists involved in the Manhattan Project, after the war Seaborg became passionately involved in arms control and the regulation of nuclear energy. But he also found time for other interests—in 1958, for example, he was appointed chancellor of Berkeley. Hey, he named an element for the place. It's a fair trade.

## ROBERT OPPENHEIMER
It was never boring being Robert J. Oppenheimer. The man was brilliant—he jumped into the field of quantum physics while it was still young, and helped train an entire generation of American physicists—but he was also fragile, with at least one nervous breakdown on his mental ledger (it was while he was a grad student, which means it's entirely understandable). And his politics were just the sort that make the Feds twitchy. In the 1930s the rise of Hitler made him very nervous (which was good), but his opinions about the Spanish Civil War had him consorting with communists (from the Feds' point of view, not so good). Oppenheimer never was a communist, in point of fact—from Soviet scientists he learned about Stalin's evil side, which gave him appropriate pause—but back in those days, just hanging around with communists was apparently bad enough.

### Old School Ties

Not that any of this mattered during the actual Manhattan Project. Intrigued by the possibilities of nuclear fission, Oppenheimer, who in the early 1940s was teaching at Berkeley, started looking into ways to separate the fissionable isotope uranium 235 from uranium ore. This dovetailed into the U.S. Army's mission in 1942 to organize U.S. and British scientists into a coherent unit to create a bomb. Oppenheimer was given the task of creating a lab to make the bomb; he selected the Los Alamos site in New Mexico because it was close to Santa Fe, where he'd gone to boarding school—a sequestered experience that the secret Los Alamos lab no doubt resembled in many ways.

Coordinating scientists is something like herding cats, but Oppenheimer got the job done, and delivered the bombs (though not personally) that ended the war in the Pacific.

### Life After Death the Destroyer

After the war, Oppenheimer served as the chairman of the General Advisory Committee for the Atomic Energy Commission from 1947 through 1952, and it was in that capacity that he went on record as opposing the development of the hydrogen bomb.

In December 1953, Oppenheimer's past came back to haunt him when he was informed that he was being investigated by the military for his previous interactions with communists, and for opposing the hydrogen bomb. At a security hearing it was decided that he wasn't actually treasonous, but that he should be stripped of his security clearance, just to be safe. This naturally caused an uproar among scientists, and Oppenheimer became a cause celebre as an example of how a scientist following his moral code can get trampled by the military-industrial complex.

The military-industrial complex came to its senses for a moment or two in 1963, and Oppenheimer was reinstated and presented with the Enrico Fermi Award of the Atomic Energy Commission by none other than President Lyndon Johnson himself. Isn't that a happy ending?

**Frank Lloyd Wright coined the word "carport."**

# CLOWNING AROUND

*Uncle John wants to take you to clown school.*

E veryone loves clowns, except for the people who hate and fear them. But how did clowns evolve into the rainbow-clad arooogah-horn honkers we know so well?

## B.C. (BEFORE CLOWNS)

Clowns' earliest relatives were court jesters. The first documented jester was a pygmy who performed for Pharaoh Dadkeri-Assi during Egypt's Fifth Dynasty (about 2500 B.C.). China has an almost equally illustrious clowning history, with jesters performing for emperors from about 1818 B.C. on.

Around the seventh century B.C., ancient Greece had "deike-liktas" (meaning "those who put on plays"), strolling comic actors who imitated Greek gods, soldiers, slaves, and other icons in street-theater skits. Because performance spaces were usually poorly lit, white makeup with black markings around the eyes and lips helped reveal features and facial expressions. These were the earliest predecessors of the whiteface clown, the most common clown type.

Aztecs were equally fond of their funnymen. When Cortez conquered the Aztec Nation in A.D. 1520, he found Montezuma well-stocked with jesters (including dwarfs and hunchbacks)—which he took back with him to Spain, along with all that gold.

## COURT JESTERS

The function of a court jester was to keep monarchs laughing—a happy monarch is a benevolent monarch. In the evenings jesters would while away a monarch's cares with funny dances, silly stunts, and pointed commentary on court happenings. As jesters evolved, they also began to take on some of the responsibilities of social critics. By poking fun at current happenings, they making political points to authority figures, their satire could sometimes be a catalyst for social change.

Colorful costumes originated with jesters who wore bright green and gold coats, tights, and caps decorated with jingling bells. This costume remained unchanged throughout the Middle Ages,

Norman Rockwell was only 22 when he illustrated his first *Saturday Evening Post* cover.

but the role of clown continued to evolve. Jesters weren't confined to court stages anymore—they took to the streets, performing magic, juggling, telling stories, puppetry, acrobatics, contortion, singing, and improv comedy. They were known variously as jesters, fools, mimes, and minstrels. In the 16th century they became known as clowns.

## THE WHITEFACE CLOWN

The 1600s were harsh for English clowns—Puritans closed English theaters in 1642. When they were reopened in 1660, only somber, socially meaningful Restoration dramas were welcome. Clowns performed mainly at fairgrounds and on the streets for spare change.

But a clown-friendly movement was thriving in Italy. The commedia dell'arte was a new and wildly popular form of theater that relied on stock characters for improvisational comedy skits. From the 1500s to the 1700s, characters like Harlequin (a zany cutup with a well-known patchwork costume) and Pierrot (a clown who wore the same sort of white makeup as the Greek clowns) were the popular icons of their day.

By the time the English pantomime theater (a British take-off on commedia dell'arte) came into fashion in the 1700s, Harlequin was a heroic character and Pierrot and other whiteface clowns were set up as the butts of Harlequin's pranks. But there was one whiteface clown who wasn't willing to play the patsy.

### Joseph Grimaldi: First and Famous

Joseph Grimaldi (1778–1837) was determined to stand out from the pack of whiteface clowns. He brightened up his makeup and painted large red triangles on his cheeks. He created routines in which whiteface clowns took a starring role and dispensed prankish abuse instead of absorbing it. Grimaldi didn't walk through stock routines and pratfalls; he invented his own characters and routines. His shows were fast and furious, as play-violent as *Roadrunner* cartoons. By the time he'd reached his 20s, he was a big star, performing in theaters under the name Joey—now a generic term for clowns in the biz. By the end of his life he was so famous that Charles Dickens wrote his biography.

Grimaldi's enduring legacy was his creativity—clowns today are expected to create their own gags rather than just play a part in the same old scenarios. Even though his makeup techniques

---

*The Long Riders* used real sets of brothers to portray the James and Younger outlaw brothers.

made a unique face an important part of a clown's look—alas, "alive" didn't really describe the many early clowns who died of lead poisoning from lead-based white face paint.

## THE GROTESQUE CLOWN

Thanks to Grimaldi, the white-faced clown was now the most intelligent buffoon, at the top of the clown pecking order. But someone had to take pies to the face and buckets of water over the head. So a second type of clown developed: the white-faced grotesque clown. This type of clown wears a base of white makeup, but outlines the eyes and mouth with bright, exaggerated makeup and often wears bright artificial hair, sometimes with a partial bald cap. Bozo the Clown is a perfect modern example of this type of clowny stooge.

After Grimaldi opened the door to original clown acts, many clowns weren't satisfied with the same old routines. The gags had evolved somewhat with time, but still relied on the same old pratfalls, pies, and fake punches. It was time for a new type of clown—the character clown.

## THE CHARACTER CLOWN
### Philip Astley: The Ringleader of the Ringmasters

Most trace the evolution of the character clown to the invention of the circus in England in 1768. A savvy clown named Philip Astley created the first circus clown act, known as Billy Buttons. The act was based on a popular tale in which a buffoonish tailor attempted to ride a horse to vote in an election (still a popular routine).

Billy Buttons was popular enough, but the idea of the circus was unstoppably infectious. In 1782 Charles Hughes, who'd worked with Astley in the Buttons act, founded the Royal Circus in England just as Astley was opening the first circus in Paris. By 1793 Hughes had opened another circus in St. Petersburg, Russia, and one of Hughes's students, John Bill Ricketts, opened the first circus in America—in Philadelphia. Circuses were (and still are) a clown-hungry maw that demanded audience-pleasing skits. Performers interested in developing new characters found fertile ground for their talents. Clowns could even make a buck without resorting to pratfalls; witness the story of Dan Rice.

### Dan Rice: Strike Up the Bandwagon

Dan Rice (1823–1901) was a Civil War–era character clown with a typical act when he first hit the circus stage in 1840. He'd left home at 13 to join the "traveling shows," second-class vaudeville acts that played in theaters around the country. Rice had a "learned pig" who could supposedly tell time. Before too long, Rice found his services useful at traveling circuses as well. He progressed to blackface routines, then other animal acts—he trained pigs, mules, and even a rhinoceros. He once trained an elephant to walk a (very strong) tightrope.

Eventually he moved on to topical humor, writing and performing songs satirizing the news with a homespun, sly viewpoint. His act, which combined weight lifting with animal routines and his oratories, was a huge hit in his self-produced circus events in the 1850s through the 1870s. And his satire was so on the mark that the very politicians he lampooned became his buddies. In 1848 Rice stumped for Zachary Taylor's presidential campaign. Part of his Taylor shtick included inviting Taylor onto the circus bandwagon to ride during parades. Local politicians at whistle-stop towns were hot to get in on the act, inspiring the phrase "jump on the bandwagon." Taylor responded by making Rice an honorary colonel.

Abraham Lincoln was another Rice fan. In fact, Rice was widely known as Lincoln's "court jester." Luckily, their friendship was able to survive a little competition. At one point Rice was making $1,000 a week, twice as much as President Lincoln.

By 1864 Rice was running for office himself. He even made an unsuccessful bid for the presidency in 1868. His increasingly boozy habits spelled the end of his circus career in the 1880s. He started walking out of gigs, and in 1885 walked off his last tour. Incidentally, Rice had another important effect on clowning history. When his show played McGregor, Iowa, in 1870, five brothers were so enthralled by his performance that they decided to start their own circus. Their name was Ringling.

## CIRCUSES GET BIGGER, CLOWNS DON'T

In a curious way, the growing popularity of circuses in America spelled the death of clown characters like Dan Rice. As three-ring circuses became more popular and circus tents grew bigger—and louder—the audience couldn't hear commentary or much of anything at all. Also, the circus had become thought of as too lowbrow for its audiences to interact with performers the way they once did (another problem in Dan Rice's later career; his act relied on a lot of give-and-take with the crowd). Clowns were relegated to oversized visual gags that could be funny even when silent.

With fewer nuances available to them, American clowns were forced to revert to clown "types" and stage their acts accordingly. If audience members saw a whiteface clown, they expected him to order the other clowns around; if a whiteface grotesque clown appeared, the audience knew he'd soon be pranked. A need arose for other clowns whose type could be easily gauged by their makeup. It was during this period in the mid-1850s that the Auguste clown was born.

## THE AUGUSTE CLOWN

Auguste clowns are the least-intelligent clowns in a clown act, the ones at the very bottom of the heap. They're recognized by their flesh-colored (rather than whiteface) makeup, frequently topped off by exaggerated outlines around the mouth and eyes. Clothes are also exaggerated: tiny hats, giant lapels, big shoes, oversized ties. The Auguste clown we know best is Clarabell, Howdy Doody's clown friend. What you may not know about Clarabell is just who was behind that wild makeup.

### Bob Keeshan: Captain Clownaroo

Though he'd eventually become famous as morning TV's Captain Kangaroo, Robert James Keeshan started his TV career as a sidekick to a puppet. Keeshan started as a page for NBC, but his career was interrupted by a stint in the Marines during WWII. When he returned in 1947, he started working for a radio host named Bob Smith. Smith had just been asked to transfer his kids radio show *Puppet Playhouse* to a television format. As the fortunes of Smith (a.k.a. Buffalo Bob) rose with his new blockbuster show *Howdy Doody*, so did Keeshan's.

At first Keeshan played gofer on the set, ushering crowds of kids around. When a producer spied Keeshan in a background shot, he got upset that a "normal" person could be seen in a show that was supposed to be a make-believe show.

---

**"Happy Trails" was the theme song of Roy Rogers and Dale Evans.**

So they turned Keeshan into a clown—a seltzer-spewing, bicycle-horn-blowing sidekick to Buffalo Bob and Howdy Doody. For three years Clarabell chased Bob around the studio, until he was fired for overly aggressive behavior and his failure to learn to play a musical instrument. They replaced him with a quiet and sweet-natured Clarabell. The kids could tell the difference and clamored for the other Clarabell's return, so he was rehired for a time. Eventually the rebellious clown got himself fired again in 1952, along with many other *Howdy Doody* staffers, when he led an uprising for higher pay minutes before going on the air live.

Another Clarabell soon replaced him, this time for good. Keeshan had the last laugh; he was back on TV on a new kids program by 1953, and by 1955 he'd created what would become the most successful kids program ever—*Captain Kangaroo*, which aired for almost three decades.

## THE TRAMP
The end of the Civil War also gave rise to another type of character clown—the tramp, best exemplified by Charlie Chaplin's "Little Tramp" or Emmett Kelly's "Weary Willie." Tramp clowns are generally world-weary types, with sad makeup and ragged clothes. They either originated from blackface minstrel clowns or from itinerant farm workers who hopped freight trains in the lean years following the war. Known as "hoe-boys," they'd usually end up covered with soot, which they'd wipe away from their eyes and mouth, creating a dark face with white circles around the mouth and eyes. However the tramp clown got its start, Emmett Kelly was the man who made it a lasting icon.

### Emmett Kelly: In the Right Face at the Right Time
Emmett Kelly was born in Sedan, Kansas, on December 9, 1889, to working-class parents. He worked various farm jobs in his youth, but he dreamed of more creative work, which is what he seemed to find when he began working as a cartoonist for a Kansas City silent film company. His true aspirations lay elsewhere, though, and he'd while away his time in the office drawing the tramp clown character he hoped to someday perform.

He bought a trapeze and practiced an aerial act in his spare time. He finally landed his first circus job in a roundabout way. The owner of a small "dog and pony show" advertised a job painting a merry-go-round. Kelly got the job. The show owner liked him—and his trapeze skills—so much that he hired Kelly as an aerialist. The show was small so Kelly ended up filling in wherever he was needed, sometimes selling popcorn or painting scenery or even working as a whiteface clown.

By 1923, he was doing a combination clown/trapeze act in the Yankee Robinson circus when he met and married Eva Moore, another trapeze artist. Together they traveled around the country as the "Aerial Kellys," with Emmett still doing occasional stints as a whiteface clown.

In 1924, Eva became pregnant, and working an aerial act in her condition would have been a little funny-looking, as well as dangerous. With their salary cut in half, Emmett made a bid for a bigger paycheck by pitching a new clown character based on his earlier sketches of Weary Willie. The circus' head clown didn't go for it—audiences wouldn't relate to a dirty-looking, scruffy tramp. Nothing doing. Kelly went on swinging on his trapeze and performing in whiteface for almost another decade. Then the Great Depression hit America and tramps and hobos were suddenly a commonplace sight. The time was right to try Weary Willie again.

In 1933 Weary Willie made his circus debut, and from there on out it was clover for Kelly. He worked at various circuses in America and England. In Europe he performed for the queen of Spain and Winston Churchill, among other notables. After his triumphant tour of London, he was given an invitation he couldn't refuse, and by 1942, the name on Kelly's paychecks was Ringling Bros. and Barnum & Bailey Circus.

Emmett Kelly performed with the Greatest Show on Earth for 14 seasons, taking the 1956 season off to perform as the "mascot" for the Brooklyn Dodgers. He was so famous he even appeared in Broadway shows (1940's *Please Keep Off the Grass*, in which Kelly stole the show from the likes of Jimmy Durante and Jackie Gleason) and in movies (including *The Greatest Show on Earth* and Fellini's *The Clowns*). Toward the end of his life, he appeared mostly on television variety shows and commercials. He also had a long-running act at nightclubs in Tahoe and Reno. His most popular and enduring bit involved Willie's attempt to sweep a moving spotlight up off a patch of floor.

## THAT'S NOT ALL, FOLKS

We've covered the major types of clowns you'd see at a circus, but there are still a few more famous names in clowning you may not know a lot about. Put that red nose back on and get comfortable.

## WALKER AND WILLIAMS: THE CLOWN COLOR BARRIER

Most famous clowns throughout history were Caucasian. Black performers weren't welcomed in circuses or on vaudeville stages. The closest thing to an African American circus act in the late 1800s was the minstrel-tramp act performed by the white duo McIntyre and Heath...until Bert Williams made a name for himself.

Bert Williams was born on November 12, 1874, in the West Indies. He started as a song-and-dance man and did pantomimes in segregated (black-only) vaudeville shows. He was just another run-of-the-mill minstrel-style clown in the mode of McIntyre and Heath, albeit an extraordinarily talented one, until he met George Walker.

Walker was considered one of the best "straight men" in vaudeville, and in 1893 Williams hired Walker to be his comic foil. The show they put together was a smash. They introduced a new dance, the "Cakewalk," and together performed all over the U.S. They even performed in some white vaudeville shows—the first black entertainers to break the barrier. And that's not all. Williams was the first black performer to star in a motion picture, and his recordings with George Walker are the earliest documented by blacks on phonograph records.

In 1898 Walker and Williams formed their own production company. They hired all black performers and created shows of African American interest that performed to sold-out crowds on Broadway. They toured Europe and America, where they were still forced to stay in segregated hotels. The success of their productions made a real difference in the reception later black performers received on Broadway and in vaudeville.

When Walker died in 1908, Bert Williams did a solo clown act. He joined the cast of the Ziegfeld Follies two years later and starred in every Folly for the rest of his career. Booker T. Washington once said of him: "Williams has done more for the race than I have. He has smiled his way into people's hearts."

Merle Haggard was in San Quentin prison in 1959 when Johnny Cash performed there.

## OTTO GRIEBLING: THE SILENT CLOWN

By the time Otto Griebling (1896–1972), a German immigrant, came to America at 14 in 1900, he was already an accomplished bareback rider. Good enough, in fact, to get an apprenticeship at Ringling Bros. and Barnum & Bailey Circus. But he wasn't happy there—his boss was an ogre (not literally, just a mean guy). At one point Griebling's trainer gave him five dollars and told him to go out and buy some milk and bread. Griebling fled instead. He hopped on a freight train and ended up working on Wisconsin dairy farms for a while. His love of the circus broke his resolve and when the circus came to Madison, Griebling bought some bread and milk and returned to his trainer, who put him back to work.

Griebling is best remembered for his Ringling work as a character clown. His most famous routines were juggling metal pie plates and an act where he kept trying to deliver a block of ice, which melted noticeably throughout the show. Griebling's acts were always silent, a lucky break for the final years of his career, as his larynx was removed in 1970 and he could no longer speak. He was able to go on performing for Ringling for two more years until his death in 1972.

Audiences today can see Griebling's work in Cecil B. DeMille's 1952 movie *The Greatest Show on Earth*.

## WILLARD SCOTT: THE FIRST RONALD MCDONALD

The most ubiquitous clown nowadays is Ronald McDonald. But Ronald's origins aren't as well known as he is. He was the creation of the man who became better known as *Today*'s goofy weather guy, Willard Scott.

Scott got bitten by the clown bug while playing Bozo the Clown on a Washington, D.C., kids show from 1959 to 1962. He liked smearing on whiteface and wearing big shoes so much that he modified his Bozo suit just a bit and pitched the character to the owners of a D.C. McDonald's franchise. They liked it, and Scott played Ronald McDonald for local promos for the next few years. He was shafted in the end when McDonald's hired another actor for their national TV commercials. Guess he didn't predict that one.

---

**Aaron Copland wrote "Appalachian Spring" and music for a ballet on gunslinger Billy the Kid.**

# HYSTERICAL SCHOLARS

*Our contributors. Proud members of the*
*Bathroom Readers' Hysterical Society.*
*We couldn't have done it without them.*

Bernadette Baillie
Bruce Carlson
Susan Elkin
Stephen Fishman
Kathryn Grogman
Francis Heaney
Heather Holliday
Vickey Kalambakal
Diane Lane
Arthur Montague
Julianne Nardone
Ellen O'Brien
JoAnn Padgett
Ken Padgett
Debra Pawlak

Leslie Ridgeway
John Michael Scalzi
Joyce Slaton
Betty Sleep
Stuart Smoller
Stephanie Spadaccini
Susan Steiner
Johanna Stewart
Richard Stim
William Stoddard
Steve Theunissen
Diana Moes VandeHoef
Jessica Vitkas
Amanda Wilson

# INDEX

# PLUNGE INTO MORE
# BATHROOM READER TITLES

## The best-selling *Uncle John's Plunges Into...* Series:

*Uncle John's Bathroom Reader
Plunges into History*
Copyright © 2001.
504 pages, $16.95

*Uncle John's
Bathroom Reader
Plunges into the Universe*
Copyright © 2002.
504 pages, $16.95

## The new *Uncle John's Presents* Series:

*Blame It on the Weather:
Amazing Weather Facts*
Copyright © 2002.
240 pages, $12.00

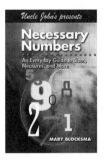

*Necessary Numbers:
An Everyday Guide to Sizes,
Measures, and More*
Copyright © 2002.
304 pages, $12.00

*Uncle John's Bathroom
Reader Puzzle Book*
Copyright © 2003.
240 pages, $12.95

# TO ORDER

**Contact:**
Bathroom Readers' Press
P.O. Box 1117,
Ashland, OR 97520
Phone: 541-488-4642
Fax: 541-482-6159
brorders@mind.net
www.bathroomreader.com

**Shipping & Handling Rates:**
- 1 book: $3.50
- 2 – 3 books: $4.50
- 4 – 5 books: $5.50
- 5 – 9 books: $1.00/ book

Priority shipping also
available.
We accept checks &
credit card orders.
Order online, or by fax, mail,
e-mail, or phone.

Wholesale Distributor
Publishers Group West (U.S.):
800-788-3123
Raincoast Books (Canada):
800-663-5714